Jazz Scores and Analysis

Vol. I

Richard Lawn

Graphic Design : Chris Goodmiller and Richard Lawn
Cover Design : Linda McLaughlin
Cover artwork : Lissa Herschleb

©2018 Richard Lawn. Published by Sher Music Co., www.shermusic.com
P.O. Box 445, Petaluma, CA 94953
All Rights Reserved. International Copyright Secured. Made in the USA
No part of this book may be reproduced, posted online or duplicated in any
way without written permission from the publisher.
ISBN 978-0-9976617-3-6

Contents

Jazz Scores and Analysis, Vol. I

Preface vi
Acknowledgements x

Chapter I – John Fedchock, "Ten Thirty 30" 2

Selected Discography 3
"Ten Thirty 30" 3
    Lead Sheet Reduction Melodic Overview 3
    "Ten Thirty 30" Lead Sheet 5
    Lead Sheet Reduction Harmonic Overview 6
    Basic Lead Sheet Form 9
The Arrangement: Form 10
    General Observations 15
    Chord Voicings 19
        Saxophone Voicing 19
        Brass Voicing 21
        Ensemble Voicing 22
Bass Doubling 30
Solo Backgrounds 30
Harmonic Embellishments 30
    Passing Chords and Substitute Chords 31
The Interview 31
Annotated Full Score 34

Chapter 2 – Bob Mintzer, "Ellis Island" 78

Selected Discography 79
"Ellis Island" 80
    Lead Sheet Reduction Melodic Overview 80
    Lead Sheet Reduction Harmonic Overview 84

Chapter 2 – Bob Mintzer, "Ellis Island" cont.

    Lead Sheet Reduction Rhythmic Overview..88

    Basic Lead Sheet Form 88

The Arrangement..88

    General Observations 88

    Form 89

    Chord Voicing 93

        Saxophone Voicing...93

        Brass Voicing 93

        Bass Doubling..95

    Solo Background Writing 96

    Development Section 96

    Interview with Bob Mintzer...97

Annotated Full Score 104

Chapter 3 – Vince Mendoza, "Homecoming".. 125

Selected Discography 127

"Homecoming" 128

Lead Sheet Reduction 129

    Melodic Overview.. 129

    Harmonic Overview... 133

    Basic Form... 134

The Arrangement.. 135

    General Observations 137

    Orchestration 138

    Chord Voicing 139

        Woodwind Voicing.. 145

        Brass Voicing 145

        Bass Doubling... 145

    Solo Background Writing... 146

    Fugato Section 146

    Final Shout Chorus.. 148

Interview with Vince Mendoza.. 151

Annotated Full Score 159

Chapter 4 – Jim McNeely, "Absolution".. 204

Selected Discography 205
Basic Score Reduction 206
    Formal Design 209
    Melodic Elements.. 209
    Harmonic Elements 210
The Arrangement.. 211
    General Observations 215
    Rhythm... 216
    Harmony and Voicing 218
    Orchestration 222
Solo Backgrounds.. 223
    Development Section (Shout Chorus).. 226
Interview with Jim McNeely 229
Annotated Full Score 238

Chapter 5 – John Hollenbeck, "A Blessing" 267

Selected Discography 268
"A Blessing" 269
    Melodic Overview... 269
The Song Lead Sheet 270
    Harmonic Overview.. 271
The Arrangement.. 272
    Overview 272
    Form 273
    Melodic Elements.. 275
    Harmonic Elements 282
    Solo Section 286
    Orchestration 288
    Final Observations... 289
Master Class Excerpts and Interview with John Hollenbeck 289
    Interview with John Hollenbeck... 291
Annotated Full Score 296

Chapter 6 – Darcy James Argue, "Transit" 337

Selected Discography 337
"Transit" 338
Lead Sheet Reduction Overview 343
    Formal Design 343
    Rhythmic Elements 343
    Melodic Elements 345
    Harmonic Elements 346
The Arrangement 347
    General Observations 353
    Rhythm 353
    Harmony, Voicings, and Orchestration 355
    Bass Doubling 360
    Solo Backgrounds and the Shout Chorus 360
Interview with Darcy James Argue 362
Annotated Full Score 370

Appendix I – Conventions, Assumptions, and Definitions 417
Appendix II – Additional Suggested Listening 421

Preface

In 1982 Rayburn Wright, head of the Jazz and Contemporary Media Department at the Eastman School of Music, published what has become an iconic book that occupies a special place on many writers' bookshelves. It has become an important teaching and learning resource for many of us since its release. Published by Kendor Music, *Inside the Score* is revered by students and professionals worldwide. If you want to learn about jazz arranging and composition techniques employed by three master composer/arrangers from the 1960s and '70s, this has been one of the best resources to consult. The book offers in-depth analysis of several scores by Sammy Nestico, Thad Jones, and Bob Brookmeyer.

Ray was my mentor at Eastman, and his approach to analyzing nine big band jazz ensemble scores by these three composers was thorough, revealing, and a revelation to many of us learning the art and craft of jazz composition. With his guidance the reader learns, through analysis, about pacing, voicing techniques, orchestration, harmonization, and re-harmonization techniques, form, solo background writing, balance, and other essential aspects of writing for the jazz ensemble. I treasure the complimentary copy of his book Ray sent me, one of the first graduates of the MM program he created, shortly after its publication. At the time I was Director of Jazz Studies at The University of Texas at Austin, my second such position.

I had been contemplating the need for a sequel to this book for some time, hoping to one day take on this challenge. Aside from some work by the late Fred Sturm, another Wright protégé, no one has followed a similar approach to examining scores by more contemporary jazz composers since Wright's book was released in 1982. Jazz composition for large ensembles has developed significantly, and in some cases has made what could be described as quantum leaps since the 1960s and '70s. Just as small group jazz has evolved, so has composition for the large jazz ensemble. It was therefore because of Ray's early inspiration, and my desire to learn about and share the work of more contemporary composers whose work I have enjoyed playing and rehearsing, that I decided to tackle the task of creating what I hope to be the first of two volumes.

Aside from the debt I owe to Ray for putting me on the right track in 1976, I am very grateful to the six composers who contributed scores to this project, which could best be described as six case studies. Grammy nominated composers and arrangers John Fedchock, Bob Mintzer, Vince Mendoza, Jim McNeely, John Hollenbeck, and Darcy James Argue are among the jazz composers whose work I have admired as a performer, teacher, and writer. Their willingness to share their art in this way is quite extraordinary, especially in this age when work is pirated from artists on a daily basis. Despite this climate, "Les Six" were enthusiastic about the project. We worked together in the selection of a score, and they proofed my work to ensure I hadn't missed an important detail or misrepresented an aspect of their score. Selecting a score was a difficult process, since in many cases composers' early works are exciting for first revealing their unique, signature characteristics, which then mature over time. In most cases we decided together to use more mature examples of their work for these case studies. Each chapter dedicated to one of these six composers will include recommendations for other recordings and scores of interest that could serve equally well as an outstanding study, revealing aspects of their style that might not appear in these pages.

Many of these other scores are available for purchase from their websites or publishers, and you are encouraged to dig further on your own.

It is no surprise that two of the writers included in this book are students of Rayburn Wright, so it is most fitting that they are included. Ray always encouraged originality in his students, never telling us how to write, or what to write, but instead guiding us along the way and asking us just the right questions. While John Hollenbeck only studied briefly with Ray, nothing could be more contrasting than the two scores by the writers who studied with him – John Fedchock and Hollenbeck. It is also interesting to note that three of these composers, Hollenbeck, Argue, and McNeely, were either close cohorts of or studied with Bob Brookmeyer, the innovative composer whose earlier works for the Thad Jones/Mel Lewis Jazz Orchestra were dissected by Ray Wright in *Inside the Score*.

Who has been omitted and why? Scores by Kenny Wheeler and Maria Schneider and later work by Bob Brookmeyer are not discussed, and there are reasons why these writers have been omitted. Scores by Schneider and Wheeler have already been made available in volumes published by Universal Edition. In each case, however, their scores are made available without any significant analysis. Sadly, Wheeler and Brookmeyer have passed away, making access to the rights to use full scores challenging. Earlier works by Brookmeyer were the subject of Rayburn Wright's *Inside the Score*, and late Brookmeyer works are now available through his website. They are being reissued through the work of Ryan Truesdell. Schneider's later works are written for a specialized instrumentation that goes beyond the traditional big band instrumentation that I wanted to remain primarily focused on. An Appendix to this volume recommends recordings by these writers.

There are of course many other creative and original jazz composers and arrangers who could have been included, and for that matter each one of "Les Six" has many outstanding arrangements to his credit as well as original compositions. I made a conscious decision to limit this study to original compositions for the standard, or close to typical, big band instrumentation. If I am fortunate enough to be the beneficiary of Father Time, I hope to pursue a second volume to feature other deserving contemporary jazz composers not included in this first volume.

An interview with each composer is included at the close of each chapter. Interviews explore the composers' creative process, how they learned their art/craft, who influenced them, and particular aspects concerning the featured score. In some cases I learned as much from these conversations as I did from the hours spent combing through their scores and recordings.

A best effort has been made to overturn every rock in these great scores, but that's not to say there isn't a remaining hidden pearl left for you to find.

While recordings of all six compositions are readily available, the temptation to include them with this book was resisted in an effort to keep the cost down. You can get them at a much greater savings than what it would have cost to include them with this book.

As a special bonus, a link is included to download a computer application developed by the author and Steve Tjernagel as a tool that composers and arrangers might find useful. *The Orchestrator's ToolKit* is compatible with Windows and Apple operating systems and is designed to quickly provide instrument ranges, transpositions, and various writing suggestions as well as cautions. The *ToolKit* provides a large menu of instrument sounds recorded over their full range. All of the sounds in the *ToolKit* library were professionally recorded and were produced by real instruments, not synthesized by machines. The *ToolKit* also includes a variety of brass mute sounds and pitched percussion instruments with different mallet strengths. Our *ToolKit* provides a handy reference to help writers to acquire an aural memory while also providing useful information about the instruments including ranges, transpositions, special techniques, idiosyncrasies, and hints about effective orchestrations. An additional note palette menu, accessible from anywhere in the *ToolKit*, provides a way to quickly see and hear what instruments are capable of playing a particular concert pitch. Not every pitch over an instrument's entire range is available, but close neighboring pitches to your choice provide an accurate idea of what the pitch area will sound like on a particular instrument.

Over the course of many years of teaching I have learned that beginning and intermediate arrangers and composers often lack an aural memory of the sound of instruments at various pitch levels, or brass mute possibilities in various ranges, making it difficult for them to make their scores both player friendly and orchestrationally colorful. We hope the *Orchestrator's ToolKit* will help to overcome such shortcomings. Download your copy of the *Orchestrator's ToolKit* by following the link. No support is provided by the authors, but none should be required.
https://www.dropbox.com/sh/79etjk2bhr9kaca/AAA1XwSGFsxGL_jVry3ilRXya?dl=0

The *Orchestrator's ToolKit* is made available to you at no cost but without any support, so please don't write me asking. On the other hand, if you find a mistake I encourage you to email me specifics so it can be corrected.

A special thanks to Chuck Sher, who believed in this project from the outset. I am of course grateful and indebted to the composers for their generosity and cooperation. I also owe a debt of thanks to the many students and colleagues I had the pleasure of working with at the University of Northern Iowa, The University of Texas at Austin, and the University of the Arts. May we all continue to write music that matters to people who want to listen.

March 2018

THE AUTHOR

Richard (Rick) Lawn has been widely published throughout his career. Kendor Music, C.L. Barnhouse, Walrus Music (now eJazzLines), Concept Music, Alfred Music, eJazzLines, Warwick Music, Dorn Publications, Baker's Jazz and More, LawnWorks Publications, and UNC Press, among others, publish his music. His books, *The Jazz Ensemble Director's Manual* (in its fourth edition), *Jazz Theory and Practice* (in its second edition, which includes interactive ear training software and an additional chapter), and *Experiencing Jazz* (now in its second edition), are considered staples among jazz educators and students. *Jazz Theory and Practice* users have said:

> "I would never want to part with this invaluable book. I think this is one of the best books on the subject of jazz theory because the content is appropriately concise, clear, and very well organized. I can't thank the authors enough for making the contents of the book so readable and enjoyable to learn about. I find myself wanting to run to the piano to test out the concepts in this book."

> "This might be the most useful, and thorough, music theory book on my shelf. It's not just a useful resource for Jazz, but for music in general."

> "I have gone through a lot of jazz theory books, but this one is my favorite by far."

Rick has received several significant composition grants from the National Endowment for the Arts, and as a member of the Nova Saxophone Quartet he has recorded his music on the Musical Heritage Society, Crystal, and Equilibrium labels. The Sea Breeze record label issued *Unknown Soldiers*, a CD recorded by the Third Coast Jazz Orchestra that features his compositions and arrangements, including his arrangement of "Donna Lee" recorded by Bobby Sanabria's New York Latin big band on his 2001 Grammy nominated CD. In the fall of 2011 his Philadelphia based little big band Power of Ten released *Earth Tones*, which includes his original compositions and arrangements. The CD received coast-to-coast radio play and favorable reviews. Most of the material from this recording is available from eJazzLines.

Performances in addition to his own ensembles include extended engagements earlier in his career with Lionel Hampton, Chuck Mangione, the Rochester Philharmonic, and the Austin Symphony. He has also performed in backup orchestras with Dizzy Gillespie, Ray Charles, Joe Williams, Natalie Cole, Marian McPartland, the Temptations, the Four Tops, Dianne Schuur, Rosemary Clooney, Nancy Wilson, Aretha Franklin, and a host of others. Visit his website at http://www.RickLawn.com.

Richard Lawn is the former Dean of the College of Performing Arts at the University of the Arts in Philadelphia, where he is now Professor Emeritus. He continues to teach various subjects, including Jazz History and Jazz Theory online for VanderCook College of Music and the University of the Arts. Formerly, he was affiliated with The University of Texas at Austin, serving as Director of Jazz Studies, Chair of the Department of Music, and Associate Dean for Academic Affairs. He began his collegiate teaching career at the University of Northern Iowa and Hartwick College.

Acknowledgments

Dr. David Aaberg, Professor, Director of Jazz Studies at Central Missouri State University, a good friend, a great musician, and one of my first successful doctoral students at the University of Texas, used his laser-sharp eyes and theorist radar to proof my work. His advice in the early and final stages of this project was of great help. Paul Baker, my old Austin, Texas, friend, section mate, and now occasional publisher of my high school–level charts, helped me on several occasions to sort out Sibelius software problems and discover some features that after years of use I didn't even know were there! Thanks, Paul!! And speaking of help with software issues, Dr. Tom Rudolph, who is an adjunct instructor for Berklee Online, the University of the Arts, Central Connecticut State University, VanderCook MECA, and the Rutgers Mason Gross School of Music, is considered a Finale and Sibelius expert, with publications on using both applications. Tom was an excellent resource when I needed to sort out Finale issues and got me back on track in using it. He has authored multiple online courses in music technology and music history. My lifelong partner Susan has always been there for me in such endeavors, and I'm grateful for her patience and support. Chuck Sher agreed to work with me on this project, though we had never met, and still haven't! He put trust in the outcome and value in its worth. It's not easy to find publishers like Chuck, who get it and understand the musician's point of view. Lastly, this project would never have gotten off the ground had it not been for "Les Six" – the six composers who agreed to take part and offer their scores for dissection and discussion. The greatest artists are those willing to share their work and aspects of their creative process with the world so that we can better understand how they think, work, and create. The world is certainly a better place because of their work.

Trombonist, bandleader, composer, and arranger John Fedchock

Photo by Joseph Verzilli

Chapter 1

John Fedchock – "Ten Thirty 30"

John Fedchock first emerged as a world-class jazz trombonist in the 1980s while serving as the lead trombonist and featured soloist in Woody Herman's last "Herd." During the seven years he spent with Herman he rose to become the band's musical director and often featured soloist. In this capacity, Fedchock served not only as musical coordinator but also as chief arranger in the production of Herman's last two Grammy Award nominated recordings – *50th Anniversary Tour* and *Woody's Gold Star.* Famed journalist and historian Leonard Feather described Fedchock as the "unsung hero" of Woody's *50th Anniversary Tour* album. Herman often referred to Fedchock as his "right hand man" and a "major talent." *DownBeat* magazine stated that "it was the young blood of musicians like Fedchock that helped keep Woody Herman's last years musically healthy and growing."

Striking out on his own career centered in New York City, the multi-talented trombonist has established himself as a renowned trombone soloist, Grammy nominated arranger, and bandleader. His big band has recorded five albums to date on the MAMA and Reservoir music labels, including *Like It Is*, which includes the original composition "Ten Thirty 30" discussed in these pages. Fedchock has been found in *DownBeat* magazine's Readers and Critics polls in multiple categories and has received countless reviews and notices in journals and prestigious newspapers such as the *New York Times.* His appearances are not limited to big band showcases, as his small group projects with his quartet and NY Sextet showcase A-list sidemen. His "incomparable trombone playing, which seems to have no limit, technically or musically" is the centerpiece of all of these groups (JazzReview.com).

Fedchock has gained global recognition and visibility through numerous tours and recordings with other groups such as T. S. Monk, Gerry Mulligan Concert Jazz Band, Louis Bellson Big Band, Bob Belden Ensemble, Manhattan Jazz Orchestra, Jon Faddis Jazz Orchestra, and the Carnegie Hall Jazz Band. He has been showcased as a soloist and composer/arranger in concert halls and festivals worldwide. John divides his busy schedule between professional engagements and educational clinics, workshops, and performances.

Born in Cleveland, Ohio, Fedchock holds degrees from The Ohio State University and the Eastman School of Music, where he became a protégé of Rayburn Wright, author of *Inside the Score* (Kendor Music, Inc.), which serves as the inspiration for this study. His compositions and arrangements are published by eJazzLines Publications and Kendor Music, Inc. While he is perhaps more well known and recognized by the Grammy organization as an arranger, he willingly agreed to contribute this original score to the project for close examination.

Selected Discography

<u>John Fedchock Big Band Recordings</u>
Woody Herman and His Band 50th Anniversary Tour – Concord Jazz, Inc., 1986
Woody Herman and His Big Band Woody's Gold Star – Concord Jazz, Inc., 1987
John Fedchock New York Big Band – Reservoir, 1995
On the Edge, John Fedchock New York Big Band – Reservoir, 1998
No Nonsense, John Fedchock New York Big Band – Reservoir, 2003
Up and Running, John Fedchock New York Big Band – Reservoir, 2007
Like It Is, John Fedchock New York Big Band – MAMA, 2015

<u>Sextet Recordings</u>
Hit the Bricks – Reservoir, 2000
Live at the Red Sea Jazz Festival – Capri Records, 2010

"Ten Thirty 30"

To paraphrase from liner notes that accompany the MAMA CD *Like It Is*, "Ten Thirty 30" was commissioned for the Clifford Brown Symposium through a grant from the Philadelphia Music Project of the PEW Charitable Trusts and the University of the Arts. Fragments in the composition were drawn from "Brownie's" tunes and solos. The somewhat cryptic title references Clifford Brown's birth date – October 30, 1930.

The arrangement could best be described as a modern big band composition that builds on that tradition. While influenced by Thad Jones, Fedchock's style goes beyond this earlier master. Generalization is always risky, but Fedchock's overall writing style seems more conversational in terms of arranging for the full ensemble. The three horn sections are in constant dialogue. His harmonic ensemble language and voicing techniques also favor a modern, denser, and at times more polychordal approach, as can be seen and heard in the score chosen for this case study.

Lead Sheet Reduction — Melodic Overview

"Ten Thirty 30," as shown in the lead sheet reduction (Example 1.1), is an illustration of the classic hard bop style. It is angular at times, sequential on occasion, and organized in what first appears to be the predictable AABA song form associated with the tradition, and it is difficult to tonicize because of shifting accidentals and melodic/harmonic resolutions. This last attribute is likely why the composer chose to write this score without a key signature, though it is essentially in G minor.

It should be noted that the first measure gives the illusion of a pickup or a break to lead into the start of the form, but measure one is in fact the beginning of the tune. The fact that the melodic line in measure one is unaccompanied, aside from the downbeat, and that the rhythm section drops out for the balance of the bar, contributes to this illusion. The syncopated nature of this tune also strongly suggests its intended roots in the hard bop tradition and dedication to the music of Clifford Brown. Example 1.1 illustrates the unique and time honored devices associated with the bebop and hard bop styles, such as sequences or near sequences, lines composed of diatonic and chromatic neighbor tones, surround tones, or simple passing tones, and a contour with lines that constantly shift direction.

The melodic material frequently represents upper extensions and altered chord tones of the given harmony, a characteristic also typical of the hard bop style. These altered tones are labeled in Example 1.1.

The melodic rhythm is also very reminiscent of the bop and hard bop styles, as it is highly syncopated. Twenty measures, or just over 50 percent of this unusually structured thirty-eight measure tune, show lines that begin on the second half of beat one. The first four measures of the A section in fact show melodic upbeat entrances after beat one. Five additional measures throughout the tune show melodic entrances occurring on an upbeat at some point in the measure. These upbeat entrances tend to propel the melody forward, creating a constant sense of anticipation and over the bar line phrasing while also serving to anticipate changes in harmony.

Example 1.1 – Lead sheet

Lead Sheet Reduction – Harmonic Overview

As previously suggested, the melody and harmony interact in such a way as to discourage the composer from using a particular key signature. This becomes even more evident when analyzing later sections of this score. While the tune appears to be fundamentally in G minor, there are numerous implications through ii^7–V^7 progressions that suggest new tonicizations to different keys even though these cadences may never resolve to the anticipated tonic.

The first phrase of the tune through measure 4 is quite predictable, showing classic i$^{6/9}$–ii^{ø7}–V^7–iii^7–VI^7 movement. What is unusual, however, is the sequence of these four chords. The more typical movement is reversed, e.g., iii^7–VI^7–ii^7–V^7. In the fourth measure the V^7 dominant chord resolves down a step to the IV^7 chord rather than tonic. A chain of ii^7–V^7 chords follows, moving down chromatically and without resolution until returning to the home key, with a ii^7–V^7 progression in the last bar of the A section.

A¹, the near repeat of the A section, shows much the same harmonic motion but without the chromatic digression to the ii⁷–V⁷ in the key of A.

Chromatic motion can be found once again in the bridge or B section, especially in measure 20 (♭II⁷ – tritone substitution for V⁷), measure 23 (chromatic resolution from the preceding bar), and m.27, with a clear return to the VI⁷ chord in the home key. The A♭ dominant chord in measure 30 serves as a tritone substitution for the V⁷ chord in the home key (D7). The progression in the final 8 measures of the tune is identical to A¹.

The movement to the E7 chord on the seventh bar of the B section feels like a deceptive harmonic movement to the VI chord.

What is very unique about this tune is its unusual length, 38 measures, since most tunes from the period that served as its inspiration followed the 32 measure AABA song form model. More discussion about this unusual aspect of the form will follow.

Example 1.2

Ten Thirty 30
Harmonic Scheme

John Fedchock

Basic Lead Sheet Form

This tune is basically structured in traditional AABA song form, with each A section being 8 measures. The unusual section is the bridge or B section, which is 14 measures, 6 more than typical. Measures 23–30 serve as an extension of the first six bars of the bridge. Within that eight bar extension are two four bar harmonic phrases. It is the strength of the half step dominant chord motions and ii^7–V^7 chord progressions in the first six bars that make the form of the entire bridge feel less unusual than it is.

Example 1.3

Ten Thirty 30
Solo Chord Progression

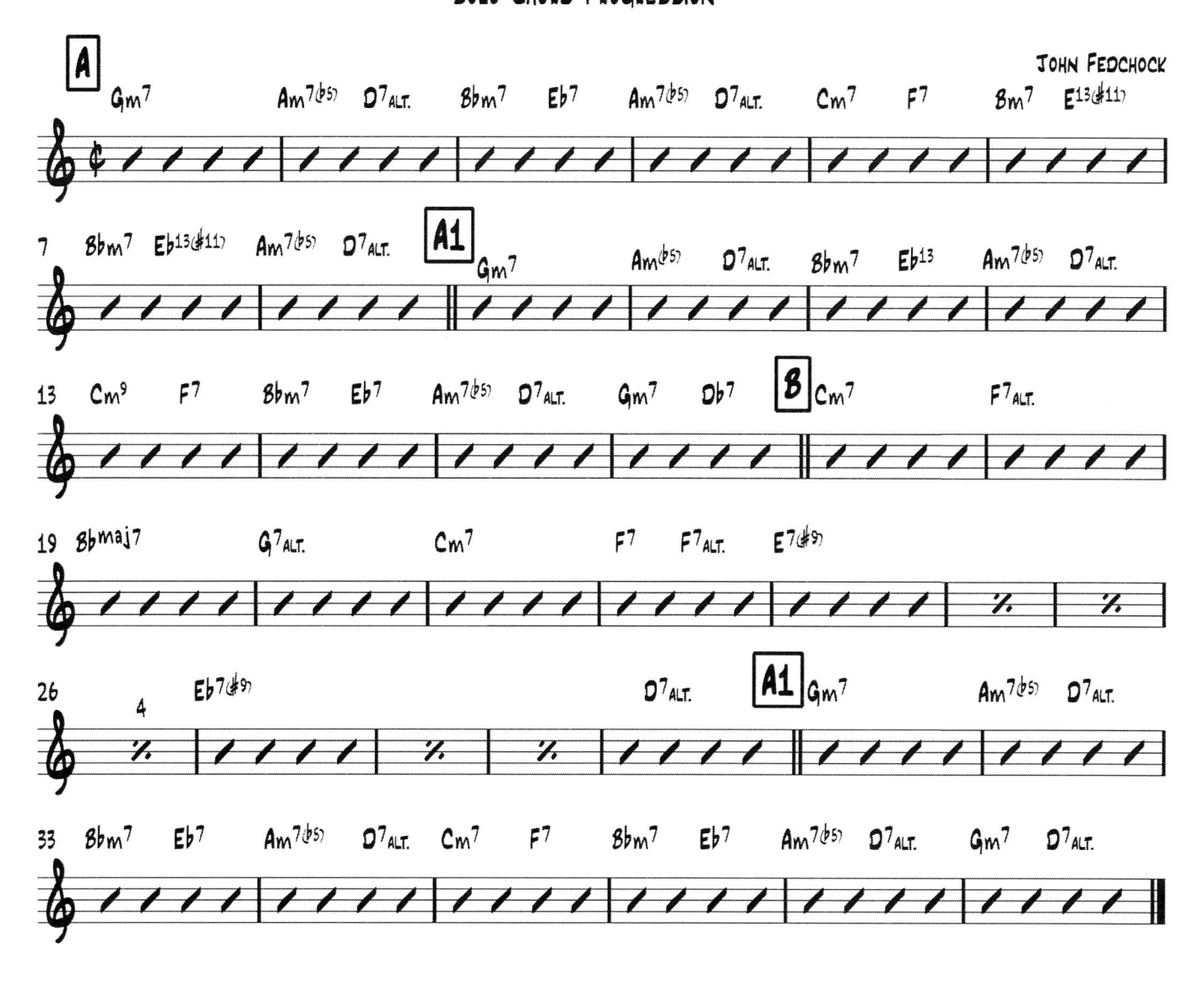

John Fedchock

The Arrangement

Form

Several factors contribute to make this score somewhat unique, not the least of which is the lengthy introduction, and that it begins with a solo. The pianist solos for sixteen bars in a modal fashion over Gmi13. What follows at measures 9, 15, 22, 31, and 41 is a series of exchanges between this soloist and the entire ensemble. What is even more unusual is the uneven, irregular groupings of these phrases. For example, the first exchange is 3 measures of ensemble followed by 3 for the soloist for a six bar phrase. Each of these ensemble sections exposes material that will appear later in the arrangement. Example 1.4 shows the scheme for this unusual introduction.

Example 1.4 — Timeline

[1—8] 0:00—0:16	[9—14] 0:17—0:23	[15—21] 0:24—0:30
Piano solo	2 bars of Ens followed 4 bars of Piano solo	2 bars of Ens followed by 5 bars of Piano solo
8 bars repeated	6 bar phrase	7 bar phrase

The AABA song form tune begins at m.53. The A and A^1, only a slight variation of the initial A section, is predictably followed by a B section or bridge, which is an unusual length at fourteen bars before the expected return to A. The second 8 measure phrase that follows a 6 measure phrase at the start of the B section appears in contrast as an extension of B and in a Latin rhythm section feel. The final A section appears as a slight variation in its final 3 measures when compared to either previous A section. A brief four bar ensemble section serves to introduce the first soloist with a four bar break for trumpet. Trumpet and trombone solos are based on the entire AABA form on the chord progression (see Example 1.3).

Once again, the composer presents an ensemble section of an unusual length, 20 measures, that serves to introduce the final soloist, who improvises on a lengthy harmonic pedal point ($D13^{(\sharp 9)}$). The solo ends with thick ensemble backgrounds over a chromatically descending progression of dominant seventh chords, with one whole step exception, to return to the V^7 chord in the home key.

A full ensemble development section consisting of new material based harmonically on the entire form begins at measure 239, concluding at measure 276. A final eleven bar coda, or tag based largely on material borrowed from an earlier interlude, brings the chart to a dramatic close.

Example 1.5a – Graphic waveform analysis of "Ten Thirty 30"

Peaks show ensemble exchanges with piano trio in introduction

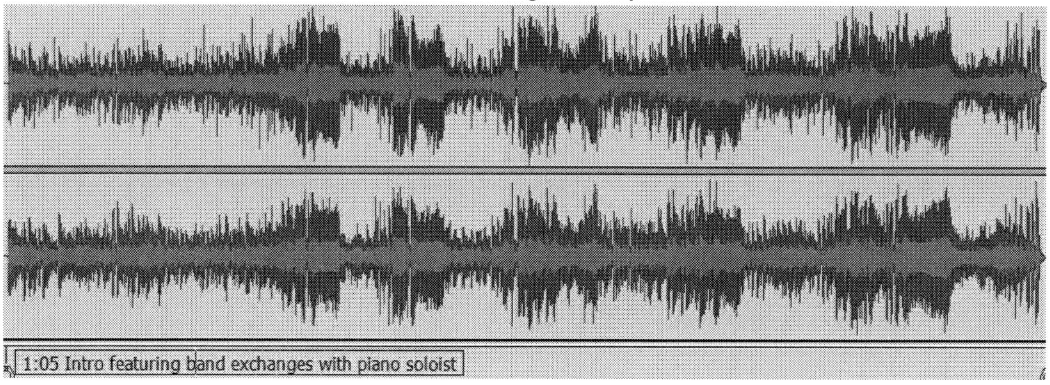

1:05 Intro featuring band exchanges with piano soloist

1:06   1:39   1:52

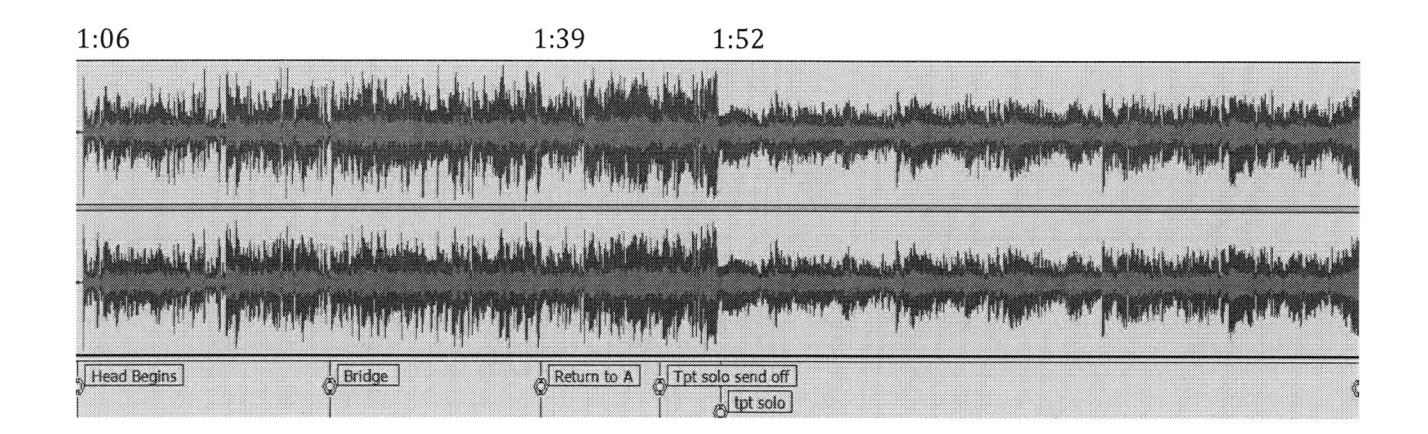

Head Begins | Bridge | Return to A | Tpt solo send off | tpt solo

1:56   3:21

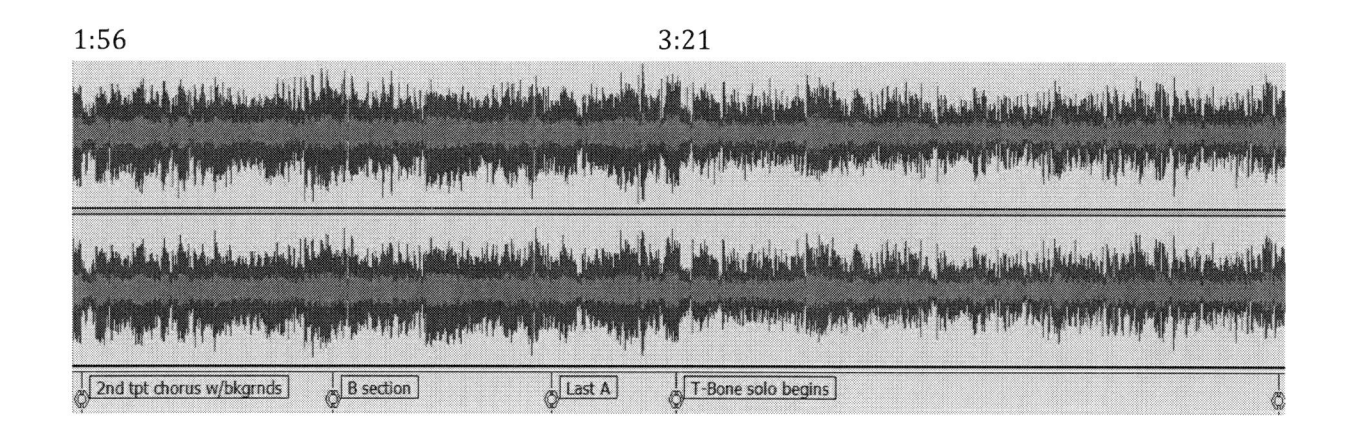

2nd tpt chorus w/bkgrnds | B section | Last A | T-Bone solo begins

4:01 4:42

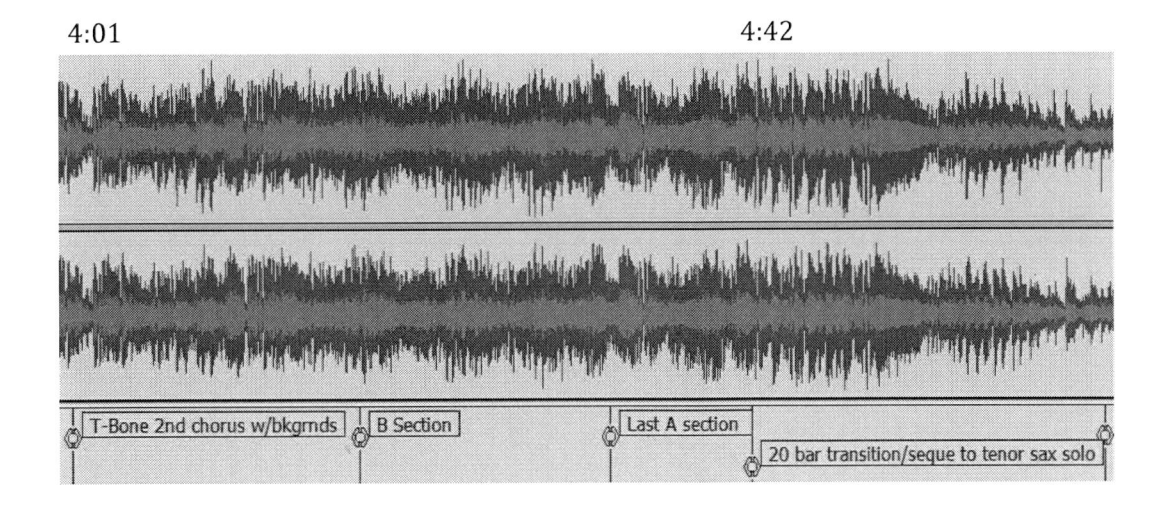

T-Bone 2nd chorus w/bkgrnds | B Section | Last A section | 20 bar transition/seque to tenor sax solo

5:04

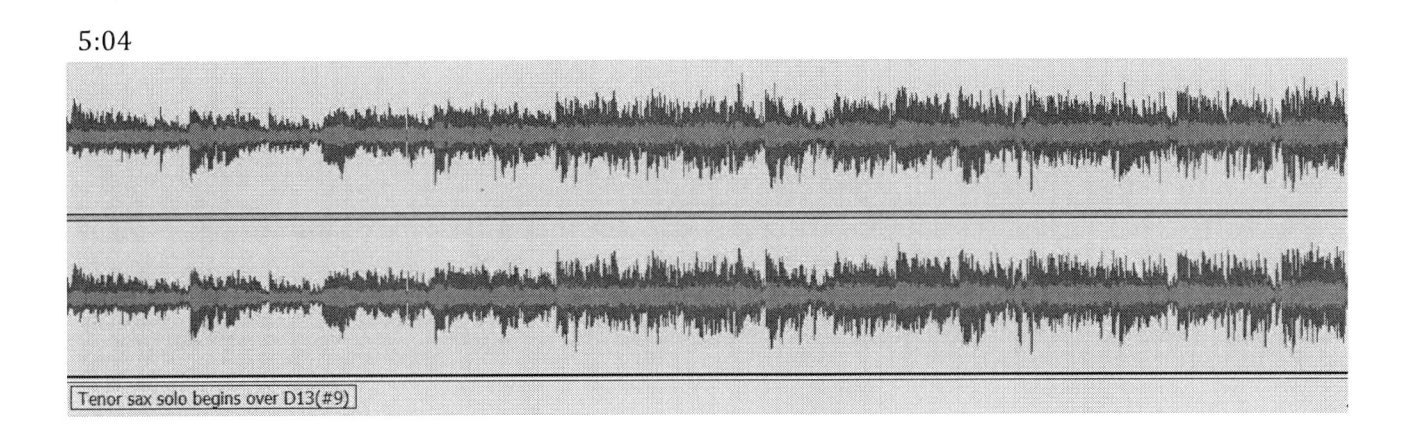

Tenor sax solo begins over D13(#9)

6:31 7:06

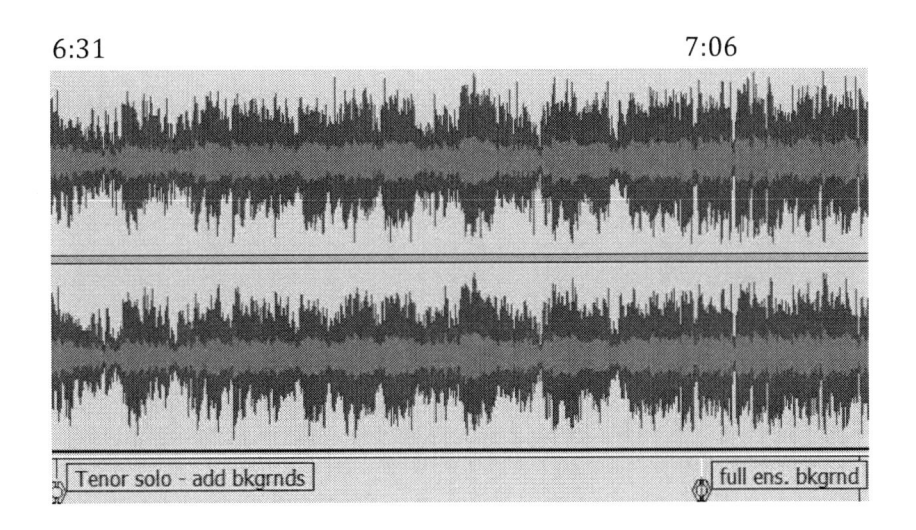

Tenor solo - add bkgrnds | full ens. bkgrnd

7:15

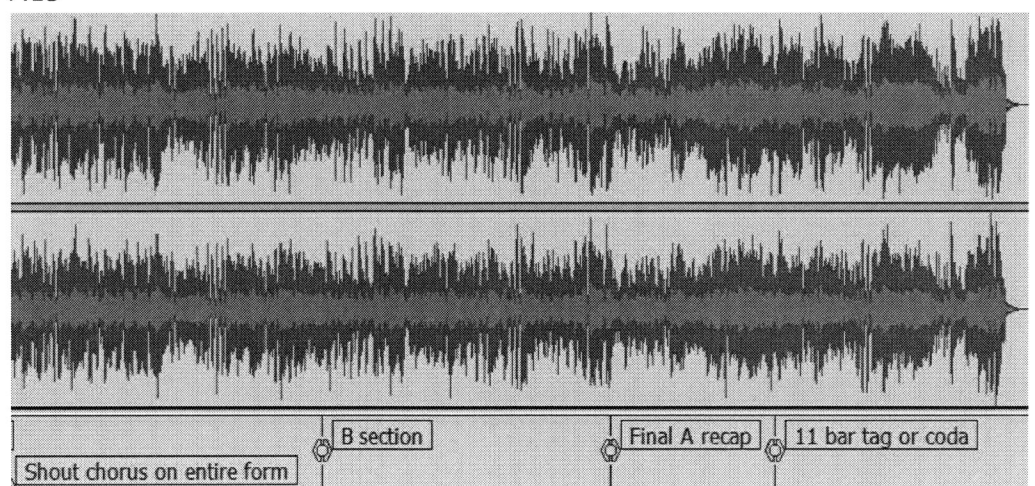

[waveform image with labels: Shout chorus on entire form | B section | Final A recap | 11 bar tag or coda]

Clearly the sections on this graphic analysis marked at 1:39–1:52, 4:01, 4:42, and from 7:06 to the end of the piece are the high points of this score. In each instance these sections either lead into a solo from a transitional ensemble section, serve to build a solo section to a climax using dense and weighty ensemble backgrounds, or constitute the shout chorus occupying the last minute of the piece. The full ensemble exchanges with piano during the intro also stand out as high points and are unsettling since nothing seems grounded to a melody or key center. Consequently the listener is left to wonder where this musical journey might be headed. But as the score unfolds it becomes clear that this material is associated with the tune and Clifford Brown references. The more detailed timeline that follows serves as a good listening guide.

Example 1.5b — Timeline

[1—8] 0:00—0:16	[9—14] 0:17—0:23	[15—21] 0:24—0:30
Piano solo	2 bars of Ens followed 4 bars of Piano solo	2 bars of Ens followed by 5 bars of Piano solo
8 bars repeated	6 bar phrase	7 bar phrase

[22—30] 0:31—0:40	[31—40] 0:41—0:52	[41-53] 0:53—1:04
3 bars of Ens followed by 6 bar Piano Solo	4 bars of Ens followed by 6 bars of Piano solo	4 bars of Ens, 6 bars Piano solo, 1 bar rhythm section figure, and 1 silent bar to close unusual intro
9 bars	10 bars	12 bars

[53] 1:06	[69] 1:23	[83] 1:38
A Section — 8 bars Repeats with thicker texture	B Section — unusual length at 6 bars plus 8 bar Afro-Latin extension	A¹ — slightly altered A section material
Ten Sax & Tpt state A theme with added Ens punches	Saxes and Tpts volley with Tbn harmonic punctuation	Sax and Tpt unison interplay
16 bars	*14 bars*	*8 bars*

[91] 1:47	[99] 1:56	[137] 3:20	[175] 4:41
Solo send off	Trumpet Solo — two 38 bar choruses	Trombone Solo — two 38 choruses	Transition — Full Ens
Full Ens alludes to earlier melodic and rhythmic shapes	Solo based on form; Brass and Sax bkgrnds 2nd time	Based on form with Ens bkgrnds 2nd time	Based on fragments of earlier material with variation and sequences; Moves to D7(#9) for second 8 to introduce soloist
8 bars	*76 bars*	*76 bars*	*16 bars*

[195] 5:04	[199] 6:31	[215] 6:49	[213] 7:06
Tenor Sax solo over harmonic pedal	Sax solo continues	Solo continues	Solo continues
Rhythm section accompanies; bass gradually moves away from D pedal to walking style	Tbns & Saxes alternate bkgrnd figures; Tpts added	Brass-Sax interplay	Full Ens bkgrnds
20 bars	*16 bars*	*16 bars*	*16 bars*

[195] 5:04	[199] 6:31	[215] 6:49	[231] 7:06
Tenor Sax solo over harmonic pedal	Sax solo continues	Solo continues	Solo continues to end
Rhythm section accompanies; bass gradually moves away from D pedal to walking style	Tbns & saxes alternate bkgrnd figures; Tpts added	Brass-Sax interplay	Full Ens bkgrnds; Pedal gives way to dense dominant harmonies that lead to shout chorus
20 bars	*16 bars*	*16 bars*	*8 bars*

[239] 7:15	[255] 7:32	[269] 7:47	[277] 7:56
Shout Chorus — Top of form (A & A¹ Sections serve as basis)	Reflects B Section	Final A Section	Finale Tag or Coda
Full Ens	Unison Saxes & harmonized brass	Brass and Sax interplay	Full Ens builds to dramatic close featuring dense harmonies and large spans.
16 bars	*14 bars*	*8 bars*	*11 bars*

General Observations

Fedchock arranges his score by choir almost exclusively, keeping like instruments together by family and/or section. The number of these choirs active at any one time ranges from one to all three depending on the circumstances, and their roles are constantly changing. In one instance the sax section might be the predominant choir while the brass is used in an accompanying role. The following phrase is just one example of many such shifting role reversals. At times there is melodic counterpoint between choirs. The following excerpt is a good example of such an occasion at measure 70. The eight bar passage also is a good illustration of the back and forth interplay between sections that is common throughout the chart.

Example 1.6 – Illustrated in concert pitch

Whether in the initial arrangement of the head (m.83–90), solo background writing (m.170), where in this case trumpet sequential imitation of saxophones is evident, or newly composed ensemble material, the composer is constantly exchanging melodic material in a call-response fashion between choirs.

Example 1.7a – Measures 83–90 in concert pitch

Example 1.7b – Measures 170–173 (in concert pitch)

Analysis of the full score shows numerous occasions where material has been re-used, providing continuity to the piece. Examples where material has been either repeated exactly, transposed and repeated, or repeated with some variation are abundant and highlighted in the full score analysis. Rarely, though, is material re-used without some change in orchestration or the addition of new material along with old.

Concerted passages featuring harmonized moving eighth note and triplet melodic lines are usually brief, though there are many examples throughout the score.

This arrangement is an excellent example of how past traditions associated with bands like Thad Jones and Woody Herman, particularly during Fedchock's time as musical director, are further developed into something new. For example, there are occasions where ensemble chord voicings are reminiscent of earlier styles without being pedantic or derivative. Fedchock's use of modern voicing techniques, enhanced harmonies, and even polychords build on the earlier traditions without getting stuck in them.

It is not unusual to see many, many syncopated rhythms, phrases beginning on an upbeat, and chord changes that are anticipated by half a beat. This tendency consistently works to propel the music forward within every measure, over bar lines and across phrases. Harmonic anticipations can be found in almost any phrase as well as ensemble figures that appear immediately after a harmony changes on the previous downbeat, occurring as a delayed reaction to it.

Variety is provided throughout this arrangement by not simply stringing three different soloists together who follow the same chord progression. While trumpet and trombone soloists do improvise on the same progression and follow one another, the instrumental backgrounds are different. The tenor sax solo section, preceded by a twenty bar ensemble interlude, deviates substantially from the tune's harmonic progression, though it reflects back to the extension of the bridge. The arranger instructs the soloist to actually begin improvising before the end of this transitional interlude, which makes for a seamless transition, especially considering the unusual twenty bar length of this section. The blurring of roles occurs again at the close of the tenor sax solo, when backgrounds begin to dominate in a segue to the shout chorus.

Chord Voicing

The composer uses close, open, chorale style, and fully concerted approaches to ensemble and section voicings throughout the score. Voice leading between instruments, regardless of the type of voicing, is smooth, usually following the contour of the lead melodic line. Because Fedchock uses modern, extended harmonies that incorporate altered chromatic and diatonic extension tones above the 7th, e.g., 9th, ♯9, ♭9, 13, 11, ♯11, and 13, repeated notes in any instrumental part are avoided with only occasional exceptions. Repeated notes are easier to execute even at fast tempos if the repeated notes occur on the upbeat to downbeat rather than downbeat, e.g., m.270 in baritone sax. If a figure within a chord call (chord of the moment) is repeated the lead melodic voice usually changes, which allows all other voices to move as well, avoiding repeated notes.

Unison and octave unison lines are plentiful throughout the arrangement and almost always culminate at the end of a phrase on a harmonized melody note or short passage, taking advantage of the entire section or full horn section. This is the case in horn background writing as well as full ensemble sections.

Saxophone Voicing

It is interesting to note that harmonized saxophone solis, which were very commonplace in earlier periods, are absent from all six pieces chosen for this book, and Fedchock's score is no exception, even though it most closely resembles the more recent past big band tradition compared to the other scores. It wouldn't be accurate to say that four part or five part saxophone solis have become completely passé or obsolete, but they are far less frequent than in years past. Unison and octave unison passages are more commonplace, as is the case in this score. Only a few examples of concerted, five part writing suggesting the earlier "soli" tradition can be found. In these few cases, and throughout the score when the saxophones are playing figures alone or with brass, they predominantly show five distinctly different voices with no doubled chord tones, and many times without the root even when playing alone as a section. The following excerpt is a good example showing a background passage during the trumpet solo at measure 99. This phrase is also a good illustration of the arranger's open voicings that utilize the drop 2 technique and the concept of voicing by using substitute tones for basic chord tones. Sometimes a substitute tone is used along with its neighboring chord tone.

It is also worth noting the less common voicing on beat four of measure 102. Here Fedchock uses a dissonant chord consisting of the root of the chord of the moment (D7) along with that chord's tritone substitution (A♭7).

Example 1.8a – In concert pitch

[Musical score excerpt showing Bar 99 onwards with chord symbols Gmin7, Aø7, D7, B♭min7, E♭7, Aø7, D7, Cm9 voiced across Alto 1, Alto 2, Tenor 1, Tenor 2, and Bari Sax, with chord tone numbers labeled beneath each note.]

The techniques utilized in Example 1.8a deserve further explanation. Looking at the third measure, begin with the melody note and, using four notes, voice the basic seventh chord in the closest possible position, as shown below in the first measure labeled Example 1.8b.

Example 1.8b

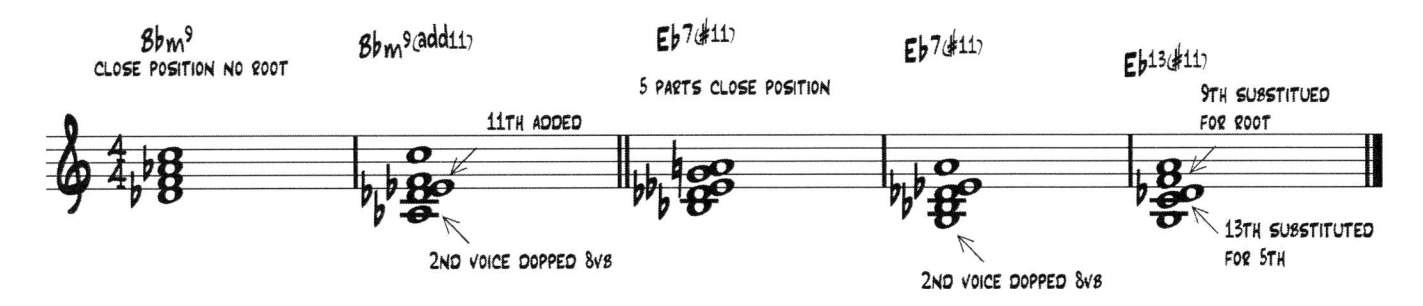

[Musical score showing five voicings:
1. B♭m9 – close position no root
2. B♭m9(add11) – 11th added, 2nd voice dropped 8vb
3. E♭7(♯11) – 5 parts close position
4. E♭7(♯11) – 2nd voice dropped 8vb
5. E♭13(♯11) – 9th substituted for root, 13th substituted for 5th]

Drop the second voice in the B♭mi9 voicing an octave as shown in the second measure of the example. The baritone is assigned to this voice. The most nonessential notes that are often omitted from chord voicings are the unaltered 5th and root. Substitute neighbor tones (e.g., 9th for root, 13th for 5th) are often used in place of these notes to add a fifth unique voice to a saxophone section chord. In this case, the arranger added the 11th (neighbor to the 5th, F) to the basic B♭mi9 and also included the 5th to create a cluster in the middle of the voicing to add tension.

Apply the same approach to voicing the next chord shown in the third measure of Example 1.8b. In this case the initial close voicing includes five unique pitches in close position. The last 2 bars in this example show how Fedchock achieved the voicing he used for the chord on beats three and four in measure 101.

These same techniques have been applied in voicing the other chords in Example 1.8a. No doubt this is all done in an intuitive manner by the arranger.

Since there are no extended saxophone solis, the following excerpt represents one of the rare passages where the section is harmonized for an entire measure of eighth notes. Like most writers, Fedchock favors player courtesy over adhering strictly to the correct spelling of accidentals. In examples such as this enharmonic respellings have been used in the interest of making examples more clear.

Example 1.9 – Measures 247–249 (in concert pitch)

Brass Voicings

Brass are voiced in close or open position and chorale style voicing. Trumpets are primarily used in close voicings over the trombones, which are either in close position or open chorale style. Figures moving at this fast tempo often dictate that trombones are voiced more often in close position. These four-part trombone voicings rarely include the root. Trombones generally feel more agile and crisp when scored in close position.

As the brass reach the culmination of a phrase, or when lead trumpet is scored closer to the top of the staff or above, trombone voicings are opened up if they have been closed. Opening up the brass voicing for a penultimate chord or final chord of the phrase helps to emphasize the impact of the phrase culmination, as shown in the example that follows. Open, chorale style trombone voicings usually show bass trombone on the low root while other key identity tones (3rd and 7th) appear in the other voices. Lead trombone often has an upper extension tone. There are of course exceptions to these observations and generalizations. In no instance are there doubled notes in the trombones.

Example 1.10 – Measures 271-273

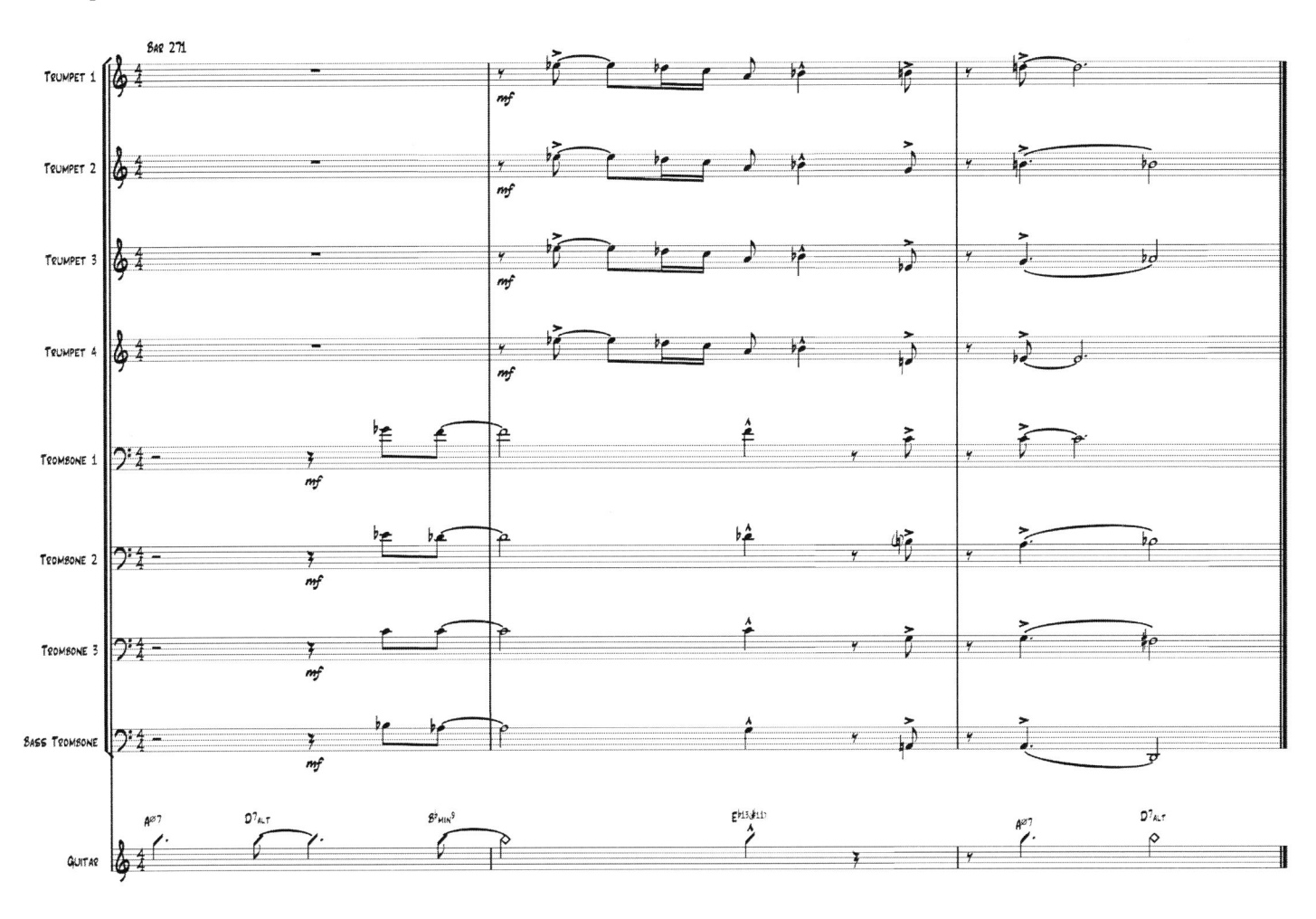

Melodic passages for trumpets are written in unison and octave unison. In harmonized concerted ensemble figures they are almost always scored in close voicings as in Example 1.10. These close position trumpet voicings are in either three or four voice structure, emphasizing upper chord extensions. Fourth trumpet sometimes doubles the lead an octave lower.

Ensemble Voicings

The final shout chorus (m.239–276), or development section, is where the composer introduces new material based on abbreviations or new representations of the original melodic material, original form, and harmonic scheme, but with much more dense and dissonant voicings than employed earlier in the arrangement. There are also many more passing chords to account for the harmonization of new melodic material (refer to the more detailed analysis in the full score). Fedchock often achieves these dissonances by adding diminished seventh chords in the trumpets built on the root of the dominant seventh chords. This is a classic technique used to vertically voice diminished or altered scales to create a more dissonant and dense dominant sonority. This basic approach was used by Thad Jones but significantly altered architecturally in this score by Fedchock. You can also think of this process by adding extension tones that are a half step below the 3rd, 5th, or 7th of a dominant seventh chord. These extension tones are the by-products of the altered and diminished scales. The altered dominant seventh chord is used throughout this score (e.g., D7^{alt}), so adding chord tones from this chord's related scale is very logical.

Example 1.11a

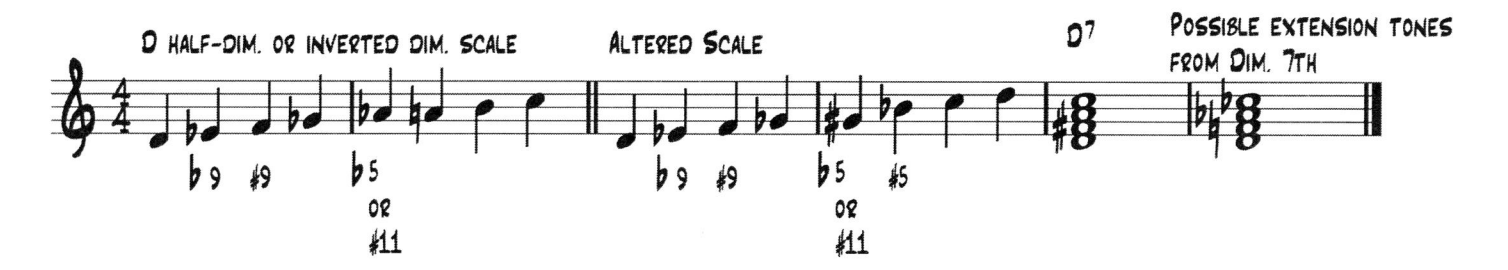

Example 1.11b – Measure 268 notated in concert pitch

The arranger in this case is careful not to make the harmonic context too murky or ungrounded by voicing chords on either side of these dissonant altered dominants as more consonant chords such as minor 9th or 11th chords. The passage beginning at measure 239 that is the first A section in the shout chorus is an excellent example of this harmonic tension and relief created by the arranger/composer, as illustrated in concert pitch in Example 1.12. The "T" indicates a chord with significant harmonic tension through dissonance, and the "R" shows a chord that relieves this preceding dissonant tension through contrasting consonance. Dissonance is created by adding fully diminished 7th and diminished major 7th chords in the trumpets as extension tones to the fundamental chord outlined by the trombones.

Example 1.12 – Measures 239–246. Enharmonics have been used to more easily realize the chords.

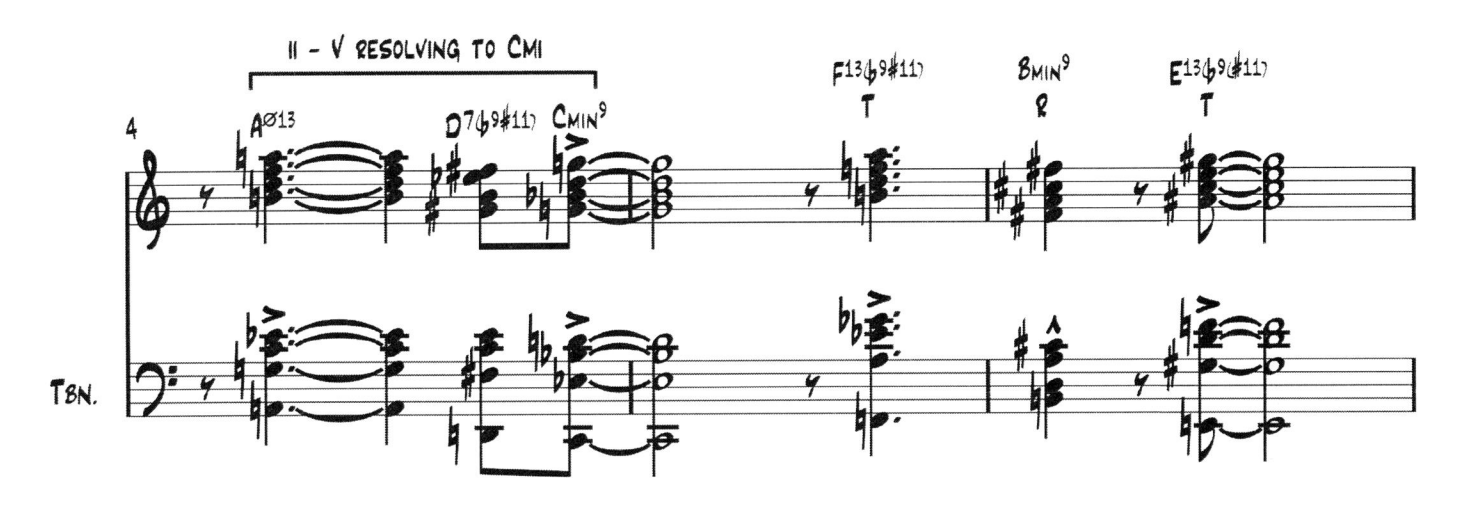

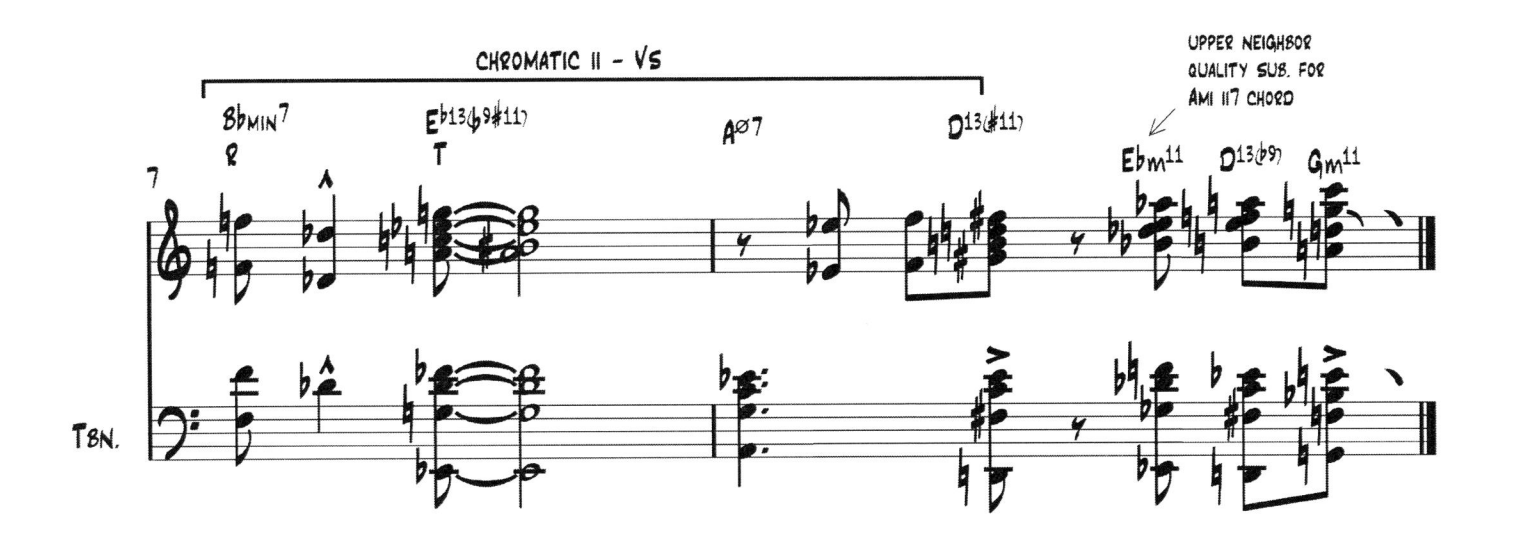

Another feature of this score is the frequent use of extension tones to half-diminished seventh chords (same as minor seventh b5). The arranger often adds the major 9th above the chord root and possibly the 11th to these chords, as seen in the first chord of measure 2 in the preceding example and in Example 1.13, which follows.

Example 1.13 – Measure 86

In concerted, full ensemble passages the saxophones are voiced to interlock with brass. First alto sax doubles trumpet three when the lead trumpet is high. When lead trumpet is scored lower, alto one sometimes doubles fourth trumpet. Typically, however, it is common for the lead alto to double a higher trumpet voice when the lead trumpet is lower in the staff. The balance of the sax section in this case doubles the next lowest brass pitch. The following example illustrates this concept.

Example 1.14 – Measures 249–250 (concert pitch)

Throughout the chart, following the tradition that preceded him, and whether in concerted full ensemble style or brass voiced as a section, the arranger ensures that each section is voiced as a complete sonority even though by itself it may not indicate the chord call. This is often the case in brass voicings where trombones outline the fundamental chord tones (1-3-7 or 9) and trumpets fall on diatonic and chromatic extension tones that often spell a different chord. Measure 159 is a particularly good example, as the saxophones alone appear to outline a B♭13$^{(\sharp 9)}$ chord while the trumpets play a C♯ diminished triad as the trombones state the fundamental chord tones of the given chord – E13$^{(\sharp 9)}$.

Example 1.15 – Measure 159 in concert pitch

There are occasions where the arranger makes use of the half-diminished 7th chord as if it were a rootless dominant from the same diminished cycle as an expected passing or substitute chord. Another way to look at this is that these passing half-diminished seventh chords are mediant substitutes for expected dominant chords. While the melody notes given might be harmonized either way, the mediant substitutes can provide the writer with another way to think about constructing smoother voice leading. In the example that follows, the two E♭ dominant chords are linked by two half-diminished seventh chords (with added 9 and 11). They could also be described as polychords. The A♭ half-diminished could be explained as a rootless E dominant chord, and the chord that follows closely resembles a rootless F altered dominant chord. The missing roots don't detract from the effectiveness of these passing chords.

Example 1.16 – Brass at measure 249

There is a useful principle, sometimes referred to as the diminished cycle, that suggests that any chord tone from a diminished seventh chord can be used as the root of a dominant seventh chord and serve as a substitute for any other chord in this diminished relationship. This is the foundation that is the basis of the tritone substitution principle. The four chords in this diminished cycle share the same parent diminished scale, and consequently the 3rd and 7th from each related chord is included. An example of the application of this principle is shown in the following example.

Example 1.17 – The sixth mode of the ascending melodic minor scale is also commonly associated with the half-diminished seventh chord.

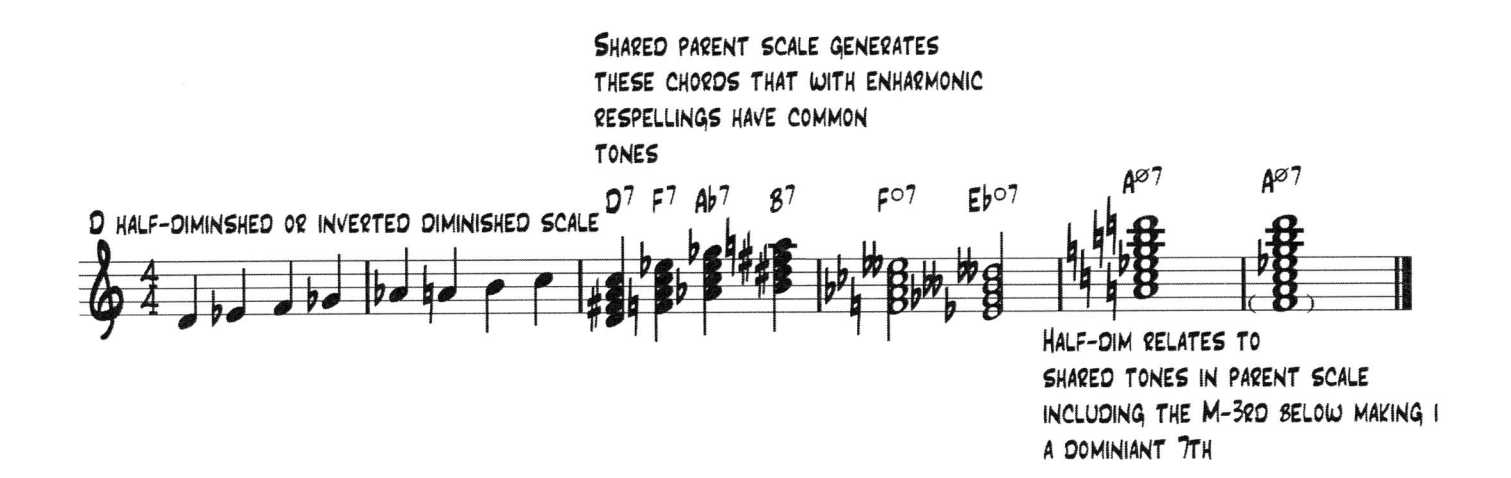

When Fedchock uses a series of passing/connecting chords in full ensemble concerted passages he leaves nothing to chance, providing the bassist with written lines rather than risk providing chord symbols. This ensures that all passing harmonies will be clear and focused.

Sustained, dense, weighty polychords appear for added dramatic tension but not until the close of the shout chorus, including the final chord. In these instances the writer uses two complete dominant seventh chords a major third apart. It is worth noting that the first occurrence of such a polychord (B♭7/D7$^{(♭13,♯11,♭9,♯9)}$) in m.250 precedes a chord that is equally dense (A♭13$^{(♯11)}$) before the phrase resolves at the end of the bar to Cmi^{11}.

Example 1.18 – Brass measure 250

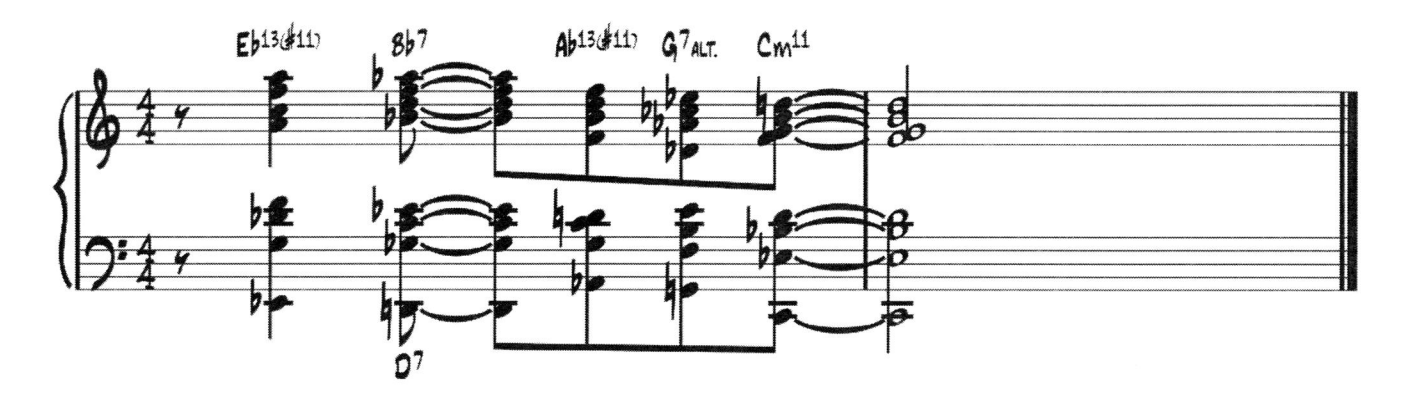

The second appearance of these dense polychords is in the last six bars of the piece, measures 282–284. Aside from chords at the ends of phrases in the introduction, this chord is the longest sustained harmony in the entire piece and the only time the trumpet section is voiced in open position, exceeding an octave between first and fourth. This B♭7/D7$^{(♯9)}$ chord, occurring five and a half bars from the end of the piece, is the first climax of the entire piece. The second falls in the final measure with a polychord as the last note (G7/B7$^{(♯5)}$).

Example 1.19 – Brass measures 282–284

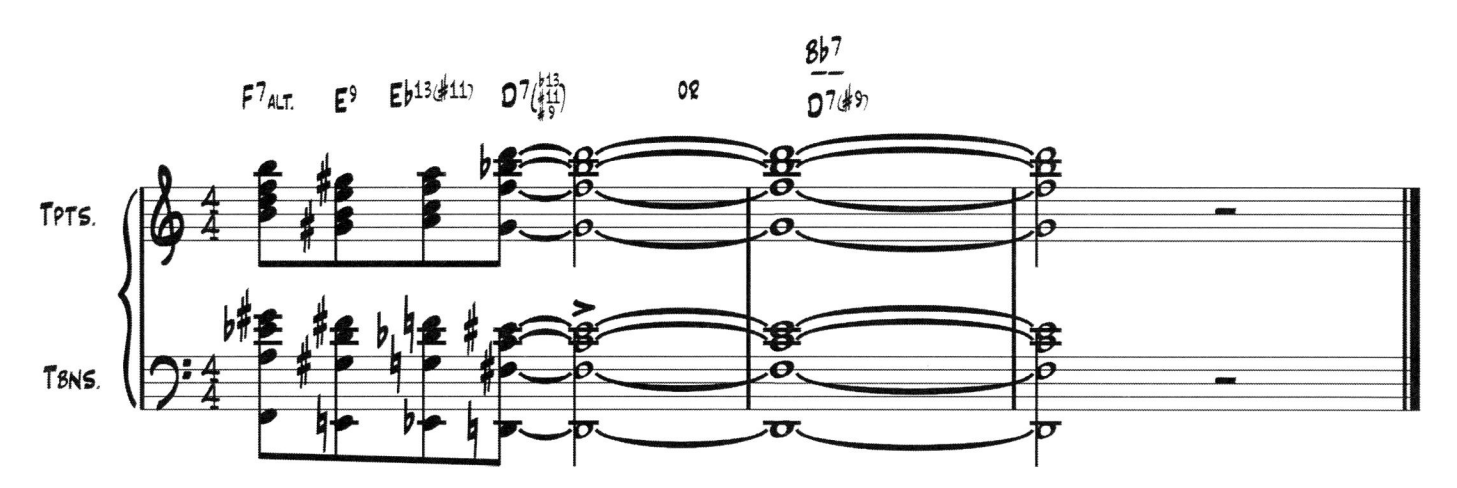

Bass Doubling

There is little to say here on this topic, as Fedchock follows the modern tradition, in a straight ahead chart, of avoiding unnecessary root doublings, particularly at the bottom of the voicing. Bari sax and bass trombone never double the root together. If the root appears in full horn voicings it falls to the bass trombone, or baritone sax if the saxophones are scored alone, or in an upper voice. In general, overuse of the root is avoided throughout the score and left to the rhythm section to define.

Solo Background Writing

The arranger constantly varies the texture by changing solo background orchestration about every four bars. This technique resembles to some extent the age-old call-response or question-answer approach used by the earliest big band writers. Trombones alone are usually scored in four part close structure. Lead voices in backgrounds create strong melodic lines, though simple enough rhythmically as to not detract from the soloist. Backgrounds build in terms of weight and density to the end of the solo section. This growing drama is often achieved by gradually moving the melodic background voice higher, pushing toward the end of the solo. Measures 211 through 238 provide a good example of this approach, and in this case the line between soloist and ensemble becomes increasingly blurred as the end of the solo section is approached (see full score analysis).

Harmonic Embellishments

Altered dominant seventh chords are abundant, along with minor and half-diminished seventh chords with added ninths and elevenths. Chromatic alterations to dominant seventh chords are also plentiful, including the addition of diminished chords built on the roots of dominants or a half step below chord tones 3, 5, and 7. Some writers think of this diminished relationship as adding tones that are a whole step above the 3rd and/or 5th of the dominant seventh chord. Either approach yields the same result. These extension tones are derived from the dominant chords related diminished scale, as previously discussed.

Interludes are created by using strong harmonic sequences such as that shown at measure 175. This passage in the full score is affectively unsettling, since it shows no clear arrival or harmonic resting point for eight bars, until measure 183.

Example 1.20 – Measures 175–178

$$\text{Gmi}^9 \quad \text{D}\flat13^{(\sharp11)} \quad \text{D7}^{\text{alt}} \quad \text{E}\flat13^{(\sharp11)} \quad \text{B}\flat13^{(\sharp11)} \quad \text{E7}^{\text{alt}} \quad \text{F7}^{\text{alt}} \quad \text{G}\flat13^{(\sharp11)}$$

Fedchock creates another harmonically strong progression, but vague in terms of establishing a key center, to close the tenor sax solo from measures 231–238. He uses this progression as a means of returning to the home key at 239, where the shout chorus begins. All strong chords, they resolve but to another temporary chord destined to move to yet another chord through primary root movements including half steps, fourths, and tritones.

Example 1.21 – Measures 231–238

B♭13(♯11)   A7alt   A♭13(♯11)   DØ7   D♭13(♯11♯9)   C13(♯11♯9)   F7(♯9)   B♭13(♯11)   A7alt   E♭7(♯9)   D7(♯9)   Gmi13

Passing Chords and Substitute Chords

Passing chords are common throughout this arrangement and are usually borrowed chords derived from secondary keys or implied secondary keys, as previously illustrated. Passing chords are parallel dominant sevenths moving by half or whole steps toward the original target chord, or dominant cycles based on root movement of a fourth. A quick look at the beginning of the B section in the final shout chorus is a good example.

Example 1.22 – Measures 255–259

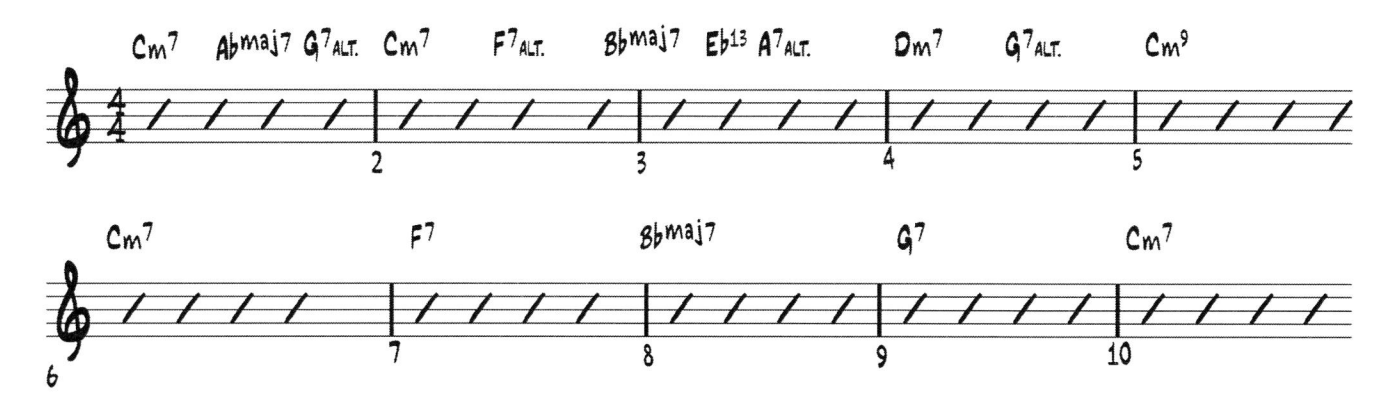

[Musical notation showing two staves of chord changes:]

Top staff (measures 2–5): Cm7 A♭maj7 G7ALT. Cm7 | F7ALT. B♭maj7 E♭13 A7ALT. | Dm7 G7ALT. | Cm9

Bottom staff (measures 6–10): Cm7 | F7 | B♭maj7 | G7 | Cm7

The bottom staff shows the original, unembellished progression. Chords are added to the original progression to connect the chords in this original model and in some cases also delay them. For example, the A♭maj7 chord is an upper neighbor resolving down to the V7 of Cmi that delays movement to its V7 chord (F7) in m.2. The third bar is embellished by moving to a V7 (and its tritone substitution) of ii in the following measure, which is a delay of the eventual movement to the original G7 chord, or V7 of Cmi. This embellished progression is motivated further by the 3 against 4 hemiola accompaniment figure in the trombones.

The Interview

RL: *Who were your formal writing teachers, and what writers did you look to for inspiration? Who influenced you and your style?*

JF: I experimented with writing a bit in high school after taking a theory class taught by my band director, Herman Treu. But I didn't take a serious interest in composing/arranging until I got to Eastman for graduate school. Studying arranging with Rayburn Wright was eye-opening. He was such a great teacher, with such a methodical and organized teaching technique, and everything just sort of clicked for me. I went on the road with Woody Herman after just one year of Ray's arranging classes, but took all my notes from class with me. Those notes formulated my arranging approach for my first charts with Woody.

I was a huge big band fan since high school, so the writers that initially inspired me were those who wrote for all the bands that were touring and recording during my formative years in the '70s. When I joined Woody's band in 1980, I had the rare opportunity to sit in the middle of the band while we played charts by Ralph Burns, Neal Hefti, Al Cohn, Frank Foster, and Nat Pierce, as well as writers of that time period like Alan Broadbent, Bill Stapleton, and Tony Klatka, as well as John Oddo, who joined the band the same day I did. This all helped me to really get a feel for the type of charts Woody was looking for. When I began writing for him, I slowly added some of Ray's concepts of voicing using extended harmony, which was inspired by people like Thad Jones. Other influences that came into the picture while I was forming a concept were Bill Holman and Bob Brookmeyer. Their linear concepts and feel for melodic development have consciously informed much of what I do.

RL: *In terms of developing the "Ten Thirty 30" score, what came first, melody of lead sheet or harmony?*

JF: In some cases melody, and in some cases harmony. In forming this tune from Clifford's solo lines and iconic tunes or arrangements, it presented the challenging task of finding identifiable material that fit well together and made sense when combined as a singular melodic idea. So in some cases, I began with changes and fit the existing melodic ideas into that framework, but in other cases, I let the melodic material I was choosing inform the harmonic choices, which is most evident at the end of the bridge.

RL: *Were you consciously thinking about creating an unusual intro, or was it intuitive and came about more organically?*

JF: I first began collecting all these little ideas that were identifiable to Clifford. Once I had several things that seemed interesting, I treated it as a puzzle to see what ideas would fit well with others to create one longer melody. Because I began the thought process with all these little ideas, I decided to approach the intro the same way, making it kind of a "genesis" section, showing many of the themes and ideas as separate thoughts and making the listener familiar to those ideas that were identifiable with Clifford and ultimately make up the tune. Setting them over a modal piano solo exchanging phrases with the ensemble not only helped to introduce the material one idea at a time, but also helped to foreshadow the modal portion of the chart that comes up later in the chart.

RL: *What was your objective in terms of paying tribute to Clifford Brown, and what/how did you decide to use source material?*

JF: Upon first receiving the commission, all the great music I've listened to over the years rushed to the surface. So I first listened to all of Clifford's iconic recordings, then went deeper into Clifford's playing. While on the road with Woody Herman, I had the great opportunity to play with trumpeter Mark Lewis. Mark was a Clifford devotee and had transcribed many of Clifford's solos. He later published one of the most complete transcription books of Clifford I've ever seen. I went through every transcription with each recording and pulled off things that I thought would carry as a strong melody. Then I had to sift through everything to see what ideas would work well together. One of my goals was to have the tune carry some of the characteristics that were identifiable with Clifford and his music.

Here are a few specific derivations:

The opening measure is a line similar to the opening line of Clifford's composition "Daahoud," but instead of using this figure as a pickup measure, I moved it to the top of the first bar of the form. This gives a feeling that the tune actually begins in measure two, keeping the listener off balance for a bit.

The chromatic ii–Vs are also reminiscent of the changes on "Daahoud." As a matter of fact, the melody in the third measure of "Ten Thirty 30" came from the opening lines Clifford plays at the top of the second chorus of his famous recording.

The triplet idea in the bridge was borrowed from the Sonny Rollins sax line within the vamp of Clifford's arrangement of "What Is This Thing Called Love." The trumpet lines that answer those sax triplets were taken from Clifford's answering lines from that same intro.

There are other themes pulled from Clifford's solos that were also used that don't appear in the actual melody, including a signature whole-tone/chromatic lick in the opening intro and several sax lines that appear throughout.

RL: *Is there any reason why you chose not to specify many chromatic altered extension tones in the soloists' parts, but of course are very specific in this regard in the rhythm section parts?*

JF: In general, I know that most modern soloists typically use alterations in their playing, so I didn't want to handcuff them to specifics. The specifics in the rhythm section were provided so that their comping would not conflict with any incoming ensemble background figures that implied alterations or extensions.

RL: *In writing the shout chorus, which begins at measure 239, what came first, sax lines or brass figures, or did it evolve in a more back and forth process as you moved from left to right?*

JF: Because it is a bit of a conversation, the brass entrance came first, although some of the following figures or phrases overall were not assigned specific notes at first. I like to sketch in shapes or contours until I get a good feeling that the phrases are well paced. My goal is to keep things moving forward so I can get a better feel for the overall chorus or section.

RL: *Much like the intro, the bridge of this chart is most unusual in that it extends beyond the expected 8, or even 12, bar length. At 14 bars it is very unusual. How did this come about? Do you view the Latin section as an 8 bar extension or elongation of the first 6 bars of the B section?*

JF: I definitely thought of the last part of the bridge as an extension. The bridge's origin was from two standards that Clifford played frequently and recorded as iconic arrangements, "I'll Remember April" and "What Is This Thing Called Love." I didn't want it to be too literal, so at about the time the end of the bridge seemed predictably like "April," I added the twist of the extension based upon Clifford's intro to "What Is This Thing." Taking a ii–V in B♭ to E13($^{♯9}$) was not a big stretch, but changing the feel gave it a totally different vibe, and continuing down another half step to E♭13($^{♯9}$) led very well to the D7alt getting back to the tune's A section of Gmin.

RL: *In general, how do you work ... what is your creative process like, and what tools do you use to assist in your writing process? Do you ever use the computer, and if so, when and how in the process?*

JF: At the time of this composition, I was still working strictly with pencil and paper. From the time I first began arranging for Woody Herman, all the way through 2010, the tool that I used to write every chart was a small Casio keyboard (non-midi) that I bought in 1982 simply because it fit in my suitcase on the road! In the '90s I started using a sequencing program and would input each chart to get a sense of what it sounded like. Before that, I had to copy all the parts (by hand) and call a rehearsal!

RL: *My last question, which I have asked everyone: as someone who has devoted a good portion of your professional life to teaching, what single lesson or suggestion can you share that might help us all to become better writers?*

JF: The most valuable suggestion I can offer to any creative writer would be to stay true to themselves. It's really important for aspiring writers to realize that everyone has something special to offer. Finding that special something is more important than any intellectual or mechanical stretching of compositional technique. There are many who feel the need to adopt a "sound" to emulate what is presently happening on the scene, but sometimes going against the grain can garner more significant results in creating a unique approach. And this is not just exclusive to moving more toward the abstract. Sometimes looking back can offer as much insight as reaching forward in taking the music to new and different places. Regardless of whatever new technique you may be exploring, always let your ear and personal sensibilities be your guide in shaping your music into something unique and personalized. Its important to remind yourself that individuality cannot be forced. It is something that is ever present within you. All your knowledge, influences, and experiences will ultimately coalesce to form your voice, but it takes time. Remember that trying to be part of the crowd will ultimately make you just that. The more honest you are to your musical instincts, the more your music will set you apart from the rest.

RL: *Once again John, I want to thank you for participating in this project!*

Annotated Full Score

The annotated full transposed score that follows provides additional details about "Homecoming," and includes concert pitch excerpts as reductions.

Transposed Score
Added concert examples

Ten Thirty 30

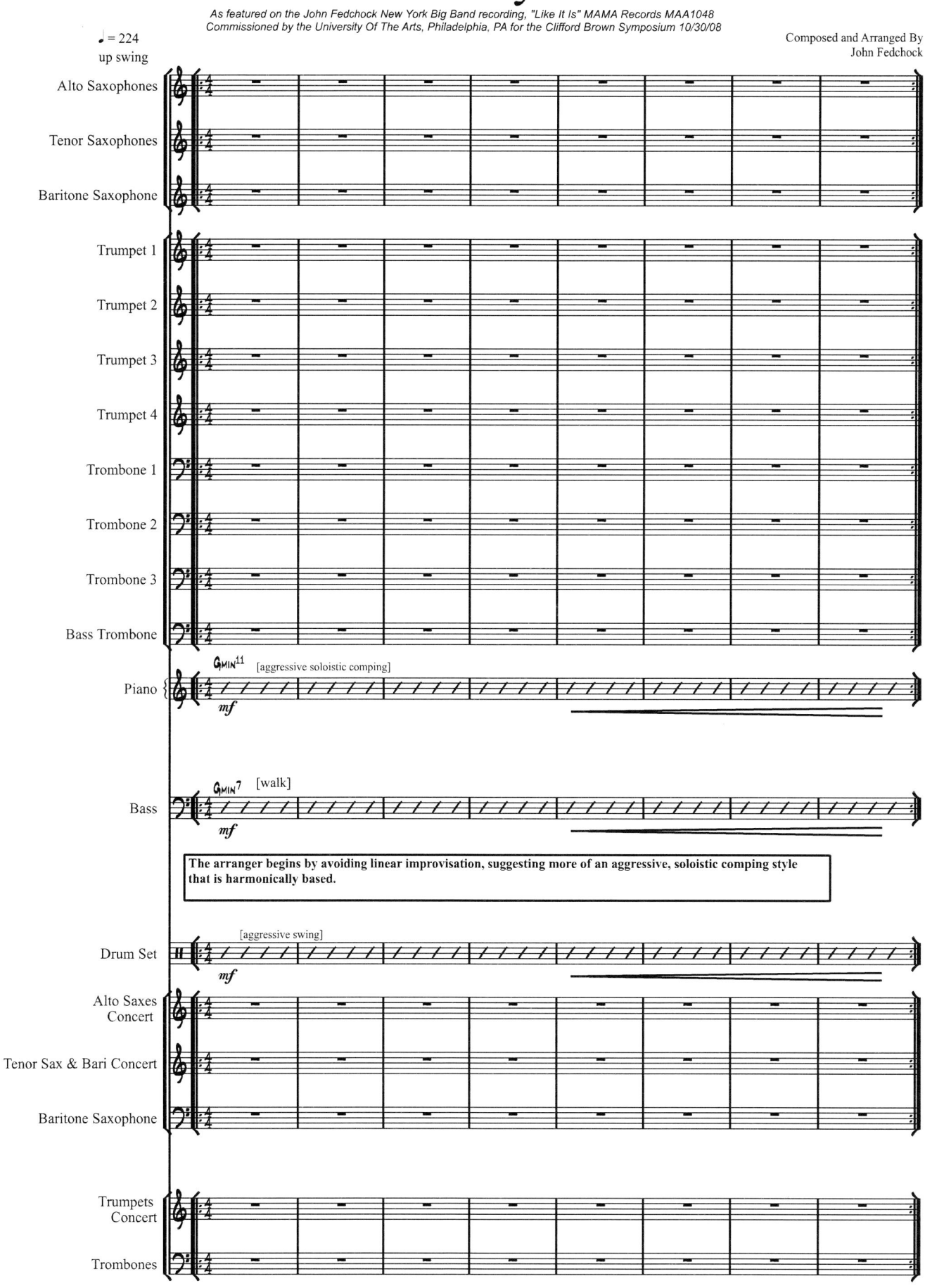

As featured on the John Fedchock New York Big Band recording, "Like It Is" MAMA Records MAA1048
Commissioned by the University Of The Arts, Philadelphia, PA for the Clifford Brown Symposium 10/30/08

Composed and Arranged By
John Fedchock

♩ = 224
up swing

> The arranger begins by avoiding linear improvisation, suggesting more of an aggressive, soloistic comping style that is harmonically based.

Copyright © 2008 John Fedchock Music

Saxes play fragment of primary A theme. Brass accompany with basic ens. voicings. Trumpets define upper extensions, tbns. define basic chord tones
9
15
Altos
Tenors
Bari. Sax.
Tpt. 1
Tpt. 2
Tpt. 3
Tpt. 4
Tbn. 1
Tbn. 2
Tbn. 3
B. Tbn.
Pno.
Bass
Dr.
Alto Sax.
Ten. Sax.
Bari. Sax.
Tpt.
Tbn.
13th
#11
9th
7th
3rd
-1
[solo continues]
g phrygian
[walk]
g phrygian
ens.
[time]
Final chord of phrase defines phrygian modal approach for soloist that follows.
Dense ens. voicings - trombones define basic chord while tpt triads emphasize extension tones 13, #11, 9; saxes interlock with brass copying them exactly starting with alto 1 doubling 4th tpt.

Saxes and tbns. in chorale accompaniment style ensure harmony is clear. Tbns. in open voicings with 4th on low roots.

Octave unison melodic sax lines based on material from extended bridge of tune but transposed. References C. Brown/S. Rollins "What Is This Thing Called Love"

Low lead tpt at start of phrase requires close parallel voicings in brass. No roots except bass & tpt 4. Brass move to open voicing to reinforce climax at end of phrase. Dense voicings with tbns in dim 7th voicing and top 2 or 3 tpts completing nearly another dim 7th. Phrase ascends chromatically to climax.

Altos
Tenors
Bari. Sax.
Tpt. 1
Tpt. 2
Tpt. 3
Tpt. 4
Tbn. 1
Tbn. 2
Tbn. 3
B. Tbn.
Pno.
[solo continues]
GMIN11
Bass
[walk]
GMIN7
Dr.
[time]
Alto Sax.
Ten. Sax.
Bari. Sax.
Tpt.
Tbn.

41
Material similar to interlude at bar 9 that introduces tpt solo break.
Altos
Tenors
Bari. Sax.
Tpt. 1
Tpt. 2
Tpt. 3
Tpt. 4
Tbn. 1
Tbn. 2
Tbn. 3
B. Tbn.
Pno.
Bass
Dr.
[ens]
Alto Sax.
Ten. Sax.
Bari. Sax.
Tpt.
Tbn.
D7ALT
C13(#11 b9)
B13(#11 b9)
Bb7ALT
A7ALT
F13(#11 #9)
E9(add13)
Eb13(#11)
D7ALT.
Open, chorale style trombone voicings with 4th on low roots
Chromatically descending dominant chords contrast with ascending lead line approaching final chord in phrase

Altos
Tenors
Bari. Sax.
Tpt. 1
Tpt. 2
Tpt. 3
Tpt. 4
Tbn. 1
Tbn. 2
Tbn. 3
B. Tbn.
Pno.
Bass
Dr.
Alto Sax.
Ten. Sax.
Bari. Sax.
Tpt.
Tbn.
-1
D7ALT
[solo continues]
[4]
[big build!]
B♭13♯11
E♭13♯11
[walk]
[build!]
f
ff

A Section of head begins here - 1:06

Trombones in comping style resemble piano left hand voicings in close position

A1 - 1:41
Near repetition of 1st A

Melody often harmonized through anticipation of the upcoming chord change. Arranger does this consistently throughout chart. Marked here with arrow and "ant." 9

B - 1:23
69
Altos
Tenors
Bari. Sax.
Tpt. 1
Tpt. 2
Tpt. 3
Tpt. 4
Tbn. 1
Tbn. 2
Tbn. 3
B. Tbn.
Pno.
Bass
Dr.
Alto Sax.
Ten. Sax.
Bari. Sax.
Tpt.
Tbn.
mf
ant.
ens.
f
D7ALT CMIN9 F7ALT B♭MIN9 E♭13 A⌀7 D7ALT GMIN9 CMIN11
A⌀7 D7ALT CMIN7 F7 B♭MIN7 E♭7 A⌀7 D7ALT

Consistently writes by homogenous choirs. First 3 bars of bridge (beginning on previous page) show 3 distinct choirs - bones, tpts & saxes. By bar 3 texture is reduced to 2 choirs - brass & saxes. Melodic exchanges move between tpts and saxes.

Brief 2-voice counterpoint between tpts and saxes in bar 70. Bass lines dictated in m. 70-71 ensure passing chords are clear.

Close tbn. accompaniment voicings opened up for added emphasis of phrase ending.

8 bar extension of B (1:31) in contrasting Latin feel. Features saxes in descending sequence based on S. Rollins/ Clifford Brown material.

Interesting rhythmic counterpoint accompaniment in brass defines harmonies.

Trombone accompaniment rhythms are always changing for added variety. Gives sense of improvised comping

A1 - 1:38
Slight variation of previous A sections. Unison tune divided between saxes and tpts with tbn accompaniment

Trombones tend to move from closed to open at ends of phrases.

variation from earlier A sections
Altos
Tenors
Bari. Sax.
Tpt. 1
Tpt. 2
Tpt. 3
Tpt. 4
Tbn. 1
Tbn. 2
Tbn. 3
B. Tbn.
Pno.
Bass
Dr.
[ens.]
Alto Sax.
Ten. Sax.
Bari. Sax.
Tpt.
Tbn.
Interesting Polychord
Ami triad over Gmi-Ma7
Target D7alt chord approached by
chromatic upper neighbor with common
tones to previous chord (A, C, Eb, G).

Solo send-off based material borrowed from intro, bar 41.

Concerted ens. section builds to solo break. All voices move following contour of lead line, concert analysis below.

Chromatic, descending passing dominants lead to final resolution chord, embellised by added 9th, 11th & 13th.

A - 1:56 1st time
2:37 2nd

Changing background textures by alternating between sax and brass. Phrase entrances often on upbeats.

Background accompaniment shows open chorale style tbn voicings at this slower moving pace. 3 Tpts in triadic-like voicings provide upper extension tones.

A
107
Background writing similar to first solo tpt. A section
Altos
Tenors
Bari. Sax.
Tpt. 1
Tpt. 2
Tpt. 3
Tpt. 4
Tbn. 1
Tbn. 2
Tbn. 3
B. Tbn.
Pno.
Bass
Dr.
Alto Sax.
Ten. Sax.
Bari. Sax.
Tpt.
Tbn.

B - 2:55
(2nd)
115
Altos
Tenors
Bari. Sax.
Tpt. 1
Tpt. 2
Tpt. 3
Tpt. 4
Tbn. 1
Tbn. 2
Tbn. 3
B. Tbn.
Pno.
Bass
Dr.
[bones]
[saxes]
Passing, chromatic upper neighbor dominant resolves by half-step. F7alt chord voicing varied on each reiteration in bar 120 providing for good voice movement on all parts.
Alto Sax.
Ten. Sax.
Bari. Sax.
Tpt.
Tbn.
Left hand piano-like voicings in tbns. Unless chord changes, upbeats always anticipate upcoming harmony. All voicings are rootless favoring use of extension tones as substitute for roots.

B extension
Latin feel
3:01
121
sequencing resembles bars 121-122
Altos
Tenors
Bari. Sax.
Tpt. 1
Tpt. 2
Tpt. 3
Tpt. 4
Tbn. 1
Tbn. 2
Tbn. 3
B. Tbn.
Pno.
Bass
Dr.
Alto Sax.
Ten. Sax.
Bari. Sax.
Tpt.
Tbn.
[latin]
[latin]
[latin]

A1- 3:10 — Similar rhythmic & voicing approach to sax backgrounds in first solo A section

129

6-part brass voicings more than adequate to create dynamic tension. Tpts on 7, 9 & 11ths while tbns. define chord with 3rd & 7th

137
A - 3:20 1st time
4:00 2nd
Similar rhythmically to backgrounds on previous solo chorus. Saxes always anticipating upcoming harmonies
Altos
Tenors
Bari. Sax.
Tpt. 1
Tpt. 2
Tpt. 3
Tpt. 4
Tbn. 1
Tbn. 2
Tbn. 3
B. Tbn.
Pno.
Bass
Dr.
Alto Sax.
Ten. Sax.
Bari. Sax.
Tpt.
Tbn.
[1st time only!]
[last X only!]
[figures last time]
[bkgds last X]
[brass]

Often uses octave unison passage culminating in harmonized phrase ending
A1 - 4:09
similarity to previous occasions in A section backgrounds
145
[last X only!]
[last time only!]
Altos
Tenors
Bari. Sax.
Tpt. 1
Tpt. 2
Tpt. 3
Tpt. 4
Tbn. 1
Tbn. 2
Tbn. 3
B. Tbn.
Pno.
Bass
Dr.
Alto Sax.
Ten. Sax.
Bari. Sax.
Tpt.
Tbn.

B - 4:18
153
Altos
Tenors
Bari. Sax.
Brass push to end of section
Tpt. 1
Tpt. 2
Tpt. 3
Tpt. 4
GMIN7 D♭7 CMIN7 F7ALT B♭Δ7 G7ALT CMIN7 F7ALT
Tbn. 1
Tbn. 2
Tbn. 3
B. Tbn.
D♭7 CMIN7 F7ALT B♭Δ7 G7ALT CMIN7 F13 F7ALT
Pno.
GMIN7 D♭7 CMIN7 F7ALT B♭Δ7 G7ALT BMIN CMIN7 F7 F7ALT
Bass
[bones]
153
[saxes]
Dr.
Alto Sax.
Ten. Sax.
Bari. Sax.
Tpt.
Tbn.

159

Largely full concerted ens. backgrounds but primarily more sustained note values so as not to detract from soloist. Backgrounds resemble same section in previous chorus but more fully orchestrated.

A1 - 4:33
167
Altos
Tenors
Bari. Sax.
Brass imitation of saxes 4 beats later
Tpt. 1
Tpt. 2
Tpt. 3
Tpt. 4
[swing]
GMIN7 A⌀7 D7ALT B♭MIN7 E♭7 A⌀7 D7ALT CMIN7 F7 B♭MIN7 E♭7 A⌀7 D7ALT GMIN7 D7ALT
Tbn. 1
Tbn. 2
Tbn. 3
B. Tbn.
[swing]
GMIN7 A⌀7 D7ALT B♭MIN7 E♭7(♯11) A⌀7 D7ALT CMIN9 F7(♯11 ♯9) B♭MIN7 E♭13♯11 E♭7♯9 A⌀7 D7ALT GMIN11 D7ALT
Pno.
[walk]
GMIN7 A⌀7 D7ALT B♭MIN7 E♭7 A⌀7 D7ALT CMIN7 F7 B♭MIN7 E♭7 A⌀7 D7ALT GMIN7 D7ALT
Bass
167
[swing]
Dr.
Alto Sax.
Ten. Sax.
Bari. Sax.
Tpt.
Tbn.

Transitional Interlude - 4:42

Brass closely resemble material found earlier at measures 41 and 91. Trumpets show near exact sequential melodic material. Notice how saxes take over melodic interest from the tpts. in the second half of bars 176, 178, 179, 180 until entire ens. climaxes to a concerted finish of this 8 bar transitional section.

12 additional bars of transitional material serving as seque to sax solo, D dominant and bass pedal reminiscent of B section extension harmonies

Similarity in brass to bars 43 & 44

In absence of 4 tbns. arranger treats 4th tpt. as lead tbn. voice through this passage.

28

Quote from bridge of tune and from Clifford Brown

Tenor sax solo begins 5:04
Static ostinato bass with harmonic pedal point as basis for tenor sax solo. Bass hints at upcoming return to walking style
A rare occasion of only 3-part sax voicings with second tenor as the doubled voice, no doubt to keep the texture, density and weight nimble and light at this point in solo. Lead alto is transposed sequence of trombone figure.
29
195
197
199
6:31
Altos
Tenors
Bari. Sax.
Tpt. 1
Tpt. 2
Tpt. 3
Tpt. 4
Tbn. 1
Tbn. 2
Tbn. 3
B. Tbn.
Pno.
Bass
Dr.
Alto Sax.
Ten. Sax.
Bari. Sax.
Tpt.
Tbn.
8xs (ostinato)
open
on cue
[backgrounds enter]
trbs 1-3 enter
[tenor solo]
[open comping]
[walk]
[driving "4"]
[4]
mf
Melodic trombone background is sequential and derived from the diminished scale related to D7(#9)

207
Altos
Tenors
- 4 -
Bari. Sax.
rhythmic repetition compared to first
4-bar phrase at bar 207
[tpt. 2 enters]
Tpt. 1
[lead]
Tpt. 2
mf
Tpt. 3
mf
Tpt. 4
mf
Tbn. 1
Tbn. 2
Tbn. 3
B. Tbn.
Pno.
[8]
Bass
[8]
A7 Eb7
207
[trpts.]
Dr.
[8]
Alto Sax.
Ten. Sax.
Bari. Sax.
Tpt melodic line also extracted from
diminshed scale. Tbns in open chorale
style voicings
Tpt.
mf
Tbn.
Eb7 serves as tritone sub of previous chord
and chromatic upper neighbor of target chord
D7. 1/2 step between bone 1 & 2 usually
avoided but voicing is low

Call-Response fashion. Full brass sustained chords now feature 4 tpts. Saxes play simple unison melodic fragment suggestive of earlier brass background and bars 7-10 of tune. Tpt. half- step motion is opposite direction of saxes.

Low tpt. voicings offer good opportunity for open chorale style tbn voicings with 4th on low root.

Brass voicings get more dense as solo intensifies. Tpts again outline dim 7th built off chord root.

Further development of previous material. Brass show rhythmic diminution of previous 8 bars and use of tritone substitution for V7 of D7 - Eb7 instead of A7. Two notes in sax & tpt. figure combine to represent original idea.

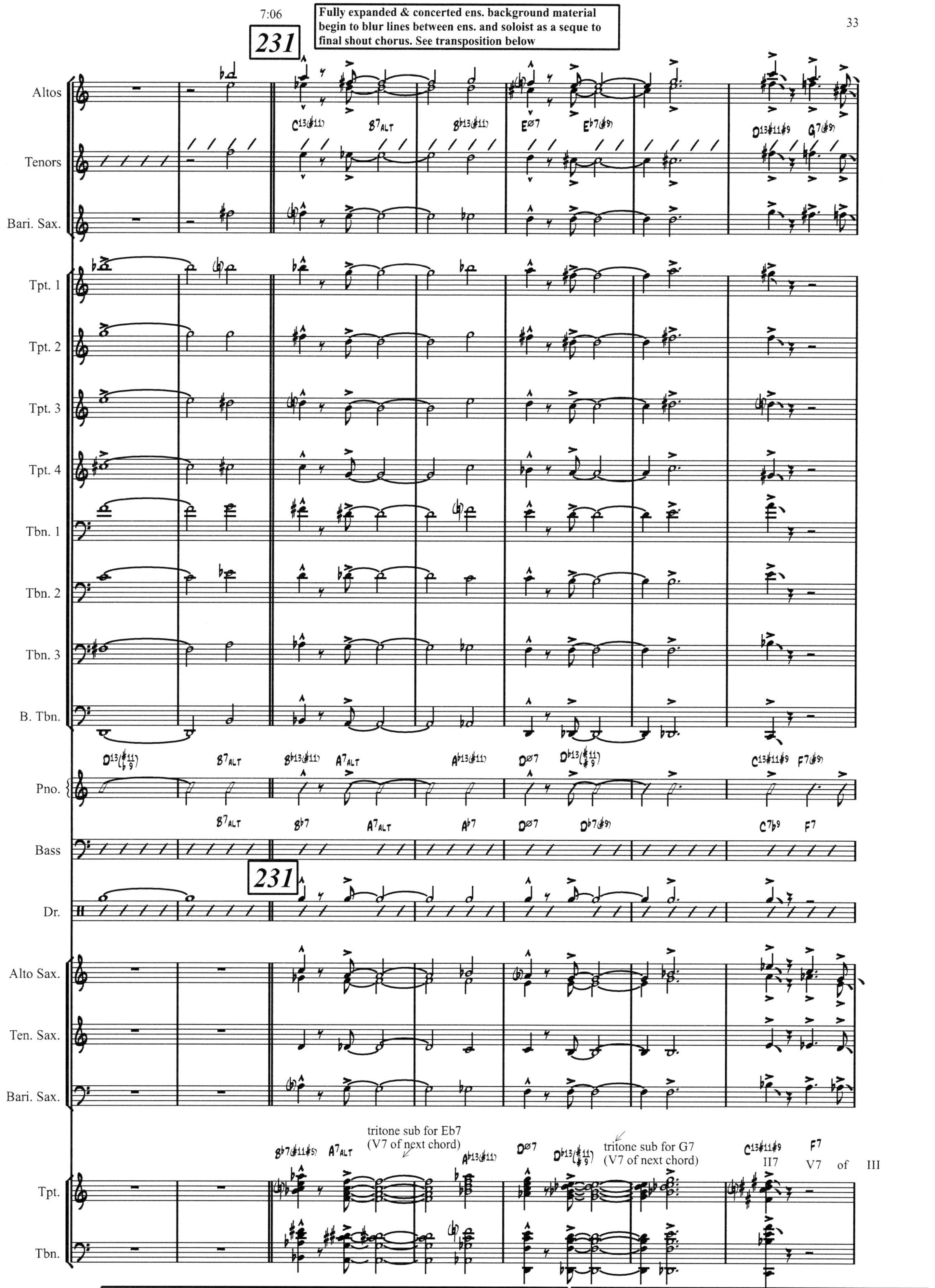

A - 7:15 Shout Chorus (m. 239)

Concerted sections avoid repeated notes by using passing chords. Saxes in octave unison for more active passages while brass accompany with more sustained chords. See concert pitch detail below.

Chord symbols followed by "P" indicate a passing chord added to original progression to accommodate lead line and ensure good voice leading in all voices. The arranger uses a series of diminshed 7th chords in tpts to stress extension tones. Defining chord tones appear in tbns. These dense, dissonant chords create a series of tensions that are relieved by the chords that follow. Chords marked with a T or R indicate Tension and Relief. Even the less dissonant chords in this ens. section are harmonically dense. Upper neighbor passing chord on & of beat 3 in bar 238 is quality sub. for expected dom. 7th (Eb7) and shares common tones with previous chord while providing good voice leading.

Altos
Tenors
Bari. Sax.
Tpt. 1
Tpt. 2
Tpt. 3
Tpt. 4
Tbn. 1
Tbn. 2
Tbn. 3
B. Tbn.
Pno.
CMIN9 BMIN9 E13(#11 b9) BbMIN7 Eb13(#11 b9) Aø7 D13(#11) GMIN13
Bass
Ab7 Aø7 D7 CMIN7 F7 BMIN7 E7 BbMIN7 Eb7 Aø7 D7
Dr.
Alto Sax.
Ten. Sax.
Bari. Sax.
quality sub
Aø7 D13(#11) CMIN7 F13(#11b9) BMIN7 E7(#5b9) BbMIN7 Eb13(#11b9) Aø7 D13(#11) Ebm11 D13 GMIN13
R T R T R T R T R T R
Tpt.
Tbn.

Saxes rhythmically & harmonically reinforce syncopations in brass. Sax voicing interlocks with brass at tpt 3
247
Altos
Tenors
Bari. Sax.
Tpt. 1
Tpt. 2
Tpt. 3
Tpt. 4
Tbn. 1
Tbn. 2
Tbn. 3
B. Tbn.
Pno.
Bass
Dr.
[saxes]
[ens.]
no root or 3rd
Alto Sax.
Ten. Sax.
Bari. Sax.
Tpt.
Tbn.
Half-dim chords as pasisng harmonies. Note poly chord on beat 2-1/2 - 3 bar 250

B -7:32

Rhythnmic interplay between saxes and trombone accompaniment. Unison saxes is contrast to previous dense harmonic section

Chords above tpt staff show how the chord progression embellishes movement of original chord progression by inserting V7 or ii7-V7 progressions to preceed the chord in the original progression, usually delaying it.

B Section
Extension - 7:38
261
Nice melodic & rhythmic interplay between saxes & brass with each section playing its own riff-like motive.
Altos
Tenors
Bari. Sax.
rare repeated note
Tpt. 1
C. Brown reference
Tpt. 2
Tpt. 3
Tpt. 4
Tbn. 1
Tbn. 2
Tbn. 3
B. Tbn.
DMIN7 G7ALT CMIN9 F7ALT E7(♯9) Latin E7(♯9)
Pno.
latin
CMIN7 F7ALT E7(♯9)
Bass
261 Latin
Dr.
Alto Sax.
Ten. Sax.
Bari. Sax.
DMIN7 G7ALT D13(♯11/♯9) Dbm11 CMIN9
Tpt.
Tbn.
G7 Cm7 F7

Return to final A section exactly as previously at bars 83-90

A1 - 7:47

CODA or TAG - Brass same as trumpet solo send- off bars 91-94 while saxes present new octave unison material

Full ensemble pushes to final climax using the largest and most dense polychords in the entire arrangement. See concert score excerpts below for harmonic detail.

Most dense polychord and largest span voicing in entire score featuring tpts in rare open voicing

Near complete altered scale in saxes

Drives to end using dense harmonic sequence resolving to final out of key polychord.

Saxophonist, composer/arranger, and author Bob Mintzer

Chapter 2
Bob Mintzer – "Ellis Island"

Many of today's jazz composers and arrangers are multitasking, diverse artists in that they are deeply committed and engaged in many aspects of the art form. There has been a great deal of discussion in recent years, especially in the ivory tower, about the need to educate entrepreneurs, not just musicians. All that's really necessary to validate this point of view is to take a look at the role models that any of the writers discussed here serve, and Bob Mintzer is a perfect example. Jazz performer extraordinaire, performance studies book author, recording artist, bandleader, composer, arranger, clinician, music director, and educator, Bob is an extraordinary example of the musician/entrepreneur who has achieved great success in all these diverse yet related areas. He was educated at Interlochen Arts Academy before pursuing advanced studies at Hartt School of Music and the Manhattan School of Music, where he seized opportunities to learn the woodwind instruments and perform in a diverse collection of classical, jazz, and early music ensembles. He was a sponge, taking advantage of every opportunity to broaden his skill set.

Mintzer's first exposure to road life as a touring professional came in 1974 as a member of Emir Deodato's large ensemble following the hit recording of Deodato's version of Richard Strauss' *Also Sprach Zarathustra*. It was during this experience that he began to learn about Latin American rhythms, an interest he continued to pursue in later years as a member of Latin bands led by Tito Puente, Eddie Palmieri, and Mongo Santamaria. The influence of Latin and Afro-Cuban music has been a lasting one that permeates his music. A year later Mintzer joined the Buddy Rich Big Band, where he spent two and a half years as featured tenor and soprano saxophone soloist and began to gain experience as an arranger. During this same period he wrote music for and performed with the Art Blakey Quintet.

Settling down in New York City in the mid-1970s, doors began to open for Mintzer including Broadway pit orchestras, a chair in the Thad Jones/Mel Lewis Jazz Orchestra, and sessions with Tom Harrell, Joe Chambers, Sam Jones, and many others. The New York loft and club scene was exploding in the 1970s and '80s, and Mintzer became a fixture on this scene. He joined Michael Brecker, Peter Erskine, and others in Jaco Pastorius' Word of Mouth band, and when the band grew in size he began to arrange for it. It was during this period that Bob also performed and recorded with Randy Brecker and Mike Mainieri. He conceived a special project for the Brecker Brothers' Seventh Avenue South club, for which he wrote all the arrangements to showcase musicians who had been featured at the club in their own groups, such as David Sandborn, the Brecker Brothers, Don Grolnick, Lew Soloff, Will Lee, and others. At every opportunity, Bob continued to develop his writing skills, making himself increasingly valuable as an exceptional performer who could also compose and arrange.

In the early 1980s and at the dawn of the compact disc and digital recording technologies, Mintzer started his big band and began a twenty-two year relationship with Tom Jung and his DMP record label. Together they produced thirteen Bob Mintzer Big Band albums, which garnered three Grammy nominations. Now with the MCG and Fuzzy Music labels, the big band has a cumulative catalogue of nineteen recordings. Soon after his success with the big band, he forged a relationship with Kendor Music, which published many of his big band compositions along with those by Thad Jones, Sammy Nestico, and Gil Evans.

Perpetually committed to education, Mintzer joined the faculty at his alma mater, the Manhattan School of Music, where he taught for twenty-five years before accepting the Buzz McCoy endowed chair of jazz studies in 2008 at the University of Southern California. The move was logical, since years before he'd found himself in a bicoastal relationship as a member of the Grammy Award winning California based small group the Yellowjackets. He has toured with this leaderless, co-op band for over twenty-six years, and his music can be heard on their nineteen recordings!

When he isn't performing or teaching at USC, or giving workshops and master classes around the globe, Mintzer is in Cologne, Germany, where he is chief conductor of the WDR Big Band. In 1994 *DownBeat* magazine described him as "a prolific composer and accomplished arranger, [who] is also a fire-breathing soloist."

There are a number of innovative scores that could have been chosen for this case study. Several earlier works were considered, including "Original People," "In the Eighties," "Like a Child," "Mr. Fone Bone," and "Camouflage," but the composer and I finally concluded that this somewhat more recent work, "Ellis Island*,*" would best serve our purposes and showcase the composer's more mature writing style. These other pieces are highly recommended for further study and will be noted in the following discography. The listing has been limited to Mintzer's large ensemble recordings, though there are many smaller group sessions with the Yellowjackets and others.

Selected Discography

Incredible Journey – DMP, 1985

Camouflage – DMP, 1986 – includes "Camouflage," "Mr. Fone Bone," and "In the Eighties"

Spectrum – DMP, 1988 – includes "Like a Child"

Urban Contours – DMP, 1989

Art of the Band – DMP, 1991

Departure – DMP, 1993

Only in New York – DMP, 1994

Big Band Trane – DMP, 1996

Latin from Manhattan – DMP, 1998 – includes "Ellis Island," which this study is based on

Homage to Count Basie – DMP, 2000

Gently – DMP, 2002 – includes "Original People"

Bob Mintzer Big Band Live at MCG with Special Guest Kurt Elling – MCG Jazz, 2004 – includes "Original People"

Old School New Lessons Featuring Kurt Elling – Telarc/MCG Jazz, 2006

Swing Out – Telarc/MCG Jazz, 2008

Get Up – Telarc/MCG Jazz, 2015

All L.A. Band – Fuzzy Music, 2016 – includes smaller band version of "Ellis Island"

"Ellis Island"

"Ellis Island" was chosen for this case study because it is in an unusual meter (6/8) for a jazz composition, and offers a glimpse into the rhythmically complex world of Latin influenced jazz, which has been a significant aspect of Bob Mintzer's musical heritage. It also features an interesting harmonic palette quite different from what is found in most big band writing, and the score shows what can be accomplished with minimal two-part linear writing. This piece has been included on two recordings, including one more recent by Mintzer's slightly smaller *LA Band*. This analysis, however, is based on the original recording for full big band that appeared on the *Latin in Manhattan* recording, one of the band's last on the DMP label.

Lead Sheet – Melodic Overview

The lead sheet that is the basis of the large ensemble score is straightforward and without great complexity, at least at first glance. It is, however, in a 6/8 Latin rhythmic style, which instantly introduces a level of complexity not associated with most big band charts. Melodically speaking, this score is an excellent example of simplicity, with much of the inspiration derived from short pentatonic scale fragments used to create motives. The A and B sections are based entirely on brief motives derived from the F and C pentatonic scales. These short phrases, never more than a measure or two, function more like gestures than long evolving melodies. These melodies are accompanied by complex harmonies and challenging 6/8 rhythms that often disguise the bar line.

Repetition or near repetition and the similarity of melodic gestures provide a cohesiveness to the melody. For example, a 16th note pair, either ascending or descending, is heard in the very first beat and occurs again in measures 2, 3, and 6 in the A sections. The two bar motive that begins and is the basis of the B section is repeated with some variation over the next five measures. The four note ascending gesture in the first and third measures of the C section, even though the intervallic shape differs slightly, provides continuity to this section, as does the similarity of the section at measures 23 and 24.

Pitch repetition within these short melodic phrases, especially in the B section, is somewhat reminiscent of Tin Pan Alley pop vocal tunes from many years earlier. The range of the primary melody, as shown in the lead sheet that follows, never exceeds a 13th. Counterpoint introduced by a secondary melodic line and the interaction of these two voices adds a great deal of interest to the arrangement.

Example 2.1 – Ellis Island lead sheet

REPETITION OF PREVIOUS 2 BAR PHRASE WITH RHYTHMIC VARIATION
10
TBNS
Bbm13/A
SAXES
Abm13/A
Eb7(add11)/A
Db7(add11)/A
Bbmaj9
C/Bb
PNO.
13
REPETITION OF 1ST & 4TH BARS OF 8 SECTION
REPETITION & TRANSPOSITION OF BAR 11
C
F7(add11)
Eb7(add11)
Db6/9(#11)
Db13(add11)
Eb7(SUS4)
E13(b9)
A+7(b9)
A7(b9)
(HARMONIES BASED ON FULL SCORE)
17
ALTO & TPT
8 FLAT LYDIAN FRAGMENT
EXTENSION TONES......................
Bbmaj7(#5)
Amaj7(#5)
Ab13(SUS4)
Ab9
G13(#9)

21
DIMINISHED SCALE FRAGMENT
TEN SAX & BARI
NEAR EXACT SEQUENCE BEGINS
C13(♯9)
F13(♯11 ♭9)
E13
F♯13
A♭13
Pno.
A1 Near exact repetion of A
24
F Pentatonic
TRUMPETS
B♭13
C13(♯11)
Dm11
Em7(♯5)
Pno.
27
F(add2)
Gm11
Dm11
Pno.

Lead Sheet Reduction – Harmonic Overview

Years after Mintzer created "Ellis Island" one can hear an extension of this rhythmic and modern harmonic style in the music he has contributed to the contemporary small group the Yellowjackets. While there are strong tendencies through the piece for one chord to move naturally to another because of half or whole step neighbor relations, functional harmonies and tendencies are almost completely absent. The unique harmonic aspects of this tune and the 6/8 rhythmic figures no doubt motivated the composer to specifically notate all voicings for the pianist rather than including the typical chord chart. The sophisticated harmonies called for specific notation rather than risk misinterpretation by the performer.

Quartal voicings, or near perfect 4th stacks, are abundant in both closed and open positions, as shown in Examples 2.2a and 2.2b. Other instances will be noted in the analysis of the full score. Example 2.2b shows open position quartal voicings. The first bar illustrates such a voicing with an added major third at the top. The second measure shows voicings that are in near perfect 4th configurations.

Examples 2.2a & 2.2b

Of particular note are several innovative and unusual aspects of the harmonic style found in this lead sheet:

1. Complex chords with extension tones above the 7th expressed with only a few voices, omitting many chord tones. The very fact that many notes are omitted often makes them difficult to label. Take, for example, the third and fourth bars of the B section, where Mintzer suggested the upper chords and the author the lower. Neither approach is wrong in this case.

2. Use of the minor seventh chord with a raised 5th, sometimes referred to as an added ♭6. This particular chord encourages quartal voicings in both closed and open positions.

3. Dominant 7th chords that include the 3rd and 4th or 11th. The 4th and 3rd are spaced widely apart at opposite ends of the voicing, creating almost perfect quartal voicings, but with an added element of dissonance.

4. Use of the augmented major 7th including the raised 5th.

5. Stepwise, chromatic movement is common, and 3rd or 4th movements between chords are rare.

6. Typical ii^7–V^7 or IV^7–V^7 cadences, even at the ends of major sections, are absent. Cadences featured include an ascending stream of dominant 13th chords beginning in m.23 that resolves to tonic in m.25 by a final major 2nd resolution, and iv^7–v^7 (both minor chords) to tonic (Dmi) motion at the end of the A section and at the end of the tune.

Key changes are implied at the B section (B♭) and C section, which stays in B♭. The strong ascending dominant chord progression in the final two bars of this section lead back to the tonic Dmi chord at the return of A.

Example 2.3

Ellis Island
Harmonic Scheme

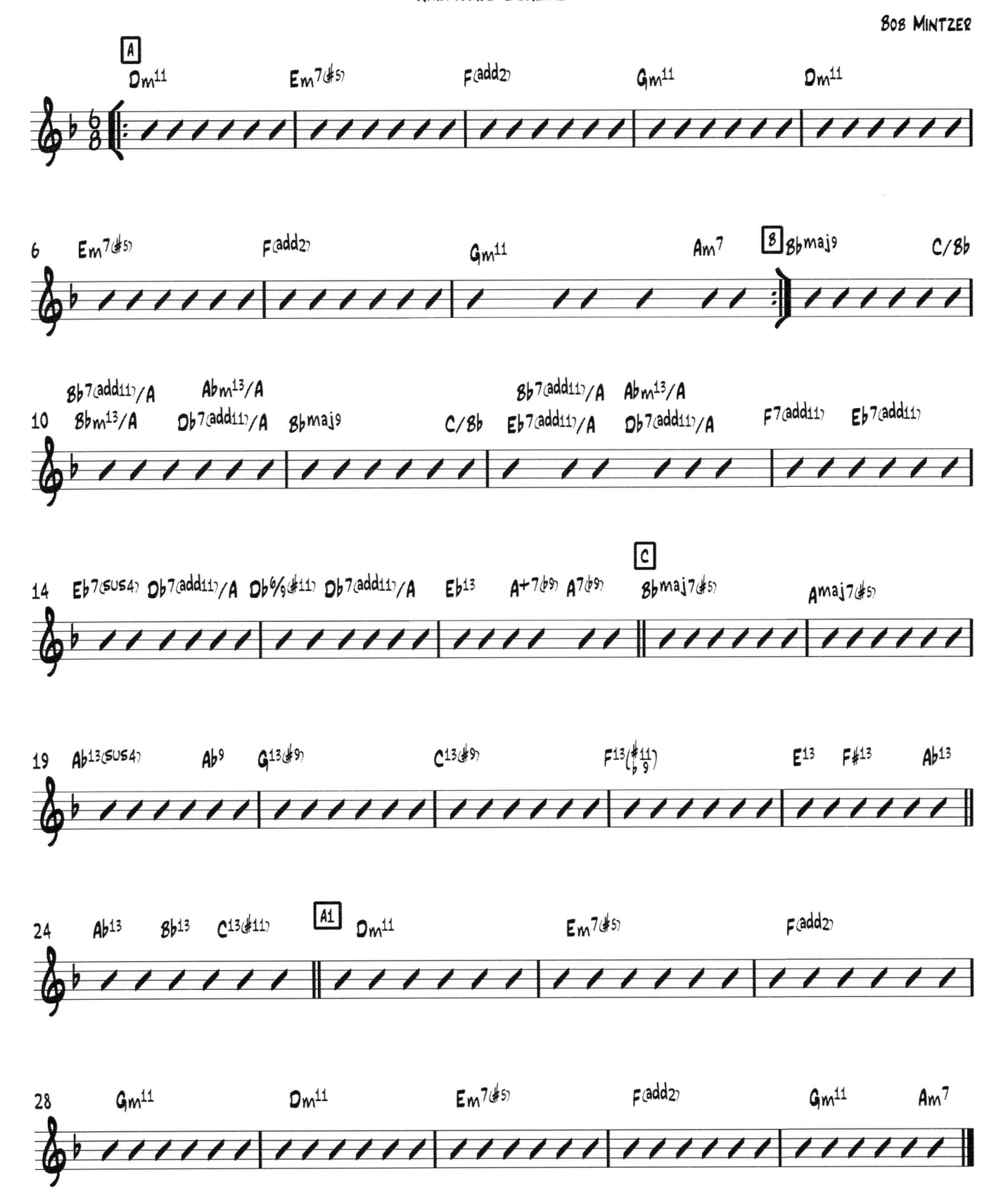

Bob Mintzer

The root movement in Example 2.3 is anything but functionally based. The C section is the closest example of functional harmonic movement.

There is a contrast and balance in this tune between the A, B, and C sections. The harmonic motion moves slowly in the A and C sections, with harmony changing only once every measure. The B section, by contrast, is much more active, with harmonies changing every three beats. The C section shows a return to slower moving harmonic rhythm until the last two measures, when the harmonic rhythm increases, pushing to the return to the A section and tonic (Dmi) in m.25.

It is important to mention that Bob Mintzer's prowess as a single note improviser no doubt leads him to make certain intuitive artistic decisions as a composer that are both challenging to analyze in a traditional manner and interesting to listen to. His harmonic structures are likely linearly derived and based on a desire for intentional dissonance resolved through voice leading, but often with a common or connecting tone that provides some sense of harmonic, gravitational stability. Some of these sonorities might also be linked to the synthetic scales that jazz players often use as source material. It is safe to say that some aspects of this score were likely guided by an organic, spontaneous, intuitive process and without any real premeditation. Jazz composition is, after all, a natural extension of improvisation. This being said, the explanations provided here are the best effort to explain some of the more unusual harmonic aspects of this score. In some cases two possible chord symbols are indicated in the lead sheet. The interview with Bob at the close of this chapter will shed further light on his intentions, premeditations, and creative process in developing this score.

Example 2.4 – Two possible ways to express chords in measures 10 and 12

Rhythmic Overview

The complex rhythmic elements throughout this score provide one of its most unique and original aspects, and this goes far beyond the unusual 6/8 meter. This complexity is apparent even in the simplified lead sheet shown in Example 2.1. Rhythmic counterpoint between voices has become a hallmark of Mintzer's style and is evident in the primary and secondary melodic voices at the A and B sections. The interplay leaves space for each voice to breathe, but as in all good counterpoint, the two lines play off one another, each melodically strong on its own though the primary voice dominates and draws the most attention. The rhythm of the accompaniment at letter B is strong enough to make this line of greater importance than merely a secondary accompaniment figure. Specific rhythms are so essential to the essence of this tune that they are notated in bass and piano parts and interpreted as written by the performers. The composer left nothing to chance, except during the solo sections.

Basic Lead Sheet Form

There are no surprises or elaborate twists in the formal aspect of this tune, though it does have one more section than the tried and true AABA song form. In this case the form consists of an added section, labeled C, before returning to the last A section, which is nearly identical to the initial statement of the A theme. Each of these sections is 8 measures long.

The Arrangement

General Observations

At first glance this rather short arrangement seems somewhat typical of a big band score. On closer examination, however, there is a great deal of subtle complexity, advanced harmonic structures, counterpoint, and rhythmic interplay. The writing is reminiscent of a small group piece. The composer paid great attention to detail in terms of the dynamics and the resulting dramatic contrasts. I had the advantage of working from Mintzer's original handwritten score, and he was very specific about dynamic markings, often writing different dynamic levels for different sections of the band, or even a single part when warranted. The nature of this piece required that he write out all piano voicings and figures except for the solo sections. The same is true for bass parts. Absent is the more typical chord symbol chart. The harmonic structures almost required a new system of symbology, since it was difficult to describe many voicings with traditional functional harmony symbols. The addition of the Latin percussionist playing conga throughout is not indicated on the score but is an important aspect of this piece. The percussionist's regular 16th note pattern keeps the groove moving forward and frees the drummer to play fills and a simple "two" groove accenting beat 4 in the 6/8 meter. Further detailed analysis in this narrative and on the score at the close of this chapter provides a microscopic look at this very unusual arrangement. Since this piece is quite different from the score discussed in Chapter 1, the organization of the analytical discussion that follows is somewhat different and is tailored to the unique aspects of this score.

The entire chart is based on a series of short one and two bar phrases. The interplay between sections splits the listener's attention at times. For example, it is difficult to decide at the B section which is primary and which is secondary material – the trombone accompaniment or the succinct sax motives especially, since they occur simultaneously.

Form

The pacing is what is striking about this score – how it gradually unfolds to just over six minutes and does so in a very dynamically changing fashion. These dynamic contrasts are easily visible in Example 2.5. There is a dynamic ebb and flow to this chart that is obvious in the graphic analysis that follows. When the composer adds additional instruments, as he does in the repeat of the A section, it doesn't necessarily mean things get louder. In this case there is a small but noticeable dynamic increase to move into the B section. This new section builds significantly to a sudden drop in dynamic level for the C section.

Example 2.5

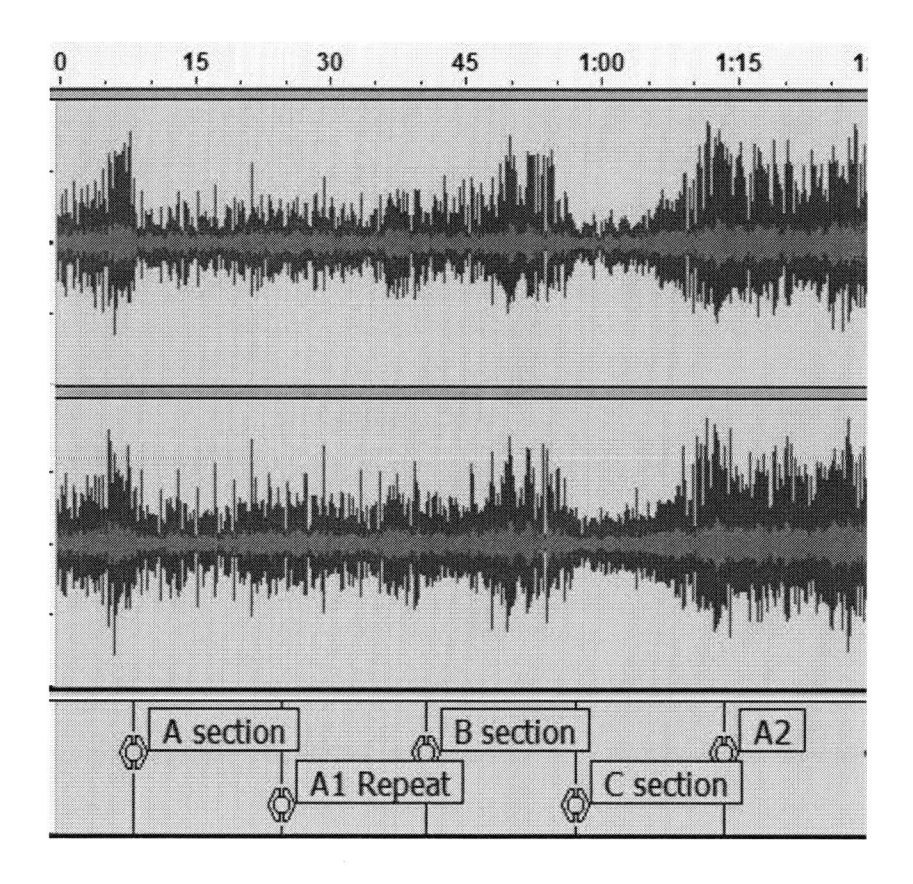

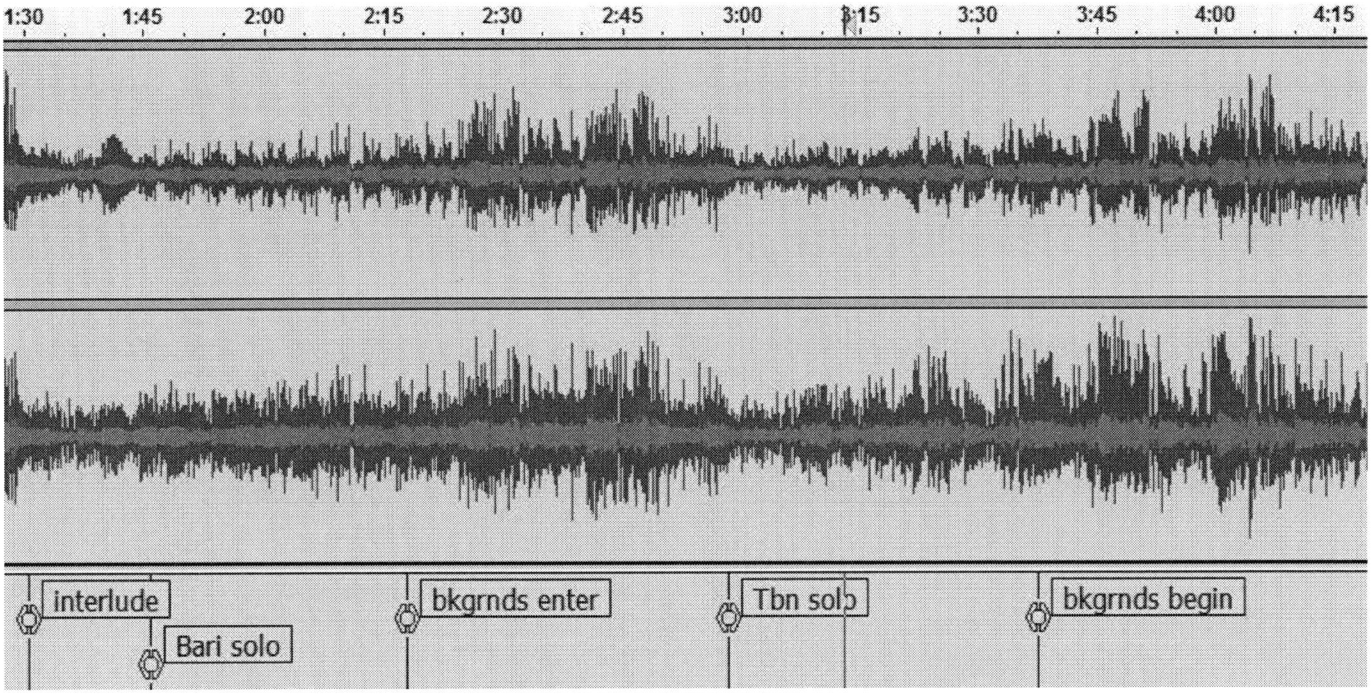
1:30
1:45
2:00
2:15
2:30
2:45
3:00
3:15
3:30
3:45
4:00
4:15
interlude
Bari solo
bkgrnds enter
Tbn solo
bkgrnds begin

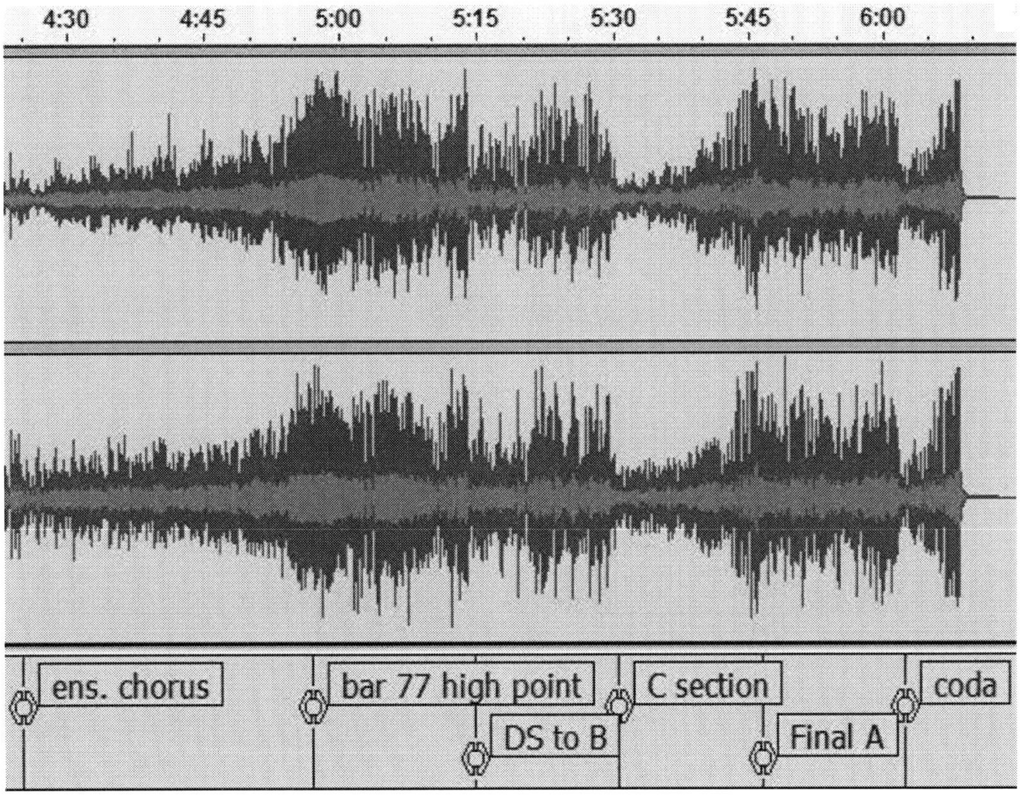
4:30
4:45
5:00
5:15
5:30
5:45
6:00
ens. chorus
bar 77 high point
DS to B
C section
Final A
coda

Example 2.6 — "Ellis Island" timeline. The top shaded cell indicates bar numbers followed by timings.

[1—8] 0:00—0:16	[9—14] 0:17—0:23	[15—21] 0:24—0:30
Piano solo	2 bars of Ens followed 4 bars of Piano solo	2 bars of Ens followed by 5 bars of Piano solo
8 bars repeated	6 bar phrase	7 bar phrase

[22—30] 0:31—0:40	[31—40] 0:41—0:52	[41-53] 0:53—1:04
3 bars of Ens followed by 6 bar Piano Solo	4 bars of Ens followed by 6 bars of Piano solo	4 bars of Ens, 6 bars Piano solo, 1 bar rhythm section figure, and 1 silent bar to close unusual intro
9 bars	10 bars	12 bars

[53] 1:06	[69] 1:23	[83] 1:38
A Section — 8 bars Repeats with thicker texture	B Section — unusual length at 6 bars plus 8 bar Afro-Latin extension	A¹ — slightly altered A section material
Ten Sax & Tpt state A theme with added Ens punches	Saxes and Tpts volley with Tbn harmonic punctuation	Sax and Tpt unison interplay
16 bars	*14 bars*	*8 bars*

[91] 1:47	[99] 1:56	[137] 3:20	[175] 4:41
Solo send off	Trumpet Solo — two 38 bar choruses	Trombone Solo — two 38 choruses	Transition — Full Ens
Full Ens alludes to earlier melodic and rhythmic shapes	Solo based on form; Brass and Sax bkgrnds 2nd time	Based on form with Ens bkgrnds 2nd time	Based on fragments of earlier material with variation and sequences; Moves to D7(#9) for second 8 to introduce soloist
8 bars	*76 bars*	*76 bars*	*16 bars*

[195] 5:04	[199] 6:31	[215] 6:49	[213] 7:06
Tenor Sax solo over harmonic pedal	Sax solo continues	Solo continues	Solo continues
Rhythm section accompanies; bass gradually moves away from D pedal to walking style	Tbns & Saxes alternate bkgrnd figures; Tpts added	Brass-Sax interplay	Full Ens bkgrnds
20 bars	*16 bars*	*16 bars*	*16 bars*

[195] 5:04	[199] 6:31	[215] 6:49	[231] 7:06
Tenor Sax solo over harmonic pedal	Sax solo continues	Solo continues	Solo continues to end
Rhythm section accompanies; bass gradually moves away from D pedal to walking style	Tbns & saxes alternate bkgrnd figures; Tpts added	Brass-Sax interplay	Full Ens bkgrnds; Pedal gives way to dense dominant harmonies that lead to shout chorus
20 bars	*16 bars*	*16 bars*	*8 bars*

[239] 7:15	[255] 7:32	[269] 7:47	[277] 7:56
Shout Chorus — Top of form (A & A¹ Sections serve as basis)	Reflects B Section	Final A Section	Finale Tag or Coda
Full Ens	Unison Saxes & harmonized brass	Brass and Sax interplay	Full Ens builds to dramatic close featuring dense harmonies and large spans.
16 bars	*14 bars*	*8 bars*	*11 bars*

As expected, the ensemble backgrounds serve to enhance both soloists and their climaxes. But there is also an opportunity to close their statements more subtly before the next soloist's entrance. The graphic analysis also illustrates the nicely shaped ensemble chorus before the D.S. to the B section. The climax to this chart and to this ensemble section comes at about 80 percent through the score. Even the short four measure coda shows the composer's concern for dynamic shaping, beginning quietly at *mp* and ending fortissimo. This sudden change in dynamic level in such a brief span creates a dramatic ending.

Chord Voicing

There is little to say about voicing techniques, since this chart is so linearly based. Scoring is largely by choir with the sections playing together. There are, however, examples of cross section orchestrating such as the A section, and the C section where saxes and trumpets are scored in unison. A high percentage of the trumpet and saxophone parts are in unison or octave unisons, while trombones are used for accompaniment figures. It is therefore the linear aspects of this arrangement, along with the very unique harmonic structures and rhythms, that are most important to consider.

Saxophone Voicing

The saxophone section is used largely to perform melodic lines in unison, octave unison, fourths, or major sixths. They are used to state primary melodies and counter lines to the trumpets. The first chord to appear scored for saxophones is not until m.37, where they state an interesting modal cluster of major and minor seconds. Modal quartal voicings are planed at bars 45 and 53 for solo backgrounds. It should be noted that since the baritone is soloing at 45 instead of first tenor, as indicated on Mintzer's original score, it is assumed that a tenor covered the baritone background parts at this point.

Example 2.7 — Quartal saxophone background at bars 45 and 53

The rare voiced chords occur at the end of the development section in bars 80 and 85, where traditional voicings occur with baritone on the low root and upper saxophones outlining chord tones. The only additional voiced chord appears at the very last note, where saxes state an incomplete Dmi^9 chord, doubling pitches in the brass. The most interesting aspect of this last sax voicing is that the baritone is playing the 11th of the chord, not the expected root.

Brass Voicing

As previously stated, the trumpets are used linearly, but also in harmonized fashion with trombones. Trumpets typically state upper extension tones that alone might state a harmony different from the chord call. In such cases the trombones provide lower voices that identify the chord of the moment. This is obvious in the final measure of the introduction.

Example 2.8 – Measure 4

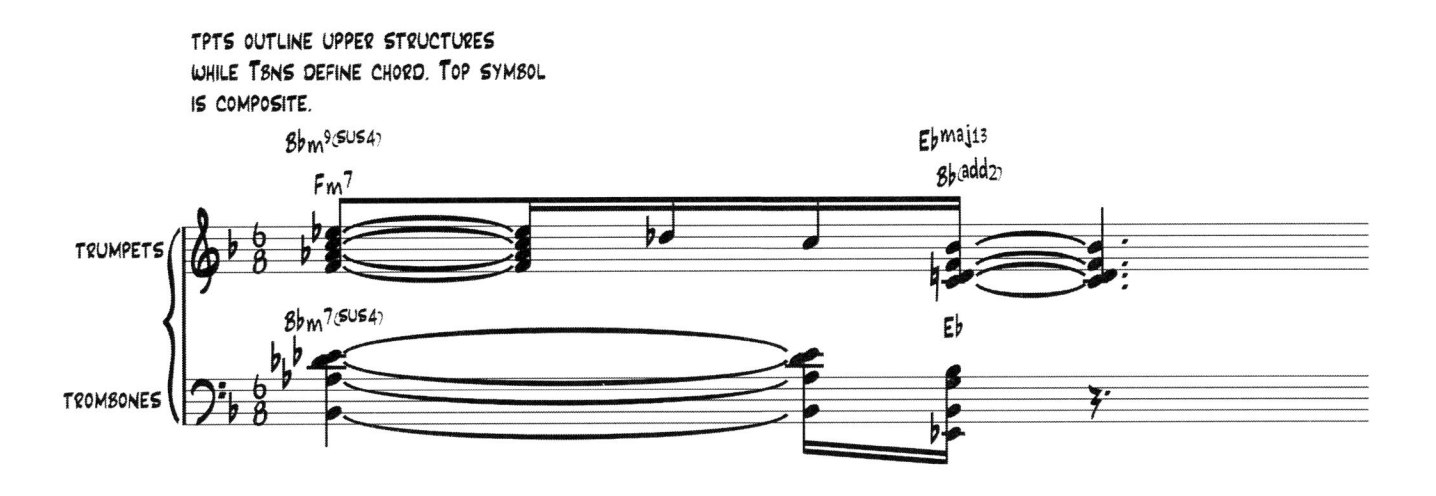

The first appearance of unusual, dissonant, and difficult to label voicings occurs at the B section, stated first by trombones and then expanded by the addition of trumpets. (See lead sheet reduction Example 2.1 for possible ways to symbolize bars 14 and 15.) Dominant and major chords that feature both the major third along with an 11th have become somewhat popular with several writers discussed in this book, and this tendency suggested the selection of the symbols used throughout this score analysis. Dominant 11th and 13th chords in measures 17–19 are far less dissonant than one would think by putting the 3rd as the highest voice, as far away as possible from the 11th or 4th, as shown in this brief excerpt from this passage.

Example 2.9 – Measure 17

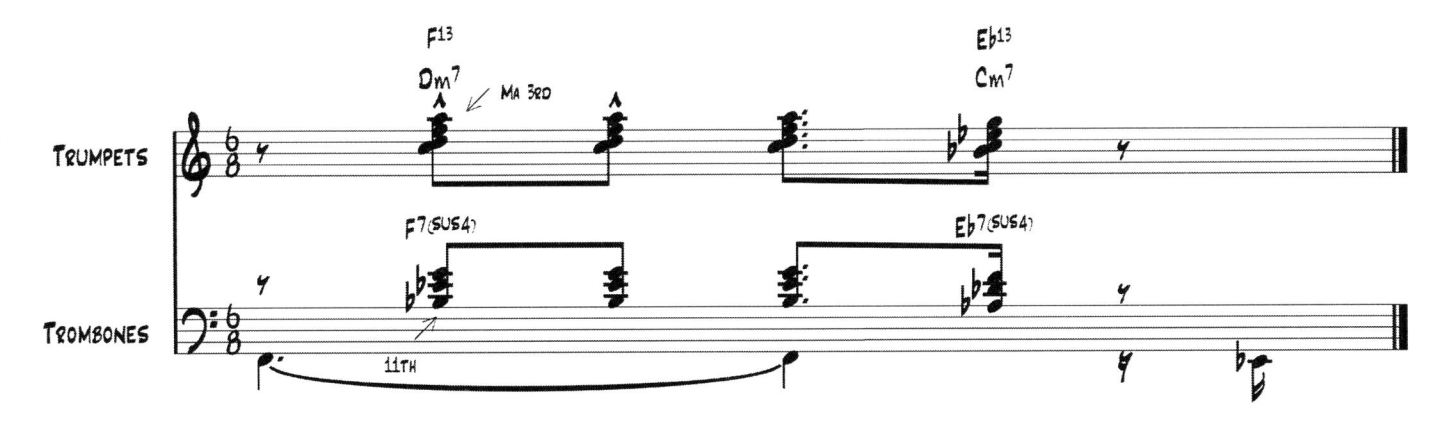

Trombones are voiced in both open position, chorale style with trombone four on low roots and in rootless close position. Quartal or near perfect quartal voicings in close and open positions are utilized. When voiced in chords, trumpets are nearly always in close position.

Example 2.10 – Measure 27. Trumpets on top include extension tones

The Dorian mode cluster voicing that immediately precedes the first soloist shows saxophones, trumpets, and trombones in close voicings. Clusters or very close voicings such as these always work best when a larger gap is maintained at the outermost voices, as is the case at measures 37 and 38 in the brass.

Example 2.11

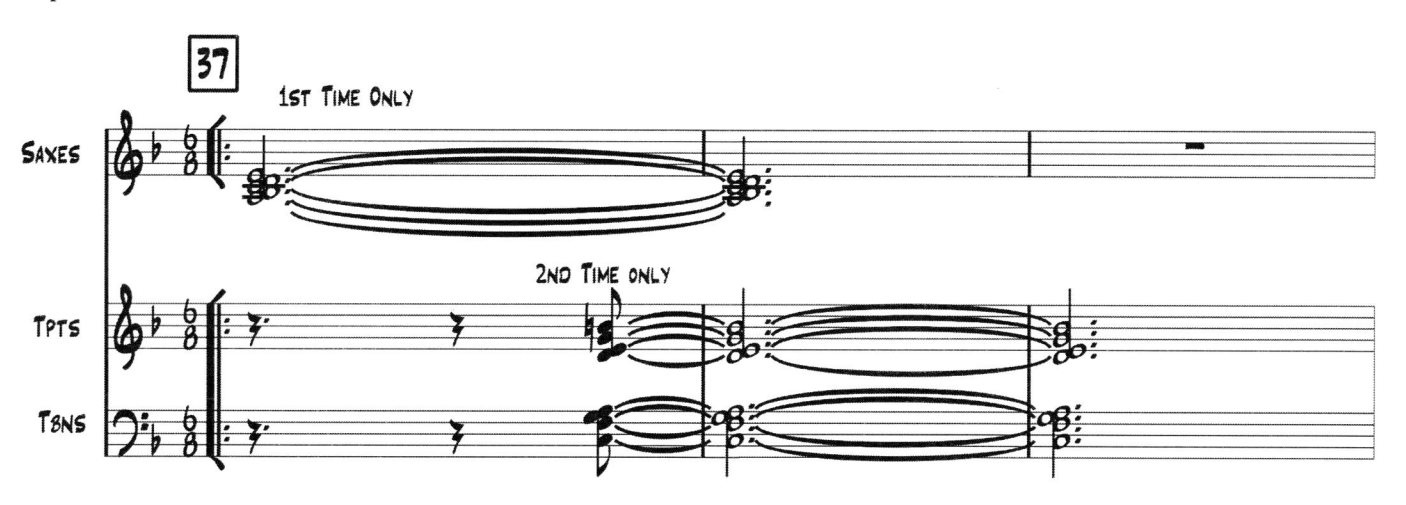

Bass Doubling

The Latin rhythmic aspect of this chart suggests that bass lines and bass ostinatos associated with this style could be an important aspect of this chart, or at least more predominant than bass lines in more traditional swing charts. The bass trombone bears much of the responsibility of doubling bass figures in "Ellis Island." The baritone sax is only occasionally used to double bass lines. Doubled bass lines in the left hand piano parts are indicated, but it is difficult to hear on the recording if the pianist is actually playing the left hand duplicate bass lines.

Solo Background Writing

Identical sax and brass background figures are used for both soloists. In both cases these background figures are quartally voiced structures based on the Dorian mode. Very similar melodic material was used earlier in the final A section scored for saxophones.

Development Section

As previously suggested, the challenging aspects of this score, from the standpoint of analysis, are found at the B and C sections as well as the development section (m.61), where the composer toys with our sense of tonal equilibrium. The bass ostinato during this section that extends through m.77 helps to add some sense of tonality and cohesion to an otherwise atonal section. This bass line along with the steady rhythm section pulse adds a sense of stability to the more dissonant, atonal melodic and harmonic aspects of the score. It is amazing how adventuresome jazz composers can get in terms of dissonance and tonality as long as there is a steady pulse and in this case bass ostinato. The interview with the composer at the close of this chapter will shed some light on how this part of the composition was conceived and whether it was the result of creative intuition or a methodical approach. The application of set theory principals of analysis might be applied to this section to explain how and why things work, but this goes beyond the scope of this analysis. This section more likely evolved in a very visceral, intuitive manner, following the composer/improviser's whims and artistic sensibilities.

The development section makes use of chromaticism to establish tensions and dissonances between melodic lines, harmonies, and the static bass ostinato. This section resembles the "sidestepping" that is employed by contemporary jazz soloists to create tension and release. The soloist intentionally plays lines a half step (or other distant key) away from the chord before releasing the tension by stepping back to consonance with the key center. Mintzer begins this section in just this way by immediately emphasizing D♭ tonality in the trombones and saxophones against the D Dorian ostinato bass line. What follows is a chromatic line in the saxophones and a unison trumpet figure that steps into and away from the tonality. These dissonant effects provide a certain shock value that is used throughout the "Ellis Island" development section.

The trombones are used during this section to provide three-part harmonic cells. The upper voice remains fixed while lower voices move chromatically in fourths. By the fifth bar of this section, the upper trombone voice is always a pitch found in the D Dorian scale while the lower voices that form a 4th move up chromatically. These harmonic cells might be best labeled using a set theory approach, which classifies groups of pitches by intervallic relationship rather than traditional functional harmony symbols.

The final ascending F pentatonic line leads into m.77 and back to tonal stability. This section before the D.S. to the B section features a strong ascending bass line and harmonic progression set against the lead trumpet line in contrary descending motion.

The brief coda provides great variety, since it is the only section in the entire chart that is based more closely on functional harmonic motion. Chord analysis is provided in the score but deserves duplication in a more concise, clearer format here. Chords have been simplified, and each line represents a full measure. Functional analysis is provided beneath.

Example 2.12

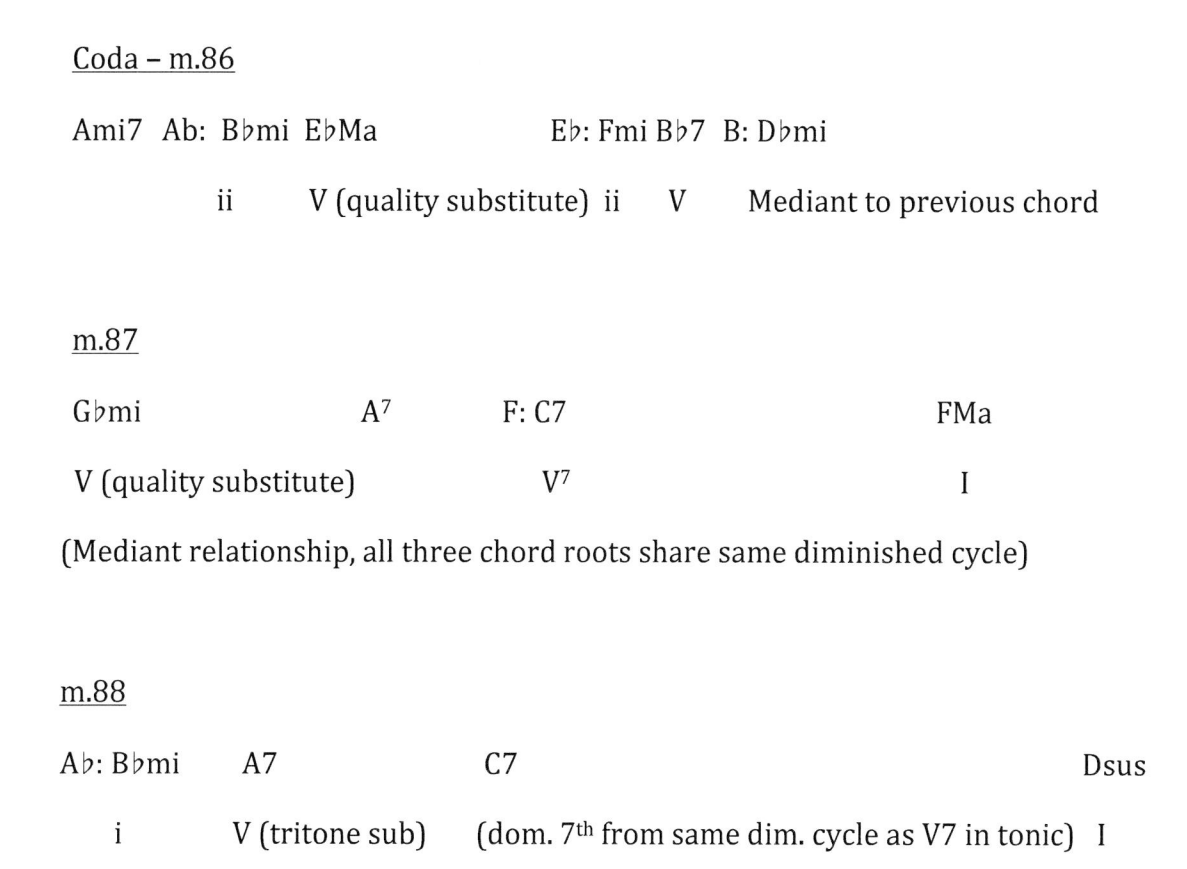

Coda – m.86

Ami7 Ab: B♭mi E♭Ma   E♭: Fmi B♭7 B: D♭mi

   ii   V (quality substitute) ii   V   Mediant to previous chord

m.87

G♭mi   A7   F: C7   FMa

V (quality substitute)   V7   I

(Mediant relationship, all three chord roots share same diminished cycle)

m.88

A♭: B♭mi   A7   C7   Dsus

  i   V (tritone sub)   (dom. 7th from same dim. cycle as V7 in tonic) I

Interview with Bob Mintzer

June 27, 2017

RL: *Tell us about your background as a writer. Did you have any formal training from teachers? Were there particularly influential writers as you began to formulate your own style early on?*

BM: No! I was self-taught. I never had a teacher who even discussed writing with me. From a very early age I just started to try and figure out songs I might hear on the radio, on a recording, or live, and try to find the notes on the piano. That ultimately led to rearranging some of this information and trying to compose my own songs. It wasn't really a concerted effort to compose. I just thought that if I took this element and that element and kind of morphed them together I'd come up with something a little different. I started doing that when I was in high school. I started writing tunes and then I found that I really enjoyed gathering a few musicians together to play this music. At that time I was in a rock band with a guy who was an aspiring recording engineer. He had a little makeshift studio in his basement and he was looking for people to record. I would go over there with a rhythm section and record my tunes. What a wonderful experience that was. I learned so much.

RL: *You got to find out what works and what doesn't. Did you do much arranging in those early days, or was it mostly original material?*

BM: I did very little arranging initially, mostly writing original tunes. I guess the most ambitious I got was writing for three horns.

When I joined the Buddy Rich band I was in the middle of making demos. I had a cassette copy of the recent one and was listening to it on the bus. Buddy asked, "What are you listening to?" I said, "It's a demo of original music." Buddy asked to hear it. He listened to it and said it sounded good. He said, "Why don't you write something for the band." I said I wouldn't know the first thing about that. But he really kind of pushed me, literally, into trying to tackle a first big band arrangement. I was excited and terrified! I hastily went to my piano and thought about how to write for these seventeen instruments I was hearing every night on the bandstand. This first chart was written in pen! I didn't know any better. It was definitely not from overconfidence. I brought the chart in and the band killed it! I was so thrilled at the results, not that it was any great arranging feat, but just to be able to realize a composition and expand it into this orchestration for a big band was such a thrill for me. It was a great band and everyone was on their best behavior because Buddy didn't want to know your problems. I went on to write six or seven subsequent pieces for Buddy.

RL: *What was that first one?*

BM: "No Jive" ... It should have been just called "Jive." And what was interesting was after that first experience I thought, "Well, I can do this on some level." Then I started to think, "What do I do next and what should I be considering?" And I thought, "This is Buddy Rich," and I thought about how he plays and how he would like to play. What would trigger him to respond favorably. And I included in that mix how I would like to play. By the way, one thing I learned early on was that when you're the arranger you can write yourself a solo. [laughs] I did that very consistently. I was the fourth tenor player in the band and didn't get many solos until I started writing. Each subsequent piece after the first one involved some thought as far as how do I frame Buddy's playing in an environment that would be comforting and encouraging to him and the band, and would create an overall positive musical event. What I realize in hindsight is that when you're sitting in a big band every night you're absorbing a good deal of information in terms of shape and sound and ultimately orchestration without realizing it. Depending upon your ability to discern pitch and hear detail in the music, one can pick up a lot of information. I was studying other people's music by virtue of sitting in it and drawing in information in general terms from the overall sound and shape of things.

RL: *I think that's the way a lot of us learned, particularly if we didn't have teachers initially. We became more aware of our environment.*

BM: Exactly.

RL: *We had a great deal of trouble deciding on a score for this study, as was the case, I might add, with the other composers in this study. We finally decided on "Ellis Island" after considering several others including some much earlier scores. Why did you encourage this particular score, and how would you say your style has changed and evolved since the 1980s and the beginnings of the Bob Mintzer big band?*

BM: I think I chose "Ellis Island" for a couple of reasons. One is that the rhythmic intricacies are in some ways a trademark of my writing. And it's something I've been working on over time. You have a contrapuntal rhythmic scenario going on. If you can fathom this, a major influence of this way of writing started when I was playing with early music groups in college. Some of these early pieces written in the thirteenth and fourteenth centuries had these wild syncopations and very rhythmically active orchestrations and that really stuck with me. I think that in conjunction with playing with all those salsa and Afro-Cuban bands I worked with in New York – Tito Puente, Eddie Palmieri, and bands like that – also added to my interest in rhythm and contrapuntal rhythmic lines. That was the main reason I chose "Ellis Island." You can see some indications of polyrhythms and over the bar line phrasing here. And of course joining the Yellowjackets was a logical progression because that band is very much about manipulating rhythm in interesting and unusual ways.

RL: *I also sensed that there is maybe a harmonic influence coming from your association with the Yellowjackets.*

BM: Well, this is pre-Yellowjackets. I think the guys in the Jackets and myself are like-minded in many ways, hence a twenty-seven year history together!

I spent a great deal of time playing the piano, finding little sounds and shapes and voicings, and I was very excited by the ability to use two hands and create rhythms. In fact I can play the accompaniment of "Ellis Island" on the piano. The idea for the tune developed out of things I was playing on the piano. It's basically a series of 1–4–5 moving voicings against a melodic bass line. I sometimes jokingly call this my "claw" piano playing style.

RL: *Interesting because that goes to some of the other questions I had … which came first, the chicken or the egg? Did you compose the harmonic/rhythmic groove and then begin to think about layering melodies on top of that?*

BM: Yes, in this tune, very much so. The comping at letter A came first. This is pre-sequencing, so I think I just tried to hear or sing the melody over the comping figures and went from there. I developed a counter melody to go with the primary melody next.

RL: *That's what I assumed, particularly because you are so specific about the piano and bass parts throughout the whole piece. You clearly had something very specific in mind rather than the open comping approach that leaves choices to the player. That is a very integral part of the piece, so you specified the voicings and the rhythms.*

BM: Yes. In this tune there are a lot of places where the piano doubles the trombones, which is something I do frequently. This orchestration has a rich texture. In the solo section things open up, and the rhythm players are free to go wherever. But in general for ensemble sections, I like using piano and bass in a specific compositional way.

RL: *You have always been one to feature counterpoint in your scores, to go back to something earlier, you said. How do you arrive at the contrapuntal lines when you are constructing a chart?*

BM: That's a good question. I'm no expert at counterpoint! I try to hear primary and secondary melodies simultaneously and see if they will fit together. There is very much a call and response scenario in play a good deal of the time, where one line sustains while another line moves, and one line rests while another is active. Sometimes you end up creating an implied harmony from the interaction of two melodic lines. I just try to have the different components complement one another.

RL: *You do that very, very well, particularly for someone who didn't formally study counterpoint with a composition teacher.*

BM: Again, I didn't specifically study counterpoint, but I've played a lot of orchestral music, I've played in concert band and woodwind quintets, chamber music ensembles, saxophone quartets. Playing this music exposed me to a good deal of information. When you start writing, you think about the big picture, how should things fit together, what are the various components, and so on. And I think you inevitably arrive at some form of counterpoint. It may not be a disciplined approach per se, but counterpoint appears in lots of different kinds of music, and you can listen for that as a means of getting some sense of how it works.

RL: *But counterpoint is certainly another hallmark of your style, because I hear that in a lot of your pieces.*

BM: Well, the way I look at it is if all the instruments are doing the same thing rhythmically there is a bit of a textural deficiency. If you have one main component and a secondary component as an accompaniment and then you add this tertiary or third component, which you might call counterpoint or a counter melody, now you have a fairly elaborate and interesting texture if you do it considerately. Not that this should be happening throughout the piece, but it adds a nice bit of variety and can add a form of tension, if you will, where there is a good deal of activity that ultimately subsides and resolves into something a little more tranquil. It's very effective. And that's my little self-taught way of viewing it. I'm sure there are more sophisticated ways at looking at all this.

RL: *Yes, but you bring the improvising horn player aspect to it, and there is a certain creative intuition at work, I think, that a lot of people who are players and writers use.*

I'm particularly intrigued by the harmonic motion and the harmonies in what I refer to as the B section in the "Ellis Island" score and found it difficult to describe the chords using functional harmonic symbols. I don't think in this case there is a right way or wrong way to symbolize these chords, and I happened to choose one way over another. Was there a method to composing this section, or was this composed through an improvisational session at the keyboard or your horn?

BM: I'm not sure. This was something that was improvised on the piano, as I remember. I did a fair amount of experimenting with pedals, playing a bass note and using either triads or 1–4–5, or 5ths or 4ths, and moving them around in different ways, and with the top note of the voicing generally creating some sort of melodic shape. I think it was something I improvised and I liked the sound of. There are certainly some polychordal moments in there as well. I relied on sound. Sometimes I think it's just trial and error, stumbling onto something and freeze-framing it, seeing what it is. And then perhaps staying with it for a while, seeing where it goes, which inevitably leads to what comes next.

RL: *That's actually what I thought you'd say about the process. And it seems there is a lot of use of common tones either in the three or four note voicing or in the bass as a pedal. And the other voices would simply move by half step while the other voices remained the same, creating some interesting motions or rotations.*

BM: That's something you hear frequently. If you had a second inversion triad like C–F–A over D minor. Now move the two lower notes down to B–E–A, and then move them down another half step and you have B♭–E♭–A all over D. I've heard this shape in other people's writing.

RL: *We sort of talked around this earlier, but I'm going to come back to it now. In more general terms, how do you work? Describe to us your creative process and what tools you use to assist in your writing process. Do you ever use the computer, and if so, when and how in the process? Do you use your horn, the keyboard, or possibly another instrument or all of the above?*

BM: There was an earlier period that was pre-Sibelius where I just used score paper and pencil and sat at a piano and would improvise a few things. It would be a confluence of things that I would play on the piano and things I would imagine. When I was introduced to the Sibelius software, which was probably about fifteen years ago, I found that I was still writing at the piano, but that ability to check things via playback gave me a little confidence in moving away from the piano and relying more on imagination, trying to hear sounds in my head, and then throw them into Sibelius and see if what I was hearing made any sense. What was a real revelation was having that ability to then manipulate things and fashion them into something that sounded good. At a certain point in time I pretty much abandoned the piano and started to just imagine sounds and shapes. I'd put the ideas in Sibelius and really start to work on it by moving things around. Again, there was a lot of trial and error – I'd inadvertently stumble onto a passage and then develop it. There is definitely an improvisatory component to writing where you do something that suggests what to do next. But all of this is in the context of having a broader vision of what kind of piece you're writing – what's the shape like, what's the form, and what's the intention?

RL: *So you have those things in mind first?*

BM: Generally, yes. Which leads me to something I do now, which is doing a sketch. It's a big part of how I now do big band arrangements; particularly when I am writing a lot of music, it is imperative that I'm not spending hours on four bars. I map my plan of attack and with each subsequent run-through access a little more detail.

I'm now generally writing eight or nine big band pieces simultaneously. Since I've joined the WDR (West German Radio Orchestra) I have to write ten pieces in a two-month period, and I can't waste time. I have to keep moving, so I find that if I do sketches it helps me feel like I'm making some progress and also allows me to jump from piece to piece, keeping things fresh. Whereas if you are laboring over one piece I don't think you move quite as quickly and you can get bogged down.

RL: *There really is a psychological component, isn't there – that necessary feeling of making progress.*

BM: Yes, absolutely.

RL: *I always used to tell my students, "Look, if you're stumped on that section, jump ahead and come back to it and work on something else." There is a psychological importance to keeping the juices going, I think.*

BM: Exactly. And also you might write something that immediately after writing doesn't sound very good, but if you let it sit for a couple of days you can come back and realize there may be something there.

RL: *Do you use your horn at all in this creative process?*

BM: Not usually. But I do imagine what it's like to play the line on the tenor. Frequently I'll be sitting on a plane just imagining I'm playing the tenor and I can hear it. I can imagine I'm actually pushing the keys down. I can do all kinds of things without actually having the horn in my hand. And you can do that with any instrument. In fact you can do that with a rhythm section. If you've spent some time with the instruments and done a good deal of listening and playing in bands, that sound, that rhythm section sound, is up in your head. And you can manipulate that any way you like, especially if you've had hands-on experience playing the instruments.

RL: *I want to get back to "Ellis Island" for a minute. I was also struck by the originality of the "shout chorus" or developmental section that follows the solo sections. Harmonically and melodically this section strays the furthest from traditional big band writing approaches. For that matter it strays pretty far from the earlier* *material except for the ostinato bass line, which serves as the cohesive glue. I know it's been a while, but can you recall anything about the motivation behind creating this somewhat atonal, or polytonal, section and how you went about creating it?*

BM: I knew that I wanted to keep the bass line from the preceding solo section and purposely stray from the D Dorian sound. I wanted to leave that in a big way and do something else. I basically just improvised, again using the 1-4-5 or 1-2-5 voicings over the pedal, and moved it around with a melodic implication on the top note of each voicing.

RL: *How much of your writing relies on creative intuition and those skills you bring to the table as a very creative improviser?*

BM: Not being a studied arranger/composer, I think the majority of my writing is intuitive and improvisatory in nature. I think most composers are coming from an intuitive and improvisatory place. Very much like when you are improvising on a saxophone, you are informed where to go next by the implication of the last two notes you wrote, and the trajectory that implies. Zooming out and considering the big picture comes into play as well.

RL: *During the shout chorus there are several different melodies and each voice seems complete. In other words, if you just heard that single voice, you'd consider it a nice little melody by itself. But the fact of the matter is it may be far-flung tonally from the D minor.*

BM: There was certainly no organized harmonic reason for any of this other than the fact that I was thinking melodically. I was thinking that it might be interesting if the sonority of the trombones, the harmonic quality of what they were doing, supported a melody that was non key center specific. I suppose there was a sense of tension/release as I would stray from the implied D minor quality of the bass line and then return, if that makes any sense.

RL: *Yes, it does. And again what struck me here was that this is what you might have played as a player, improvising off a pedal. You'd go outside, you'd come back in … sort of sidestepping to create moments of tension and release.*

BM: And again, some of the influence on this section was from the early music I played where there was a cantus firmus, a slow moving sustained line, another line that was more active, and then another line that was florid, extremely active. If you look at the ninth bar of that section, or the tenth bar, where the two altos come in with that sixteenth note line [scat sings the line]. That's the most active part of the line. The tenors and the bari are a little more sustained and they're interacting with that trumpet line … I tried to assemble these parts, like you said, with each individual part having some sort of melodic weight but related rhythmically in an interesting way and at least part of the time related to the chords being implied by the trombones.

Let me elaborate … we have a solo section that presumably builds to some level of strength and activity, and then it comes back down. And then we gradually introduce various components. There are three components going on almost from the beginning of this section, and it becomes more and more active and there are more and more sixteenth notes that lead us to the main body of the shout, which is bar 69, with these big, majestic brass chords with lead trumpet up above the staff, and the saxes break into a unison sixteenth note melody against that. I was really making a concerted effort to have a gradual but profound build to something exciting and strong.

RL: *The pacing on this chart is incredible. It's particularly evident when you look at it graphically by using the software application Audacity. It's very telling when you examine a piece of music that way, because you* *can see immediately that there is a clear effort to pace the music. There is an ebb and flow throughout the piece. You can find other pieces of music where that's not the case and it's very static and consequently there is a dynamic sameness to the entire piece. Even in your original pencil score that I worked from, there was a precision about dynamic markings, adding that element of drama to the score.*

BM: I think some of that comes from playing and being a big fan of orchestral music. A lot of orchestral writing is about the story line, drama, variety, changes in texture and dynamics, surprise.

RL: *You've mentioned early music and orchestral music several times. Do you listen to a lot of that in the course of your week?*

BM: Yes, I do. I listen to a good deal of classical music; in fact we subscribe to the LA Philharmonic. My wife and I go regularly, and it's a wonderful vehicle for inspiration. I love the music and I'm always in awe of what I hear. And always thinking how could I somehow incorporate the dramatic effect that I'm hearing or some of the orchestrational things within the context of playing rhythm section music, where things sometimes can get a bit static.

RL: *If you were to leave our readers and students with a single suggestion about composing and arranging for the large jazz ensemble, something maybe you've learned over the years, what would that be?*

BM: Well, two things: One is, whatever kind of writing you want to do, by all means bathe your brain with, first and foremost, that kind of writing. So if we are talking about big band music, then listen to the full spectrum of possibilities in terms of what the great big band composers and arrangers have done, and get that sound in your head. In listening, if something really grabs you, freeze-frame and see what it is in detail. Try to dissect it a little bit. Then listen to all kinds of music. That's one of the best ways to oil the machinery and give you some ideas. I would say 90 percent of the things I write are informed by something I've heard that really inspired me, where I take some essence of the inspirational piece and build a new piece.

The other thing is that you have to just keep writing. There is this improvisatory thing that happens when you start assembling a piece from scratch. Generally I'll think tempo, maybe key, who I'm writing for, and I just start. I might program a little drumbeat in Sibelius and then throw some chords in there. It's like practicing your instrument. The more you practice your instrument, the more fluid you become at playing any kind of music. So if you are writing all the time, there shouldn't be any shortage of ideas.

I think of somebody like Michael Brecker, who I knew fairly well. He didn't really study composition and arranging. He took a few lessons from a guy in New York back in the '80s when a bunch of the jazz guys were studying with this one guy. He was an amazing musician with incredible ears and recall ability, and I believe he was able to extract the essence of all the music he played or listened to and put his personal slant on his own resulting compositions. Mike was someone who used composition to provide a vehicle for his playing along with realizing his musical vision. The more he wrote over time, the more his writing evolved. And at the end that last album he did, *Pilgrimage*, the writing was stunning! Incredibly involved, and uniquely beautiful.

RL: *When I first heard that I wondered whether he was doing a lot of studying at that period of his life with some writing instructor.*

BM: Well I know that he allegedly became very intrigued with Bulgarian music, I think, and some of the Eastern European music, and in fact had done some sort of demo for a subsequent project of this Bulgarian music that incorporated odd meter and such. So he had his radar up and was checking out all different kinds of music. Combining that with his ability to understand how things were put together made him a really evolved composer.

RL: *He was definitely a talent without peer ... no doubt about that.*

Is there anything we've missed that you'd like to get off your chest, so to speak?

BM: Just one thing. I think this piece, "Ellis Island," is a way of looking at writing for a large horn section where you could view wind instruments as percussion instruments. I do that quite a lot. I use the horn section or individual sections in a percussive capacity where seemingly the rhythm takes a front seat to the sonorities and even the melodies sometimes. There is this very strong rhythmic component in most of my big band writing. I am very rhythmically oriented, but at the same time I love melody. For that matter I love harmonies too! [laughs] But the rhythm thing is such a big part of it. I've owned a drum set for forty some odd years. I'm very interested, intrigued, and motivated by rhythmic interplay, and it's really demonstrated in "Ellis Island" some of the possibilities of how you can shape a horn section and rhythm section and have this interesting rhythmic terrain happening.

RL: *Yes, I never felt like the meter was obvious. It was obviously influenced by your association with Latin bands, but it's not derivative of that.*

Thank you so much for participating in this project, Bob.

Annotated Full Score

The annotated full transposed score that follows provides additional details about "Ellis Island," and includes concert pitch excerpts as reductions.

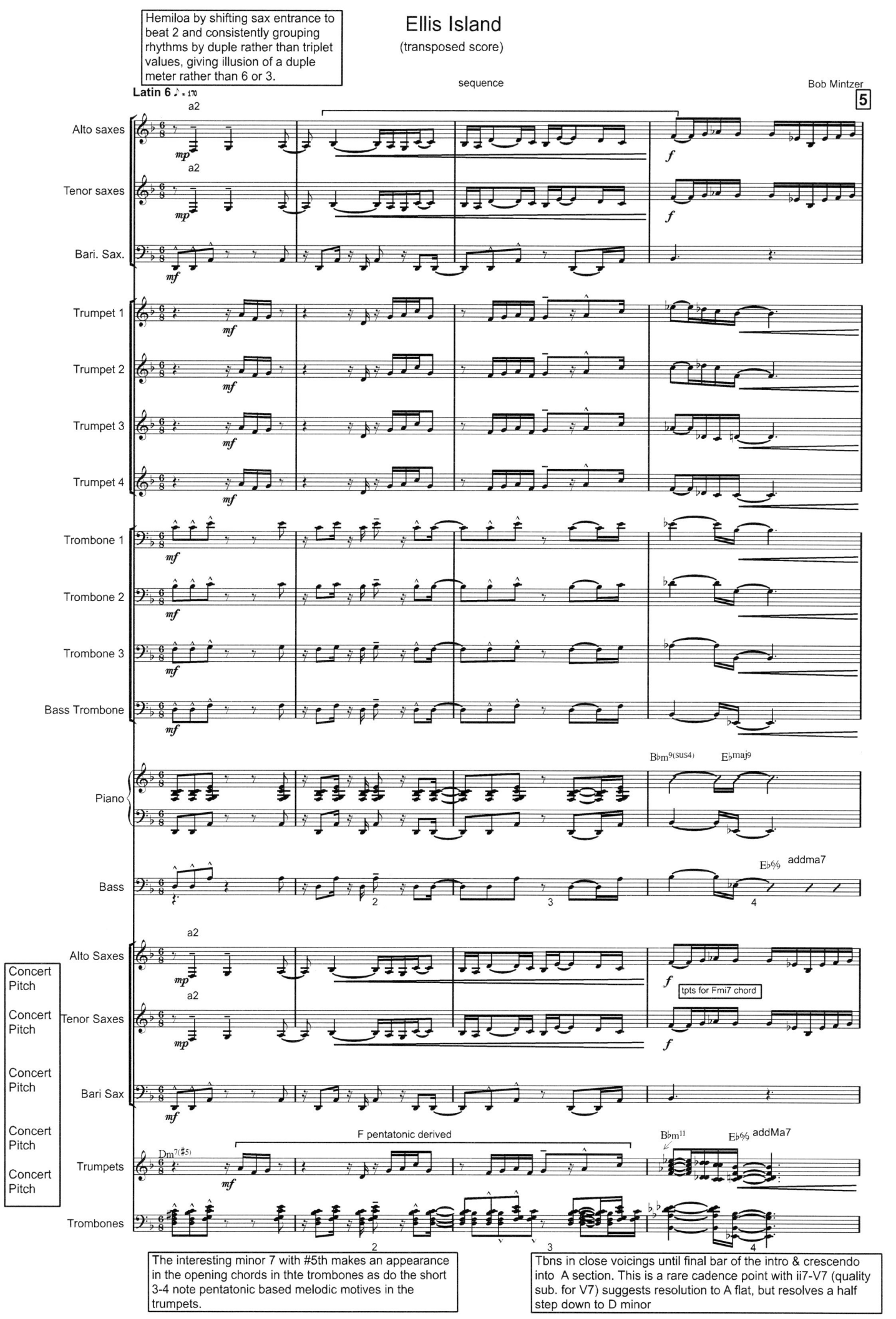

Ellis Island
(transposed score)

sequence

Bob Mintzer

Hemiloa by shifting sax entrance to beat 2 and consistently grouping rhythms by duple rather than triplet values, giving illusion of a duple meter rather than 6 or 3.

Latin 6 ♪.= 170

The interesting minor 7 with #5th makes an appearance in the opening chords in thte trombones as do the short 3-4 note pentatonic based melodic motives in the trumpets.

Tbns in close voicings until final bar of the intro & crescendo into A section. This is a rare cadence point with ii7-V7 (quality sub. for V7) suggests resolution to A flat, but resolves a half step down to D minor

A Section

Much like intro, sax counterline in hemiola rhythms gives illusion of duple meter and emhpasizes over the bar line phrasing

Appearance of both major 3rd and 11th in dominant sonority

F pentatonic

Chords: Dm11 | Em7(#5) | F(add2) | F/G C9(sus4)/G

Step wise ascending progressing leads to resolution to Bb maj

4
13
B Section
Alto saxes
Tenor saxes
Bari. Sax.
Tpt. 1
Tpt. 2
Tpt. 3
Tpt. 4
Tbn. 1
Tbn. 2
Tbn. 3
B. Tbn.
mf
Pno.
B♭maj13
C/B♭
E♭7(add11)/A
D♭7(add11)/A
Bass
B♭maj9
B♭maj13
13
14
15
16
B Section
Abbreviated version of bar 13
rhythmic variation of pantatonic motive in
Alto Saxes
Tenor Saxes
Bari Sax
Trumpets
Trombones
4.
Quartal voicings in trombones
Juxtaposition of MA 3rd & sus4 (11th) in incomplete dominant 7th chords with foreigh bass tone in tbns & piano.

Same lead line in brass as previous 2 bar phrases, but reharmonized. Wide separation of major 3rd and sus 4 makes these dominant voicings work.

6
C Section
21
similar ascending juesture gesture to previous 2 bars
1.
Alto saxes
Tenor saxes
Bari. Sax.
Tpt. 1
Tpt. 2
Tpt. 3
Tpt. 4
Tbn. 1
Tbn. 2
Tbn. 3
B. Tbn.
Pno.
Bass
mp
B♭maj7(♯5)
B♭
Amaj7(♯5)
B(omit3♯11)/A
A♭13(sus4)
no 3rd
A♭9
G13(♯9)
21
22
23
24
C Section
1.
Alto Saxes
Tenor Saxes
Bari Sax
Trumpets
Trombones
21
22
23
24
Sudden dynamic contrast makes this C section dynamically striking
Interesting harmonies are difficult to label & might be more accurately described as harmonic cells based on intervalic structures

A1 Section
sax counterpoint repeats 4 note motive.
Material used again as solo background.
29
a2
7
Alto saxes
Tenor saxes
Bari. Sax.
Tpt. 1
Tpt. 2
Tpt. 3
Tpt. 4
Tbn. 1
Tbn. 2
Tbn. 3
B. Tbn.
Pno.
Bass
A1 Section
F pentatonic harmonized with A dorian pentatonic or A natural minor fragment
Alto Saxes
Tenor Saxes
Bari Sax
Diminished scale fragment
Trumpets
Trombones
Ascending progression of altered dominant 7ths suggests a resolution to F but instead resolved to the relative minor home key of Dmin
trombones play orchestrated piano accompaniment from first A section

Alto saxes
Tenor saxes
Bari. Sax.
Tpt. 1
Tpt. 2
Tpt. 3
Tpt. 4
Tbn. 1
Tbn. 2
Tbn. 3
B. Tbn.
Dm11
Em7(♯5)
F(add2)
Pno.
Bass
33
34
35
Alto Saxes
Tenor Saxes
Bari Sax
a2
Trumpets
Trombones
4:3♪

near repetition of material from bar 29
To Coda
37
1st x only
2nd x only
mp
Alto saxes
Tenor saxes
Bari. Sax.
Tpt. 1
Tpt. 2
Tpt. 3
Tpt. 4
Tbn. 1
Tbn. 2
Tbn. 3
B. Tbn.
Gm7(sus4)
Am7
Dm7
Light fills
Pno.
Bass
36
37
38
39
40
Alto Saxes
Tenor Saxes
Bari Sax
Trumpets
Trombones

staggered sax and brass backgrounds provide variety and make section sound longer than it is.
41
45
Open
On cue: play 1st & 3rd x
Alto saxes
Tenor saxes
Open (loosely)
Dm7
Bari. Sax.
On cue: play 2nd & 4th x
Tpt. 1
Tpt. 2
Tpt. 3
Tpt. 4
Tbn. 1
Tbn. 2
Tbn. 3
B. Tbn.
Open - sparse comping
4x
Pno.
(bass cue)
A7
Bass
Background material very similar to sax counterpoint at A1 (bar 29). Variations based on 4 note pattern
Alto Saxes
Tenor Saxes
Bari Sax
Trumpets
Trombones
Parallel planed harmonies derived from Dorian scale. Sax voicings are quartal.

Alto saxes
Tenor saxes
Bari. Sax.
Tpt. 1
Tpt. 2
Tpt. 3
Tpt. 4
Tbn. 1
Tbn. 2
Tbn. 3
B. Tbn.
Pno.
Bass
A7
46
47
48
Alto Saxes
Tenor Saxes
Bari Sax
Trumpets
Trombones
46
47
48

49
53
Identical background figures in saxes and brass to previous solo section
on cue
Open
On cue: play 1st & 3rd x
Alto saxes
Tenor saxes
Bari. Sax.
end solo
Dm7
On cue: play 2nd & 4th x
Tpt. 1
Tpt. 2
Tpt. 3
Tpt. 4
(loosely, overlap with baritone)
Tbn. 1
Tbn. 2
Tbn. 3
B. Tbn.
Open - sparse comping
4x
Pno.
(bass cue)
A7
Bass
Col. bars 45-48
Alto Saxes
Tenor Saxes
Bari Sax
Col Bars 45-48
Trumpets
Trombones
49 50 51 52 53 54 55 56

57
61
On cue
Alto saxes
Tenor saxes
a2
Bari. Sax.
mp
Tpt. 1
Tpt. 2
Tpt. 3
Tpt. 4
Dm
Tbn. 1
Tbn. 2
Tbn. 3
B. Tbn.
Open
Open
(sparse comping)
Pno.
Bass
A7
57 58 59 60 61 62 63 64
ma 3rd min 3rd
motive similar to brass
Alto Saxes
Tenor Saxes
1/2 below tonic
chromatic
Bari Sax
min 3rd maj 3rd
motive
Trumpets
Trombones
Tbn chord 1/2 step from
tonic in all voices. Adding tonic
makes this Dma7(-5) chord
close position quartal tbn
voicing moves from consonance to
half step higher cluster

descending staccato fragment serves as response to tpt ascending short phrase in previous bar

saxes imply B flat major scale

chromatic line

ascending chromatic

Lower 2 tbn voices move in 1/2 steps from dissonant to consonant chord tones while lead voice remains on chord tone

3 note harmonic cells. Lower voices move chromatically to final triad at end of bar.

69
a2
Alto saxes
Tenor saxes
Bari. Sax.
Tpt. 1
Tpt. 2
Tpt. 3
Tpt. 4
Tbn. 1
Tbn. 2
Tbn. 3
B. Tbn.
Pno.
Bass
69
70
71
72
69
a2
F Pentatonic material
Similar rhythmic groupings & shape to previous bars
Alto Saxes
min 3rd followed by 4th
Tenor Saxes
Bari Sax
diminished scale fragment
Trumpets
Trombones
69
70
71
72
Once again, common consonat connecting tone in upper voice while lower voices move chromatically in 4th structure
identical harmonic and voicing approach as seen in bars 66, 68, 70 and 75-76

16

Tpts in close position, Tbns open chorale style. Trpts in contrary motion to bass line and chord progression

Chord also suggests G7/Dmi

D.S. al Coda
Alto saxes
Tenor saxes
Bari. Sax.
a2
Tpt. 1
Tpt. 2
Tpt. 3
Tpt. 4
Tbn. 1
Tbn. 2
Tbn. 3
B. Tbn.
Pno.
Bass
Dm
Em7(b6)
F11
G
E13(b9)
Am7
81
82
83
84
85
saxes perform new material compared to previous phrase but still based on F pentatonic scale
Alto Saxes
Tenor Saxes
Col Altos
Bari Sax
Col Altos 8VB
Trumpets
Trombones
Dm11
Em11(b13)
F13(sus4)
G9(add13)
a4
Am7(sus4)
Dm(sus4)
brass voicings identical to previous phrase butwith some rhythmic variation
identical cadence to previous phrase but last 2 chords show tpts in wide spaced quartal voicing with tbns in open choral voicing

a2
Alto saxes
mp
Tenor saxes
Bari. Sax.
mf
Tpt. 1
Tpt. 2
Tpt. 3
Tpt. 4
Tbn. 1
Tbn. 2
Tbn. 3
B. Tbn.
B♭m13 E♭maj9 Fm9 B♭13(♭9) D♭m9(sus4) G♭m9(sus4) A11 C11 Fmaj9 B♭m9 A13(♯11 ♭9) C(sus4) D(sus4)
Pno.
ff
Bass
86
87
88
89
3 note motive reflects back to A theme
Alto Saxes
Col altos
Tenor Saxes
Bari Sax
Latin style encourages doubled bass lines in bari sax
B♭m9(add11) A11(♭9add13) C11(add13) Dm11(add13)
Trumpets
B♭m9(add13) E♭maj9 Fm9 B♭13(♭9) D♭m9(sus4) G♭m9(sus4) A13(add11) C11 F6/9
trombone voicings are all close position and rootless
Trombones
Ab: ii7 V7 Eb: ii7 V7 Cb: ii7 V7 F: V7 I Ab: ii7 Dm: V7 Vii7 i
(quality sub) (min 3rd) (quality sub) shared dim. cycle bII7 tritone sub shared dim cyc.

Composer, arranger, and conductor Vince Mendoza

Photo credit: © Pamela Fong

Chapter 3
Vince Mendoza – "Homecoming"

Multi–Grammy Award winner Vince Mendoza stands as an exception to the norm as a jazz composer and arranger who continues to thrive as just that – a writer. Most of the writers in this study are performers as well as writers. While it is true that Mendoza teaches at the University of Southern California, where he earned his master's degree after completing a BM in composition at Ohio State University, his livelihood largely stems from his versatility as a composer, arranger, and conductor who specializes in jazz and related idioms.

The wide scope of his works demonstrates an extraordinary understanding of many musical languages. He has written scores of compositions and arrangements for big band and extended compositions for chamber and symphonic orchestra settings, and his jazz composing/arranging credits read like a who's who of the best modern instrumentalists, singers, and composers. He has written arrangements for a wide variety of pop and jazz vocalists, from Joni Mitchell, Sting, Melody Gardot, Elvis Costello, Gregory Porter, and Björk to instrumentalists Joe Zawinul, John Scofield, Charlie Haden, Al Di Meola, Dave Liebman, Gary Burton, Pat Metheny, Michael and Randy Brecker, the Yellowjackets, and the GRP All-Stars. His compositions have appeared on recordings by the likes of saxophonist Joe Lovano, guitarist John Abercrombie, drummer Peter Erskine, pianist Joey Calderazzo, and singer Kurt Elling. As a leader, Mendoza has released ten recordings for the Blue Note, ACT, Blue Jackel, and Zebra labels. Mendoza's work on John Scofield's *54* recording on the EmArcy record label earned him a Grammy, his sixth Grammy in twenty-five nominations. That same year he was nominated by the Jazz Journalists Association as Arranger of the Year.

Growing up in Connecticut, Mendoza chose as his first instrument the guitar, later turning to trumpet. His early influences ranged from Bach to Mancini and Aretha Franklin. But it was Miles Davis, Gil Evans, Igor Stravinsky, and Alban Berg who began to influence his writing. Later the music of Joe Zawinul and Wayne Shorter exerted an impact on his big band writing. While studying at USC and working at studios composing music for TV he met drummer Peter Erskine and contributed several compositions to his mixed ensemble recording *Transition*, on Denon Records. Since then they have become frequent collaborators.

Mendoza's early solo albums on Blue Note Records, *Start Here* and *Instructions Inside*, were critical triumphs and featured such artists as John Scofield, Joe Lovano, Ralph Towner, Bob Mintzer, Randy Brecker, Erskine, and others. *Start Here* was voted one of *Jazziz Magazine*'s Top Picks, and Mendoza was recognized as Best Composer/Arranger by *Swing Journal*'s critics poll in Japan.

He has become well known throughout Europe through long associations with the West German Radio Orchestra (Cologne), which has recorded several albums featuring Mendoza's repertoire, including his most recent *Homecoming* and the earlier *The Vince Mendoza/Arif Mardin Project: Jazzpaña*, which brought him a Grammy nomination for Best Instrumental Arrangement.

Mendoza's alliance with the Metropole Orchestra of the Netherlands began in 1995. The Metropole is in its sixty-first year and is the only full-time symphonic pop/jazz orchestra in the world today. Following a nine year appointment with them as the orchestra's chief conductor, he continues to work periodically with them at concerts and festivals and for recordings with artists as diverse as Elvis Costello, Herbie Hancock, Ivan Lins, Al Jarreau, and many more.

Mendoza's work as an arranger can also be heard on many expansive jazz projects from the mid-1980s that include work with the Yellowjackets, Al Di Meola, Gino Vanelli, Joe Zawinul, Mike Stern, Kyle Eastwood, and the GRP All-Star Big Band, among many others. His television music has also received nominations for an Emmy Award, while his music for the World Cup closing ceremony was broadcast worldwide.

His versatility as a contemporary jazz, chamber music, and string orchestra composer and arranger has led to commissions from renowned jazz and classical ensembles including the Turtle Island String Quartet, the Debussy Trio, the L.A. Guitar Quartet, the Metropole Orchestra (Netherlands), the Berlin Philharmonic, and the BBC. His music has been featured at the Berlin Jazz Festival, and he has performed major works at the Montreux and North Sea Jazz Festivals. Mendoza undoubtedly has more frequent flier miles than he can use, as he actively conducts concerts of his music throughout Europe and in Japan, Scandinavia, and the U.K.

Epiphany, a suite of compositions composed for the London Symphony Orchestra, is quite possibly his most compelling work, demonstrating an extraordinary ability to seamlessly move between idioms. The pieces were inspired and performed by some of the finest jazz soloists of our time. Each piece is beautifully crafted and framed to feature the unique voice of artists he had worked with before – Kenny Wheeler, Peter Erskine, John Abercrombie, Joe Lovano, Michael Brecker, John Taylor, and Marc Johnson. Perhaps the most impressive aspect of this significant episodic recording is the way the composer integrated the essential aspects of jazz with the attributes offered by a symphony orchestra. Few composers have successfully melded these diverse musical traditions as well as Mendoza has in *Epiphany*. Another ambitious and similar large scale project, his seventh as a leader, is *Blauklang*, combining jazz, classical, and modern art.

Managing to combine his own sophisticated solo work with widely acknowledged skill as a sympathetic vocal arranger has earned him the respect of many singers who have benefited from his arranging talents, including Björk, Chaka Khan, Al Jarreau, Bobby McFerrin, Sting, Gregory Porter, and Joni Mitchell. His arrangements supporting Mitchell's 2004 *Both Sides Now* brought him a Grammy for Best Instrumental Arrangement for Accompanying a Singer. The arrangements on this recording, which help to communicate and support the lyrics, are nothing short of lush and elegant.

Mendoza was called upon again by Mitchell to create arrangements for her "final" studio album, *Travelogue*. For this project Mendoza drew on many of his most important stylistic references, from Gil Evans to Brahms and Richard Strauss, Igor Stravinsky, and Gyorgy Ligeti. And once again he found himself working with the cream of the jazz world, including Wayne Shorter and Herbie Hancock, among a top-draw supporting cast of musicians featured on this album.

Mendoza's most recent recordings are his own *Nights on Earth*, again featuring an impressive all-star cast. According to *All About Jazz*, Mendoza "daringly expands the vernacular by including elements of abstract impressionism, romanticism, and a highly unorthodox palette to position him as the clear and natural successor to the late Gil Evans." This recording, which further probes one of his familiar interests, Latin American music, was followed in 2017 by the release of *Homecoming* by the WDR Big Band. The title track of this recording serves as the focus of this study. *DownBeat* magazine reviewer Kirk Silsbee aptly described Mendoza's writing and this recording in particular by writing: "Mendoza is a superb colorist who ably allows his themes to build and his textures to turn. Introspective interludes and a relaxed tone mark this album as the work of a master who has many colors in his paint box."

Selected Discography

Transition (Peter Erskine) – Denon, 1986

Motion Poet (Peter Erskine) – Denon, 1989

Vince Mendoza – Funhouse, Inc., 1989; CR Music Group, 1994

Start Here – World Pacific, 1990

Sweet Soul (Peter Erskine) – Novus (RCA), 1991

Instructions Inside – Manhattan, 1991

Mendoza/Mardin Project Jazzpaña – Atlantic and ACT4, 1992

Vince Mendoza and the WDR Big Band – Sketches – ACT 4, Blue Jackel Entertainment, 1993

Vince Mendoza and the London Symphony Orchestra – Epiphany – Zebra Acoustic and SonyBMG, 1999

Both Sides Now (Joni Mitchell) – Reprise, 2000

American Dreams (Charlie Haden with Michael Brecker) – Universal-Verve, 2002

Symphonic with Yuri Honig – Jazz In Motion Records, 2006

Vince Mendoza – Blauklang – ACT4, 2008

The Phoenix – Vince Mendoza and the DR Big Band – Red Dot Music, 2010

54 – John Scofield, Vince Mendoza and the Metropole Orchestra – EmArcy, 2010

Vince Mendoza and the Metropole Orchestra – Fast City: A Tribute to Joe Zawinul – BHM Productions, 2011

Vince Mendoza – Nights on Earth – Horizontal, 2011

Vince Mendoza and the WDR Big Band – Homecoming – Jazzline/Delta Music, 2017 (Sunnyside Communications)

"Homecoming"

With a catalogue as diverse as Vince Mendoza's, selecting a score for this case study was challenging, to say the least. Limiting the choice to typical big band instrumentation made the chore somewhat less difficult, and the objective remained the same as for the other compositions selected for this volume – choose a score that best illustrates the composer's unique and identifiable traits. No single score offers the complete spectrum of these characteristics, but "Homecoming," as a more recent score, seemed best suited after consultation with the composer. At the risk of generalizing, his many identifiable characteristics can be summarized as follows:

> Mendoza composes infectious melodies and catchphrases that are often presented as riffs or vamps. Many are guaranteed to create a lasting earworm! In the pop music world these repeated phrases might be termed "hooks." There is always an unforgettable melody, rhythmic groove, or harmonic gesture in the form of a vamp. In this way his music leaves the door open, inviting in even the less informed listener. Both his melodies and vamps provide an easy entry point to get inside and enjoy his music. In this way he could be likened to Pat Metheny in that his music offers a high degree of sophistication in the composition and arrangements but without putting one off.

> Mendoza also has a preoccupation with syncopations and rhythmic displacements that work against the sense of strong beat, weak beat within a typical meter. These syncopations create subtle and not so subtle tensions and releases at the rhythmic level that could be described as rhythmic suspensions. The rhythmic freedom of his melodies, no doubt an influence from Wayne Shorter, often defies bar lines and meter altogether. The rhythm of his melodies sometimes seems motivated by a lyric that is not there. These rhythmic characteristics, when coupled with his distinctive signature harmonies and voicings, especially chords that include a major third and suspended 4th, helps to explain why he calls his publishing company Suspended Music. His music is filled with rhythmic and melodic/harmonic suspensions.

> His orchestrations range from the quiet and at times sensual to the bold and brassy big band sound. Dynamically speaking, these moments can change in an instant, which is another dramatic feature of many of his scores.

> His voicings, whether for individual sections or across the ensemble, often break from conventions and are based on a personal sense of resonance and individual voice leading.

> Woodwind doubles for saxophonists are a norm in Mendoza's scores, and he uses them to great advantage in colorful combinations, especially with guitar, which in this score is used as another melodic voice more than a rhythm instrument.

All these characteristics and more will be illustrated in the analysis of "Homecoming" that follows.

Lead Sheet Reduction — Melodic Overview

The principal melody introduced following a brief introduction has a quaint, simple, folk song quality, constructed of "white notes" and composed of stepwise and other small intervals that outline the C Ionian mode. Motifs are of unequal length but when combined create two larger 8 bar phrases. The second 16 measure section is labeled as A². The first 8 bar phrase repeats A nearly exactly, though it does not begin on the second measure as it does in the first A section. The second 8 bar phrase in A² is new, but related, material that continues to utilize C Ionian as source material.

The B section is somewhat of an anomaly in that it is never repeated again, though it does present the seeds of ideas that germinate later in the piece. These ideas include a stepwise ascending gesture and the 4 measure phrase that begins in m.59 and ends this section. A bit more will be said about this section in the following section exploring the harmonic structure of "Homecoming."

Example 3.1

Homecoming

Lead Sheet

♩=155

Vince Mendoza

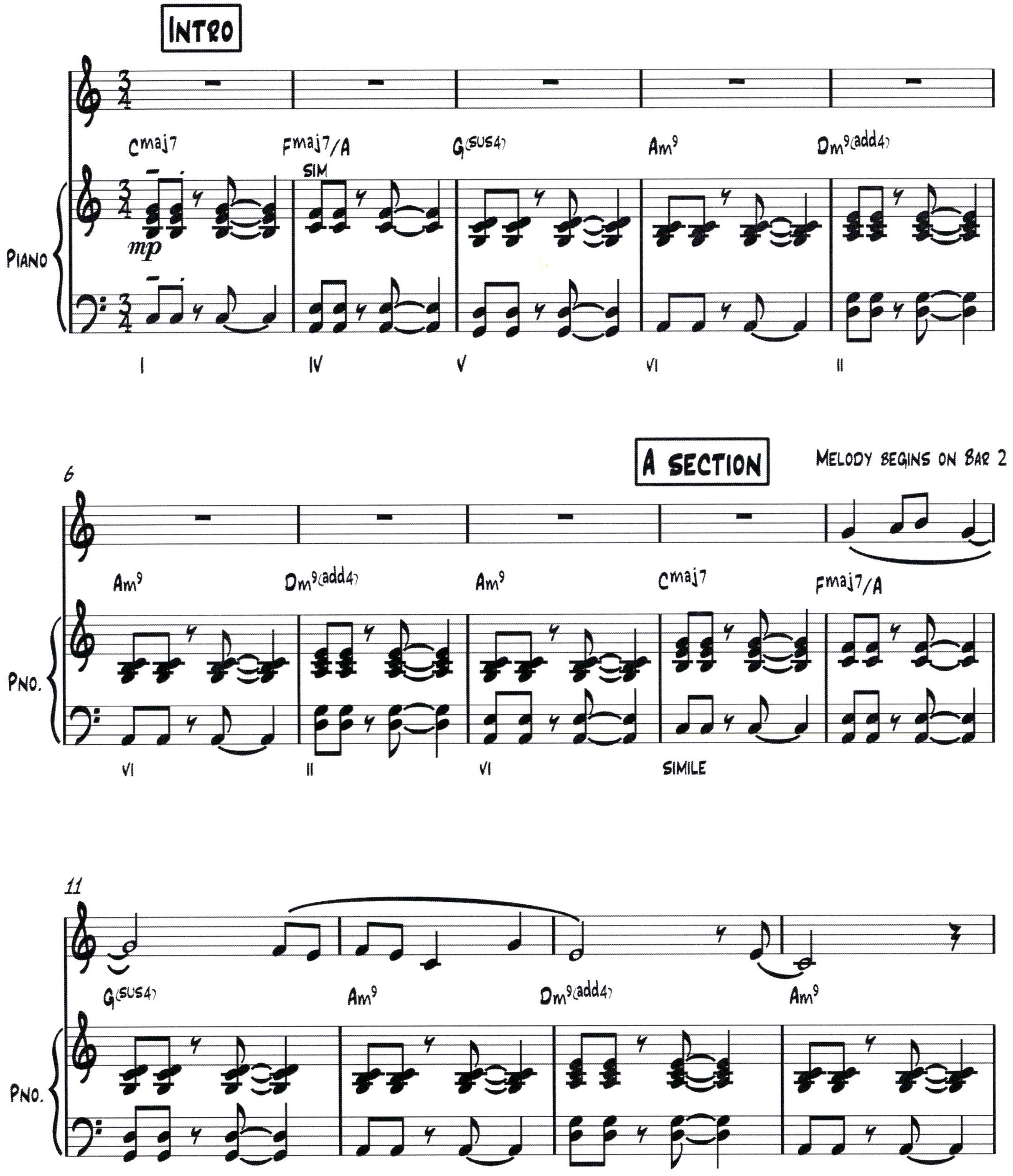

15
Dm9(add4)
Am9
Cmaj7/E
Fmaj7/A
Em7
A9(sus4)
Pno.
I
VI
III
V7 of II
20
Dm9
C7(add4)/Bb
C/F
G(sus4)
3
Pno.
II
I7
IV
V
A2
BEGINS ON BAR 1 OF PHRASE RATHER THAN BAR 2
OTHERWISE IDENTICAL TO A SECTION
24
Am7(add4)
Cmaj7
Fmaj7/A
G(sus4)
Am9
Pno.
VI
I
IV
V
VI
29
Dm9(add4)
Am9
Dm9(add4)
Am9
Pno.
II
VI
II
VI

2ND 8 BAR PHRASE DIFFERS FROM A SECTION
33
Cmaj7/E
Fmaj7/A
Em7
G/A
Dm9
Pno.
37
C7(add4)/Bb
C/F
G(sus4)
Am7(add4)
Pno.
B SECTION
41
Cmaj7/D Dmaj7/E Emaj7/F#
3 ASCENDING NOTES ARE KEY MELODY
Cmaj7/D Dmaj7/E Emaj7/F#
MELODY DISPLACED BY 1 BEAT
Pno.
47
Cmaj7/D Dmaj7/E Emaj7/F#
Pno.

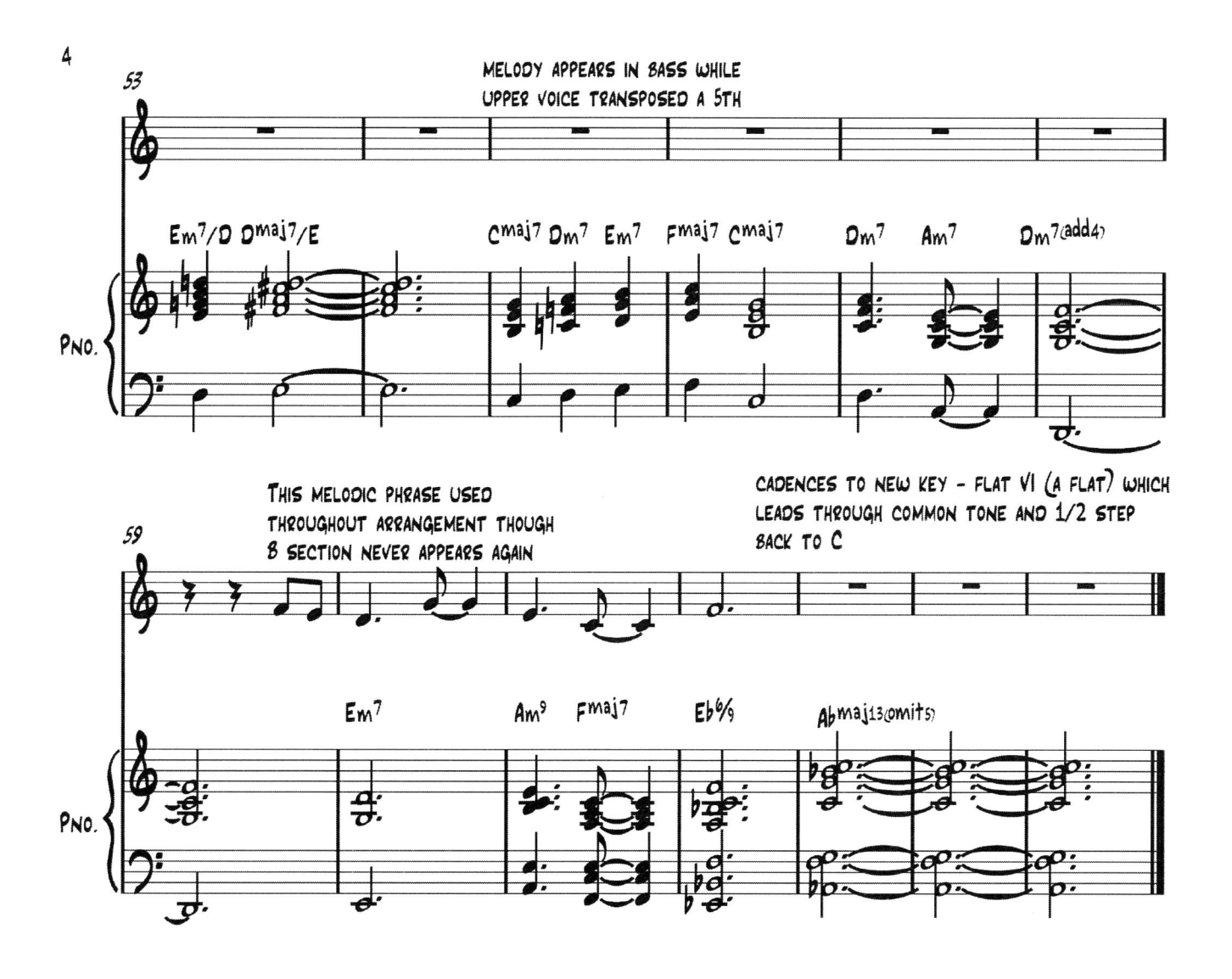

Lead Sheet Reduction — Harmonic Overview

As previously suggested, Mendoza often creates memorable moments in his scores that are either harmonic vamps or repeated melodies that are accompanied by such figures. He usually reserves these "hooks" for later in the score, but in this case he introduces a catchy rhythmic figure that lays out the chord progression at the outset, as shown in Example 3.1. These opening bars establish both a hypnotic, rhythmic gesture and harmonic scheme that will serve as the basis for much of the entire arrangement. As is the case with most Mendoza vamps, they have as much melodic value as they do harmonic and rhythmic, and the riffs used in this score follow his established trend. Roman numerals have been added beneath the bass clef staff merely to show basic root movement within a functional harmonic framework. While the cadence using Amin to return to Cma^7 is less typical and less strong, especially because of the minor quality, it does make complete sense based on voice leading, since the C, E, and G are common tones and the A and D (if included in the Ami7) can move stepwise to chord tones in CMa^7. A minor is of course also the relative minor to C major. It is important to note that a dominant 7th, or for that matter a ii^7–V^7 progression, is nowhere to be found in this entire score.

The idea of parallel ascending chords used in the B section will surface at several points in the arrangement, as indicated later in the analysis.

Mendoza trademark harmonic structures are apparent in this basic lead sheet. For example, the use of triads with suspended 4ths (measures 3, 11, etc.) and minor chords with added 4ths or 11ths (m.5, 24, etc.) are found throughout Example 3.1. But even more characteristic of the composer's style is the use of major triads, seventh chords, or dominant 7th chords with the added 11th. This introduces a dissonance created by the added minor ninth or minor 2nd, which is the distance between the 3rd and 11th or 4th. Mendoza makes this work by using sufficient spacing and strong voice leading. It is another way that he achieves tension by adding suspensions to his music that are often not resolved. Measures 21–24 in Example 3.1 show a series of unresolved suspensions leading back to the top of the form at A². The following example illustrates the resolutions that never take place to these four chords.

Example 3.2

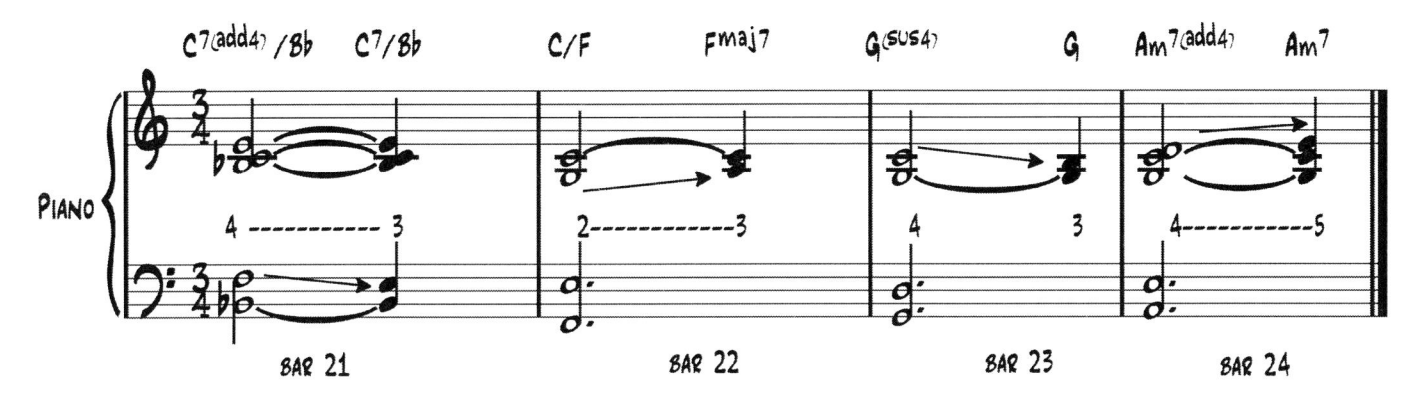

The B section, which establishes a few ideas used later in the arrangement, does not repeat in its entirety. It does feature parallel Ma⁷ chords with foreign bass tones. Another way to look at this is to classify these chords as major 9ths with the 9th in the bass. The composer exhibits a preference for using extension tones at the bottom of voicings rather than at the top, which is more typical. Examples of such voicings will be shown in the upcoming section and highlighted in the full score analysis. Stepwise, parallel motion is found later in the arrangement, especially the sudden and unexpected cadence to A♭ major at the end of this section. A quality change is substituted for the expected V⁷ of A♭ (E♭⁶/⁹) and it is approached from the IV⁷ in the home key a major second above. The new temporary tonic (A♭maj¹³) moves smoothly by half step and common tone to resolve back to C major. Much of the composer's voicings and the harmonic motion he favors is achieved through a concept of smooth and melodic voice leading rather than functional harmony principals.

Basic Form

As previously suggested, this form is basic and straightforward, though it took some thought to finally justify the second section as a true B section, especially since there is no return to A. The B section stands in significant contrast rhythmically, tonally, and melodically to the A section, but since it never repeats in the arrangement there was some debate as to how best to architecturally describe the section. But this dilemma of architectural description presented itself more than once throughout the analysis of the entire arrangement because Mendoza is a master at doing the unexpected and creating suspenseful moments of expectation.

The Arrangement

The graphic outline that appears as Example 3.3 offers an overview of how the entire arrangement unfolds and is architecturally conceived. It is a balance of composition, improvisation, and sections that are the result of the composer's improvisations. Follow it as you listen to the recording.

Example 3.3 — Top line shows bar numbers in brackets followed by timing

	[17] 0:17	[33] 0:33	[49] 0:49
Intro	A Section	A¹ Section	B Section
8 bars of piano Add Tbns	Alto Sax and Flugelhorn	Add Gtr and Flute to previous texture	Ens. plays contrasting material
16 bars	*16 bars*	*16 bars*	*14 bars*

[74] 1:21	[113] 2:07	[129] 1:29	[145] 2:43
Fugato Section	Alto Sax Solo	Second Alto Sax chorus	Third Alto Sax chorus
5 voice counterpoint with all winds leads to 3 bar solo send off	Rhythm section accompaniment	Bkgrnds added	Soloist trades 4 bar phrases with Ens riff
36 bars	*16 bars*	*16 bars*	*16 bars*

[164] 3:18	[180] 3:36	[227] 3:31	[251] 4:59
Interlude	Incomplete arpeggios in melodic, improvised style becomes counter-line to new melody	Trumpet Solo	Trumpet solo continues for 2 choruses
Ens.	Based on harmonic scheme of A theme	Soloist in dialogue with Ens	Rhythm section accompanies
16 bars	*47 bars*	*24 bars*	*32 bars*

[267] 5:34	**[285] 6:07**	**[300] 6:28**	**[331] 7:02**
Two more Tpt solo choruses; Soloist trades with Ens	Transitional seque section	Shout Chorus	Reprise of Piano intro
Brass riff as bkgrnd with unison Saxes on final chorus	Section includes mixed meters and builds with Ens to shout chorus	Full Ens — unison sax lines with brass punch chords. Harmonic references to A section material	Comes to close with quiet muted brass
30 bars	*15 bars*	*33 bars*	*8 bars*

One of the important aspects of any composition is pacing and dynamic contrast. The graphic analysis provides an opportunity to see how this chart is paced from beginning to end. Nothing is more tiresome than maintaining a constant dynamic level for too long, and the graph clearly shows how this score has an ebb and flow, building to the final thirty seconds or so of the shout chorus. There is a dynamic peak leading into the first solo and coming out of each solo. Call and response sections with the band and soloist are presented as their final solo choruses, helping to advance these sections of the score dynamically. But the most exciting dynamic peak comes in the full ensemble shout chorus, or development section, and falls about 90 percent into the piece, as shown in the third frame of the graphic analysis in Example 3.4.

Example 3.4

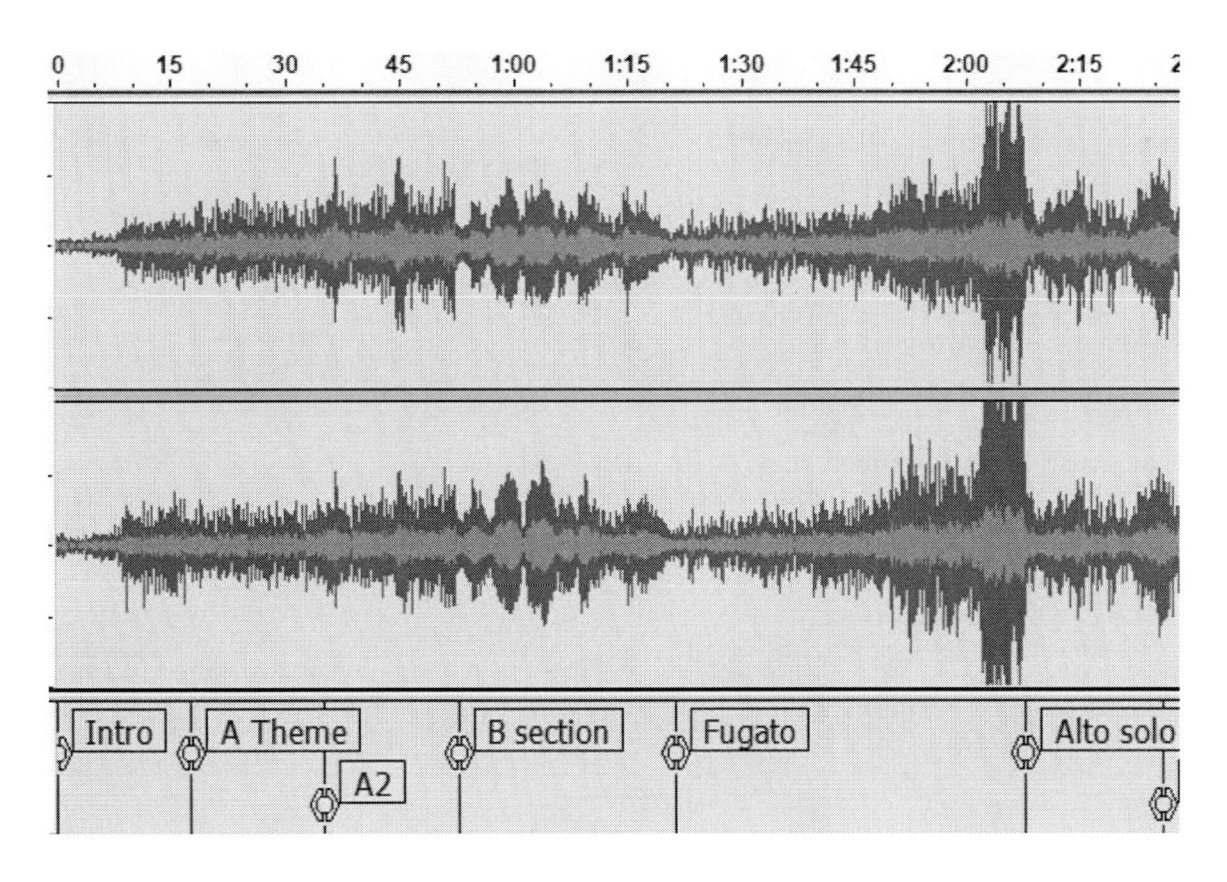

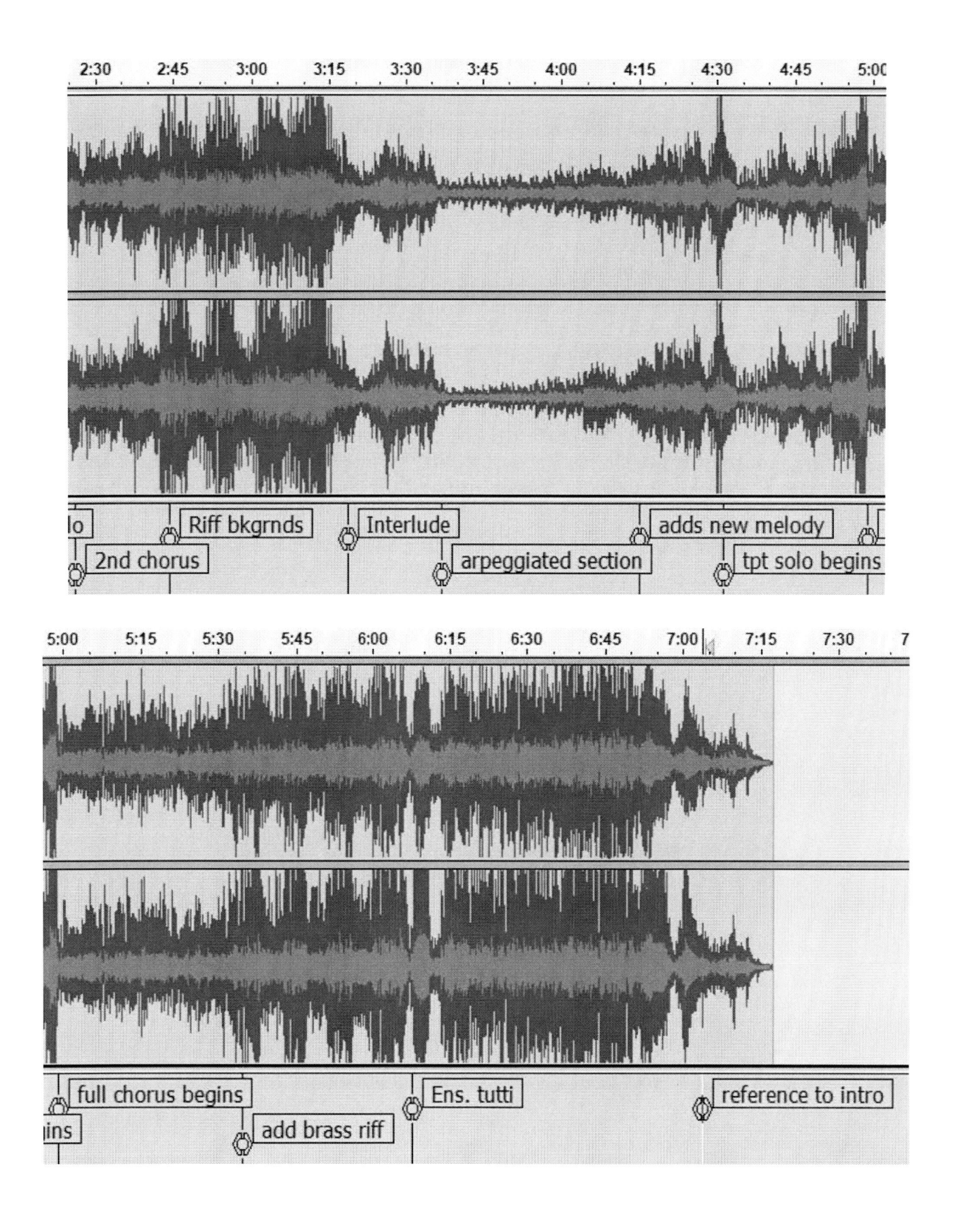

General Observations

As is the case with many innovators, the originality of their work is often based on finding ways to break from the norm, defying rules that are often taught, and forging new sounds by the way they work with melody, harmony, form, rhythm, and orchestration. The typical big band instrumentation, even when augmented by a percussionist, French horns, or woodwinds, is by nature somewhat limiting, but Mendoza, through his use of woodwinds and guitar in particular, finds new colors that dress this timeless ensemble in new clothes. Through unique harmonic structures, and the ways in which they are voiced and orchestrated, Mendoza has established a very personal sound. Rhythmically, his sense of phrasing also stands out as unconventional and free of the constraints of bar lines. It is in the phrasing of his melodies where one can hear the influences of Wayne Shorter. Mendoza scores are also very driven by melodic movement. Harmonies seem to move and exist in a linear fashion rather than as vertical blocks, though there are moments where the rhythmically concerted, cohesive, vertical punches of the traditional big band sound emerge. Such is the case in this score during the final solo choruses and the shout chorus.

Two sections in this score that, on first glance, seem to deviate significantly from the primary thematic material are the sections labeled "fugato" and "arpeggiated section." Fugato is defined as a fugal style passage that is usually a contrapuntal section that appears as a component of an otherwise non-fugal composition. Such sections are typical in classical sonatas and quartets or within the development section of a symphony. In the case of this score, the composer subtly introduces melodic and rhythmic fragments from the original theme with newly composed material. Annotations on the full score at the close of this chapter will point out some of the references to the original theme as Mendoza ultimately introduces five independent voices to his fugato.

As previously suggested, it is difficult to label the section that follows the interlude after the alto sax solo. The outline describes it as "incomplete arpeggios in an improvised style." This is in fact what initially occurs at this section – broken and incomplete arpeggios that suggest the sixteen bar harmonic progression used throughout the piece. But the suggestion of a harmonic progression is subtle at best and similar to how an improviser would hint at a chord progression without blatantly arpeggiating the chords. One could also view this section as a melodic counter line to a primary melody not yet introduced. This section keeps us in suspense for two choruses before new melodic material is introduced at measure 212 by flute and muted trumpets while the haunting, arpeggiated section now more obviously serves as a countermelody. Just prior to this entrance the trombones introduce an additional simple counter line that suggests prior melodic material. Aside from the melodic invention, the beauty of this section once again is in the orchestration, combining clarinets with guitar and piano to present a very subtle line that eventually serves as a countermelody to a more predominant new melody that is held in reserve. This section conjures a sense of anticipation, prompting listeners to wonder what might come next while they wait for a melody to be embraced by this unusual accompaniment or improvised-like countermelody.

Orchestration

Orchestration is one of the striking aspects of this score, which is at times elegant, much like the composer's orchestral scores. Of particular note is the use of woodwinds in combination with brass, both open and muted, to provide a dusky, darker quality. Two bass clarinets are used for well over half of the arrangement and often combine with the trombones as a choir. The bass clarinet is consistently used as the lowest voice in such cases, leaving the fourth trombone to state a chord extension tone, as seen in many of the examples that will follow. There are many such passages throughout the full score.

Flute is often used to double the lead trumpet line, either in unison or an octave higher for added punch and clarity, especially when the lead trumpet is written in the staff.

Mendoza makes use of the guitar as another linear instrument, rather than unnecessary rhythm section chording. Guitar often doubles lead lines and in combination with the woodwinds. The guitar exerts an influence on wind instruments it is combined with, transforming the collective sound into something entirely new.

Excessive doubling is not found in the score. If only three trombones are necessary to express a sonority, that is all the composer uses.

The rhythm section is removed from traditional responsibilities almost completely for about sixty-four measures of the score. Drums might be contributing only light cymbal work suggesting the pulse during these sections while bass is used melodically rather than in a timekeeping role.

Chord Voicing

Voice leading is important during the development of a Mendoza score, and that is obvious through full score analysis. The composer frequently adds motion inside of a sustained harmony to make it less static through the melodic motion of inner voices, as illustrated by the following example. This melodic motion helps to connect the changing harmonies, giving them a smoother connection. The two examples that follow illustrate this principle.

Example 3.5a – The ascending harmonic scheme in m.53 is found throughout the score in different keys.

Critics have compared Mendoza's work to that of Gil Evans, and that may in part be due to his frequent exploitation of Spanish and Latin American styles. But this association is also based on Mendoza's tendency to add one unexpected note to a simple triad or dominant chord, and where he places such tension tones and their weight in terms of doublings within the voicing. He may also omit a note that is most often included, for example, the third. The following examples illustrate a few such circumstances.

Example 3.5b – D dominant 9th chord with a suspended 4th or 11th

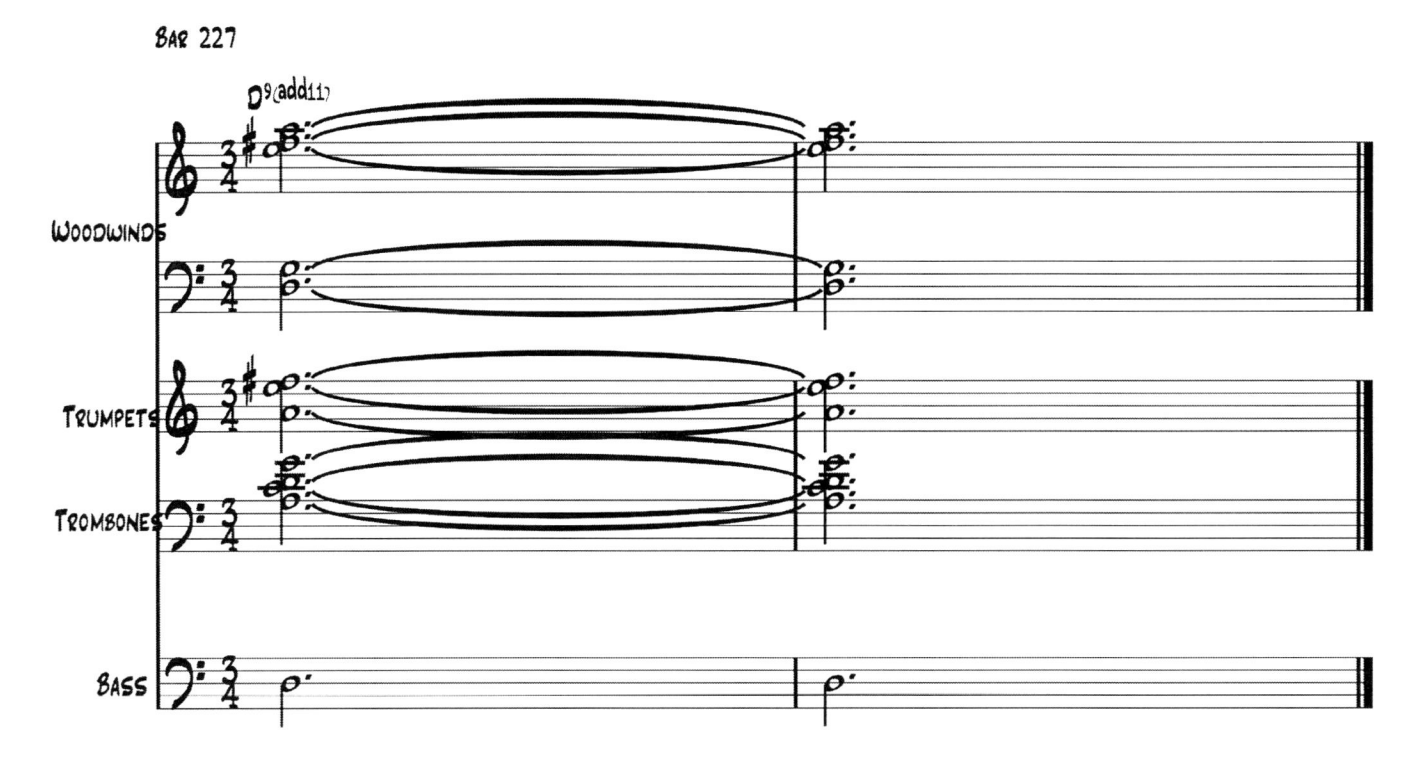

Example 3.6 – F major triads with added suspended 4th

Mendoza often disregards one of the Arranging 101 class rules in favor of creating harmonic resonances unique to his sound. Grinds or dissonances within a voicing such as minor seconds traditionally are located in the middle of a voicing, between trumpets or trombones two and three. It is for this reason that these sections are typically seated from left to right, as 2nd, 1st, 3rd, 4th, which keeps the dissonant interval separated, facilitating good tuning by the performers. The trumpet voicing at the beginning of Example 3.7 illustrates this more traditional approach. Mendoza's voicings that put dissonances between outer voices are more difficult to tune by less skilled musicians, unless of course the seating order is changed to resemble a concert band – 1st, 2nd, 3rd, 4th. It is not uncommon in this score to find minor second dissonances between the top or bottom two voices, as seen in the following example.

Example 3.7

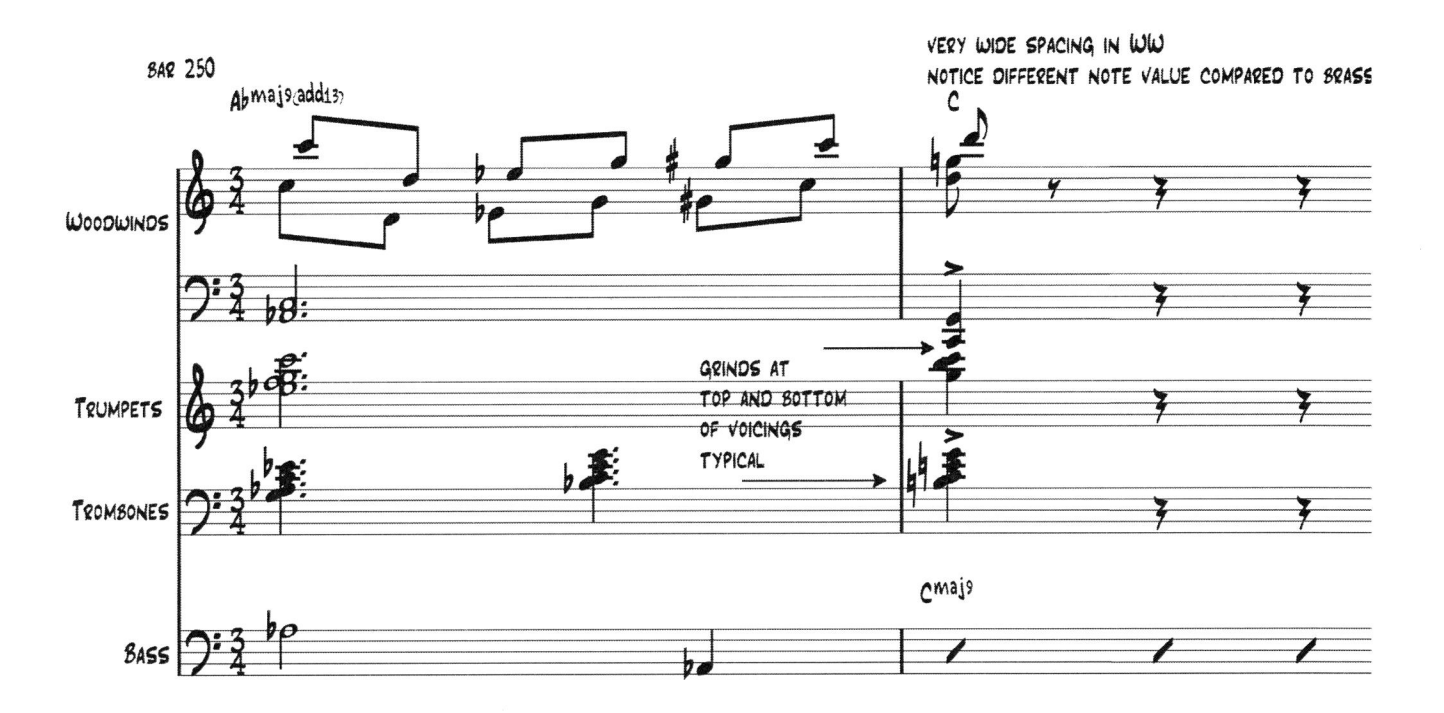

Example 3.8

Spacing between section voicings as well as within a section voicing is also a striking aspect of this Mendoza score. When not playing in unison, the woodwinds are often spaced very widely, as shown in the earlier Example 3.7. Sometimes the spacing is larger than one might expect, or closer in cluster-like voicings as shown in Examples 3.10 and 3.11.

Example 3.9

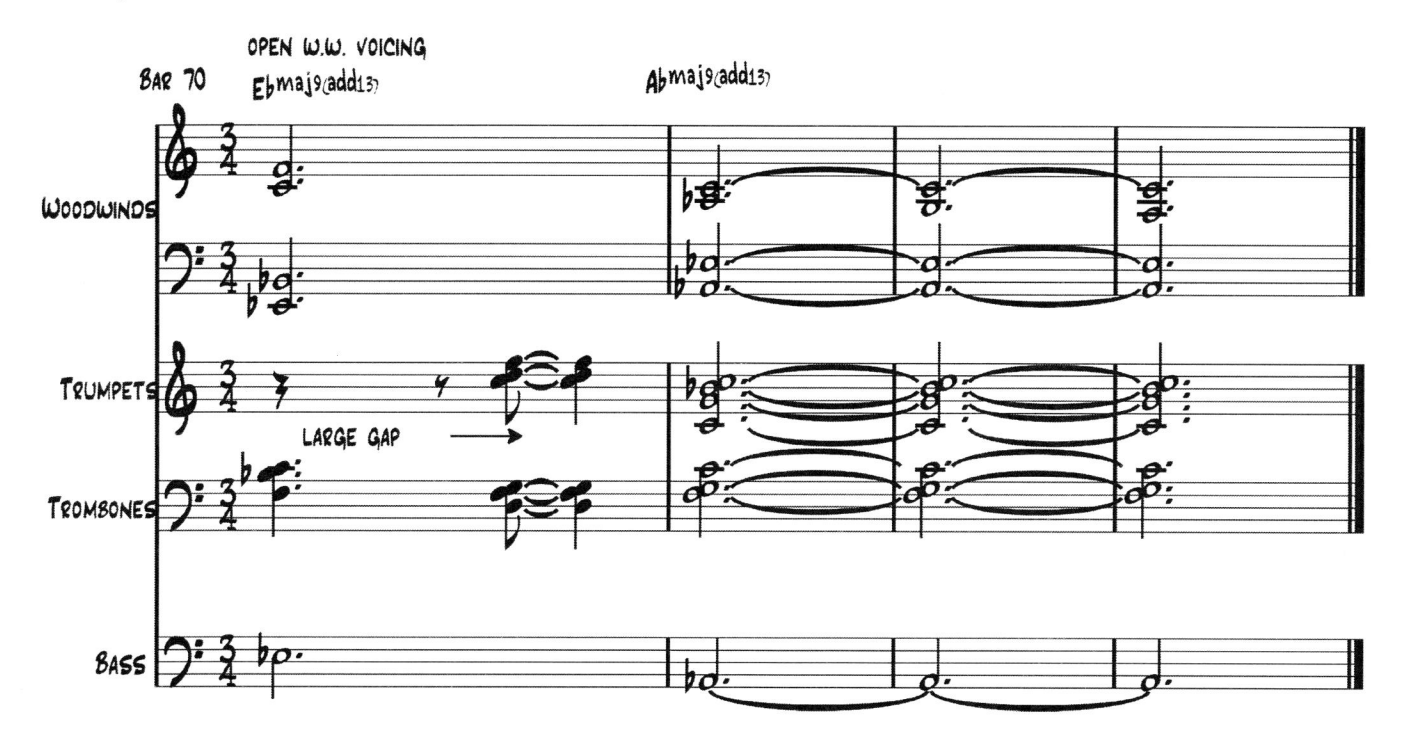

Example 3.10 – Note wide woodwind spacing.

143

Example 3.11

[Musical score excerpt showing Bar 140, with Woodwinds, Trumpets, and Trombones parts in 3/4 time. Chord symbols: Dm9, Bbmaj9(omit3), C/F, G(sus4), Am9. Annotations: "CLOSE, CLUSTER-LIKE" and "PIANIST GIVEN Bbmaj7"]

Example 3.12 – Parallel ascending passages are found throughout the score. Note the fairly large gap in m.286 between trumpets and trombones.

[Musical score excerpt showing Bar 285, with Altos & Tenors, Bari, Trumpets, Trombones, and Bass parts in 3/4 time. Chord symbols: C/D, D/E, E/F#, F#/G#, Am9, ETC. Annotation: "VOICE LEADING"]

Several passages in "Homecoming" feature triads over foreign bass tones. Example 3.13 is more dissonant in this regard than Example 3.12, which is are more diatonic in nature and consequently less dissonant. Only a fairly knowledgeable guitarist or someone who knows this instrument well would write the guitar part shown in the following example.

Example 3.13

Woodwind Voicing

When the woodwinds are not in unison or octave unison they are often used in a cross section doubling with brass. When used to voice a harmony they are frequently spread as much as three octaves or more. The woodwinds frequently fill the larger gaps that might appear between trumpet and trombone voicings.

Brass Voicing

Trumpet voicings have already been discussed with numerous examples; however, there is a section that deserves special mention. Harmonized trumpets alone appear very rarely in jazz scores and are a bit more common surrounded and supported by other instruments. This is the case at measure 212, where four cup muted trumpets in harmony are joined by flute to express a new melody. The cup mutes take an edge off the trumpet's timbre to blend well with the accompaniment.

Trombones are primarily voiced in close spacing with occasional examples of chorale style open voicings. Trumpets are also generally voiced in close position; however, larger than expected gaps between second and third or third and fourth can be found, as shown in the score analysis. The gaps help to create less tertian-like voicing structures. Sometimes these section and brass voicings are almost cluster-like, as previously illustrated. (See Examples 3.10 and 3.11.)

Bass Doubling

It is rare to see the bass trombone on a low root, a task more likely assigned to the bass clarinet or baritone sax once the woodwinds finally move to saxophones. The bass clarinet doubling is far less cumbersome and plodding and leaves possibilities for the assignment of extension color tones to the trombones, as is frequently the case.

In the shout chorus the baritone sax doubles bass lines also played by fourth trombone and bass. This practice is not followed consistently through this entire section, however.

Solo Background Writing

Solos are important to this chart and Mendoza introduces their entrances dramatically, as is the practice of most writers. He follows this tradition in introducing the alto sax soloist but more subtly introduces the trumpet soloist, first segueing from ensemble to soloist before bringing the soloist into full spotlight. This is just the opposite of how the previous alto soloist interacts with the ensemble in that ensemble backgrounds are not introduced until the end of the solo section. These solo backgrounds introduce a four bar call and response with the soloists, and it is a memorable riff that stays with the listener much like the opening piano and trombone introduction (see Example 3.10, m.145). Once again Mendoza creates in his fashion a very memorable, short rhythmic motive whose melody is strong and unforgettable.

We learn in Arranging 101 that it is best to use saxophone backgrounds behind brass solos and brass behind sax solos so as not to distract from the soloist. This is likely why Mendoza reserves the sax linear backgrounds for the final trumpet solo chorus, although since the backgrounds interact with the soloist as four bar exchanges, the old rule is less of an issue.

Fugato Section

A unique aspect of this arrangement is the fugato section, and it warrants special consideration, since such things are rarely found in a big band jazz score. Not only does this section add an element of unexpected variety, it showcases the composer's skill in writing linearly. It is not uncommon to find three voice counterpoint, or even four voices, but in this case five different voices are eventually introduced.

The cross section, mixed orchestration also contributes to the unique sound of this section. The orchestration of these lines is as follows:

Voice 1 – 2 bass clarinets, bass trombone, and bass, later adding guitar and 2 trombones
Voice 2 – bass and 1 bass clarinet
Voice 3 – 1 bass clarinet and 2 trombones
Voice 4 – 4 trumpets and clarinet
Voice 5 – 2 trumpets and flute

The free counterpoint throughout this section is somewhat new material but not without significant references to rhythm gestures and melodic shapes found in the original thematic material. These references are highlighted in Example 3.13. The rhythmic figure highlighted in the last four measures of this section in voice 2 (and also found in voices 1 and 3) is also a common denominator throughout the fugato.

Example 3.14 – References to the original melodic and rhythmic material are boxed.

Fugato Section

Final Shout Chorus

A series of odd meters (5/4 and 3/2) at m.296 features borrowed melodic, rhythmic, and harmonic elements from the theme and solo backgrounds to segue back to 3/4 meter and the tutti shout chorus that follows, beginning at measure 300. These shifting odd meters set up the return to 3/4 in such a way as to obscure bar lines even when a regular 3/4 meter is established at m.300. Coupled with highly syncopated and over the bar line brass figures, these changing meters leading to m.300 help to completely obscure any sense of meter regularity through the balance of the shout chorus. It is the drummer's reinforcement of these syncopations that really makes this section work and propel things forward in an exciting way.

The saxophones are sometimes in rhythmic unison with the brass and at other times function on their own with brass harmonies punctuating their lines that spin out new melodic material. Once this section begins to evolve there is little melodic reference to the original thematic material aside from maintaining very non-chromatic, "white note" shapes. While the brass accompaniment references the original harmonic scheme, it is not at all bound by it.

Brass are well paced with lead trumpet mostly in the staff until the final culmination with a deceptive move to Ami at m.323, and then again briefly in a very abrupt, subito crescendo in Mendoza fashion at m.329 before winding down to finalize the arrangement.

Example 3.15

As is the case with many contemporary jazz composers, Mendoza never returns to thematic material following this development section and only briefly alludes to it by reintroducing six bars from the opening piano progression. Consult the full score analysis for additional details.

Interview with Vince Mendoza

August 19, 2017

RL: *While I've followed your work for many years and of course become familiar with your bio, I'd like to learn more about your influences as a writer, and who your teachers were.*

VM: It's funny that you mentioned earlier [in our email discussion] a "fly by the seat of your pants" approach to writing, because my influences were really more the function of my experience as an instrumentalist. I started as a young guitar player listening to classical music, but at the same time wanting to play jazz by learning the repertoire of "standards." I learned a lot of them from my mother, and her brothers, who were all musicians. That's who I learned the standard repertoire from, and my chord language immediately came from that standard repertoire. My approach to linear writing really didn't happen until I became a trumpet player and discovered Miles [Davis] and Freddie [Hubbard], and started to hear both the language of jazz and their unique linear approach to improvisation. I started to concentrate more on creating lines and less in terms of the structural motion of chords. And that was an important moment. Being an instrumentalist opened up for me the study of the linear aspect of improvisatory expression.

When studying classical music as a composer I studied further the aspect of linear writing and how it controls harmony. Harmony in classical applications, for the most part, is a function of the linear motion, scales, sets, and modes. A more traditional jazz or "songwriting" approach would have an emphasis in writing melodies from similar scales and modes, but based on established chord changes. In other words, a melody on this phrase has to be a certain scale because the chord is C7. A "classical" approach would involve deciding that a melody is going to have particular shape and as a result guides the eventual motion of the harmony.

The more I learned about counterpoint and intervallic writing, the more I realized that the harmony associated with Debussy and Stravinsky and Bartok and Boulez is dictated by the intervals, scales, and modes that they chose in their music. So, for instance, it's not really a $C^{9(\#11)}$, but rather about the whole tone scale and its combination of scale tones. That was a liberating moment for me, making the jump from a jazz musician using extensions on chords to being open to non-functional harmony through my choices of intervals and shapes. This is really the basis for my approach to writing.

RL: *Did you discover that on your own?*

VM: I discovered it from my score study, and of course from my composition teachers. Obviously, Debussy wasn't referencing chord changes in his music. He was for the most part interested in scales, modes, and linear motion. For me that was the ticket, as was the study of serial composition. Even though most of us don't use it very often, some of the aspects of serial composition technique are useful, most notably generating harmonies from the grouping of notes in the set. You can use a certain set of intervals that will generate your melody and resulting harmony. Another good example would be the synthetic chords generated by the melodies in the music of Eric Dolphy and other jazz musicians playing in that style.

RL: *But you nevertheless chose to write in a jazz/pop related direction rather than writing classical music, although I know you have written some more classical oriented music.*

VM: Right. I think that whenever I try to go too far into the "classical" direction I start losing the visceral sense of satisfaction with my own music. I start losing *myself*. I talk about that with my students all the time. You really have to find out what your own path is going to be. In that way I think there is a certain place where my music lives, which isn't to say that I can't challenge the paths that I take to get to that place.

RL: *I think that approach has led you to create a voice that is very unique.*

VM: If I had followed the path that some classical composers might have taken, in particular with serial and textural writing, I might have lost my personal voice.

RL: *Before we look specifically at "Homecoming," can you tell us about how you work? I'm interested in creative processes that composers use and what tools they use, and how they start with that blank piece of paper.*

VM: I think that it's important to understand that whatever result we get, not to mention the work that we put into creating a piece, the music should in the end have a development of form, the management of energy, as well as all the other things that we think about as composers. As jazz composers, we are charged with a certain duty to include in the development of the piece an opportunity for improvisation. And in addition, what I add is that the ideas that I come up with are somewhat improvisational in nature. So my process has to begin with a certain amount of improvisation in various forms. It could be keyboard improvisations that I record or through playing guitar, drumming, singing, dancing – thinking of things and writing them out. It's a very unstructured, visceral period of improvisation that is unedited. That's something that I've always done. Then there will be much work put into giving shape to all these improvisations. Anytime that I've tried to just structure something mechanically it has always lacked that individual voice that I feel should be in the music, so maybe part of that individuality has to come from those original improvisations from whence those pieces grow.

"Homecoming" actually is a great example of that process. The beginning piano introduction was something that immediately appeared to me (in the office of my former orchestra) [Metropole Orkest]. It was a visceral response to going in that room after a long period of time and all of those years that I spent in that room just coming out, you know.

Those improvisations are important to me; although I may use very, very little of what I improvised, the original ideas are usually the basis of pretty much everything I will use in a piece.

That's the start of my process, and the next portion of it has to do with listening, deciding what I think is useable and what is redux, what is aimless. Maybe there will be one little diamond in the middle of all of that. And I'll realize I like that particular idea, which is great, and get rid of everything else. And then that idea becomes the basis for the piece. Then I start asking questions – what's the piece about? Is it about a song, is it about the organic development of ideas, is it about a groove or a texture, or is it about the blues? Those are the things I tell my students. If they come up with improvisations, I don't want them to edit themselves right at that moment. I want them to explore things and then come to it [later].

RL: *So the editing comes later.*

VM: Exactly. The thing that I notice most often with my students is that they edit themselves so deeply that either they come up with nothing or whatever they come up with is so minuscule that it's not possible to embellish upon it or develop it. The editorial process for me is based on what I think is interesting and what I would want to develop. And then I ask myself those questions I described to you. The answers to those questions guide my decisions about the piece.

RL: *Are you still using paper and pencil, maybe not exclusively? That's probably a loaded question because I think that we all use computers and sequencers at some point in the process. But are you still fundamentally in that early process using pencil and paper?*

VM: At this point I'm not using pencil and paper much, unless I'm quickly sketching something out. Or maybe I feel that there is some kind of detail that I really need to work out, in particular with regard to rhythm. I might work on a shape that is worth exploring but I don't yet know how it's going to be notated. So I'll work through it rhythmically based on how I feel it. When I am using the computer for notation I have to know how it's going to look and feel before I enter it in the software.

RL: *I like your last point! But I suspect that you've gradually come to this place of how you rely more on computers and less on paper and pencil. I think a lot of us have evolved as we've become more mature, experienced writers and have a better ability to put it into the computer and know what it's going to eventually sound like. We've learned how to use this twentieth century tool, in other words.*

VM: Yes, I think so. I think the younger generation of writers are now able to work right into the software.

RL: *But don't you find that there are a lot of problems with the younger generation who fall into the "copy and paste" habit, and as a result there is this danger of losing a sense of the bigger picture of their piece and variety? How long do they dwell on something before moving on to something else? You can lose the listener's perspective when you're looking at the screen and that's all you are seeing.*

VM: That's right. In the old days, and this is more of a formal consideration, when my students brought in their score paper I used to take pages of their score and line them up in the hallway of our house so I could see where they were going texturally and formally. You would really get an idea of the density of a piece that way. When you are looking at a little window you can't see anything in that way.

RL: *You can easily lose sight of pacing and a number of other aspects of a score.*

VM: The paper part of it for me is most useful if I want to think about the fluidity of linear motion – like Miles or Ornette and the way that they played their melodies freely over the bar line. I like to write the dots of the pitches on paper and then maybe try to figure out some way that it can be made into a line. I want to find out how fluid I can be with a particular melody before I enter it into the computer.

RL: *You talked about reaching that point after you've gone through the organic improvisational step in creating work that is going to contribute to a new piece. And the next step is asking the big questions – "What's this piece about and what are the goals?" and so on. What can you tell us about "Homecoming" in regard to that second step and how much of that was planned out ahead of time.*

VM: Well, as I said, "Homecoming" was born out of that first line. Of course, at the beginning, it wasn't *exactly* how it needed to be, so I had to distill it into a phrase that made sense. But it was clear that I wasn't going to be able to sustain the entire piece with just that, so there had to be some melodic interest as well. From then it was about deciding where the high point of the piece was going to be and how that line was going to function to get us there. It was clear that most of the piece was going to be built around that initial six bar phrase and some variant of it. The variants ended up as the fugato section and the other interlude to get from one place to another, and the shout chorus. The shout chorus was another one of those exercises that I just sort of *felt*. It came from the brass section figures, which were written first. The saxophone line was written as an improvisation over the brass figures. My shout choruses are often composed that way, i.e., there is some kind of reinforcement of the feeling of rhythm by the brass section, and the saxophones are an improvisation to whatever the brass section is doing.

RL: *Did you work from an outline that imagined the flow of the entire piece, or did sections evolve one to another in an improvised, more organic process?*

VM: Before I work on a score, I generally have an idea of what the piece is going to look like in terms of form. It isn't always a written outline or sketch, but usually I will be thinking about those issues for a while before I decide that it is time to put notes on paper or into the software. It is important to note that these days I tend to make changes in the master plan as I am writing, especially in terms of form. I didn't do that much in the paper days … Things might get longer or shorter, or some portions of a piece that were originally intended to be at the end might wind up at the beginning. I am happy with being fluid in this regard and encourage my students to be so as well.

Having said all that, "Homecoming" didn't really have much of a formal master plan going in. The organization was pretty organic. I was finished when I couldn't take the piece any further, and that sign was at the high point of the shout chorus. Where can you go from there? In that way I prefer to find "moments" that can be signposts in the development of a composition.

RL: *When you composed the brass aspect of the shout chorus, with all the hits and syncopated rhythms and such, was that created first as a non-pitched line that you may have sketched out before you thought about harmony and voicing?*

VM: Yes; in fact I'll often do that with shout choruses. I'll write out a shout chorus rhythmically with two lines: brass and woodwinds. I want to get a rhythmic idea of the interaction of the sections. Also, it's important to make the distinction between horizontal and vertical writing, which I do quite often. If you are thinking about "Homecoming," for example, the brass section is almost entirely vertical and the saxophones are horizontal. Sometimes in a shout chorus I'd want to make a shift and maybe the trumpets are horizontal and the trombones and saxes are doing something else. That's something that Thad and Bob Brookmeyer of course did quite often. When my students are daunted by the notion of writing a shout chorus, working it out rhythmically on paper takes a lot of the pressure off. They don't have to think about chords and the melody and all of that. If a shout chorus doesn't feel like a rhythmic expansion of what we're wanting to hear, then it isn't right. The shout chorus should be an inevitability. You get there because you have to.

It's just like the role of the improvised solo. The solo should be there only because we *need* to go there.

RL: *I also think that there is a certain psychological advantage, particularly with a student but even with an advanced writer, where when you are working on a section like that you aren't so worried about pitch content. You are concerned only with sketching out rhythms, and you are making forward creative progress without having to worry about the details that can come later. It is a good confidence builder.*

VM: Yes, and then when you are working with a computer it's especially true that you can work a little that way and decide to come back and deal with that later, as long as you remember to do it! [laughs]

RL: *While you've already touched on this a bit, it seems to be that voice leading and melodic motion within a harmony and between changing harmonies also seems to be an important feature in your writing. It seems that you are less concerned about harmonic flow and verticality and more about linear flow and connectivity, except in the contrasting shout chorus, maybe.*

VM: Yes, that's true. If I find that there is a particular note in a vertical texture that may not exactly be reflective of the chord symbol in the piano part, it's not something that I'm too concerned with, except with regard to how it's approached and how I leave it. If you notice that there isn't a chord tone in the structure, something is missing or something is there that shouldn't be there, and it's only because I'm trying to get from point A to point C in a way that makes sense in that individual voice.

RL: *That's clear in the entire score, although I think you purposely leave out a note from a chord that would be an expected note, which gives it a kind of resonance that is much more unique than the chord would have been had you included all the pitches.*

VM: Right, and that's somewhat of a Stravinsky-ism too, treating lines individually from other lines. It might lead to open fifths or octaves as opposed to thirds or seconds.

RL: *Let's talk about counterpoint for a moment, as this to me seems to be such an important aspect of your style and particularly in this score. At one point in the fugato section just before the first solo there are, as I recall, five independent voices moving. What was your approach to writing a section like this?*

VM: I recall that section was written away from the main score. I sketched that five-part fugato and then went back and made decisions about how it was going to be orchestrated. And the same is true of the other interlude, but that fugato is decidedly more complicated. It was an idea that I had while walking around town or in the shower or something. The actual execution of it had to be done on paper, as counterpoint exercise. It is much easier for me to write on paper this way so I can see the relationship of the parts, keeping in mind what the intervals are and how I am moving, and when I might be getting into trouble! [laughs] For students of counterpoint, as you are, Rick, it is easy to get into trouble, and once you get into trouble you're in *deep* trouble! [laughs]

RL: *Oh yes, it's very much like painting yourself into a corner.*

VM: When you start a voice, if your other voices aren't moving properly, you're really digging a big hole. So that fugato section needed to be written out on five lines to see how it was going to work out, especially with regard to interval relationships. And then I orchestrated it from there.

RL: *You bring up an interesting point that I hadn't actually thought about until now, though I do it myself. There are two ways of writing for the ensemble – one in which you are literally writing for the band, where from square one you are thinking – "Saxes are doing this while trumpets are doing that," and so on; and then there is this other way of writing where you are actually composing with the notion that it's going to fit in the score at a certain point, but you worry about orchestrating it later. They are two different processes in a way.*

VM: Yes, I think that way as well with symphony orchestra. There is a way to work directly onto an orchestral score and make your painting that way, but also there is a way to make a five to seven line sketch of your music without regard to how it's going to be orchestrated. But then you have to think about the answer to the question that you ask way far back in the process – "What's this piece about?" If it's going to be about the blues or about Kansas City or in the Basie style, then you're not really going to be sketching outside the score as much as thinking "The saxes are doing this figure," and "This is a good bone line," and "The brass have to be doing that," and so on.

RL: *And that is even going to dictate how you voice things.*

VM: Yes, often when I'm writing orchestral music I might make sketches and think later about who's going to play it: "Who would best bring this character to life?" – as opposed to sketching and saying, "This melody will be played by the oboe."

RL: *This next statement is more of my own comment or observation, and I'd like you to reflect on it and tell me if I'm on track. It seems to me that the rhythmic aspect of your melodic lines, and the resulting phrasing, is also a very unique aspect of your style – defying bar lines and meter and disguising them at times; and your music is highly syncopated. I sometimes feel that it's guided by the rhythm of a lyric that of course isn't there because they aren't vocal scores. But I often get that impression. This aspect of your writing also strikes me as being somewhat Wayne Shorter inspired – that unique way he has of rhythmically improvising, not just melodically but rhythmically. Is my description of your rhythmic invention at all accurate?*

VM: Well, Doctor Lawn, you *nailed* it! [laughs] And I'll add one thing to that. My approach to writing linearly almost always relates somehow to what Wayne or Miles *might* have played, even though in my construction of counterpoint it probably is closer to what Stravinsky might have done. Stravinsky's construction was somewhat less, believe it or not, improvisational to my ears than Wayne would have been. I suspect that if you asked Wayne about it he probably would tell you that there were probably some words or images that would go with what he just played. He's always connecting his melodies to a story.

RL: *Well, he's a poet.*

You have made a reputation as both an arranger and a composer. Do you find one benefits the other – arranging benefits composition and vice versa? How did you begin as a young writer in this regard? Did you focus on arranging, more on composition, or did you focus on both evenly?

VM: I think it's significant to know that I grew up listening to the radio, and I always dreamed that I could be this guy in the studio conducting that orchestra on the record. That's part of my early inspiration to be a musician. But I was never an arranger until I started doing radio orchestra gigs [in Europe] and they started asking for guests to come and play their own songs. I would have to arrange things for them, so in a way I sort of fell into that.

And then I started working with singers. I think that working in that capacity has definitely informed my music in a dramatic way. As an arranger and working with a text, you really have to think about what you want the listener to feel about the meaning of the text and how to get that. If you're not doing that properly, you're not really doing a service to the song or the artist. That's a concept that I wasn't that aware of before working with singer/songwriters. When you're a jazz musician and you're doing yet another arrangement of "Cherokee," or "Body and Soul," or "Lush Life," and in particular as a young jazz musician, you're thinking about the changes and the extensions and the cool textures you could put in there. But you're not so much thinking about the story of the song and any kind of emotional thread that you might want to generate, which by the way could give you a lot of assistance in your decisions and the writing of the piece. In the end it is a disservice to the song not to think these things. So that aspect of arranging really informed my composing activities. And it goes without saying that composition informs my decisions as an arranger – to have so many more tools to use to get that emotional quality or the emotional thread through an arrangement. I think arranging is very important, and in discussion with my students there would be no difference between arranging and composing. We are all working toward the same end, which is to have an emotional experience in whatever form. We want to be moved, we want to tell a story. We can use someone else's text or our own.

RL: *I have a couple of questions that are more about mechanics and why you do what you do in a score layout. For example, why lay out the score, as you did in "Homecoming," with trumpets 1/2 and 3/4 on one line and the same with the trombones? And the piano appears at the very bottom of the score. I'm not being critical; I'm just curious.*

VM: You know, the piano on the bottom ... I don't know where I got that from, but I've always done that. I do know that [Hollywood] Judy Green Music paper was always like that. Did you look in Mancini's book, *Sounds and Scores*?

I have to say that now that I'm spending a fair amount of time at the universities and master classes telling people what to do, I'm asking myself the question as well: why am I doing this? [flips through the Mancini book in his library] Of course, he has no full scores in this book. The "Peter Gunn" score is even weirder, as this score has the bass on the bottom. So I don't really know; I just know that the Judy Green paper had piano on the bottom.

RL: *I suppose if you are a conductor and you want to grab important information quickly in a rehearsal, putting piano at the very bottom of the score really makes it pop out and easy to see.*

VM: Okay, I accept that answer [laughs]; and I hope the next question isn't about chord symbols because I'm even more wishy-washy about chord symbols than I ever was. Twenty years ago I was a chord militant – how something should be spelled and so on. And now as long as it is consistent, especially since I'm a slave to software and have to spell it the way they want, I'm much more open about it. I still maintain to use chord symbols that most accurately tell the rhythm section what notes should be played and not so much give them springboards to their improvisation. I know that there are various schools of thought on this. And, for Pete's sake, get rid of the triangles!

And the practice of putting instruments 1 and 3 on one line and 2 and 4 on the other line has more to do with the classical approach and the need to not have seconds on the same line, to have some spacing. But I don't really care about that these days because they're not actually reading from the same part. For most projects I might send the copyist all of the trumpets on one or two lines and would split them out. It could just as easily be 1/3 and 2/4 and 5th on the bottom. Then the lines are condensed again for the conductor score. [The "Homecoming" score shows trumpets 1 and 2 on a line and 3rd with 4th on a line and 5th on its own staff.]

RL: *I think it also helps to free up space, create more real estate on the score, so things aren't so tightly jammed.*

VM: If you are doing a big band score, and I do the same thing for orchestral scores, I almost always condense the trumpets and trombones because it gives you more real estate, and I want to have adequate space between the lines for articulations, bar numbers, slurs and so on. The only way to get all that information on a page is to use a super small staff size. And I don't know about you, but the 3mm staff size is too small for me.

RL: *You're right about that! Speaking of bar numbers, you're not the only writer in this project who shows every measure with a large measure number in the middle of the bar throughout the score. I've removed them for the sake of space in the book design and for annotations. But I assumed that the numbering was for convenience in rehearsals and the conductor. I assumed it was to expedite things and save time in rehearsal.*

VM: I do that with all my scores. I think it's a Hollywood thing. I want to be able to say bar 32 trombone 2 is a B♭, and you're not wasting time. I flip out with my students about that. I hate rehearsal letters. I want to see the bar numbers because again, pragmatically speaking, I don't have a lot of time to discuss "15 bars after letter B" in Budapest with the 3rd trombone player.

RL: *Getting back to "Homecoming," how would you describe the transitional section that begins at bar 180, scored very sparsely for two clarinets, guitar, and piano? I was really struck by this section because of its simplicity as nothing more than abbreviated arpeggios outlining, in a somewhat disguised way, the* *harmonies that support the primary theme. When I first heard it and saw it on paper I had one of these "Why haven't I ever thought of doing that?" moments! The beauty of that section for me is what it doesn't do rather than what it does.*

VM: If you are thinking of the role that the clarinet and guitar play, I think that what these instruments are playing have a melodic curve to it. Although it has an arpeggiated nature, it still has a melodic curve. I'll bring you back to your comments about Wayne [Shorter] because that clarinet part is what I could definitely hear Wayne playing. If you gave him those changes and told him to play something, I could imagine he might have played that, except that he wouldn't have played everything on the downbeat. That would have been an interesting way of approaching it too if I had my druthers, but I felt that having it on the downbeat helps propel the time a little bit because otherwise there isn't anything else propelling the time [there are no drums or bass involved in timekeeping at this point]. If you think that an improviser would have played these shapes, then you are more inclined to think that it's melodic.

RL: *For that matter, the opening sixteen bars of "Homecoming" is a melody.*

VM: Yes, it has a certain curve to it. If we had used just the first bar sixteen times, then it would be another story. There's a fine line between accompaniment and melody, and I talk sometimes in lectures about role playing in ensembles. I divide it into the lead role, a support role, and accompaniment. You'd think that there would be an element of what you discern to be the lead part, and the support part would somehow be a commentary on what they're doing, e.g., counterpoint, someone improvising. And then the accompaniment would be something that propels the time or gives you harmonic information. In most music that we listen to, even *The Firebird*, you'll have elements of accompaniment and so on. But the lines between those three things are ever so vague, and constantly shifting. Imagine a triangle with the three roles represented by the points. When you're thinking of free improvisation and what people are doing in the ensemble, the lines between them are very vague or at least constantly changing. In this case in this section of "Homecoming" I think the accompaniment is really the open fifths in the piano part because it gives you a downbeat and harmonic information.

RL: *As I recall, the guitar, clarinet, and upper piano part, the triplets, very subtly hint at the harmonic form that you used throughout the whole piece, but in such a way that it's more like an improviser who hints at the changes and doesn't just arpeggiate them.*

VM: Right. And we did need to have that final melody there [measure 212].

RL: *And as I recall that becomes the link to the next solo section.*

What single lesson, or suggestion, can you leave composers and arrangers with that might help us all to become better writers? Tell us something, in other words, that you find yourself often telling your students.

VM: I think that the main thing I tell my students is to try to find a way to be free in their writing, and in particular (in the big band context) to understand that the big band is a collection of musicians and not an entity responsible for maintaining a *particular* sound or style. I want the writers to be free to create their own vision of their emotional thread and to tell their story in a way that they want to tell it in the context of the collection of these musicians, and not so much think that because it's a big band they need to write a certain way. If you go down that road you're going to lose all your individuality. Part of your voice, your personal approach, is based on how you treat this group of musicians and how you exercise your emotions.

RL: *Once again, let me thank you for sharing your music and your ideas about writing with our readers.*

Annotated Full Score

The annotated full transposed score that follows provides additional details about "Homecoming," and includes concert pitch excerpts as reductions.

Homecoming

Transposed Score

Vince Mendoza

9
Fl.
Alto Sax.
Cl.
B. Cl. 1
B. Cl. 2
Tpt. 1/2
Tpt. 3/4
Tpt. 4
Tbn. 1/2
Tbn. 3/4
sim.
mp
Gtr
Bs.
Time (swinging)
Dr.
(8)
Cmaj7
Fmaj7/A
C(add2)
Am9(omit5)
Am9/D
Am9
Am7/D
Am9
Pno.
W.W
Tpts.
Tbns copy piano voicings
Tbns.
9
10
11
12
13
14
15
16

A Section
17
Fl.
Alto Sax.
Cl.
B. Cl. 1
B. Cl. 2
Tpt. 1/2
Tpt. 3/4
Tpt. 4
Tbn. 1/2
Tbn. 3/4
Gtr
Bs.
Dr.
Pno.
W.W
Tpts.
Tbns.
Alto Sax
mp
Flugelhorn
4.
mp
Time (swinging)
(8)
Cmaj7
Fmaj7/A
G(add4)
Am9(omit5)
Am7/D
Am9
Am7/D
Am9
Alto Sax
flugel
mp
17
18
19
20
21
22
23
24

Fl.
Alto Sax.
Cl.
B. Cl. 1
B. Cl. 2
Tpt. 1/2
Tpt. 3/4
Tpt. 4
Tbn. 1/2
Tbn. 3/4
Gtr
Bs.
Dr.
(16)
Cmaj7
Fmaj7/A
Em7
G/A
Dm9
C7(add11)/B♭
C/F
G(sus4)
Am7(add11)
Pno.
W.W
Tpts.
Tbns.
25
26
27
28
29
30
31
32

A1
Flute used throughout to double lead tpt line 8va
same as measures 18-24 but begins at A1 a bar sooner
33
Flute
soli
Fl.
mp
soli
Alto Sax.
mp
Cl.
B. Cl. 1
B. Cl. 2
Tpt. 1/2
soli
Tpt. 3/4
mp
Tpt. 4
Tbn. 1/2
Tbn. 3/4
Uses guitar as a linear instrument throughout
soli
Gtr
mp
Bs.
Time (swinging)
(8)
Dr.
Pno.
plus Fl. & Gtr
W.W
mp
Tpts.
mp
Tbns.
33
34
35
36
37
38
39
40

new material begins here at second 8 bar phrase
Fl.
Alto Sax.
Clarinet
Cl.
mp
Bass Clarinet
B. Cl. 1
B. Cl. 2
doubles tbn. line
Tpt. 1/2
Tpt. 3/4
Tpt. 4
unison counterline
Cup
a2
Tbn. 1/2
Tbn. 3/4
Gtr
Bs.
Dr.
(16)
Pno.
W.W
Tpts.
Quartal voicing
Tbns.
41
42
43
44
45
46
47
48

This section never reappears though ascending parallel harmony gesture does.
Movement in Clar., 4th Tbn., Fl., Gtr., and Piano provide motion within sustained chord.
B
49
Fl.
mp
Alto Sax.
w/alto
Cl.
Embellishment of Flugel/Alto sax line
B. Cl. 1
melody is embellished & moving chord tones provide further harmonic montion within chord
B. Cl. 2
Tpt. voicings give the impression of suspended chords without 5th which is in Tbn.
Rhythmic variation of bar 49
Cup
Tpt. 1/2
melody appears now in middle of chord
Tpt. 3/4
4. Flug/alto
Tpt. 4
Tbn. 1/2
1.
4.
Tbn. 3/4
Gtr
Bs.
Time on cymbals
Dr.
Pno.
W.W
Cmaj7/D
Dmaj7/E
Emaj7/F♯
Tpts.
tbn
bass
Tbns.
49
50
51
52
53
54
55
56

Voice leading gives motion to sustained chord & added disonnance
to Sop. Sax
Fl.
Alto Sax.
Variation of melody bar 41
Ellaboration of bar 53
mf
Cl.
mf
B. Cl. 1
mf
B. Cl. 2
Tpt. 1/2
Tpt. 3/4
Tpt. 4
mf
Tbn. 1/2
mf
Countrary motion to other voices
Tbn. 3/4
Gtr
Bs.
fill
Dr.
Pno.
W.W
Tpts.
Tbns.
57
58
59
60
61
62
63
64

Sop. Sax.
Alto Sax.
Cl.
B. Cl. 1
B. Cl. 2
Tpt. 1/2
Tpt. 3/4
Tpt. 4
Tbn. 1/2
Tbn. 3/4
Gtr
Bs.
Dr.
Pno.
W.W
Tpts.
Tbns.
melody reoccurs at bar 245
ascending 3-note B section melody
Fairly wide voicing gap filled by W.W.
a2
w/tpt&alto
Dm9
C/E
Am9
EbMaj7
C(SUS)/Ab
65
66
67
68
69
70
71
72

10

Fugato loosely follows primary harmonic scheme
Sop. Sax.
Alto Sax.
Cl.
B. Cl. 1
V3
B. Cl. 2
V2
Rhythmic reference to A section accompaniment
Tpt. 1/2
Tpt. 3/4
Tpt. 4
Tbn. 1/2
V1
a2 Open
mp sempre crescendo
Tbn. 3/4
V3 Open
a2
mp sempre crescendo
Gtr
V1
mp sempre crescendo
Rhythmic reference to A section accompaniment
Bs.
V2
Dr.
Pno.
W.W
Tpts.
Tbns.
81
82
83
84
85
86
87
88

90
Sop. Sax.
Alto Sax.
Cl.
V4
mp
sempre crescendo
Gesture reflects back to A theme
B. Cl. 1
V3
B. Cl. 2
V2
Gesture reflects back to A theme bars 19-20 in different pitch level
Open
V4
2.
Tpt. 1/2
mp
sempre crescendo
Open
4.V4
Tpt. 3/4
mp
sempre crescendo
Tpt. 4
V1
Tbn. 1/2
Gesture reflects back to A theme
V3
Tbn. 3/4
V1
Gtr
V2
Bs.
Dr.
Pno.
W.W
Tpts.
Tbns.
89
90
91
92
93
94
95
96

5th voice enters making this sound like first bar of new phrase; phrases now seem to overlap
Soprano Saxophone
V5
mf
Sop. Sax.
Alto Sax.
Thematic refernce to B Section dbled in Tpts.
Cl.
Alludes rhythmically to previous material and makes this sound like start of phrase
B. Cl. 1
Alludes rhythmically to previous material and makes this sound like start of phrase
B. Cl. 2
Tpt 1 Thematic reference
Tpt. 1/2
Tpt. 3/4
Tpt. 4
Thematic reference
Thematic reference
Tbn. 1/2
Alludes rhythmically to previous material and makes this sound like start of phrase
Tbn. 3/4
Thematic reference
Gtr
Alludes rhythmically to previous material and makes this sound like start of phrase
Bs.
Dr.
Pno.
W.W
Tpts.
Tbns.
97
98
99
100
101
102
103
104

14

Alto Solo

113 — Soloist does beautiful job on recording of capturing essence of theme in improvisatory fashion

Alto Sax chord changes: AMaj7 | D/F# | E | F#m9 | Bm9 | F#m9 | Bm9 | F#m9

Bass chord changes: CMaj7 | F/A | G | Am9 | Dm9 | Am9 | Dm9 | Am9

Drums: Swinging (8)

Piano chord changes: CMaj7 | F/A | G | Am9 | Dm9 | Am9 | Dm9 | Am9

Measures: 113, 114, 115, 116, 117, 118, 119, 120

Fl.
AMaj7/C♯ DMaj7/F♯ C♯m7 F♯m7 Bm9 GMaj7 A/D E(SUS) F♯m9
Alto Sax.
Cl.
B. Cl. 1
B. Cl. 2
Tpt. 1/2
Tpt. 3/4
Tpt. 4
Tbn. 1/2
Tbn. 3/4
Gtr
CMaj7/E FMaj7/A Em7 Am7 Dm9 B♭Maj7 C/F G(SUS) Am9
Bs.
(16)
Dr.
CMaj7/E FMaj7/A Em7 Am7 Dm9 B♭Maj7 C/F G(SUS) Am9
Pno.
W.W
Tpts.
Tbns.
121 122 123 124 125 126 127 128

129
Fl.
Alto Sax.
AMaj7
D/F♯
E
F♯m9
Bm9
F♯m9
Bm9
F♯m9
Cl.
mp
B. Cl. 1
mp
B. Cl. 2
clar., bs clar., and flugel provide dark, woody quality
Tpt. 1/2
Tpt. 3/4
4. Flugelhorn
Tpt. 4
mp
1/2 step disonances more typically found in middle of voicing not top or bottom as is case here
Tbn. 1/2
mp
Tbn. 3/4
mp
Gtr
CMaj7
F/A
G
Am9
Dm9
Am9
Dm9
Am9
Bs.
(8)
Dr.
CMaj7
F/A
G
Am9
Dm9
Am9
Dm9
Am9
Pno.
W.W
Tpts.
Tbns.
129
130
131
132
133
134
135
136

Flute dbls lead Tpt line 8va
Flute
Fl.
AMaj7/C♯ DMaj7/F♯ C♯m7 F♯m7 Bm9 GMaj7 A/D E(SUS) F♯m9
Alto Sax.
Cl.
B. Cl. 1
B. Cl. 2
mf
Cup
a2
Tpt. 1/2
mp
Close voicing as shown below
Tpt. 3/4
Tpt. 4
No 3rd or 7th in voicing
Tbn. 1/2
Tbn. 3/4
Gtr
B♭Maj7 C/F G(SUS) Am9
Bs.
CMaj7/E FMaj7/A Em7 Am7 Dm9 B♭Maj7 C/F G(SUS) Am9
Dr.
(10)
Pno.
W.W
Tpts.
Tbns.
137 138 139 140 141 142 143 144

Ensemble figures represent classic Mendoza style - memorable, vamp-like "hook" repeated multiple times

Once again, fl. dbls lead tpt. 8va
1.
Fl.
Alto Sax.
AMaj7/C♯ Bm9 GMaj7 A/D E(SUS) F♯m9
Cl.
B. Cl. 1
B. Cl. 2
Tpt. 1/2
Tpt. 3/4
Tpt. 4
Tbn. 1/2
Tbn. 3/4
Gtr
CMaj7/E FMaj7/A Em7 Am7 Dm9 B♭Maj7 C/F G(SUS) Am9
Bs.
CMaj7/E FMaj7/A Em7 Am7 Dm9 B♭Maj7 C/F G(SUS) Am9
Dr.
Pno.
CMaj7/E FMaj7/A Em7 Am7 Dm9 B♭Maj7 C/F G(SUS) Am9
W.W
Tpts.
Tbns.
153 154 155 156 157 158 159 160

Variation on progression segues to temporary new key center for transitional interlude
Interlude
164
2.
Fl.
Alto Sax.
Cl.
B. Cl. 1
B. Cl. 2
Tpt. 1/2
Tpt. 3/4
Tpt. 4
Tbn. 1/2
Tbn. 3/4
Gtr
Bs.
Dr.
Pno.
W.W
Tpts.
Tbns.
G(add9) A/D A/D E(SUS) DMaj7/F♯
to Clar.
end solo
a2
B♭(add9) C/F C/F G(SUS)
Time (sort of in 1)
B♭(add9) C/F C/F G(SUS) FMaj7/A G7(sus4) Dmi/F
161 162 163 164 165 166 167 168

Contrary motion
transposition of 3 bars earlier
Fl.
descending
Clarinet in B♭
Cl.
Cl.
descending
B. Cl. 1
B. Cl. 2
Cup
Tpt. 1/2
Cup
Tpt. 3/4
Tpt. 4
descending
ascending
Tbn. 1/2
Tbn. 3/4
Gtr
descending
Bs.
Dr.
G/B
B♭(add9)
E♭Maj7
Fm7
A♭Maj7
B♭Maj7
C(add9)
D6/9(♯11)
B♭6/9(♯11)
Am7(♭6)
Pno.
Wide spacing in W.W.
W.W
Tpts.
Tbns.
169
170
171
172
173
174
175
176

Incomplete arpeggios feel improvised and based loosely on 16 bar harmonic progression from theme. Chords added below for analysis sake
180
Fl.
Cl.
Cl.
B. Cl. 1
B. Cl. 2
Tpt. 1/2
Tpt. 3/4
Tpt. 4
Tbn. 1/2
Tbn. 3/4
Gtr
Bs.
Dr.
l.v.
Very sparse accompaniment sometimes only stating 1 & 5
Fm(add9)/A♭
or Abma7(13, #11)
Cmaj7(6)
Fmaj7/A
G7(sus4)
Am9
Dm9
Pno.
W.W
Tpts.
Tbns.
mp
177
178
179
180
181
182
183
184

Fl.
Cl.
Cl.
B. Cl. 1
B. Cl. 2
Tpt. 1/2
Tpt. 3/4
Tpt. 4
Tbn. 1/2
Tbn. 3/4
Gtr
Bs.
Time (light on cymbals)
Dr.
mp
Am11
Dm9(add11)
Am11
Emi7
Fmaj7/A
Em7
G/A
Dm9
C7sus4/B♭
Pno.
W.W
Tpts.
Tbns.
185
186
187
188
189
190
191
192

196
Fl.
Cl.
Cl.
B. Cl. 1
mp
B. Cl. 2
Tpt. 1/2
Tpt. 3/4
Tpt. 4
Tbn. 1/2
Tbn. 3/4
Gtr
Bs.
(8)
Time
Dr.
mp
C/F
G7(sus4)
Am7(♯5–add11)
Simile
Dbls melodic line
Pno.
W.W
Tpts.
Tbns.
193
194
195
196
197
198
199
200

Fl.
Cl.
Cl.
B. Cl. 1
B. Cl. 2
mp
Tpt. 1/2
Tpt. 3/4
Tpt. 4
Counter line hints a main theme; surfaces again a bar 287 in saxes & guitar
Cup
a2
mp
Tbn. 1/2
Tbn. 3/4
Gtr
Bs.
(8)
Dr.
Pno.
W.W
Tpts.
Tbns.
201
202
203
204
205
206
207
208

Previous arpeggiated melody leads one to anticipate this new melody with continuing arpeggios which now seem more like a contrapuntal accompaniment; harmony however is different
27
212
Fl.
Cl.
Cl.
B. Cl. 1
B. Cl. 2
Tpts are in cup mutes are harmonically planing related scale/mode
Tpt. 1/2
Tpt. 3/4
Tpt. 4
Same melody as bars 204-211
Tbn. 1/2
Tbn. 3/4
Gtr
Bs.
(16)
Time
Dr.
CMaj7
Am7
G7(sus4)
Am9
Dm7
Pno.
W.W
close voicings with dissonances primarily at top or bottom of voicing
Tpts.
Same melody as bars 204-211
Tbns.
209
210
211
212
213
214
215
216

Fl.
Cl.
Cl.
B. Cl. 1
B. Cl. 2
Tpt. 1/2
Tpt. 3/4
Tpt. 4
Tbn. 1/2
Tbn. 3/4
Gtr
Bs.
(8)
(10)
Dr.
FMaj7/A
Dm9
Am9
Em7
Am9
CMaj7/E
mf
Pno.
W.W
#11 added
Tpts.
Tbns.
217
218
219
220
221
222
223
224

227
Tpt. solo emerges from ensemble transition rather than beginning abruptly as alto solo began
Triads over foreign bass tones as shown in analysis below
Fl.
Cl.
Cl.
B. Cl. 1
B. Cl. 2
Tpt. 1/2
Tpt. 3/4
4. Trumpet
E(add9)
Tpt. 4
C(add2) G(sus4) add2
Tbn. 1/2
Tbn. 3/4
Gtr
Bs.
fill
Dr.
Pno.
E
F♯
C/D♭
D/E♭
Gm7
C/A♭
W.W
Wide W.W. Spacing
Tpts.
Close cluster-like voicings
Tbns.
225
226
227
228
229
230
231
232

Fl.
Cl.
Cl.
B. Cl. 1
B. Cl. 2
mp
Tpt. 1/2
Tpt. 3/4
Am7
Tpt. 4
chords added for analysis sake
B♭(add2) Gm7 Am(add4) C/F Gm9
Open
Tbn. 1/2
mp
Open
Tbn. 3/4
mp
Gtr
Bs.
Dr.
Gm7
Pno.
Am9 B♭ G(sus4) Gm(add9)
W.W
Tpts.
Tbns.
233
234
235
236
237
238
239
240

Used earlier in the B section
Chord progression leading to 251 is identical to end of B section; concludes in interesting cadence from bVIMa7 back to tonic CMa7
Fl.
Cl.
Cl.
B. Cl. 1
B. Cl. 2
Tpt. 1/2
Tpt. 3/4
Tpt. 4
Tbn. 1/2
Tbn. 3/4
Gtr
Bs.
Dr.
Pno.
W.W
Tpts.
Tbns.
mf
Open
a2
Near repetition of bars 237-239 in Tbns.
(8)
(12)
Dm7(♭6) Gm7 Am7(add4) Fmaj9 Gm7 Gm9
Dm7 Gm7 Am7 FMaj7 Gm7 Gm7 Em7 Am9 F E♭maj9(add13)
cluster-like voicing
241
242
243
244
245
246
247
248

251 Trumpet Solo

Sop. Sax.
Alto Sax.
Ten. 1
Ten. 2
Bari.
Tpt. 1/2
Tpt. 3/4
Tpt. 4
Em9 Bm9 DMaj7/F♯ GMaj7/B F♯m7 Bm7 Em9 CMaj7 D/G
Tbn. 1/2
Tbn. 3/4
Gtr
Bs.
Dm9 Am9 CMaj7/E FMaj7/A Em7 Am7 Dm9 B♭Maj7 C/F
Dr.
(8)
Pno.
Dm9 Am9 CMaj7/E FMaj7/A Em7 Am7 Dm9 B♭Maj7 C/F
W.W
Tpts.
Tbns.
257 258 259 260 261 262 263 264

Soloist trades 4s with ens.
267
Soprano Saxophone
Alto Saxophone
Tenor Saxophone
Tenor Saxophone
Baritone Saxophone
Sop. Sax.
Alto Sax.
Ten. 1
Ten. 2
Bari.
Tpt. 1/2
Tpt. 3/4
Tpt. 4
Tbn. 1/2
Tbn. 3/4
Gtr
Bs.
Dr.
Pno.
W.W
Tpts.
Tbns.
2xo
A(SUS)
Bm9
DMaj7
Em9
(4's with the band)
dbls sax line
G(SUS)
Am9
CMaj7
F/A
G
Dm9
(16)
angular melodic line accompainied by brass figure
265
266
267
268
269
270
271
272

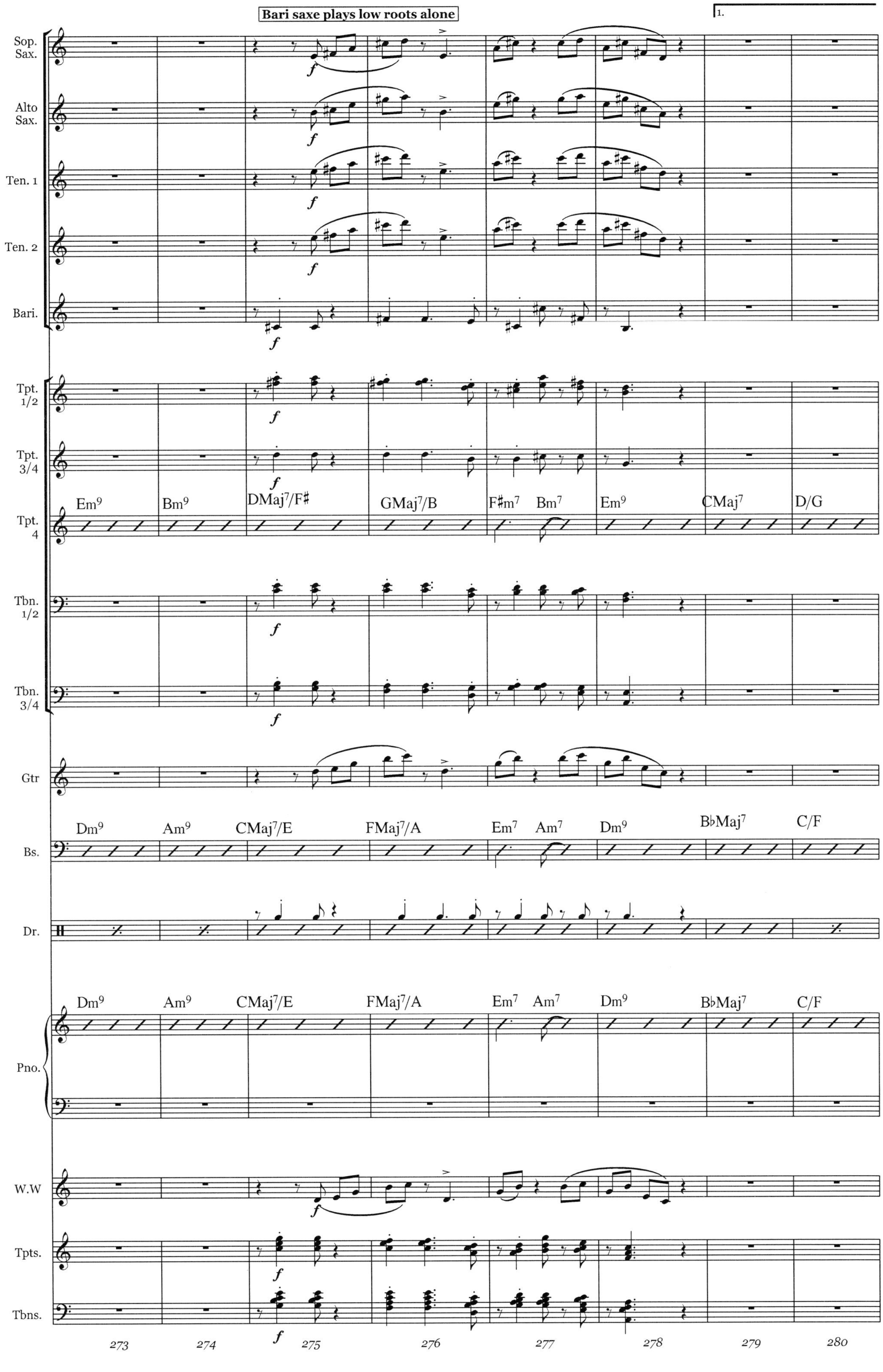

High unison sax line with with guitar is favorite of composer; features common tone with changing harmony; similar to m204-208
Segue to Shout
285
Subito crescendo is composer trademark
Sop. Sax.
Alto Sax.
Ten. 1
Ten. 2
Bari.
Tpt. 1/2
Tpt. 3/4
Tpt. 4
Tbn. 1/2
Tbn. 3/4
Gtr
Bs.
Dr.
Pno.
W.W
Tpts.
Tbns.
unis.
mf
f
2.
A(SUS) Bm9 CMaj7 D/G D/E E/F♯ G♭/A♭ A♭/B♭ Bm11
G(SUS) Am9 B♭Maj7 C/F
G(SUS) Am9 B♭Maj7 C/F C/D D/E E/F♯ F♯/G♯ Am11 Dmi/A Dmi/E♭
Ascending progression has been used before
281 282 283 284 285 286 287 288

New Harmonic material in this section
Brief reference to earlier arpeggiated section
A theme quote begins
296
Sop. Sax.
Alto Sax.
Ten. 1
Ten. 2
Bari.
Tpt. 1/2
Tpt. 3/4
Tpt. 4
Tbn. 1/2
Tbn. 3/4
Gtr
Bs.
Dr.
Dm7
A♭maj9
E♭/D♭
Cm7 Fm7
B♭7(sus4)
E♭maj13
G7(sus4)
CMaj7
Pno.
W.W
Tpts.
Tbns.
F(add2)/A
289
290
291
292
293
294
295
296

Mixed, changing meters and syncopations in brass and rhythm tend to mask return to consistent 3/4 meter and erase bar lines
Quote from A Theme
Melodic lines in saxes remain true to original Ionian context (see concert key versionbelow)
Sop. Sax.
Alto Sax.
Ten. 1
Ten. 2
Bari.
Bari covers low chord roots alone or with 4th Tbn.
Same as previous 2 bars with added beat at beginning of bar
Brass figure much like solo background riff
Tpt. 1/2
Tpt. 3/4
Tpt. 4
Tbn. 1/2
Tbns show more open chorale & concerted voicings during shout chorus
Tbn. 3/4
Gtr
Bs.
Dr.
Piano is omitted since it is unnecessary & could clutter horn textures
Pno.
W.W
Dm7/G
G/A
Am7
Dm9
Am9(omit5)
Dm11
Am9(omit5)
Em7(b6)
Am7(b6)
G(sus4)
Em7(add11)
Am9
Tpts.
Tbns.
297
298
299
300
301
302
303

Longer sustained notes in sax line often emphasize extension tones as labeled
308
Sop. Sax.
7th
sus4
9th
7th
unis.
Alto Sax.
Ten. 1
Ten. 2
Bari.
Tpt. 1/2
Tpt. 3/4
Tpt. 4
Tbn. 1/2
Tbn. 3/4
Gtr
Bs.
Dr.
Pno.
W.W
Tpts.
Tbns.
B♭maj7(♭5)
Am7
Am9(♭13)
C/F
F(add2)
Am9
Em7(add11)
Fmaj7
Fmaj7/A
G(add2add4)
Am11
Dm9
Am11
304
305
306
307
308
309
310
311
312

Sop. Sax.
11th
Alto Sax.
9th
Ten. 1
Ten. 2
Bari.
Tpt. 1/2
Tpt. 3/4
Tpt. 4
Tbn. 1/2
Tbn. 3/4
Gtr
Bs.
Dr.
Pno.
W.W
Tpts.
Dm9 Am11 Dm9 Am11 Dm11 G(add2sus4) G(add2) Am9(♭6)
Tbns.
313 314 315 316 317 318 319 320

Contrary motion in upper and lower most voices

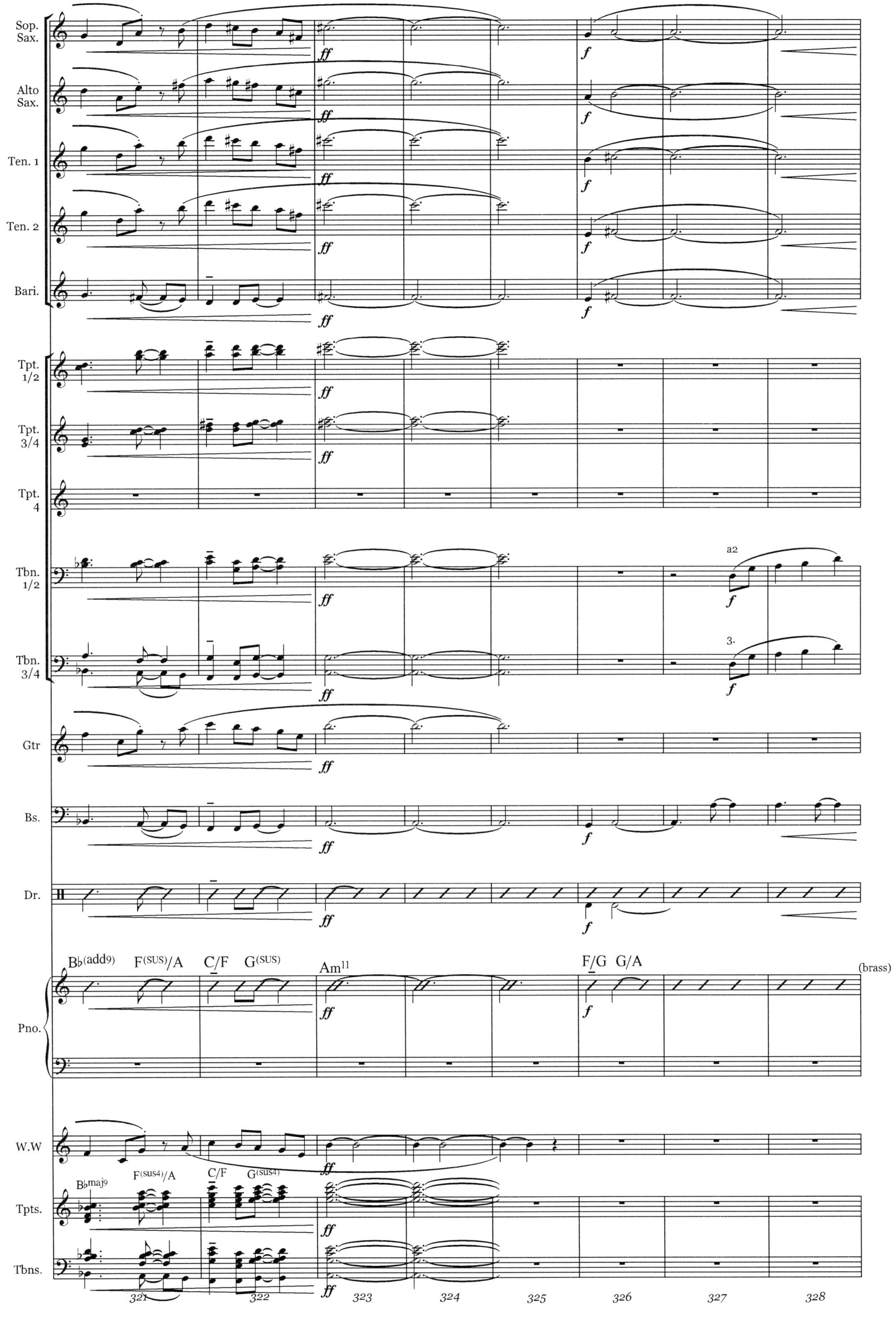

331
Piano briefly returns to introductory gesture
to Fl.
Fl.
Alto Sax.
Ten. 1
Ten. 2
Bari.
Tpt. 1/2
Tpt. 3/4
Tpt. 4
2.
Tbn. 1/2
Tbn. 3/4
Gtr
Bs.
Time
(6)
Dr.
sim
Pno.
W.W
B♭maj9(♯11) Fmaj9 E♭maj9 A♭maj13(♯11) Cmaj7(add11)
Tpts.
Tbns.
329
330
331
332
333
334
335
336

Flute
Fl.
Alto Sax.
Ten. 1
Ten. 2
Bari.
single harmon mute on lead tpt only gives added bite to lead note and combines well with flute 8va.
Harmon
Tpt. 1/2
Cup
Tpt. 3/4
Cup
Tpt. 4
Cup
Tbn. 1/2
Cup
Tbn. 3/4
Gtr
Bs.
Dr.
l.v.
Fmaj9
C7(add11)/B♭
Pno.
W.W
Fmaj9
C7(add11)/B♭
Tpts.
Tbns.
337
338
339

Composer/arranger and pianist Jim McNeely

Photo credit: Ben Knabe

Chapter 4

Jim McNeely – "Absolution"

Jim McNeely is a native of Chicago and attended the University of Illinois. He was admitted to UI as a music education major but quickly realized that this was not the right direction for him, ultimately changing his major to composition. It was here that he studied twelve-tone composition techniques and counterpoint and was active in the vibrant chamber music scene. He moved to New York City in 1975 following his studies at UI, and in 1978 he joined the Thad Jones/Mel Lewis Jazz Orchestra. He spent six years as a featured soloist with that band and its successor, the Mel Lewis Jazz Orchestra (now the Vanguard Jazz Orchestra). McNeely began his four year tenure as pianist/composer with the Stan Getz Quartet in 1981, and from 1990 until 1995 he held the piano chair in the Phil Woods Quintet. At the present time, he leads his own tentet and trio, and he appears as soloist at concerts and festivals worldwide.

McNeely's reputation as composer/arranger and conductor for large jazz bands continues to flourish, earning him nine Grammy nominations. In 1996 he re-joined The Vanguard Jazz Orchestra as pianist and Composer-in-Residence. This relationship led to several significant recordings, including *Lickety Split*, to which he contributed the composition that is the subject of this analysis, and *Up from the Skies*. Europe has become a harbinger of American jazz artists and particularly serious composers, including many of those discussed in this book. Following this trend, McNeely became chief conductor of the Frankfurt Radio (HR) Big Band. Other such associations include projects with the Danish Radio Big Band (where he was chief conductor for five years), the Metropole Orchestra (Netherlands), the Swiss Jazz Orchestra, and the Stockholm Jazz Orchestra. McNeely also contributed scores to the Carnegie Hall Jazz Band, conducted by former Mel Lewis Jazz Orchestra lead trumpeter Jon Faddis. The *New York Times* has called his writing "exhilarating," and *DownBeat* magazine has said that his music is "eloquent enough to be profound."

As a pianist, Jim has appeared as a sideman on numerous recordings led by major artists such as Thad Jones, Mel Lewis, Stan Getz, Chet Baker, Bob Brookmeyer, David Liebman, Art Farmer, Robert Watson, and Phil Woods. He has recorded numerous albums under his own name. One of his more recent is *Up from the Skies* with the Vanguard Jazz Orchestra on the Planet Arts label, described by *DownBeat* as "concert jazz at its headiest."

Teaching is also an important aspect of Jim's work. He is currently on the faculties of both the Manhattan School of Music and William Paterson University, where he is Professor of Graduate Arranging. He was Musical Director of the BMI Jazz Composers' Workshop from 1991 to 2015, serving with Manny Albam. He has appeared at numerous college jazz festivals as performer and clinician, and he has been involved regularly with several summer workshops. He has also done clinics and major residencies at dozens of institutions in the U.S., Canada, Europe, China, Australia, New Zealand, and Egypt.

Selected Discography

East Coast Blow Out – WDR Big Band – Lipstick Records, 1991

Sound Bites, Stockholm Jazz Orchestra – Dragon, 1995

Carnegie Hall Jazz Band – Blue Note, 1995

*Lickety Split – The Vanguard Jazz Orchestra Music of Jim McNeely – New World Records, 1997

Nice Work, Danish Radio Orchestra – Da Capo Records, 2000

Group Therapy – Omni Tone, 2001

Swiss Jazz Orchesta, Paul Klee – MOHS, 2006

Up from the Skies, The Vanguard Jazz Orchestra Music of Jim McNeely – Planet Arts Records, 2006

Quest for Freedom – Sunnyside, 2010

Dedication Suite, DR Big Band – Cope Records, 2011

Danish Radio Orchestra Play Bill Evans – Stunt Records, 2012

The Frankfurt Radio Big Band Jim McNeely: Barefoot Dances and Other Visions – Planet Arts, 2017

"Absolution"

The analysis that follows in this chapter will build on the following brief analysis provided by the composer in the notes that accompany the CD *Lickety Split*:

"This is another instance in which the sound of the major soloist (Rich Perry) served as the impetus for the piece. The opening section is a dialogue between two melodic groups. They're working out a couple of different pitch groups and a couple of different rhythmic cells. This occurs over a three measure vamp." (Shown in Examples 4.1 and 4.2.)

Example 4.1 – Primary pitch groups

Example 4.2 – Bass ostinato

"They finally conclude with the ascending "agreement" in ¾. Using an octave triplet figure they then eject Rich from their number, leaving him to solo and work out his inner voice over a two measure isorhythmic vamp in E minor."

Example 4.3 – E minor vamp

"It's a five-attack rhythmic pattern with a six pitch cycle, so it keeps spilling over itself."

Example 4.4

"The ensemble offers a brief 'prayer' (chorale), then ensues a litany in which all the wind players offer a series of brief solo statements, each one answered by the full band. The band builds to a climax, then Rich emerges for a final cathartic solo statement. The ensemble restates the ¾ phrase and extends it to become a final statement of absolution."

McNeely's brief explanation of "Absolution" is actually quite good as a "Cliff Notes" analysis of a very complex composition based on simple ingredients. Analysis of this score requires a somewhat different approach from that used on the other scores in this study. For that matter, each of these contemporary scores has required a somewhat unique approach. What follows will expand significantly on McNeely's brief description of this very contemporary score.

Basic Score Reduction

While the nature of this composition does not lend itself well to lead sheet reduction, what appears as Example 4.5 is a best effort at condensing the essence of melodic, rhythmic, and harmonic material that serves as the basis for the arrangement.

Example 4.5 – "RC" refers to rhythmic cell, and "PG" abbreviates pitch group.

RC1 rhythmic expansion
29
3
Pno.
Random rhythmic improvisation 4 note motive
35
B
melodic line suggests E Mixolydian
parallel voicings from mode
non-functional harmony
3
transposed bass isorhythmic ostinato
40
3
3
consonance
3
3
modal shift to E Dorian
varying consonance & dissonanc
bass ostinato
44
A2
PG1/RC1
PG1/RC1
PG1/RC1
48
PG1/RC1
PG1/RC1 transposed rhythmic augmentation
3
3
3
improvise rhythms using 3 note motive
isorhythm transposed up min. 2nd

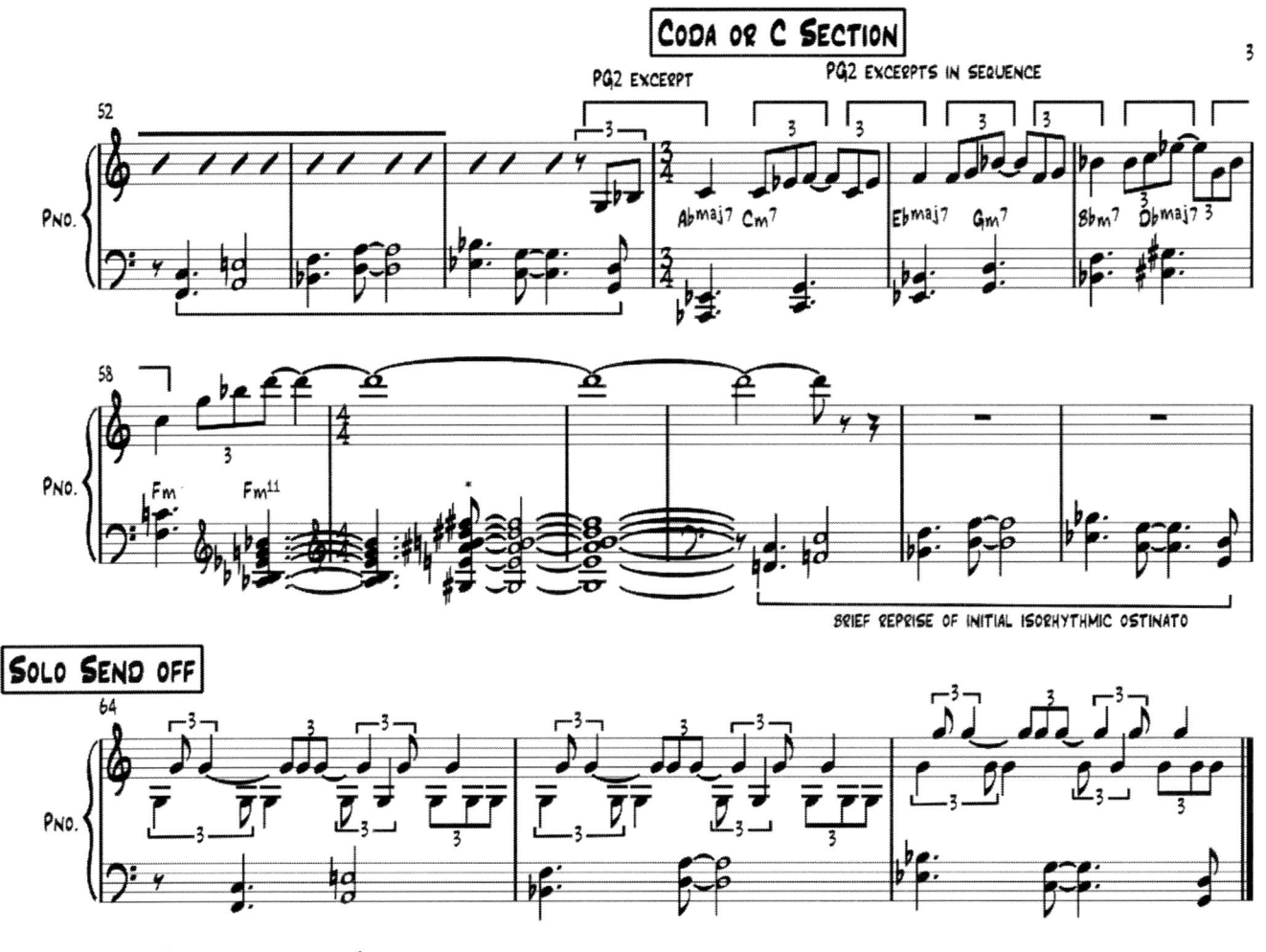

Formal Design

To facilitate discussion of this piece, it has been divided into sections labeled A, A1, B, A2, and Coda or C section. While A1 and A2 are significantly different as compared to the first A section, included are many familiar ingredients, such as pitch groups and rhythmic cells, that are found throughout the initial A section. The section labeled as the Coda might also be described as a C section, making the overall form appear to be similar to a classic rondo form.

Melodic Elements

This composition is all about melody and rhythm, with harmony playing a somewhat secondary role, and harmonies are largely derived from the scales/modes that serve as the basis for melodic content. Melodies used throughout the lead sheet are compact cells or pitch groups consisting usually of not more than four notes, as shown in Example 4.1. These pitch groups undergo manipulation through transposition and rhythmic variation. In some cases rhythm takes precedence over the melodic content, which may be only one or two notes that constitute a complete phrase. The primary pitch groups and rhythmic cells are identified as shown in the following example. Abbreviations for these groups and cells are used throughout the lead sheet analysis and the full score analysis that follows at the end of the chapter.

Example 4.6

PG1 (pitch group 1)   PG2 (pitch group 2)

RC1 (rhythmic cell 1, usually associated with PG1)   RC2 (usually associated with a single note or two)

Rhythmic cell 1 (RC1), or some slight variation of it, is almost always associated with pitch group 1 (PG1), which often appears transposed from the original or manipulated rhythmically and sometimes melodically, though reference to the original is always obvious. RC2 also appears varied throughout the score, usually appearing as repeated notes or two pitches a major second apart moving downward. A high percentage of this eight and a quarter minute score is derived from these basic melodic and rhythmic building blocks that are first presented in the opening bars, shown in the condensed lead sheet as Example 4.5.

The section labeled as the Coda or C section is based on an excerpt of pitch group 2 (PG2) and has an interesting similarity to the very spiritual and important work by John Coltrane titled *A Love Supreme*. This may or may not be a coincidence, given the religious connotations of the title and structure of this piece, but more about this theory in the next section.

Harmonic Elements

The basic lead sheet shows very little harmony whatsoever, with the exception of the isorhythmic ostinato in the form of open 5ths that occurs as a form of glue that helps hold the piece together while providing a sense of regular rhythmic forward momentum, and the contrasting B section that consists of the E Mixolydian mode harmonized using three note voicings. The fifth and fourth bars immediately preceding the B section expand on the isorhythmic ostinato bass line by adding an additional 5th to create an even greater reference to a Gregorian chant–like texture. The B section makes use of both perfect 4th and 5th relationships in a closer voiced structure to form three note voicings.

The section labeled as the Coda or C section introduces for the first time supporting harmonies that are fully developed 7th chords, deviating from the open, chant-like textures that had been the basis for the entire piece up to this point. This more fully developed harmonic section also helps to build to the introduction of the principal soloist. This section shows an interesting progression of major and minor 7th chords moving by major and minor thirds. The major 7th progresses up a major 3rd to a minor 7th, which then progresses a minor third up, returning to a major 7th. This progression is used several times throughout the full arrangement and will be discussed in more detail in the following section. (I learned later that McNeely borrowed this progression from the piano part of Darius Milhaud's "Duo Concertant" for Clarinet and Piano.)

The Arrangement

As suggested by the composer in the recording notes previously quoted, the composition is greatly inspired by the soloist, in this case Rich Perry on tenor saxophone. It is not a great leap to assume that this score was influenced in some way by the composer's encounters with religion, even if one considers only the title of the piece. This composer is sometimes influenced by theater and films, so it stands to reason that "Absolution" may have been influenced, or at least inspired in some way, by his previous experiences with worship services. For anyone who has attended an ecumenical service of any denomination, it is undeniable that there is an element of theater and drama. To continue this metaphor or analogy, the chant-like element (especially the open parallel 5ths), the abundant isorhythmic ostinatos, the call-response litany section featuring soloists and ensemble (congregation), and the overall religious service organizational aspects of this piece are all elements that justify this comparison. The architectural scheme of this piece could be described generally as follows, though I am undeniably mixing denominational practices to suit my own purpose and making some assumptions about the composer's influences.

> **Penitential Rite** – Formula A, B, and C represented by the opening thematic material that suggests the confession of sins and the plea for mercy. This section is represented by the first line of the timeline that follows – sections A through Coda (C).
>
> **The Message or Sermon** – In this case, the tenor saxophone soloist serves as the pastor or priest. The ensemble figures might represent organ interludes or background music. This section is represented by the solo section, measures 65 through 104 in the timeline shown in Example 4.7.
>
> **Hymn or Anthem** – What is expected here is a chorale, and that is exactly what the composer gives us at m.112, as seen in the timeline that follows.
>
> **Altar Call (Litany)** – At this point in a jazz score it is typical to find the "shout chorus," or development section. In this case, however, individual members of the ensemble appear as soloists followed by a reprise from the ensemble (congregation). The communal response is phrases with a speech-like quality, an instrumental version of "sprechstimme." This section appears in the timeline that follows as measures 121 through 172. The section could justifiably be described as the "litany" aspect of the service. Litany is described as a prayer consisting of invocations and supplications by a leader with responses by the congregation. In this case there are many leaders.

Prayer – This brief section in the score alludes to the Penitential Rites granting absolution by the pastor. This section appears at m.173 in the timeline.

Benediction – A brief closing section featuring the full ensemble in very open, slow moving parallel minor 11th, major, and dominant suspended chords. This final section can be seen in the outline from m.189 through the end of the piece.

It would be wrong to suggest that the composer consciously followed this entire model, and I suspect he did not; but it is not unlikely that his life experiences had some influence on the development of the composition, through either conscious or subconscious memory. This will no doubt come up in the interview, which will either confirm or disprove this theory.

The timeline that follows as Example 4.7 shows more clearly how this score unfolds.

Example 4.7

	[22] 0:54	[37] 1:32
A Section — Introduction of primary pitch groups and rhythm cells presented in dialogue between instrument groups in unison or octaves	A^1 Section — development of rhythmic cell 2	B Section — contrasting material based on mode
3 bar bass isorhythmic pattern from F Mixopydian	Section ends in open 5ths	Ens in vertical planning; Isorhythm transposed down mi 2nd to E Mixolydian
21 bars	*15 bars*	*9 bars*

[46] 1:55	[53] 2:18	[65] 2:47
A^2 Section — Reprise of PG1 Rhythmic diminution and augmentation	Coda or C Section — Coltranesque transition	Tenor Sax Solo Begins
Isorhythm returns to original key center	Based on PG2 & reaches climax and solo send-off.	New 2 bar bass isorhythm derived from E Dorian
9 bars	*12 bars*	*12 bars*

[77] 3:47	[89] 4:08	[104] 4:51
Sax Solo Continues	Sax Solo Continues	Solo Concludes
Bkgrnds derived in part from thematic material	Expanded PG1 material as bkgrnds; 3rd mode of Eb melodic minor	F# bass pedal; Gma7 over pedal implies Phrygian
12 bars	*15 bars*	*8 bars*

[112] 5:11	[121] 5:35	[165]
Full Ens Chordal planning on GbMaj & Mixolydian	Call-response between many soloists and octave unison Ens figure derived from PG1/RG1. Meter oscillates from 4/4 – 3/4	Full Ens. frenzy builds to staggered octave unison
F# bass pedal continues	& 3 chord progression continues to rise through key centers making new relationships and identities to Ens line while events come closer and closer together building to a frenzy	Section peaks at sustained polychord
9 bars	*52 bars*	*8 bars*

[173] 7:11	[189] 7:48	[193] 7:55
Tenor Sax soloist re-emerges from previous Ens high point	Reprise of PG2 material from bar 55	Rhythmic pace slows with full Ens
Alludes to opening bass ostinato in 5ths	Reference to "Love Supreme" re-emerges	Open voiced minor 11th chords move to final chord
15 bars	*4 bars*	*6 bars*

The graphic depiction of this score, with timings shown along the top scale and brief synopsis of the musical activity, illustrates how and where McNeely achieves the most dramatic points in the score. These three high points occur predictably at important times. The first serves to introduce the tenor saxophone soloist, Rich Perry, at 2:45 into the piece. The second builds more and is more sustained, coinciding with the peak of the solo section, where full ensemble background material contributes to the soloist's dramatic conclusion (4:20–4:45). The final climax is achieved as the ensemble builds to a frenetic close of the call-response development section (shout chorus) that leads to a sustained, dense polychord (6:45–7:12). This final climax occurs about 86 percent of the way through the piece, with the first coming at about a third of the way and the second just over halfway through the score.

Example 4.8

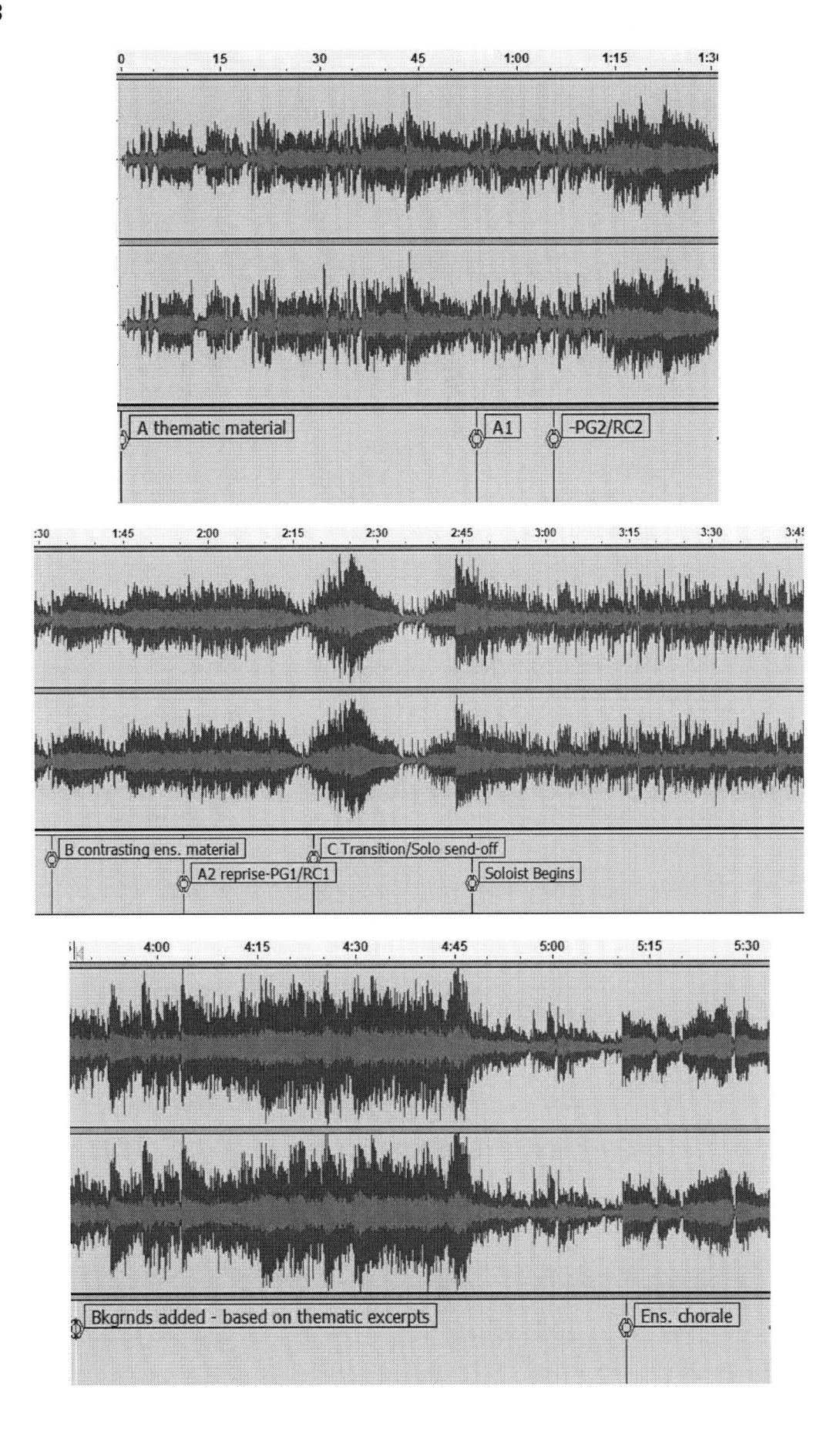

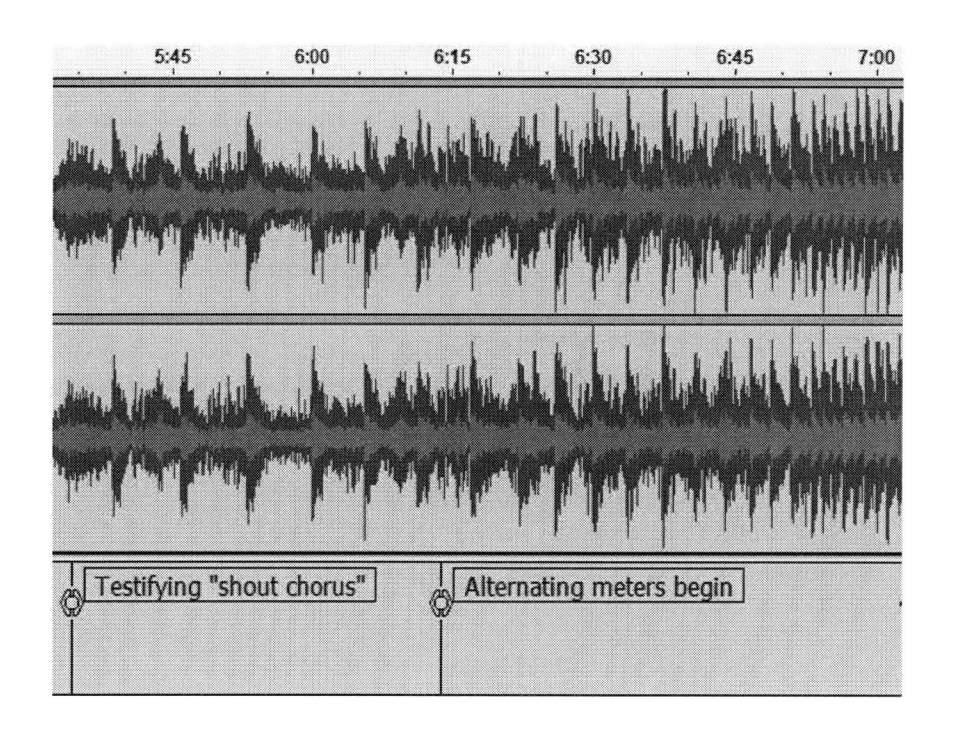

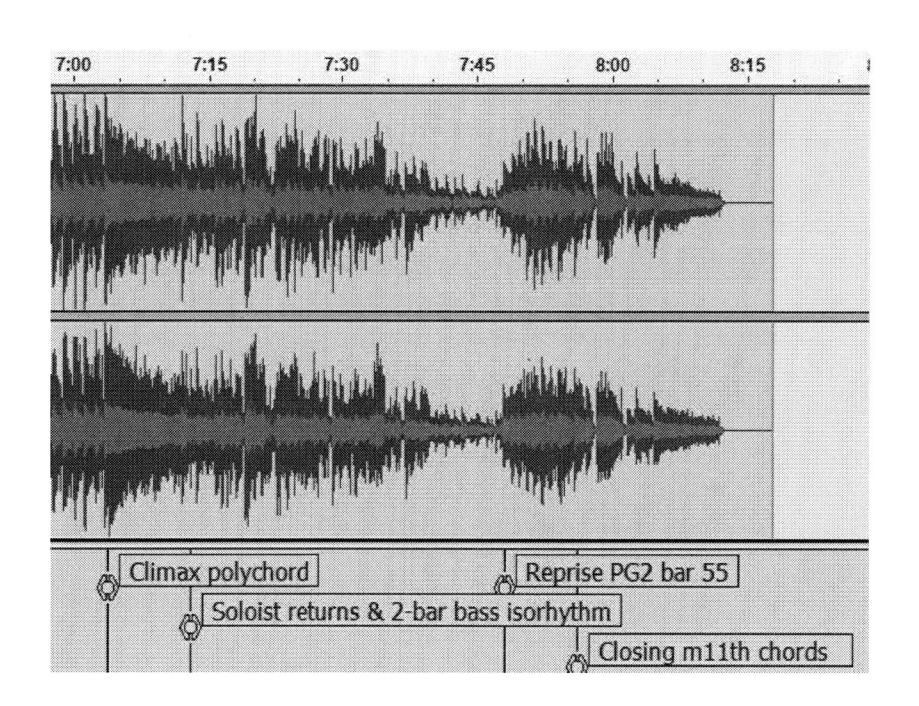

General Observations

The first noticeably unique characteristic of this score is that it is missing something that is usually commonplace in most jazz compositions. There is no introduction, though the first measure suggests for an instant that there might be a predictable ostinato isorhythmic vamp of some sort, but the first melodies emerge by the second bar. Right from the outset this composer defies the norm. McNeely wastes no time in getting to the meat of the composition. The ending is just as unusual as this unexpected beginning in that there is no effort to reprise any thematic material. Undoubtedly the composer felt that this was unnecessary, since his primary thematic pitch groups had been used throughout the entire piece.

McNeely is known for breaking away from the norms associated with this genre, but in doing so he maintains his commitment to certain aspects of the jazz tradition. For example, his commitment to the importance of improvisation as an overriding element is apparent in "Absolution." There is always a preponderance of improvisation in his scores, even when a motive is composed for the players, who use it as a springboard for their own improvised variations. This technique, which has appeared in other McNeely scores, is evident early on in this composition, appearing first at m.19 and then again from measures 33 through 36, and at m.50 lasting for 5 measures. The mere fact that he incorporates this form of controlled ensemble improvisation this soon in a composition, and even before the first formal soloist is introduced, speaks volumes about the composer's commitment to interpretation and improvisation as important aspects of the jazz tradition.

Another aspect of the jazz tradition, whether in big band writing or small group performance, is the idea of call and response. Traditional call and response writing usually suggests that there is some regularity in that one or both groups repeat an idea in answer to the other group. McNeely uses this back and forth musical dialogue from the outset of this composition as he moves motives throughout the wind section through varied orchestration but without the repetition associated with strict call and response. In fact, it is always a surprise where the musical volleyball is being bounced as one listens.

Variation permeates this score, and there is hardly a case where anything is repeated without some alterations. The variations come through either player interpretation or the composer's ability to always find a new way to state the same or similar idea.

Unison and octave unison writing is predominant throughout this score and harmony is kept in reserve, even during the shout chorus, for contrast when needed and/or to help achieve a dramatic high point.

McNeely is at the forefront of contemporary jazz composition, showing here, as he has so often, that anything is possible when there is sufficient grounding through repetitive rhythms and bass lines to provide the momentum and glue-like underpinnings that encourage experimentation in other voices. This approach is very apparent throughout the composition, where linear motion is so much more important than concern for vertical harmony or consonance. In fact, it is safe to say there is no functional harmony at any point in this piece other than a few traditional chords that do not move in any functional way.

Rhythm

As has been suggested, isorhythmic ostinatos serve as bonding agents throughout this piece. The first of such groups is the seven note phrase in perfect 5ths that begins in measure 1 and continues unchanged as an F Mixolydian ostinato for 36 bars. At m.37 it changes, but only to a new mode – E Mixolydian, where it settles for 12 measures before returning to the initial key center at measure 49.

Example 4.10

[Musical notation: Bars 1-36, F Mixolydian; Bars 37-48, E Mixolydian]

McNeely creates a new, two measure isorhythmic ostinato based on E Mixolydian that serves as a foundation for the soloist at m.65. While this rhythmic pattern repeats every two bars, a six note line, which also repeats, spills over into the first half of the following measure. This is a similar yet slightly different rhythmic arrangement from the earlier seven note grouping and further disguises bar lines and sense of regular meter, though the entire piece remains in 4/4. This pattern continues until m.89, where it is then based on the third mode of the E♭ melodic minor scale with a chord call for the soloist and pianist of G♭Ma$^{9(\#5)}$. The rhythm of the previous E Mixolydian isorhythm is maintained while the pitches are altered to conform to the new mode. The following examples clarify these changing patterns.

Example 4.11 – Notice that the isorhythm is two bars long but the ascending, repeating line consists of six notes, spilling into the next measure. This forces the repetition of the isorhythm to begin on a different pitch of the isorhythm each time.

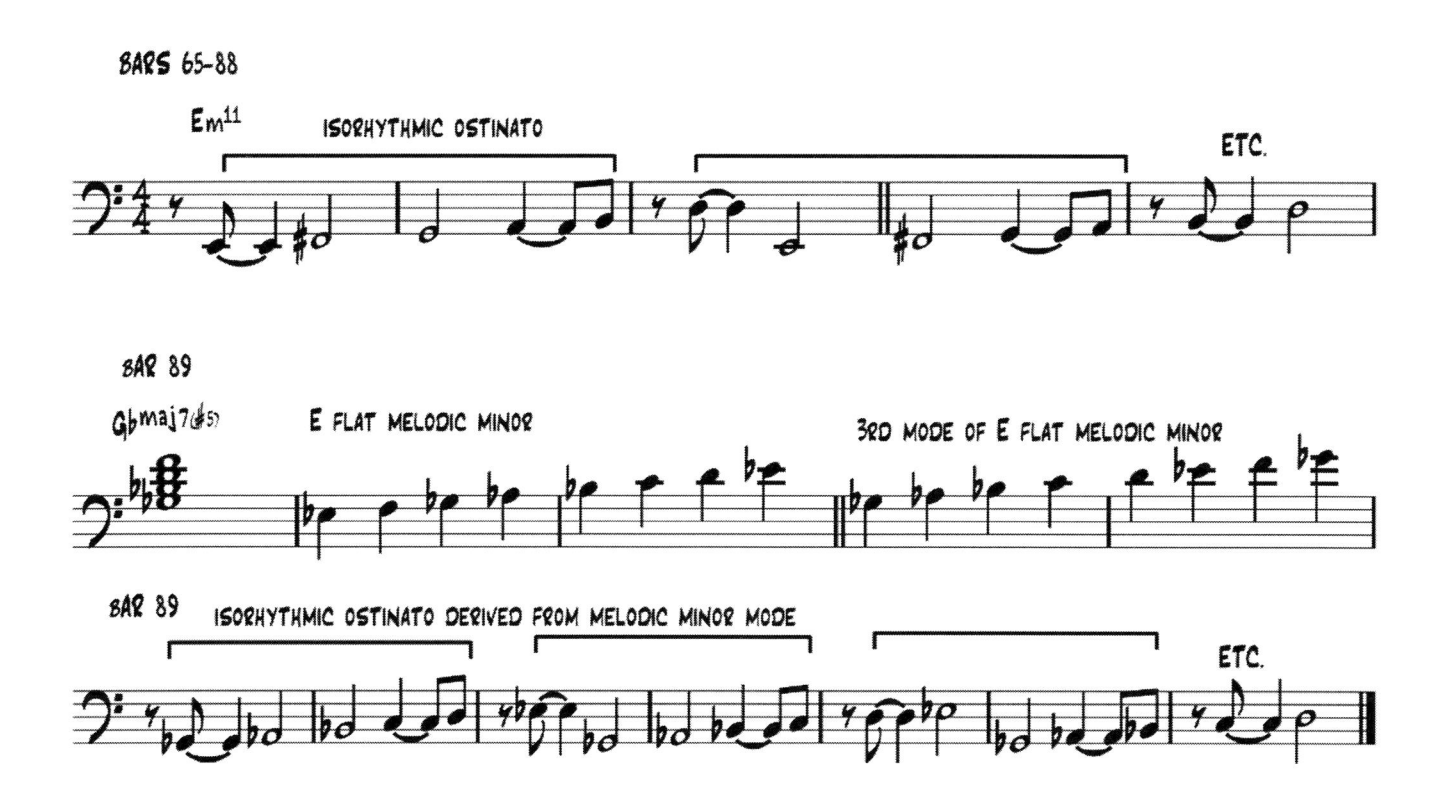

[Musical notation: Bars 65-88, Em^{11}, Isorhythmic Ostinato; Bar 89, G♭maj7(♯5), E Flat Melodic Minor, 3rd Mode of E Flat Melodic Minor; Bar 89, Isorhythmic Ostinato Derived from Melodic Minor Mode]

Harmony and Voicing

As previously suggested, harmony is used sparingly throughout this composition and largely in contrast to the predominance of linear, melodic textures. Much of the harmony is based on only two or three voices – open 5ths including the initial isorhythmic ostinato and 6ths used in the development section (shout chorus). As stated previously, aside from a few dense polychords, the composer never goes beyond three voice textures. And aside from the open 5ths used as the isorhythmic bass ostinato, the first introduction of two voice harmony in the winds (above the bass isorhythmic ostinato) occurs at bar 32, again with a stack of 5ths.

Example 4.12

When McNeely does introduce harmony it is frequently to achieve an added dramatic effect through contrast and/or tension of dissonant polychords, as shown in the following examples. Example 4.13 shows the polychord that serves as an introduction to the soloist. This dissonant chord is framed by a consonant approach chord, Fmi[11], and an octave unison rhythmic figure that is the immediate springboard to the solo section. The dissonant polychord in the middle of m.57 is reached through smooth voice leading in all voices.

Example 4.13

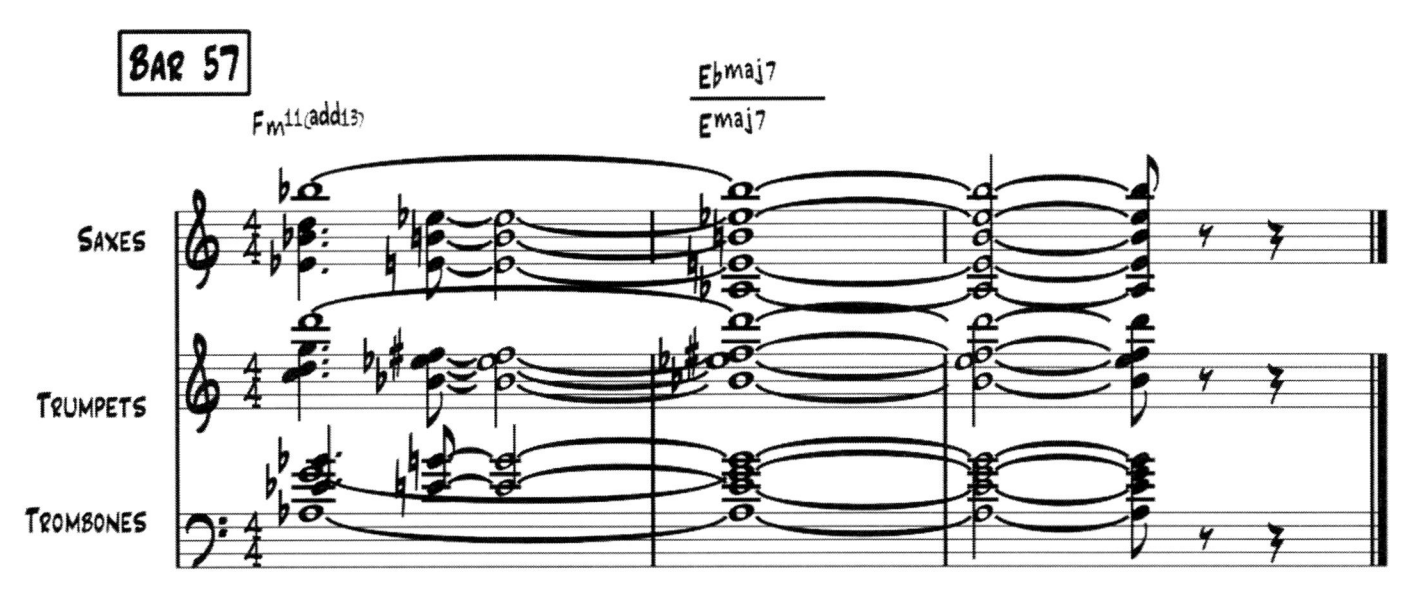

The following example shows a brief ensemble transitional passage leading to the close of the tenor sax solo and as a means to arrive at a new mode center – F♯ Phrygian for the final eight bars of the saxophone solo. The harmonies accompany a descending triplet melodic line, shown in Example 4.15, that is not unlike PG1.

Example 4.14 – Some pitches have been harmonically respelled from the score.

Example 4.15

At m.169, the culmination of the development section, the composer once again uses a dense polychord sustained for fifteen beats to reintroduce the soloist for the final "benediction."

Example 4.16

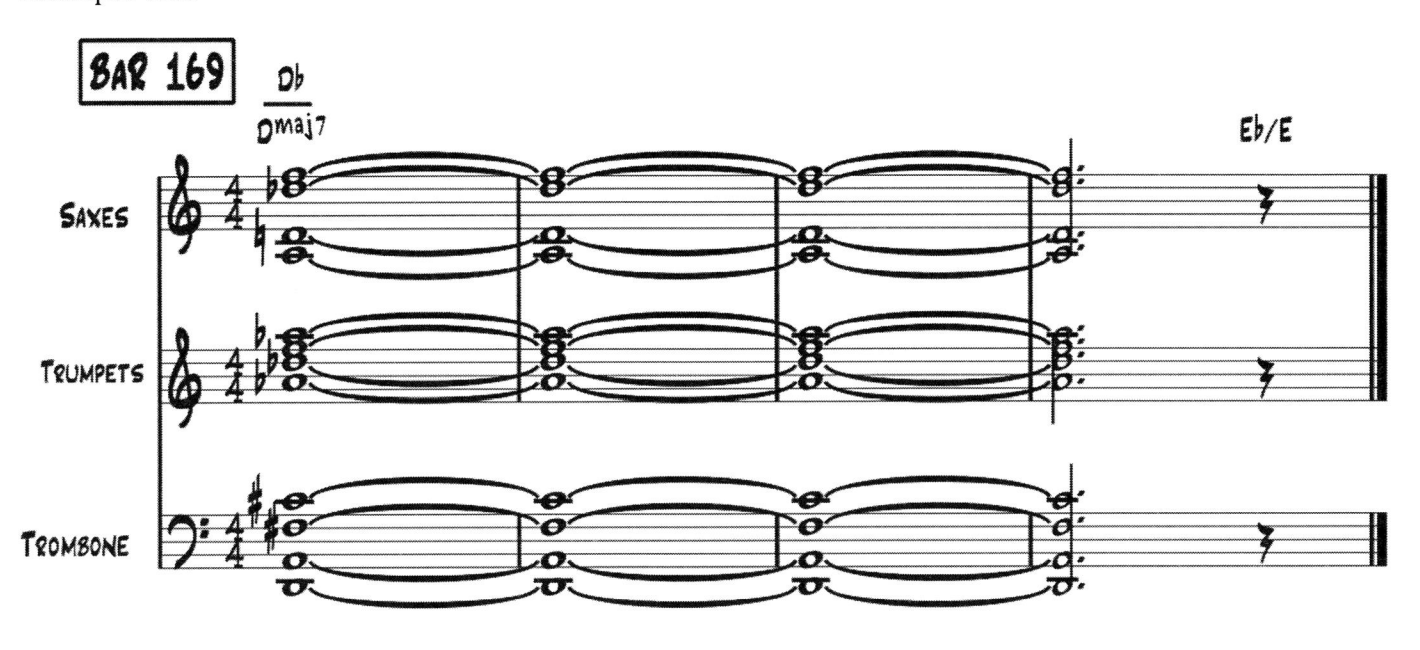

When McNeely uses concerted textures they appear in stark contrast to linear passages, and some are melodies harmonized by planing the given scale or mode. Take, for example, the passage that follows, labeled as the B section in the full score and lead sheet reduction.

Example 4.17 – Labeled as the bridge in the score reduction and the full score analysis.

Such four voice textures are not always based on the chant-like open fourths and fifths heard throughout most of the piece. For example, the final chorale just before the piece comes to a close is very reminiscent of Bob Brookmeyer's later style in planing G♭ major and Mixolydian harmonized scales over a G♭ pedal in the bass, as illustrated in Example 4.18. It is worth also noting that while these passages are in different modes and harmonic structures, there is a striking similarly to the shape and rhythm of the melodic line that rises and falls in approximately two measure phrases while making use of triplet rhythms. While McNeely may reuse the essence of material, he rarely if ever simply repeats himself.

Example 4.18 – Four voice texture in third inversion with 7th on the bottom maintains 4th structure between outer voices.

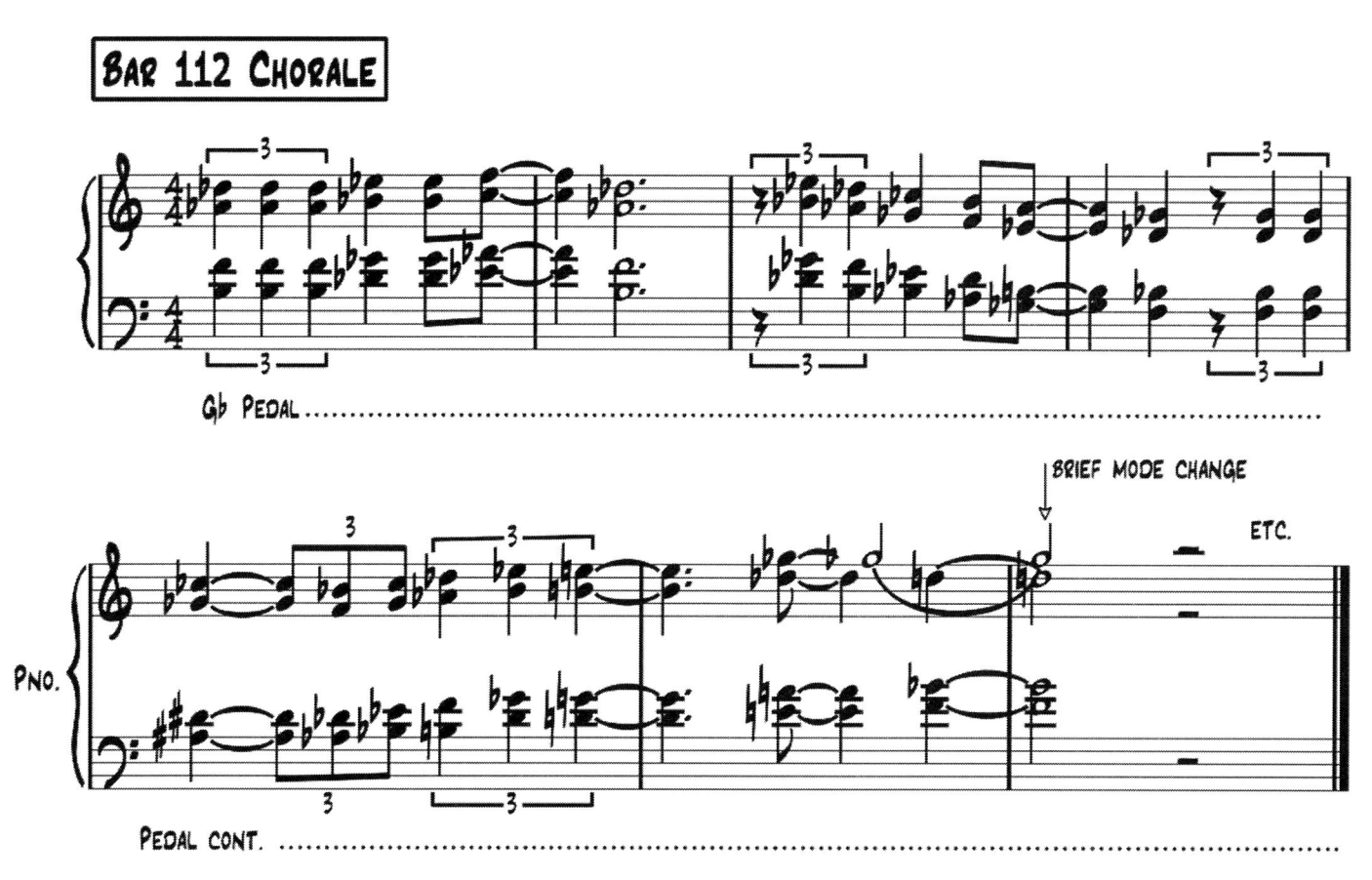

The progression of major and minor 7th chords at measures 53 and similarly near the end at m.188 is interesting in that it capitalizes on the common tones that exist between chords that enjoy a third relationship. All of these ascending chords are derived from the A♭ major scale, but ascend by skipping a note. In each case McNeely uses this cycle to reach the same target chord – F minor, which is essentially the basis of this harmonic planing. This is the section he borrowed from Milhaud's "Duo Concertant."

Example 4.19

The final phrase of McNeely's "Absolution" returns to the harmonic essence of the piece and its roots in Gregorian chant. This chain of minor and dominant suspended and major chords composed largely of stacked fifths are all voiced in wide, open spacing, as shown in Example 4.20. This example, like many of the others in this section, has been reduced to a great staff for easy realization at a keyboard. This could be viewed as the perfect closing hymn or postlude following the granting of absolution.

Example 4.20

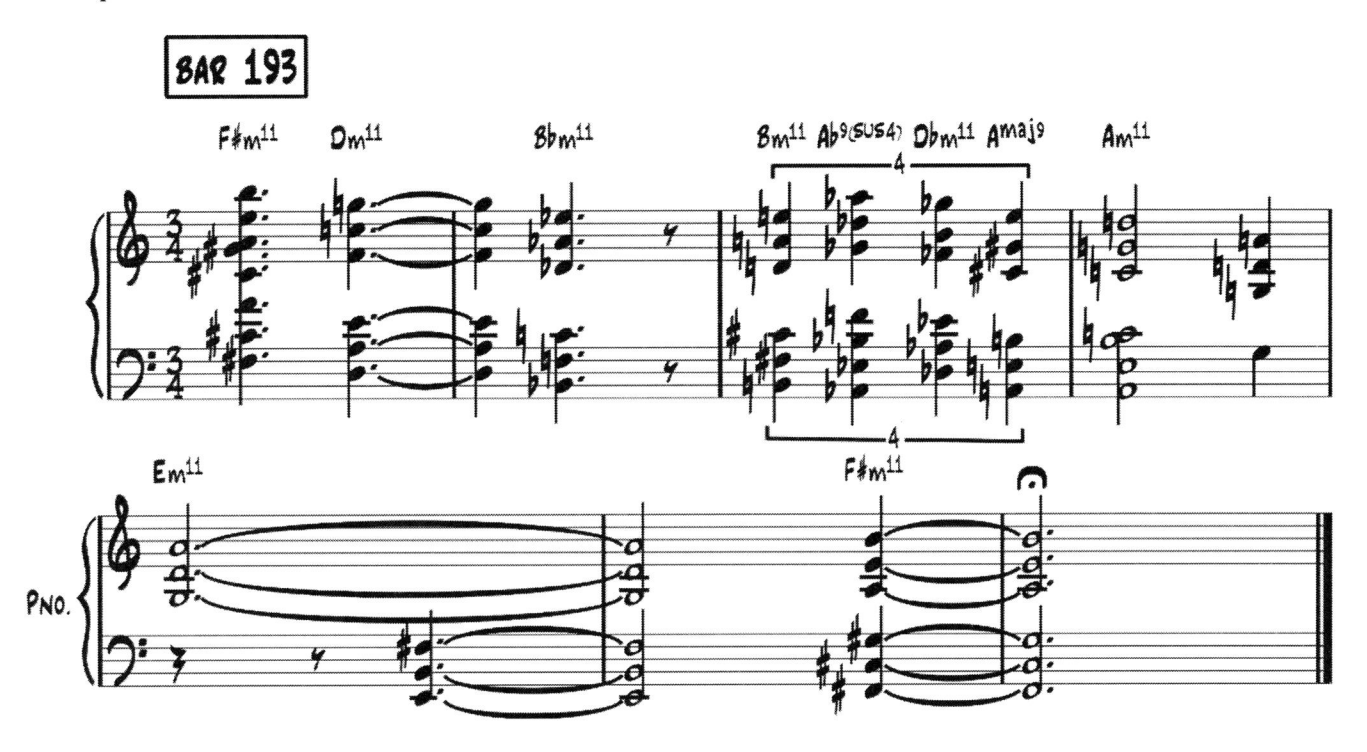

Orchestration

As previously suggested, this piece, with the exception of the few more densely populated harmonies discussed in the previous section, could almost be realized with four voices, since the composer rarely exceeds this limit. But in doing so he would have sacrificed the richness, weight, and timbral variety provided by the octave unisons, losing the sense of "congregation" as well as the impact of the phrases presented as a dialogue between instrument groups. There are many occasions where no more than two different voices are scored for both trumpets and trombones, for a total of four different brass voices. Example 4.17 is a good illustration of this full ensemble scoring of a simple four note voicing where the top three notes of the voicing are scored for three saxophones with four trumpets and only one trombone on the bottom voice. Baritone sax and third and fourth trombones have nothing written in this section. Obviously, McNeely does not use instruments just for the sake of keeping musicians occupied!

Example 4.18, the ensemble chorale section, is also a good example of the composer's approach to orchestrating four voice textures. In this case the example is played by four saxophones (soloist is resting) while the trumpet section doubles the top two saxophone parts and the trombones double the bottom two sax parts. This is a quite simple but very effective approach to orchestrating for only four voices, and similar voicings and doublings have been used by Bob Brookmeyer, John Hollenbeck, and Kenny Wheeler. A review of the full score will make this approach even more apparent at measure 112.

For readers less familiar with the Vanguard Jazz Orchestra, formerly the Mel Lewis Jazz Orchestra and before that the Thad Jones/Mel Lewis Jazz Orchestra, they did not use a guitarist (except in the very early years). McNeely added a guitar part, but since it was not part of the original orchestration and recording it was removed here in the interest of space conservation and to make it easier on the eye to read the full score at the end of this chapter. Aside from this aspect, the piece is scored for the usual big band instrumentation. The top voice in the saxophone section is soprano, something pioneered by this band in the early days when Thad Jones and Bob Brookmeyer were its primary composer/arrangers.

Solo Backgrounds

McNeely uses a two bar isorhythmic ostinato again during the tenor sax solo. This rhythmic pattern obscures bar lines and obvious references to a meter, as shown in Example 4.21. Notice how the six repeated pitches in this causes the figure to spill into a third measure before the pitch repetition begins again. Each time he changes the mode, he adjusts the bass line pitch content appropriately while maintaining the same rhythm.

Example 4.21

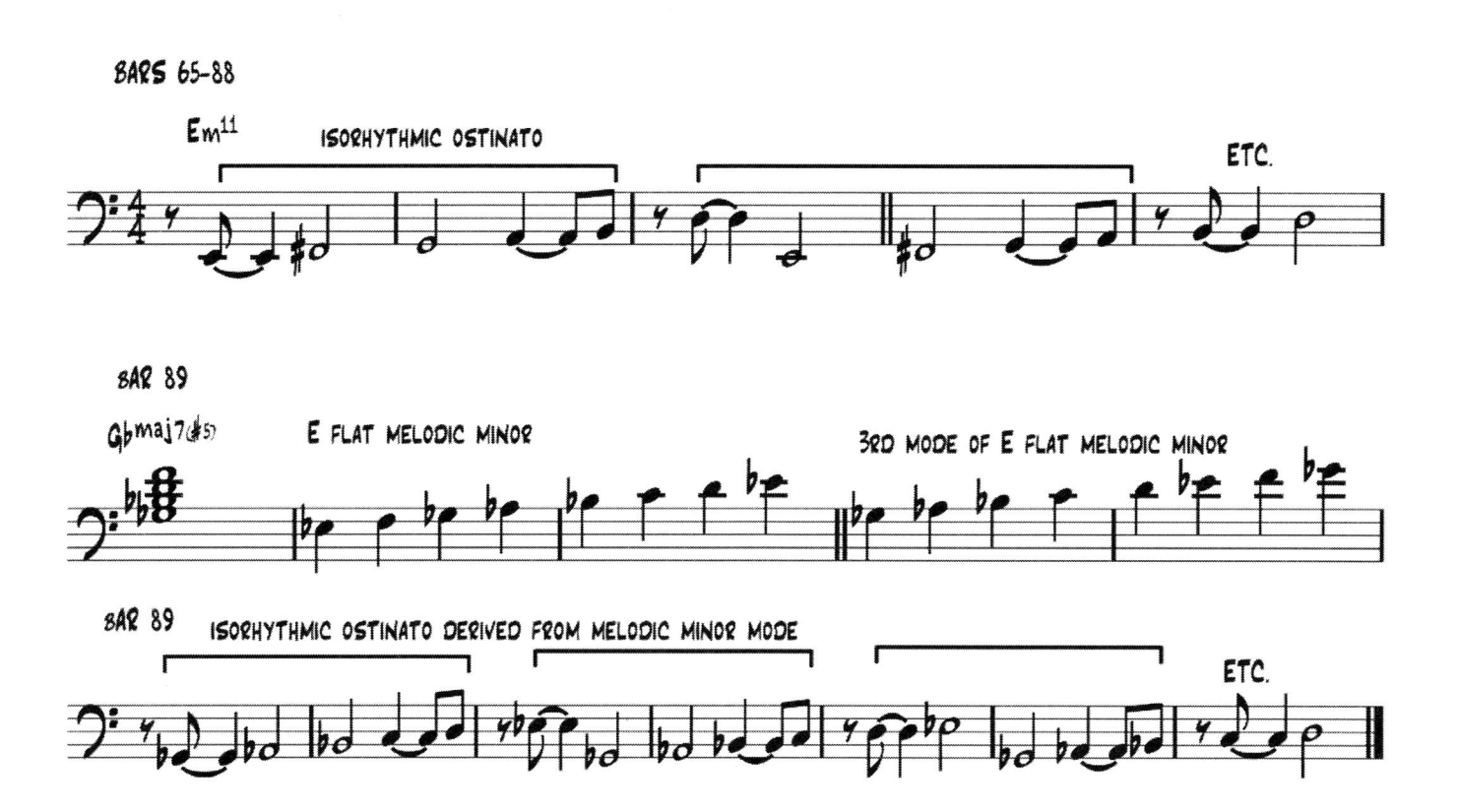

Once again, the composer makes use of PG1/RC1 thematic material, this time as background material in support of the tenor saxophone solo. He begins by stating only one note of PG1 by the trombones, which is highlighted in the full score analysis. As notes are added, the expanding motive works in dialogue with harmonized flugelhorns until it reaches its complete form in m.86. At this point the call-response interplay based on E♭ melodic minor, or modes of this scale, is between trombones and saxophones who respond a perfect 4th away, as shown in Example 4.22. McNeely never does the same thing twice during these backgrounds. To provide variety, he adds a prefix to the beginning of the original PG1, and this prefix is never stated the same way twice. These background gestures between trombones and saxophones are structured in overlapping two bar phrases, in contrast to the bass isorhythmic ostinato, which is two bar phrases but with a line that spills into the third bar after the isorhythm repeats at the start of every other measure. These backgrounds gradually expand, reaching a high point in polychords at measure 101 while continuing to make use of transpositions of PG1 leading to the final eight bar solo section in yet a new another new mode – F♯ Phrygian. The backgrounds serve to bolster the soloists' increasing intensity.

Example 4.22

Development Section (Shout Chorus)

The development section of this piece is unique in that the expected drama achieved by dense harmonies and syncopated rhythms is completely absent until the last few bars. Escalating drama is achieved through rhythm, changing meter, somewhat repetitious octave unisons, and improvising soloists. As suggested earlier in the outline and in describing the composition's similarity to an ecclesiastical experience, this section could imply that moment in a service when individual members of the congregation are encouraged to testify. The full congregation (ensemble) then responds to the solo testimonies with a descending pentatonic scale refrain that uses extreme dynamic contrast ranging from forte to piano in the course of one measure. This pentatonic phrase is very striking, almost speech-like in quality, and the short phrase ends leaving a sense of incompleteness, setting up the entrance of the next soloist. This pentatonic refrain is also similar in terms of shape, pitch, and rhythmic content to PG1/RC1.

Example 4.23 shows how the composer gradually manipulates the meter and the motive, compressing the call and response events between soloist and ensemble to eventually reach a frenzied state that culminates in a cascading, overlapping presentation of the motive building to a polychord. The example shows excerpts from this section to illustrate how the composer manipulates the simple material. The full score analysis will show much more detail.

Example 4.23

The composer uses a three chord harmonic gesture to accompany the pentatonic refrain and soloist. This refrain illustrates not only how important voice leading is as a guiding principle for this composer, but also how a melody can be given a new identity when it is accompanied by changing harmony. The three chord gesture ascends in contrast to the melodic refrain that descends and is based on the same chord qualities each time it is transposed. Sometimes the melody changes with the transposed harmony, and other times it does not. For example, compare bars 129 and 148 in Example 4.23.

Harmonic transposition is achieved by changing the target chord in this three chord progression. Rather than approaching it from a major 2nd, which creates a consistent relationship of whole steps between each chord root, a new target chord is approached by a leap. The new target chord sets up the new relationship of major second root movements (Ma7(#11)–Dom7–Dom7) in the next phrase. This progression is achieved through smooth voice leading, as illustrated in Example 4.24, which follows. Chord voicings in this example are not stipulated in the piano part in the score but are used here only to illustrate the strong minor and major second voice leading as well as common tones that connect these three or four note harmonies. Many different voicings of these chords are possible but would show a similar result in terms of smooth, strong voice leading.

Example 4.24 – "CT" indicates common tone between voicings.

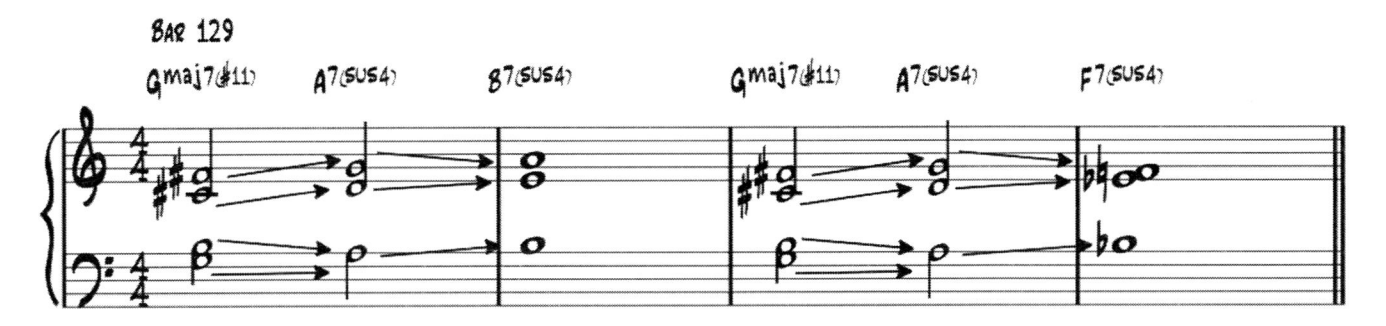

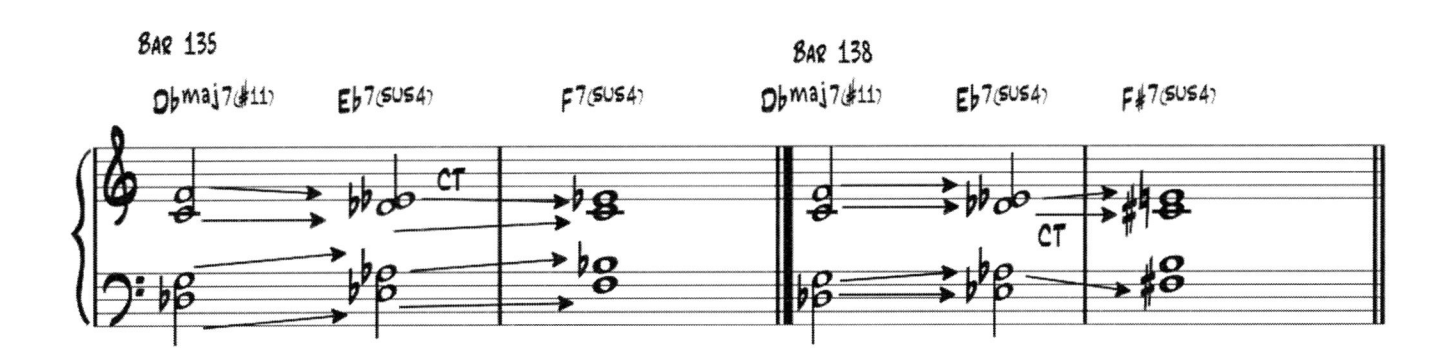

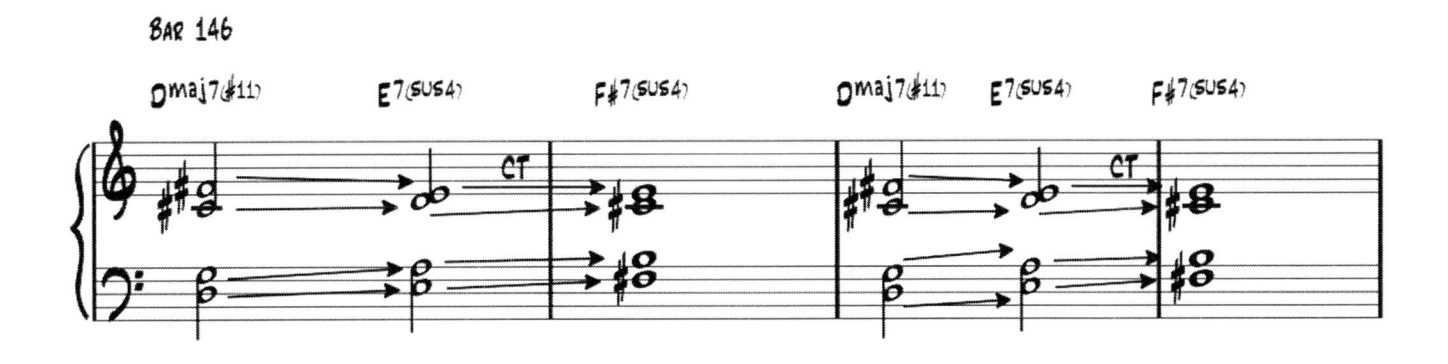

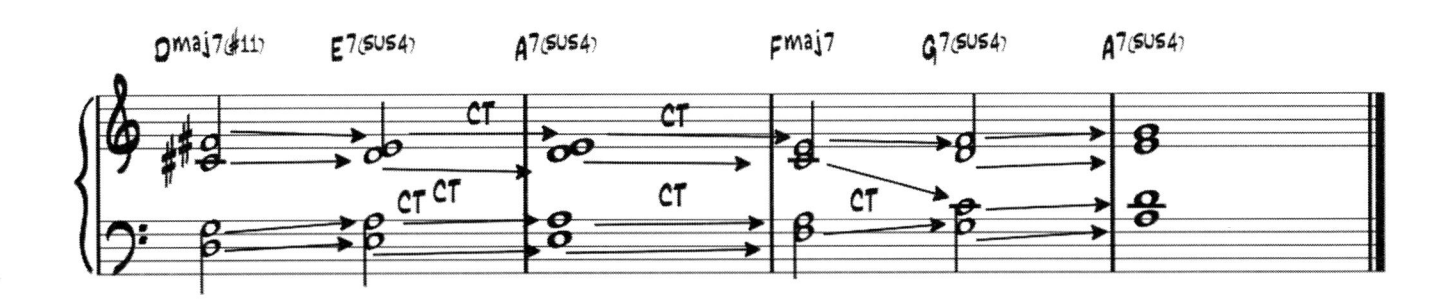

In the final analysis, Jim McNeely shows with this score why he is considered to be one of the leading influential composers of our time, whose many innovations are illustrated in this score, not the least of which is the value of simple unisons or octave unisons and in developing simple motives.

For additional details, see the analysis of the full score that follows. In an effort to improve legibility, some dynamic markings in a few individual parts have been removed from the original score to make it less visually cluttered. The score is transposed; however, excerpts of some passages appear at the bottom of the score in concert pitch to more easily show analysis of significant aspects of the composition.

Interview with Jim McNeely

Author's note: The interview was conducted both in real time via FaceTime on 12/19/17 and by email, giving the composer time to jog his memory about the creation of this older score.

RL: *While I've followed your work for many years, I'd like to learn more about your influences as writers and teachers. Who and perhaps what music has had an impact on you as a writer?*

JM: In high school, Rev. George Wiskirchen (band director) encouraged me to write; Oliver Nelson [was an influence], and at the University of Illinois Jim Knapp and Morgan Powell, who was also my composition teacher. The Basie band always killed me; I heard them live a couple of times. But the first time I heard Thad and Mel on WAAF in Chicago, probably 1966, set off a little explosion in me. Then, when Thad and Mel's first live album came out, I knew that Thad was "it" for me. There was a density to his writing that I didn't quite figure out, but it also swung like crazy, thanks to Thad's writing, Mel's playing, and the musicians in the band. And the soloists, including Thad, played in a language that reflected what I was hearing in small group recordings at the time.

The next big influence was Bob Brookmeyer. Of course I knew who he was and [had known] his playing and writing since the mid-'60s. But I'd joined Thad and Mel in 1978. Thad left in early '79, and Mel asked Bob to come in as musical director. The music he wrote in those few years, including "First Love Song," "Ding, Dong, Ding," and the *Make Me Smile* album, really turned my head around. Playing his and Thad's music every Monday for years was the greatest arranging lesson of my life.

RL: *Thad certainly did it for all of us. I had no idea you were a Father George disciple.*

Do you remember anything in particular that one of your teachers had you do that had an impact on your writing?

JM: There are two things off hand that come to mind, maybe even three. Number one, Father Wiskirchen had a six or seven line template for how to arrange for marching band. I forget who put that together … some rather well known figure in the marching band world. When I was a senior, he would have me and a friend of mine write the shows for the marching band, and that was my first experience writing to a deadline. We'd have a meeting on Monday and he'd say, "OK, by next Monday I need … ," and I remember one time he needed thirty-two bars of "She's Only a Bird in a Gilded Cage" to modulate into Coltrane's version of "My Favorite Things," and I played soprano sax. And you know in those days you didn't call some big music publisher and buy it off the shelf, so he would get us to custom write what he needed. And another time I did an arrangement of "Intermission Riff," the Kenton thing. It was kind of jazz oriented writing, but it was also writing to a deadline, and it was the first time I had experienced that.

Another thing that he did that really made an impression on me – he called me into his office one day and he said, "I've got two of Oliver Nelson's original scores for things he's written for Jimmy Smith, I think, or Jimmy McGriff. [**RL:** *Well, he did a lot of things for Jimmy Smith, just about all his records, so it was probably for him.*] And he said, "Can you copy out the parts? I have to have them back in a couple of days." I don't know where he got them and I didn't ask [laughs]. So I said sure, and there I was at my little clunky spinet piano at home looking at Oliver's manuscript and checking out the voicings and saying, "Ah … so that's how you do that." So that was a great experience for me. And then I would bring in recordings of things to just try and piss him off! Here I was, this young teenager, getting into these wild things. I brought in an Archie Shepp record because I was into Archie back in those days. I played something for him and thought, "This will really get under his skin," and he looked at me and said, "Write something like that for the band." He completely called my bluff. And I did. He was great in that way, encouraging me to write, and that was the first time I had a band at my disposal, and for the day it was a very good high school big band in the Chicago area.

When I got to college, my composition teacher was Morgan Powell, who was writing music that was really in the cracks between big band music and contemporary chamber music. He wrote a massive piece for orchestra, and he had me copy and prepare the score for him. And that was a big thing for me … looking at how he did things and trying to learn from that. I've always found it valuable to look at scores and figure out how they did that. And I also learned to look with my eyes if I'm playing something, and if I heard a sound that is attractive I'd just look up and see who's playing.

The more I think about it, Wiskirchen really is the guy who messed up my life [laughs]. He's the reason why I'm doing what I'm doing today; at least he was the first one.

RL: *He was also the first one to write a pedagogical book about running a jazz ensemble in the precollege schools.*

JM: Stage band, as they had to call it back then.

RL: *Yes, and that book was very formative for me when I was working on my first book.*

JM: I think that was his master's thesis, I think from Quincy College, though I'm not sure. I was impressed because I knew this guy who wrote a book. I was impressed with that, thinking he must be famous. He had a great attitude, too, because I think the few bands around Chicago at that time, the few schools that had bands, those directors were more into Stan Kenton and Maynard Ferguson, and Wiskirchen was into Count Basie and getting the band to swing. He really worked us on that, and that was really valuable.

RL: *Copying parts can really be a valuable exercise. I remember when I was a TA and doing some work for Bill Dobbins. He had transcribed and sort of merged the two recorded versions of George Russell's "All About Rosie," and I copied it all in felt tip pen. There was a lot to be learned by doing that, even though I was cursing him under my breath! [laughs]*

Do you see an advantage of writing arrangements as well, and not just focusing your time on composing original work? It's a lesson I didn't learn until very late in life. I was always writing original music, though

I'm not sure why I did that, and it's only been in the past ten to fifteen years that I've done a lot more arranging, and I think it's had a positive impact on my compositional skills.

JM: Yes, I think so. I'm kind of the same way, although the first couple of things I wrote while I was in high school were arrangements. I found an Ernie Wilkins blues head in a book and I did an arrangement of that. And then I found a lead sheet for "In the Land of Oo-Bla-Dee," that Mary Lou Williams tune, and I did an arrangement of that. But then I started to do mostly original compositions in college.

When I started to write for the first European band I wrote for, which was Umo up in Helsinki, that was all original stuff. And what I was doing for the WDR band in Cologne was original with an occasional arrangement. It wasn't until I started to work with the Carnegie Hall Jazz Band in 1994 that I really started to write a lot of arrangements. And that was a great learning experience for me. At that time Manny Albam and I were the directors of the BMI Jazz Composers Workshop, and of course Manny had come up writing arrangements. He was the staff arranger for Charlie Barnet's band and wrote three arrangements a week. They had relationships with music publishers, and the publishers would give them the new tunes that were coming out. He said that your job was to make sure the singer could hear the key and the people knew the melody and they could dance to it. He said you could be creative maybe in the intro, but that was it! Later in life he got into composing for big band. We used to talk about the fact that I came about it from the other way. I was writing all this original material and then finally learning all the discipline involved in writing an arrangement. When Jon Faddis called me to write this program for the Carnegie Hall Big Band based on the music of the Benny Goodman Orchestra, he said, "As long as people can hear the melody, that's what we have to have. You can do whatever you want, but they have to hear the melody," which was fine with me because there are a lot of great melodies there. It forced me to put a kind of discipline on my writing that I hadn't done much of in writing original compositions.

And the same thing is true with all my work with the Frankfurt Radio Big Band; most of that is arranging. You have to play it pretty conservatively because you don't have a lot of rehearsal time with the guest soloist. We've done a couple of projects with Oregon [Ralph Towner and Paul McCandless], and these guys have been playing some of their tunes for thirty years, and you can't expect them in two rehearsals to learn some Brookmeyer deconstruction of their song, you know. I imagine them playing as a quartet and then just drop a big band around them and let them do what they do normally. You learn how to make the most of certain resources in the band but keep the form so that they know what's going on and it's familiar to them. It is something I had to learn, and that's not a "dis" on Brookmeyer. I love his "My Funny Valentine" and "King Porter 94," the way he deconstructed those songs. It was pretty remarkable, but there's a time and place for that, and there is a time and place for playing it pretty close to the vest.

RL: *Before we look specifically at "Absolution," can you tell us in general about your creative process in developing a new score? In your response you might explain how you started to develop "Absolution," though I realize I'm asking you to stretch your memory back quite a few years.*

JM: Hmm, time to get into the Wayback Machine! I do remember that the working title was "New Slow Groove," or NSG. "Absolution" is not an arrangement of a song – in a way there are a lot of melodies, but no one theme that is the central focus of the piece. When I start a piece like that I begin with a very general conception of the whole thing. Sometimes just one word to describe the feeling of the piece; what the listener might feel; what the players might feel. With "Absolution," I started with two general ideas: the slow groove, and Rich Perry's sound and melodic language. I also had one very specific idea: the first note ["C" unison with trombone and tenor]. I'd played a gig with Ed Neumeister [trombone] and Billy Drewes [tenor] where they started a tune together on that note. Something went "boing" in me; I said, "I've gotta use that sound as the first note of a piece!"

At that time I was just beginning to figure out how best to use the computer in my process. As a pencil-and-paper guy, I was still discovering the computer's strengths and weaknesses. I was running some kind of sequencing software in those days. I never used it very much, but I remember that I put in the opening three bar vamp and improvised over it. I kept coming back to a couple of small motives – kind of like a guy standing off in the corner mumbling to himself, always returning to the same couple of phrases. Then I took what I'd had, and printed it out. It was a mess; I did it with no quantization! So after a lot of editing, and throwing out some things, I developed the first section. I also had the image of Rich and Ed as the main voice, and occasionally the other voices would chime in to reinforce a phrase, a Greek chorus. And at times the focus would get blurry, then snap back again.

When I was young I was raised in the Catholic Church. There's a call and response prayer that can go on a long time – seemingly forever, to a ten year old kid! It's called a litany. Say, the litany of the saints – the priest calls out the names of various saints and the congregation responds with the same phrase – maybe "Pray for us." I've used this idea in several pieces over the years, and I knew that I wanted to incorporate it into this "New Slow Groove."

So it all started with the groove, the sound of the first note, Rich's sound, the Greek chorus, and the litany.

The beginning stage of a piece is a lot like a brainstorming session, but with yourself. There are no bad ideas, in fact, no good ideas, only ideas. If you think of something and don't know how it might fit in the piece, never mind. Just write it down. It will either find its place later on, or not, and you can set it aside. Let the ideas flow, with no judgment.

I have some devices to get the process going. Sometimes I make up negative rules. I'm not sure what I'm *going* to write, but whatever it is, it will *not* be X or Y or Z, things I've used too much in the recent past. I will also occasionally use pitch cells or even serial technique to force me to come up with material I wouldn't normally sit at the piano and improvise. Brookmeyer once told me that if you sit at the piano and improvise, you end up trying to remember the last thing you wrote. So sometimes I use these techniques to artificially jump-start the process.

Sometimes I approach my piano thinking about the sandwich I just ate, or the discussion I just had with my accountant. Sit at the piano and hear what comes out of my hands. I want to hear the phrase the way that the other 8,000,000,000 people on the planet would hear it – unattached to any baggage. I'm the only person in the world who might hear the phrase with expectation, or disappointment. So I try to neutralize those things.

I also find it important not to take my ideas at face value. I like to work with them. I think of them as having physical properties, like bread dough. I can stretch it, compact it, cut it up into little pieces, rearrange them, and mash it all into a big ball. Then, if I decide to go with my original idea, I do it informed with what I've experienced in the process. It's all process. I once read about a technique in pottery where you throw a pot, fire it, and then smash it against the wall. After a while you've got enough shards to grind up and make more clay to make more pots. You don't get attached to your pots. I don't get attached to my musical ideas. I work with them.

I also discovered that musical ideas sound different depending on the instrument you're playing them on. When I bought my first DX-7, in about 1982, I realized that some simple little idea I wouldn't think twice about on the piano would sound different played in, say, a warm analog-sounding patch. So even now, sometimes I write at my Steinway, sometimes at my old Fender Rhodes.

RL: *Looking now at "Absolution," one of the questions in your written response that you sort of sidestepped or didn't entirely answer – and I know how difficult it is to go back in your time machine, since this is not a recent piece – but I am curious, as I have been with all the writers I'm working with on this project: how much of the real architecture of the piece, either in outline form or in your head, was conceived before you actually put notes on paper?*

JM: That's a good question, and I really can't remember. These days, especially when I'm doing arrangements for people, I really plot the whole thing out in outline form before I get to work. I'd like to say that I did that with "Absolution," but I doubt it. I do remember I started to improvise off the bass line and knew I wanted to do this section where there is a melody. I used to think that a melody was an agreement by a group of people who would say the same thing together at the same time. It didn't have to be a real identifiable tune, like "I've Got Rhythm" or "Mean What You Say." It's melody but not a theme that keeps reoccurring. So I knew I wanted a section like that. And I was also playing around with these vamps that spill over themselves where the number of rhythmic hits and the number of pitches are different so it keeps churning around and it takes a long time for it to come back to the downbeat. I was probably working on these two things at the same time. I also knew I wanted to write something for Rich [Perry] with his sound and the way he plays. I think the idea of the litany section came later as I was working on the other sections. Thinking of what could come next, I didn't think that the [plays block chord traditional shout chorus on the piano] ... I didn't think a shout chorus was appropriate.

RL: *The piece strikes me as more of an organic process of development because it is not an arrangement of a composition. The piece is a composition that's been orchestrated.*

JM: Yes, that's right. And I had this idea of this melodic thread being spun out by just two people, and sometimes others would join in just to highlight a certain phrase. And it would build to a point where it would reach a climactic. It's kind of unelegant, but it's a phrase I like to use – it kind of dumps Rich off, like dumping him off the back of a truck and he starts playing out of that. I also know that I wanted a couple of places where the focus became very blurry and then would snap back into more sharp focus. If there is any unifying element to the piece, it's the fact that Rich is the solo character. I've talked a lot about my feeling about the dramatic element to my music; Brookmeyer used to talk about that, too. By dramatic we don't mean [plays series of chromatically ascending diminished chords]. I mean it's moving toward a climax. It does that through character development and then conflict and resolution of the conflict. So I have the soloist working out some issues that he has, and then the band takes over with a kind of prayer, and then the litany section, where each guy puts in his two cents' worth and the band answers with the same phrase. When I originally wrote that section, the answer was the same all the time. We played a few times, and I thought I could at least change the key so it would keep building up, and then I had the idea that I could keep compressing the answers so that gradually it gets shorter and the solos get shorter, too. It then builds up to another peak, and Rich comes out of that with all burners on, and then the final phrase from the band. So I'm pretty sure that wasn't all laid out beforehand and it kind of grew on its own.

RL: *In a way, then, it seems like this piece was workshopped with the Vanguard Orchestra.*

JM: Yes. Several pieces on that album were brought in in one form and then tweaked. At this point I wasn't back in the band yet. I would bring something in, and then two or three weeks later I'd make little changes before it reached its final form.

RL: *There are two of the features of this piece that jumped out at me as being unique and unusual. One is the fact that there is no intro; you just jump right in. There isn't the expected intro, even though there could have been, using that isorhythmic ostinato to sort of set things up, but you didn't, which I found very refreshing. I also liked that the expected shout chorus isn't there, though there is a dramatic buildup, as you described. But the way you achieved that is so unlike most pieces in our world, and for me that really worked. And also I appreciated how important the soloist was to this piece, and it made me think of Bob Brookmeyer and the way he talked about how to introduce a soloist, or if it's even appropriate to have a soloist.*

JM: We used to talk about that, and he was kind of misquoted on that. People on the Internet were saying, "Bob Brookmeyer hates solos," and that's the furthest thing from the truth. What he didn't like is that when it's finally time for a tenor solo, somebody just gets up and plays all the Michael Brecker licks he's been working on in the practice room, you know. He wanted somebody to really respond to the surroundings and make musical sense and not just say, "Well, it's my solo and I can do anything I want."

I've done "Absolution" with a number of different bands, and Rich was always the voice I had in mind for that. But on the other hand, if you just limited it to Rich Perry you're not going to get played very much, so … I've done it with a number of college bands where I've had different degrees of success. We did it one time at IAJE with Chris Potter, and that was tremendous. It works with a soloist who really listens to and responds to what's going on around him. That vamp that the tenor solo starts on was designed to kind of throw the soloist off because every time we hear the low E, that feels like a downbeat, but it's not. The low E comes at different parts of the rhythmic cycle. Even now, and I think I mentioned this in the stuff I sent you, people still ask me what meter is that in, and it's 4/4 all the way, but the low E is shifting.

RL: *Yes, bar lines are sort of erased through those sections, which is the beauty of it.*

JM: Yes, and oddly enough it's a twelve bar cycle, but it's not a blues. The soloists who are most successful with it are the ones that give in to the feeling – someone who just thinks, "You know, I'm not quite sure where we are, but that's OK and I'm just going to play." And that's what I was going for. If the soloist starts to worry about where [beat] 1 is, then they're dead. You have to forget [beat] 1 and just play over what you hear. And finally the mode changes and that's your cue for the next section. Even before that, the background comes in. You have to just give in to the moment and play with what you hear. And I think the comping is important. When I play it with Rich, we develop a little chromatic thing that helps build the shape. [*Author's note: Of course, this aspect is not indicated in the score with any specifics and left to the improvising, comping pianist, who is serving more as a collaborator than in more traditional situations, where he might be considered more of an accompanist.*] You can't worry about where [beat] 1 is because you'll probably never find it and you'll spend your time trying to find 1 [laughs], so forget about it and just play.

RL: *At what point to you make use of a computer in your creative process and how is it used, or is it used at all? I ask this question because of the significant influence the computer has exerted, particularly on the* *younger generations of writers, and to some degree even those of us who started by pushing pencils around on paper and have done so for years.*

JM: Like I said, I needed time to figure out how to use it well and efficiently. I was writing a piece and I'd decided to just open my notation software – Encore, back in those days – and start composing. I wanted to write thirty-two bars of counterpoint. I entered a little motive, and was trying to develop it, with little success. I felt that I was looking at a picture of the music; I was detached. I finally said, "This is silly." Grabbed a pencil, turned to my keyboard, and everything started to flow. So I need the feel of a pencil in my hand, and paper underneath. The smell of the eraser. Composing and arranging still has this sensual element – I'm not just hearing the music but feeling it, smelling it, seeing it. I still take great pleasure in meticulously writing notes on the page; it feels good. Sorry, I don't get this from the computer.

So the beginning stages of a piece are all paper-focused. In the middle, I start sketching. I have a seven staff sketch template in Finale where I enter everything from the sketch. This is where I start making more detailed decisions about form. I move things around in the sketch. Still, a lot of it is blank. Then I print the whole thing out and start writing on the blank paper. As I go along, I enter material into the computer. By the time I'm finished with the sketch, it has all the formatting, all the harmonic and rhythmic details, and a complete bass part. Now I'm ready to paste that into the score. I have starter templates for the several ensembles I write for regularly.

This is where the practical advantages of the computer kick in, so I now do my scoring on the computer, then send it off to a copyist. I do find it a help to play passages back, to check for errors. But I don't trust the computer for things like balance and timbre. I rely on experience and memory for that.

RL: *This piece, like some of your other compositions, seems to be motivated by a personal experience. I know that you often think of developing your compositions as if they are a movie or theater piece unfolding. You treat the musicians like characters in a play. In this particular case, the title initially led me to suspect that it is your musical interpretation of a church service complete with preacher, congregation whose members testify in call and response format, hymns, and closing benediction. The more I listened to and studied the score, the more convinced I became that I was right, especially considering the theatrical aspect of a religious service. Am I at all close in this description of "Absolution"?*

JM: I spoke earlier about the litany idea. That came pretty early on, and I called it that. But the "New Slow Groove" title stuck for a while. It wasn't until I'd played the piece for a while with the VJO that I started to have this image of a young Catholic lad, wracked with guilt and trying to work out some kind of bargain with God. I'm sure it's autobiographical [smiles]. It was then that I changed the title to "Absolution." It's not meant to literally depict a religious service, but to evoke the different feelings involved with dealing with guilt and your relationship with God.

RL: *Another thing that struck me about the piece was lack of harmonic structure. It is so melodically driven, and when you do introduce some kind of harmony it's often based on 4ths and 5ths. Were you thinking about the religious vibe, this context, almost chant-like, and was that at all part of your thinking?*

JM: Not really. I think I was just playing around with things and the 4ths and 5ths seemed to make sense. The only time any kind of religious thinking came in the writing process was the litany section. I've used that a couple of other times in smaller contexts, and I knew I wanted to do that in this piece. I didn't have any kind of association with any kind of religious overtone to the harmonic language; I was just thinking of this real open sound with a lot of 5ths in the bass and in the vamp. At one point it gets into that G♭ scale and gets kind of chromatic and there is that ascending set of changes, which, as I said, I copped from this Milhaud "Duo Concertant," which I played when I was a kid and that little progression always caught my ear. In my mind, even though Milhaud was a twentieth century composer, this was classical music, and I thought, this guy was hip. He was fusing this kind of harmony, so that's always stayed with me and I used that kind of motion in a number of pieces, where it keeps ascending and you finally get back to the I [chord]. You're going through all the possible diatonic chords, but not in scalar order, as you're moving up in thirds.

RL: *Yet another thing that interested me about the piece, and I've seen this approach in some other scores that are actually part of this project, is the fact that in a way you could have written this for a small band with four voices and a rhythm section. There are a few occasions with the dramatic big polychords, but other than that there are generally not more than four voices, with various octave and unison doublings. How did you come about that approach, and is it something you've been using a lot?*

JM: I had been using it a little bit and with another piece on that record called "Reflections." That was part of a suite I wrote for Phil Woods originally and the WDR band. In that I was using a three note structure like that [plays example on Fender Rhodes], and it has a lot of tripling of voices in it. That might have been the first time that I had done that. I liked that sound, and in talking with Bob [Brookmeyer], who got to a point where he was writing a lot that way. There is a thing he wrote for Jim Hall and the WDR Band and I performed it with him in Rotterdam in the Conservatory there, with Jim playing guitar. I don't think there were more than three voices in the whole piece, and everything was tripled and quadrupled. I think the band probably hated it because there was never any place where there was a big satisfying chord where everyone had a different part to play. But it had a real sound to it. If I was writing for a small group, it wouldn't occur to me to write that piece because I was going for a sound with all these tripled lines. It's a wider sound than you get from single voices, so I probably wouldn't have written that piece if I had four or five horns. It came to me as a big band piece, but there isn't much in terms of vertical harmony.

RL: *What I was implying was more about the sparsity of uniquely individual voices. I wasn't implying that the piece would sound the same if you wrote it for four horns. It would miss that density and richness and timbre you get out of the octave doublings and triplings and so on.*

The last question, which I have asked everyone: as someone who has devoted a good portion of your professional life to teaching, which has been true with all the other writers in this project, what single lesson or suggestion can you share that might help us all to become better writers?

JM: Two of the things that helped me – first of all, brutal honesty in listening to what you've written when it's played. When I was younger I used to get defensive about things, and I realized I wasn't really being honest with myself about something that didn't work. I learned to be honest with myself, and if something doesn't sound the way you thought it would, find a different way to achieve what you're after. Also, courage to try things is important. You know Stravinsky said speculation is one of the most important jobs of a composer – to ask "What if." And rather than asking "May I," ask "What if I did this and do that." In the BMI workshop, once in a while we would get someone who seemed like their main objective was to please me and Manny, not to discover their own voice. We would get into this situation where one week Manny would tell the guy to voice something a certain way and the next week I'd tell him to voice it a different way, and he'd say, "Well, Manny told me to do it this way." And I'd say, "Now you've got two opinions, what are you going to do?" It's nice to get positive feedback from somebody, but don't be afraid to take risks and then accept the consequences of the risks. Sometimes they don't pay off and sometimes they do. Don't be concerned about just pleasing the status quo. To find your own voice means you've got to take some chances.

And a modern-day piece of advice is get the hell off your computer!

RL: *Bravo!!*

JM: Hey, I use the computer, too. I use it to make sure the notes are correct and so forth. But unless you have $1,000 worth of great samples and you spend significant time tweaking them, the computer is just not going to give you the right idea in terms of balance. It will also give you a false sense of how a piece is going to sound. I've had students complain that a reading session doesn't sound like it was supposed to, and they'll play me the computer version. On the computer that may be how it goes, but with real people … you've got to learn that interface with humans is such an important part of the process. Whether you are using a computer or pencil and paper you have to learn to deal with that first step in putting things in front of humans and dealing with how they respond to it. The human element is still there. Learn to use the computer wisely. Use it as a tool to write music that is really playable and sounds good with human beings.

RL: That is great advice, and I couldn't agree more.

JM: I still have my trusty Rhodes, and I do a lot of writing on that. But I'll still go over to my Steinway and play on that because it just feels so good. I still love playing the piano. I may not have the technique I used to have, but in a way that's a good thing because it makes you think and play what you hear and hear what you play. It all goes back to that. I remember Dizzy Gillespie saying, "You spend a lifetime learning what not to play." Hopefully we all learn that lesson and learn what not to write. Just because you can doesn't mean you should. You learn to edit yourself and not overdo things. Which is a lesson that took me a long time to learn, and I'm still learning that.

Years ago at a BMI reading, somebody wrote a lot of woodwind stuff and one of the flute players finally raised his hand and said, "Excuse me, are we supposed to play this in tune?" [laughs]

Author's note: We went off on some tangents telling war stories about reading sessions and the unforgiving, or misunderstanding, nature of some student writers. The conversation then turned to tuning.

JM: There is a section in "Absolution" with all those open 4ths and 5ths, and that's rough. I was reading Gary Lindsay's book and he said more or less "Don't do that" because tuning is really hard, and he has a point.

RL: *Some of those minor 11ths – I call them the Joe Schwantner voicings because I think he used that sound in the piece he won a Pulitzer for – I think it was "And the Mountains Rising Nowhere." It's a beautiful minor 11 sound, but it can be a bear to tune if you don't have great players. But I've done it anyway. [laughs]*

JM: Yes. For a while I used to say the 4ths and 5ths have to be in tune, and the unisons and octaves have to be in tune, and the 3rds have to be in tune [laughs], and the 6ths … the half steps, they all have to be in tune! And that's another place where the computer … I remember rehearsing, I think it was "First Love

Song," with a college band and at one point there's a place where the voicing is [plays chord on Fender Rhodes]. The voicing puts the first and second trombone on an E and E♭, and I had to really work with them to get each player to really believe in their note and make it a great big fat half step, because if the 3rd player tried to slide up a little closer to his neighbor, it just wasn't going to work. You really have to sell those half steps like they are big and juicy and really mean it. At some point they all have to be in tune.

RL: *I noticed that you mentioned two mid-career Brookmeyer pieces as important to you. "Ding, Dong, Ding" was one of his from this period that we both share a love of. That and "First Love Song" showed me that there was an entirely new way to think about writing for big band.*

JM: Yes. He wrote both of those as vehicles for me. I remember it was like looking for an elevator and the door opens up and there's no elevator car there; you just jump into the empty shaft. We still play those with the Vanguard Band today, and it took me a while to really get a handle on them, an approach to playing on them.

With "First Love Song" the band would finish playing their first big opening section and I would be calculating how I was going to start my solo while they were playing. The band stops, and I would play what I had worked out in my head for the first few bars, and then I was lost. I'd sit there and think, now what am I going to do? Now when I play that piece I don't think of anything. The band stops and I just put my hands on the keyboard and see where it goes. You can't really overthink or plan on that piece.

RL: *Thank you so much for agreeing to be part of this project and sharing your music with us. I'm glad we finally found a convenient time to hook up, as you've been traveling a lot in Europe.*

JM: Yes, the history at least from the 1980s on of American big band composers is not complete without talking about these European bands, especially the German, Scandinavian, and Dutch bands that have kept us afloat.

RL: *Yes. Everyone in this project is always abroad working. Thank you again, Jim, for sharing your great music with us.*

Annotated Full Score

The annotated full transposed score that follows provides additional details about "Absolution," and includes concert pitch excerpts as reductions.

ABSOLUTION

Jim McNeely

PG1/RC1
S. Sx.
A. Sx.
T. Sx. 1
T. Sx. 2
B. Sx.
Tpt. 1
PG1/RC1 rhythmically augmented & transposed
PG2
Tpt. 2
Tpt. 3
Tpt. 4
Tbn. 1
Tbn. 2
Tbn. 3
B. Tbn.
Pno.
Bass
D. S.
Saxes
Tpts
Tbns.

15
Preface to PG1
similar to RC2
PG1/RC1
PG1/RC1 transposed
rhythm ad lib
improvisation around PG1
occurs here on recording
S. Sx.
A. Sx.
T. Sx. 1
T. Sx. 2
B. Sx.
Tpt. 1
Tpt. 2
Tpt. 3
Tpt. 4
Tbn. 1
Tbn. 2
Tbn. 3
B. Tbn.
Pno.
Bass
D. S.
Saxes
Tpts
Tbns.
mf
15
16
17
18
19
20

A1 section
22
as written
RC2
Based on PG2
RC2
RC2 augmented
RC2 anticipated
S. Sx.
A. Sx.
T. Sx. 1
T. Sx. 2
B. Sx.
Tpt. 1
Tpt. 2
Tpt. 3
Tpt. 4
Tbn. 1
Tbn. 2
Tbn. 3
B. Tbn.
Pno.
Bass
D. S.
Saxes
Tpts
Tbns.
21
22
23
24
25
26
27

abbreviated PG1
3 note harmony in
5ths and 2nds
Rhythm ad lib....
RC2 augmented
S. Sx.
A. Sx.
T. Sx. 1
T. Sx. 2
B. Sx.
Tpt. 1
Tpt. 2
Tpt. 3
Tpt. 4
Tbn. 1
Tbn. 2
Tbn. 3
B. Tbn.
Pno.
Bass
D. S.
Saxes
Tpts
Tbns.
28
29
30
31
32
33
34

B Section

Planing through E mixolydian mode - 3 note texture

deviates from mode here
A2 Section
octave unison section Based on PG1/RC1 with entrances overlapping
7
S. Sx.
A. Sx.
T. Sx. 1
T. Sx. 2
B. Sx.
Tpt. 1
Tpt. 2
Tpt. 3
Tpt. 4
to open
to open
Tbn. 1
Tbn. 2
Tbn. 3
B. Tbn.
Pno.
Bass
D. S.
Saxes
Tpts
Tbns.
42
43
44
45
46
47

49
rhythmically augmented & transposed version of PG1/RC1
53
Coda or C Section & Solo send Off
etc.
1.
2.
S. Sx.
A. Sx.
T. Sx. 1
T. Sx. 2
B. Sx.
anticipates transposition of PG1
open
Tpt. 1
Tpt. 2
Tpt. 3
Tpt. 4
to trumpet
Trumpet
mf
Tbn. 1
Tbn. 2
Tbn. 3
B. Tbn.
A♭maj7 Cm7 E♭maj7 Gm7
Pno.
p
progression in major and minor 3rds
alternating major and minor 7th chords
account for all pitches in Ab major scale
Bass
D. S.
Saxes
Tpts
Tbns.
48 49 50 51 52 53 54

material based on PG2 reminiscent of Coltrane's A Love Supreme
*See text for explnation of this polychord chord resolves from consonant to dissonent
variation in triplet rhythm avoids duplication of rhythm across the brass
S. Sx.
A. Sx.
T. Sx. 1
T. Sx. 2
B. Sx.
Tpt. 1
Tpt. 2
Tpt. 3
Tpt. 4
Tbn. 1
Tbn. 2
Tbn. 3
B. Tbn.
B♭m7 D♭maj7 Fm7
Pno.
Bass
Light fill
D. S.
Saxes
Tpts
Tbns.
See text for explanation
55
56
57
58
59
60
61
62

65
nature of isorhythmic bass line obscures bar lines throughout solo section
Play 3x's
S. Sx.
A. Sx.
T. Sx. 1
G♯m11
T. Sx. 2
B. Sx.
(1st x only)
Tpt. 1
Tpt. 2
Tpt. 3
Tpt. 4
ff
to Fl.
Tbn. 1
Tbn. 2
Tbn. 3
B. Tbn.
Em11
Pno.
65
E Dorian Isorhythm repeats every 2 measures but the 6 pitch shape repeats every 2-1/2 bars
Bass
Harder (tenor solo)
D. S.
Saxes
Tpts
Tbns.
63
64
65
66
67
68
69
70

77
S. Sx.
A. Sx.
T. Sx. 1
G♯m11
G♯m11
T. Sx. 2
B. Sx.
Close position
flugel bkgrnd voicings see detail below
Tpt. 1
Tpt. 2
Tpt. 3
Tpt. 4
Fl.
mp
Notice now t-bone bkgrnd gradually expands from 1 note of PG1 to the entire motive
Tbn. 1
Tbn. 2
Tbn. 3
B. Tbn.
ppp
f
pp
ff
Pno.
Em11
Em11
Isorhythm continues - ascending line forms incomplete E Dorian or Aeolian scale
Isorhythm continues
Bass
D. S.
4-note tpt. chords derived from E Dorian mode
Saxes
Em(add2)
Tpts
Tbns.
71
72
73
74
75
76
77
78
79

Background material based on PG1 as indicated -
Trombones in call-response with flugelhorns & Saxes
chord symbols added to flugels for analysis only
S. Sx.
A. Sx.
T. Sx. 1
T. Sx. 2
B. Sx.
Tpt. 1
Tpt. 2
Tpt. 3
Tpt. 4
Amaj7 Cmaj7 B(add4)
2 notes
incomplete PG1 missing 3rd pitch
PG1
Tbn. 1
Tbn. 2
Tbn. 3
B. Tbn.
Pno.
Bass
D. S.
Top trumpet voice refers
back to B section material
Saxes
Tpts
Tbns.
Bm(♭6) A7
Bm(add2) C♯o
add D
Gmaj7 B♭maj7 A7(add4)
80
81
82
83
84
85
86

Mode transposition to 3rd mode of Eb melodic minor
each time a new preface is added to the PG1 bkgrnd in saxes & Tbns. as indicated below
PG1
89
PG1 answer to T-Bones transposed a 4th
Preface
PG1
13
S. Sx.
A. Sx.
T. Sx. 1
T. Sx. 2
B. Sx.
Abmaj7(#5)
Tpt. 1
Tpt. 2
Tpt. 3
Tpt. 4
to trumpet
P
PG1 in new key
Preface added to PG1
Preface added to PG1
Tbn. 1
Tbn. 2
Tbn. 3
B. Tbn.
Gbmaj7(#5)
Pno.
89
Same isorhythm in new mode defined by new pitches
Bass
D. S.
Call-Response style between saxes and Tbns.
A9(add4)
A(add4)
A9(add4)
Dmaj7
Saxes
Tpts
Tbns.
87
88
89
90
91
92

Preface
PG1
Preface
PG1
Preface
PG1
S. Sx.
A. Sx.
A♭maj7(♯5)
T. Sx. 1
T. Sx. 2
B. Sx.
Tpt. 1
Tpt. 2
Tpt. 3
Tpt. 4
Preface added to PG1
Preface added to PG1
Preface added to PG1
Tbn. 1
Tbn. 2
Tbn. 3
B. Tbn.
G♭maj7(♯5)
Pno.
Bass
D. S.
Saxes
Tpts
Tbns.
93
94
95
96
97
98

See text for harmonic analysis of polychords.
Melodic material based on PG1.
tenor sax solo concludes over F# Phrygian
15
Preface
PG1
101
S. Sx.
A. Sx.
T. Sx. 1
T. Sx. 2
B. Sx.
Tpt. 1
Tpt. 2
Tpt. 3
Tpt. 4
Trumpet
to Fl.
Complete PG1
Preface
Tbn. 1
Tbn. 2
Tbn. 3
B. Tbn.
Pno.
Bass
D. S.
Saxes
Tpts
Tbns.

Ens. chorale using only 4 voices planing primarily
G flat major scale see text for more detail

deviates from tonality briefly
S. Sx.
A. Sx.
T. Sx. 1
T. Sx. 2
B. Sx.
Tpt. 1
Tpt. 2
Tpt. 3
Tpt. 4
Tbn. 1
Tbn. 2
Tbn. 3
B. Tbn.
Pno.
Bass
D. S.
Saxes
Tpts
Tbns.
Even
swing
115
116
117
118
119
120

121 Development Section

Beginning of call-response, soloists "testifying" with ens pentatonic response
See text for more detail on this "shout chorus"

G as 6th serves as substitute tone for 5th

response and progression transposed up minor 2nd

Melodic line transposed up minor 2nd while harmonic accompaniment transposed a tritone which gives new identity to melodic line

Melodic line and progression transposed up minor 2nd & harmonized with major 6th
solo exchanges compressed to 1 bar
139
S. Sx.
A. Sx.
T. Sx. 1
T. Sx. 2
B. Sx.
Tpt. 1
Tpt. 2
Tpt. 3
Tpt. 4
Tbn. 1
Tbn. 2
Tbn. 3
B. Tbn.
Pno.
Bass
D. S.
Saxes
Tpts
Tbns.
C7(sus4)
B♭7(sus4)
F♯7(sus4)
D♭maj7(♯11)
E♭7(sus4)
Dmaj7(♯11)
E7(sus4)
138
139
140
141
142
143
144
145

3/4 ens figures adds to ever increasing frenzy, much like religious revival meeting call-response exchanges compressed further to 2/4 bars; melodic gesture abbreviated & shortened through rhythmic diminution

157

Ens. takes over completely with overlaping gestures
S. Sx.
A. Sx.
T. Sx. 1
T. Sx. 2
B. Sx.
E7(sus4)
Tpt. 1
Tpt. 2
Tpt. 3
D7(sus4)
Tpt. 4
Tbn. 1
Tbn. 2
Tbn. 3
B. Tbn.
Pno.
B♭7(sus4) G♭maj7(♯11) A♭7(sus4) B♭7(sus4) G♭maj7(♯11) A♭7(sus4) A7(sus4) Gmaj7 F♯m7(♭13) Em7 A♭maj7 D♭maj7 Bmaj7(♯5) E♭/E D♭/D
Bass
D. S.
Ens. takes over completely with overlaping gestures
Saxes
Tpts
Tbns.
161 162 163 164 165 166 167 168

Dense polychord at this dramatic high point
173
New bass isorhythmic ostinato initially reminiscent of opening isorhythm but is significantly different & accompanies closing tenor sax solo
S. Sx.
A. Sx.
F/F♯
scream!!!
G/A♭
(4)
T. Sx. 1
ff
T. Sx. 2
B. Sx.
to Harmon
Tpt. 1
to Harmon
Tpt. 2
to cup
Tpt. 3
to cup
Tpt. 4
to cup
Tbn. 1
Tbn. 2
Tbn. 3
B. Tbn.
E♭/E
E♭/E
Triads over foreign bass tones
Pno.
ff
173
new Isorhythm
Bass
ff
D. S.
ff
D♭maj7
Dmaj7
Saxes
Tpts
Tbns.
169
ff
170
171
172
173
174
175
176

S. Sx.
A. Sx.
T. Sx. 1
T. Sx. 2
B. Sx.
Tpt. 1
Tpt. 2
Tpt. 3
Tpt. 4
Tbn. 1
Tbn. 2
Tbn. 3
B. Tbn.
Pno.
Bass
D. S.
Saxes
Tpts
Tbns.
(8)
D♯/E
diminuendo to 189
B/C
diminuendo to 189
diminuendo to 189
diminuendo to 189
177
178
179
180
181
182
183

Variation on PG2 same as bar 55. This is as close as it gets to any reprise of earlier material before the final chords

Open voicings based on stacks of three 5ths a minor 2nd apart creating minor 11th chords. Aside from the few earlier polychords this section makes more full use of available voices than any other moment in the score

Composer/arranger, percussionist, and bandleader John Hollenbeck

Chapter 5

John Hollenbeck – "A Blessing"

"Musical chameleon" is a good way to describe John Hollenbeck. His work as a composer and percussionist has been described as genre crossing, blending elements that could be labeled as new music and world music with jazz. Because he draws on influences that may on the surface have little to do with music, no two Hollenbeck pieces sound the same, and this is by design. While his music occasionally demonstrates influences from other composers, no one could ever label his work as derivative and anything but original. His style is uncompromising and beyond categorization, with a unique vocabulary enriched by an astounding sense of rhythmic variety that leads his music to disregard bar lines and meter signatures. Hollenbeck's eclectic influences as a composer provide an unparalleled freshness full of surprises for the listener.

Before moving to New York City in the early 1990s, Hollenbeck earned degrees from the Eastman School of Music, where he studied beginning arranging with Ray Wright. It was in New York that he first fell under the influence of his most important mentors, jazz composer and valve trombonist Bob Brookmeyer, whom he studied with in Holland and New Hampshire when Brookmeyer returned home, and composer/choreographer Meredith Monk. Hollenbeck became Brookmeyer's drummer of choice, participating in every recording Brookmeyer and his innovative European New Art Orchestra made, and became the unmistakable ambidextrous motor of this contemporary big band.

Hollenbeck composes and performs for several different ensembles, showcasing his music with the genre hopping and award winning Claudia Quintet, the Refuge Trio, and the John Hollenbeck Large Ensemble. Make note of the fact that even in his big band, the term "jazz" is not used. While many of the key ingredients associated with this American genre are present in the Large Ensemble, one could hardly compare it to what is expected from a typical jazz big band.

His most prolific medium has been with the Claudia Quintet (sometimes sextet), releasing to date eight recordings since their first release in 2001. Despite the financial challenges contemporary large ensemble leaders face, Hollenbeck has released three recordings with his American based Large Ensemble, two receiving Grammy nominations. Because of his elevated profile throughout Europe, teaching in Berlin for many years and performing throughout the continent, Hollenbeck has released two albums with the Frankfurt Radio Big Band (Germany), including one nominated for a Grammy for vocal arrangements. He has also released recordings with the French Orchestra National de Jazz and the Jazz Big Band of Graz (Austria). His discography indicates numerous other recordings classified as contemporary chamber music collaborations.

The extraordinary vocalist Theo Bleckmann, a longtime collaborator, is heard on many Hollenbeck recordings, including the score included in this study, where he adds an ethereal, mystical quality to an otherwise uniquely original work.

Hollenbeck has received prizes, commissions, and accolades from around the globe, including four Grammy nominations, the 2012 Doris Duke Performing Artist Award, the 2010 ASCAP Jazz Vanguard Award, and a 2007 Guggenheim Fellowship. He has received Meet the Composer Grants and recognition in the *DownBeat* magazine Critic's Polls in the Rising Star Arranger and Big Band categories.

John has divided his time between two continents for over a decade, serving as professor of jazz drums and improvisation at the Jazz Institute Berlin until joining the Schulich School of Music faculty at Canada's McGill University in Montreal. He continues to maintain a busy touring schedule with the collection of Hollenbeck led ensembles and as a collaborative composer.

Selected Discography

John Hollenbeck Large Ensemble

Eternal Interlude – Sunnyside Records, 2009

A Blessing – Omnitone, 2005 (reissued, GPE Records, 2017)

All Can Work – New Amsterdam Records, 2018

Other Big Band Recordings

Joys and Desires – Jazz Big Band Graz – Intuition Records, 2005

Shut Up and Dance – Orchestre National de Jazz – Bee Jazz, 2010

Songs I Like a Lot – Frankfurt Radio Big Band – Sunnyside Records, 2013

Songs We Like a Lot – Frankfurt Radio Big Band – Sunnyside Records, 2015

The Claudia Quintet

The Claudia Quintet – CRI/Blueshift, 2001

I, Claudia – Cuneiform Records, 2004

Semi-Formal – Cuneiform Records, 2005

For – Cuneiform Records, 2007

Rainbow Jimmies – GPE Records, 2009

Royal Toast – Cuneiform Records, 2010

What Is Beautiful Featuring Kurt Elling and Theo Bleckmann – Cuneiform Records, 2011

September – Cuneiform Records, 2013

Super Petite – Cuneiform Records, 2016

"A Blessing"

Selecting a score for this case study was no less challenging than considering scores by any of the other featured composers. "A Blessing," the subject of this discussion and analysis, is considered by some to be a breakout moment for Hollenbeck. While it's been suggested that every Hollenbeck score is as unique and different as the subject matter that inspires them, many of his identifying characteristics are evident in this epic score, as are influences from Kenny Wheeler and mentor Bob Brookmeyer. The unique aspects of this score warrant special treatment that will deviate somewhat from the approach used in the analysis of previous scores.

Melodic Overview

Perhaps the most impressive aspect of this score, and there are many, is that nearly all of the melodic material in its 16 minutes is derived from the opening 2 minute and 36 second song. During this time vocalist Theo Bleckmann, accompanied by a sparse modal and mystical texture, vocalizes the text of a traditional Irish blessing. The rhythm of the text and the melodic motion make this opening statement feel much like an A, B, C format in eight bar segments. Hollenbeck uses changing meter and a somewhat rubato tempo to favor the natural rhythm of the text and achieve a sense of floating, seamless phrasing. While the bass changes about every two measures, the static harmonic accompaniment and melodic phrase endings suggest that this melody is in D minor, though there is no specified key indicated.

In setting this simple text to melody, the composer used larger ascending leaps to express the optimistic aspects of these lyrics and to also help offset the beginnings of phrases. Take, for example, the optimistic implications of the melodic leap from measures 8 to 9, "May the Sun-shine," a phrase that occurs again a few measures later. This same ascending leap at a slower rhythmic pace adds even more emphasis to the text in the final section – "May God Hold You." As this song comes to a close, the melody descends to its lowest phrase – "of his hand" – which reflects back to the end of the first phrase at m.3.

Following this song, Hollenbeck uses transitional material featuring clarinet and piano to migrate to a new key of F minor, which he essentially adheres to through the balance of the piece. Taking this transposition into account, the melodic material introduced in the initial song accounts for more than 80 percent of the entire piece. Through various manipulations, including rhythmic augmentation and diminution, retrograde, retrograde inversion, transposition, fragmentation, and contrapuntal layering of new melodic representations creating ever-changing harmonic relationships, the composer creates an evolving musical narrative through a series of variations. All of the pitch material used throughout these variations is based on source material and the intervallic relationships stated in this simple song.

Song Lead Sheet

Example 5.1

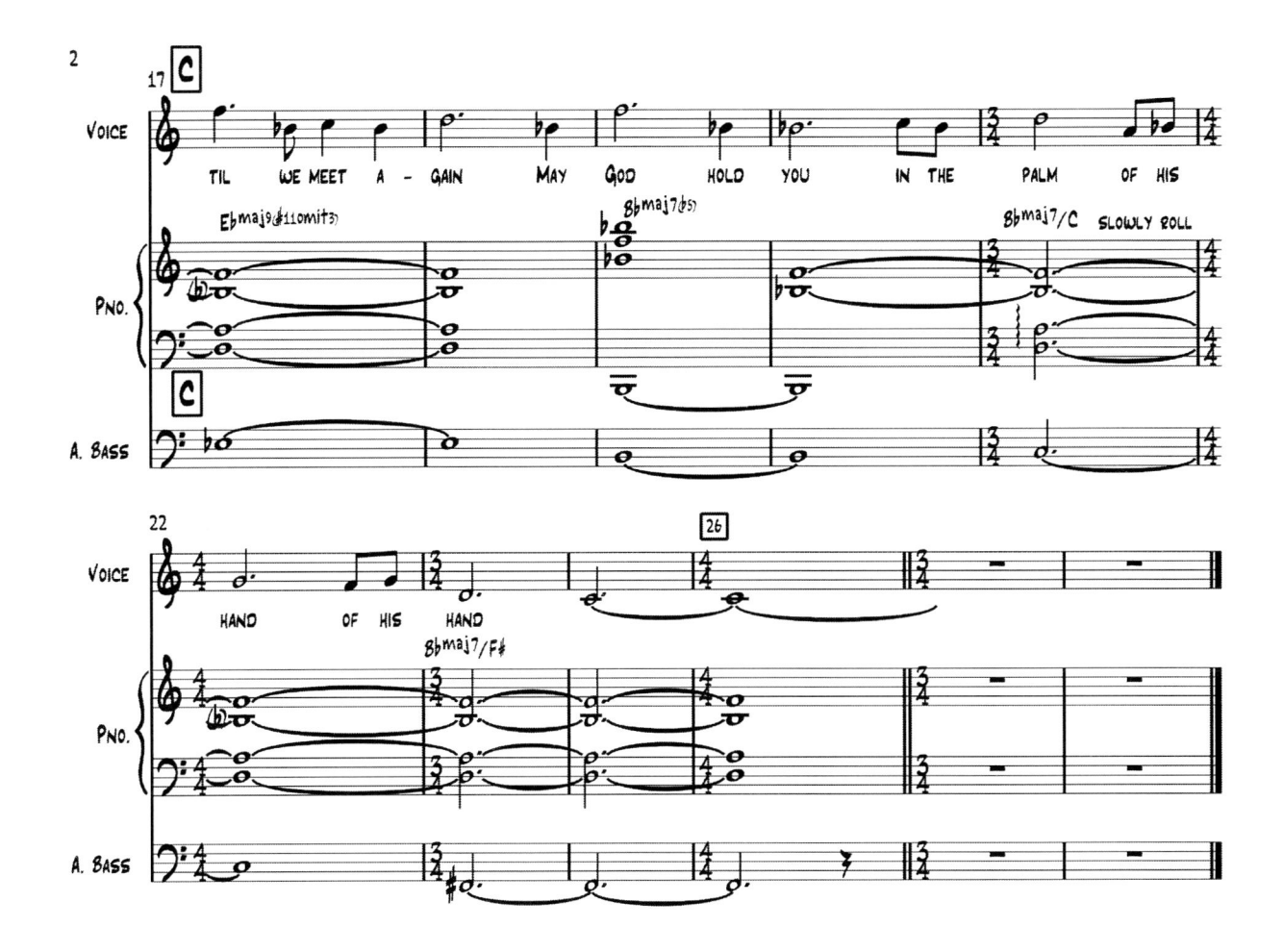

Harmonic Overview

There is little to discuss regarding the harmonic aspects of the initial song, since the harmony is static and modal. There is, however, a changing role that the four note harmony, a Dmi$^{(\flat 6)}$ (or ♯5) chord sustained throughout, plays, since the bass pitch under it changes every two bars. For example, in measures 2–4 it seems more like a B♭Ma^7 than the Dmi$^{(\flat 6)}$. The arrangement of stacked fifths a minor 2nd apart produces perhaps the most interesting of all possible major seventh chord voicings. The appearance of the E bass in both first and second endings establishes a dissonant tritone relationship with this static harmony (B♭Ma^7/E bass). This dissonance resolves to consonance throughout letter B, with bass notes creating a B♭Ma^7 chord in second inversion and the related sub-mediant Gmi^9 in bars 11–12 and 15–16. This harmonic drone (Dmi$^{(\flat 6)}$) is given additional new identities at m.17, where the bass notes change, first to E♭, then to B, C, and F♯. The shape of this bass motion is similar to that of the melody in measures 21–23, though this is likely coincidental and unplanned. In either case, these changing bass notes re-identify the harmonic drone as E♭Ma$^{9(\sharp 11)}$ with no 3rd, B♭Ma^7/B, B♭Ma^7/C, and the final restless B♭$^{\text{omit 3}}$/DMa. This final, unsettling harmony leaves the listener yearning for more and helps to segue to a transitional section and key change.

In considering the harmonies and chord symbols provided for the soloist later in the score, the composer told me, "I actually never think about [chord] changes … the harmony comes and then I try to figure out if there is a way to write it that is easily interpreted. Chord changes are problematic because I'm attracted to all the sounds that chord changes can't adequately name." This is much the same challenge that other composers featured in this study faced. It is a greater problem in solo sections than it is in the body of a composition, where such indescribable harmonies can be spelled out with pitches. Harmonic aspects of this piece will be discussed in more depth in the upcoming section, which looks more carefully at the entire arrangement and full score.

The Arrangement

Overview

"At this point in my life, I'm not a fan of most big band music." That is what Hollenbeck told a group of composers and arrangers at a 2017 gathering of the International Society of Jazz Arrangers and Composers, who met in Tampa, Florida. He seemed to have had a full dose of the typical big band arrangement in his early years and has moved as far away from the predictability that is often associated with such arrangements. He thrives on the unpredictable and the excitement of creating something that breaks the mold, even his own, each time he composes a new work. When writing for his big band, which he purposely calls his "Large Ensemble," ignoring the word "jazz," Hollenbeck thinks of it more in terms of a wind ensemble. He purposely tries to avoid what he sees as trappings of establishing a "Hollenbeck sound."

"A Blessing" is far from the traditional big band compositions that the composer became bored with, though its instrumentation follows the time tested model very closely. Exceptions to the rule are the added mallet percussionist and sometimes wordless vocalist. But even when he uses an instrument as commonplace as the vibraphone, he does something unusual by instructing the player to use a violin bow across the bars to achieve an eerie, sustained soaring timbre. Vocalist Theo Bleckmann, a frequent musical collaborator, is aptly described as an atypical vocalist more reminiscent of the high male vocals in 1960s pop groups or high countertenor than the typical big band singer. Woodwind doubles, including flute and clarinet along with soprano saxophone, muted brass and flugelhorns, help to provide a wind ensemble–like quality throughout the score.

Influences from Kenny Wheeler (utilizing wordless vocal as another instrument), Bob Brookmeyer (ideas about when and how to introduce an improvising soloist as well as melodic development techniques and working with only three voices), and the minimalist classical composers are apparent in this score. But the composer absorbed these influences without losing his own identity. Never once is there any sense of appropriation.

The piece unfolds very slowly, beginning with a spare $Dmi^{(\flat 6)}$ harmonic drone created by piano and bowed vibraphone, along with a chorus of wind players humming a pitch from this harmony (though it is nearly inaudible on the recording). This sonic combination generates a scrim-like texture from which Bleckmann emerges with the prayer song. The song is only reintroduced, and in a different key, at the very end of the piece, by which time most listeners might have already forgotten it. It is this song melody that serves as the basis for endless variations through classic manipulation techniques discussed in more detail later and highlighted on the full score analysis. Hollenbeck treats the song material like a Slinky, first stretching the melodic phrases before gradually compacting them, all the while applying numerous compositional techniques to vary the original modal song. Each variation, and there are five, or six counting the solo section, adds instrumental voices while adding density through cross choir unison and octave doubling of melodic lines. Variations are separated by brief interludes that serve as aural palate cleansers to prepare the listener for the next variation.

This piece is all about melody and much less about harmony, which is used only as sparse accompaniment and to provide new, changing tonal identities to the melodic lines as bass pitches and/or supporting harmonies change.

More detailed analysis can be found throughout the full score and the narrative that follows. Additional bar by bar, note by note analysis seemed to be unnecessary and would leave nothing to the curiosity of the reader. The score is like a map to a treasure hunt in that the origins of nearly every bar can be traced to its song antecedent, but this analysis will not divulge all of the melodic variations and relationships.

Form

The piece follows the shape of waves or series of arcs, with each section building to a new plateau before being interrupted by brief transitions between variations. The following outline should be useful in grasping the overall architecture and shape of this lengthy concert piece. Numbers at the top of this timeline indicate measure numbers and timings.

Example 5.2

0-0:31	[2] 0:32	[26] 2:28
Introductory Drone	Song — Poem sung rubato by vocalist	Interlude —rubato
Fermata over sustained Dbmi(b6)	Accompanied by sustained rhythm section and humming	Clarinet and Piano
1 bar	*24 bars*	*16 bars*

[40] 3:00	[59] 3:36	[68] 3:57
Piano	Accelerando	Variation 1
Facilitates modulation to new key	Rhythm section introduces 2 chord gesture	Voice, Flute and Clarinet accompanied by 2 chord piano gesture in call-response; sustained brass pads are added
18 bars	*8 bars*	*56 bars*

[125] 5:52	[149] 6:11	[153] 6:25
Variation 2	Brief Transition	Variation 3
Longer phrases and smaller rhythmic values; added woodwinds for thicker orchestration	Sustained AbMa7/Db	Further diminution and melodic variations; longer lines, added layers & brief key shifts builds to solo
23 bars	*3 bars*	*60 bars*

[214] 7:57	[268] 9:46	[305] 11:24
Improvised Soprano Sax solo	Variation 4	Variation 5
Sustained bkgrnds followed by thematic melodic fragments	Juxtaposed melodic fragments in shifting meters building to variation 5	3 different voices in counterpoint based on further melodic & rhythmic variations; dense, thick linear texture
7 bars	*96 bars*	*62 bars*

[368] 12:03	[390] 13:51
Transition-Reduction	Recap of Song
Begins to simplify melodic & rhythmic motion, settling on mi triad with flat 6	Accompaniment using initial mi triad with flat 6 thins to end
21 bars	*23 bars*

Digital audio analysis provides an even better view of how this piece unfolds. Notice how each section, or variation, as they are described in this analysis, builds in intensity, with variation five being the densest for the longest period of time. The scale at the top indicates real time. Notice how the composer set the text so that the highest peak in the song occurs on the word "God."

Example 5.3

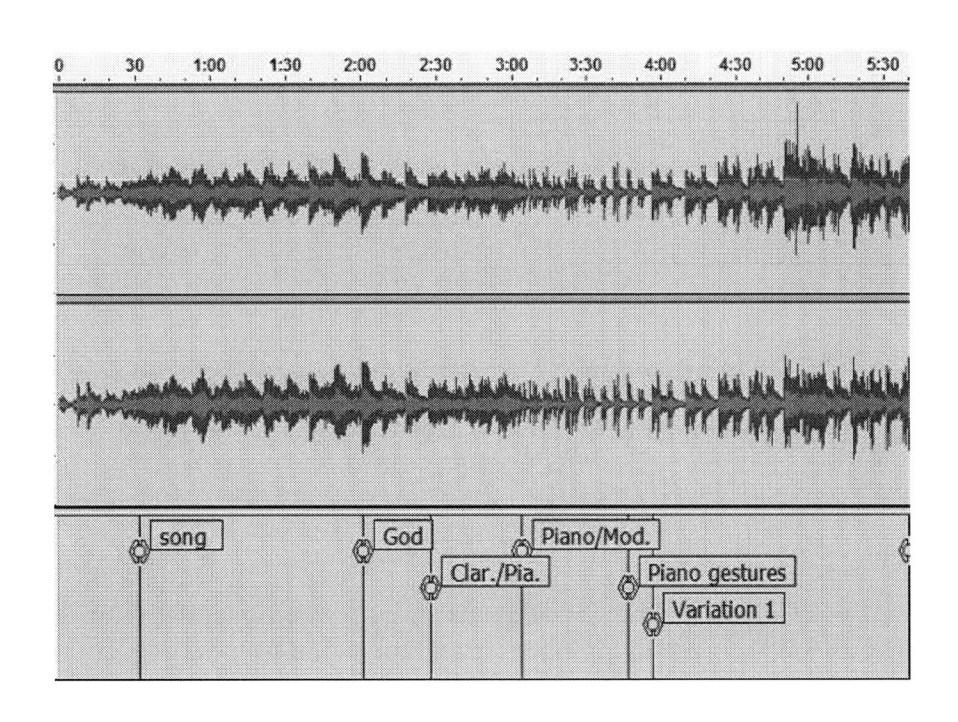

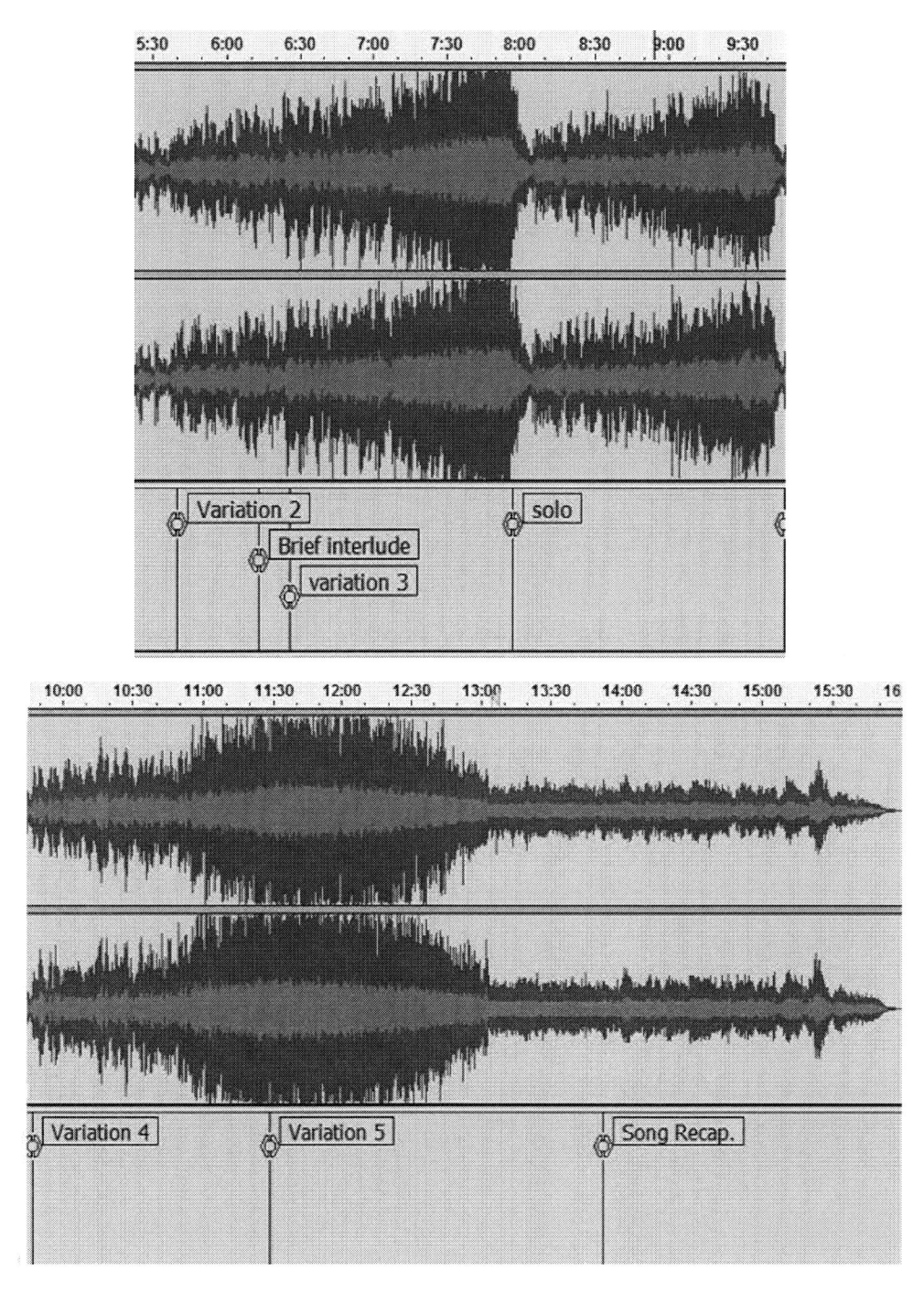

Example 5.3 demonstrates that, aside from the gradual build in intensity to the solo section, the climax to the piece occurs around 75 percent of the way through before gradually winding down to the song recapitulation.

Melodic Elements

As suggested, this piece is all about melodic development, but never exceeding more than three different simultaneous voices (pitches) plus sparse melodic accompaniment. It is not the intent to provide a bar by bar analysis here but only to point out some of the many ways the composer has applied various techniques. The following example illustrates how Hollenbeck applied rhythmic augmentation to phrases in the original song to create the first variation. He also applied combinations of techniques such as retrograde and reordering of pitches to achieve variations. Regardless of the key change, the similarity of intervallic shapes should be obvious. The original song that serves as source material for this first variation is always shown first, with the variation under it for comparison. The numbers at the bottom of excerpts indicate scale degree numbers, which will make the comparison easier given that the original song is stated in D minor and the variations are in the key of F minor. Original bar numbers appear at the top of the staff. The bracketed portion shows the specific section under comparison.

Example 5.4

The composer never planned the sections of this piece as variations on a theme, but the application of this term to describe how the piece evolves seems to provide a logical approach in helping to understand its development. Example 5.5 shows how similar melodic development techniques were carried through in crafting each of the five variations. Notice how variations 1 and 2 apply rhythmic augmentation to the original song, which has been transposed here to F minor to facilitate easy comparison and, in the case of the original song melody, re-barred to remain in 3/4 meter. To the contrary, the melody in variation 3 has been rhythmically compressed (diminution) to the point that six measures of the original melody appear in only two bars. The fragmented 4th variation leaves out notes and substitutes rests by comparison to the original song melody. In the case of variations 1 through 4 there remains a common sense of phrases strung together, much like the original song melody; however, by the final variation there are absolutely no rests to set off a melodic phrase and the pitch material is orchestrated so the variation is one long line with no breaks.

Example 5.5

Not all of the melodic phrases begin on downbeats, as illustrated in the following example showing how the entrance of a melodic phrase has been shifted to an upbeat.

Example 5.6

The fifth and final variation begins at m.305 and appears almost like a two voice fugue or simple round before evolving further to three different voices, all based on manipulations of the original song melody.

Example 5.7

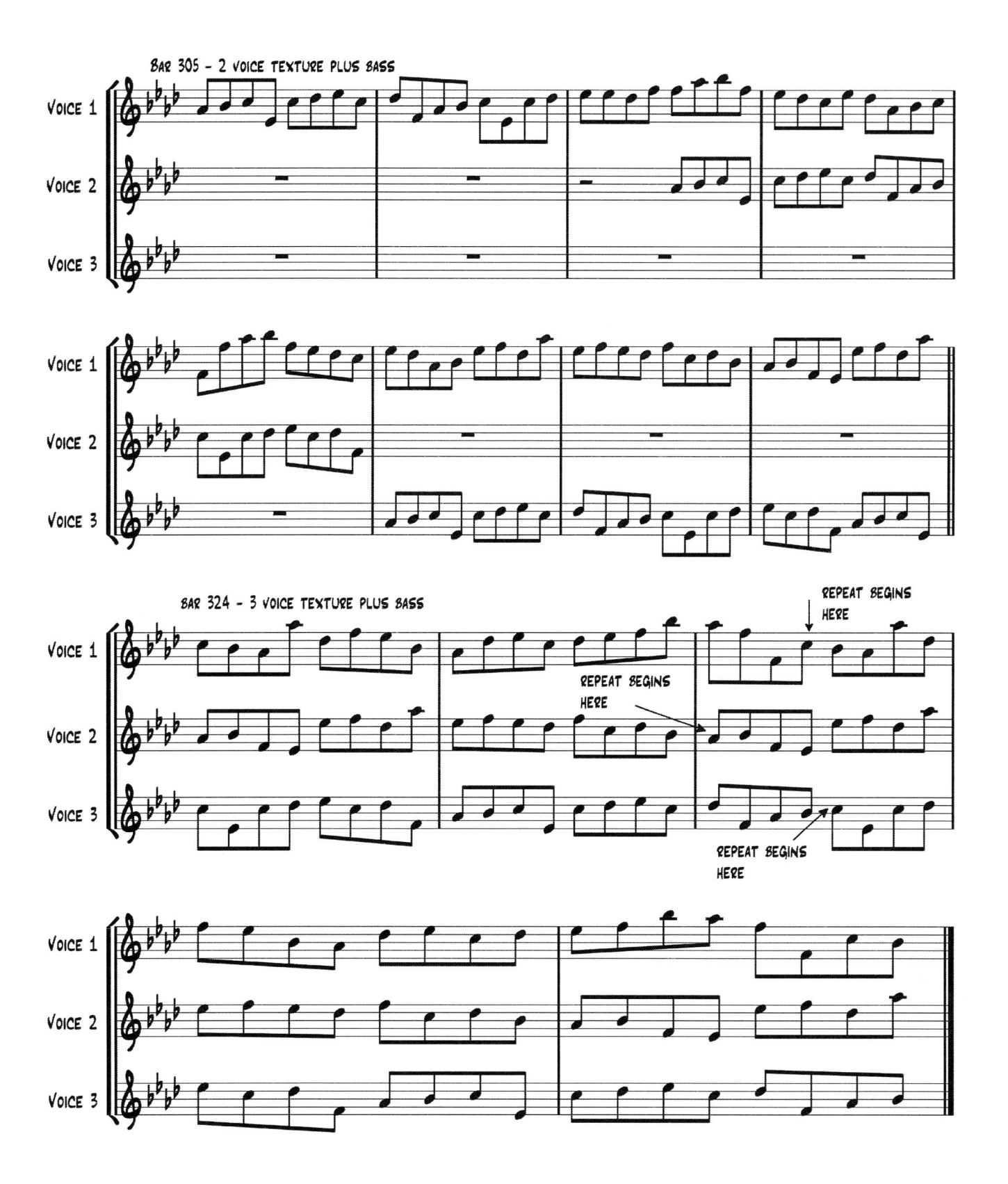

It was necessary for the composer to reduce the activity of this final, dense variation in order to facilitate a return to the original song. This was accomplished by gradually reducing the intervallic motion in each voice to only a few reoccurring pitches, which becomes apparent in m.362, where this sense of winding down begins. The eventual goal is for each instrumental voice to land on a single pitch from the Fmi$^{(\flat 6)}$ undulating chord, which is accomplished by m.386. Much like the accompaniment to the opening statement of the song, this recapitulation uses the same voicing and undulating harmonic drone but in F minor, and this time all instruments are involved, improvising a rhythm by gradually elongating the composer's suggested rhythm on an assigned single pitch. Gradually, it seems, based on the recording, players fade to nothing, dropping out completely as the piece comes to a close. By focusing on only the trombone section, Example 5.8 abbreviates the conclusion of this final variation to illustrate how the design works in leading to the recapitulation of the song.

Example 5.8

Brief chromatic excursions that resemble the improviser's practice of sidestepping (purposeful movement away from a given chord that provides momentary dissonance usually resolved) are almost essential as temporary diversions from potential listener fatigue that might stem from minimalistic music. Example 5.9 shows one such example, and there are many more.

Example 5.9

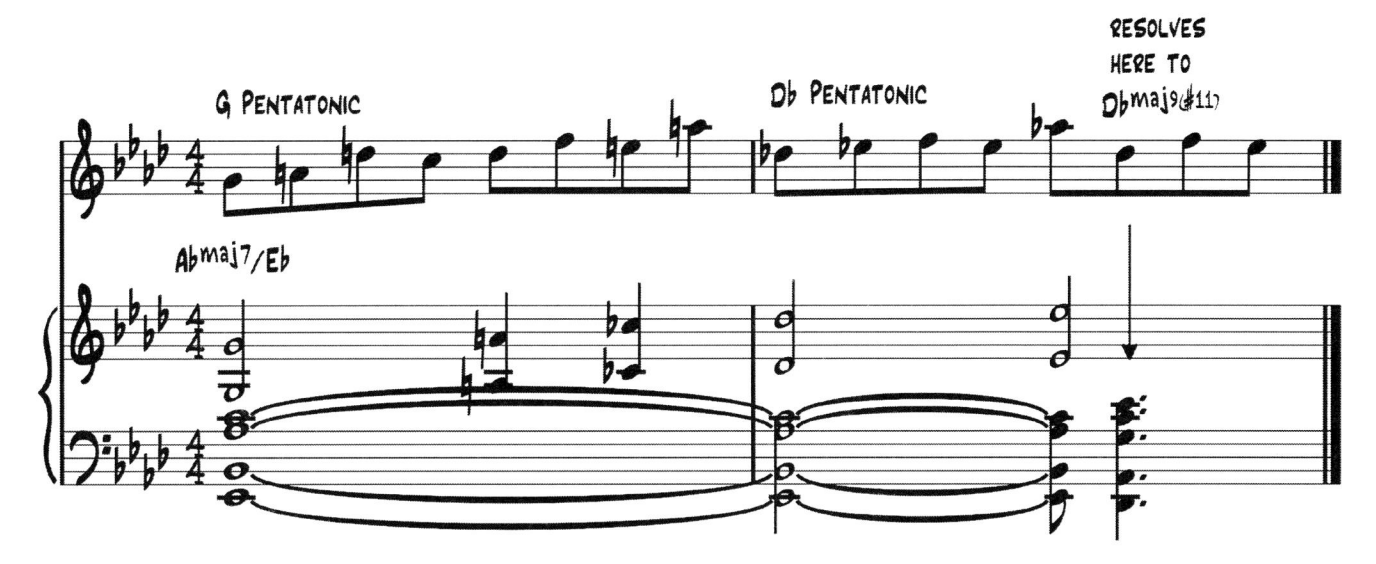

Additional analysis is provided in the complete concert score included in this chapter. Since the composer always works in concert scores, and in an effort to keep page count to a minimum, it seemed unnecessary to include a transposed score.

Harmonic Elements

Harmony throughout this piece provides yet another sense of spontaneity and improvisation, since it is somewhat organic, largely modal, and not at all bound to the expectations that accompany functional harmonic motion. Aside from the brief piano interlude at measures 41–58 composed in an improvisatory chordal style, the re-appearance of harmony following the initial song is gradual and often vague with quartal or quintal open voiced stacks and groups of pitches without any identifying third. Not one chord symbol is used until the solo section, where these are provided for convenience to the soloist. While there are root movements that are often stepwise and therefore strong, the closest thing to cadence points are those cited in Example 5.9 and the two chord gestures that accompany several variations. Examples of these cadence points follow. Bear in mind that it is the melody in these examples that helps to fill in missing voices that actually identify the chord.

Example 5.10

Measures 211–213: $AMa^7-B^{6/9\ (no\ 3rd)}-Cmi^{11}$

This same ascending cadence–like progression is found at the end of the chord progression given to the soloist through m.263 before it resolves further and back to $D\flat Ma^7$.

The composer uses the following two chord gestures as accompaniment to variations 1 through 3 in a question-answer style, with the melodic line as shown in Examples 5.11a–e.

Examples 5.11a–e

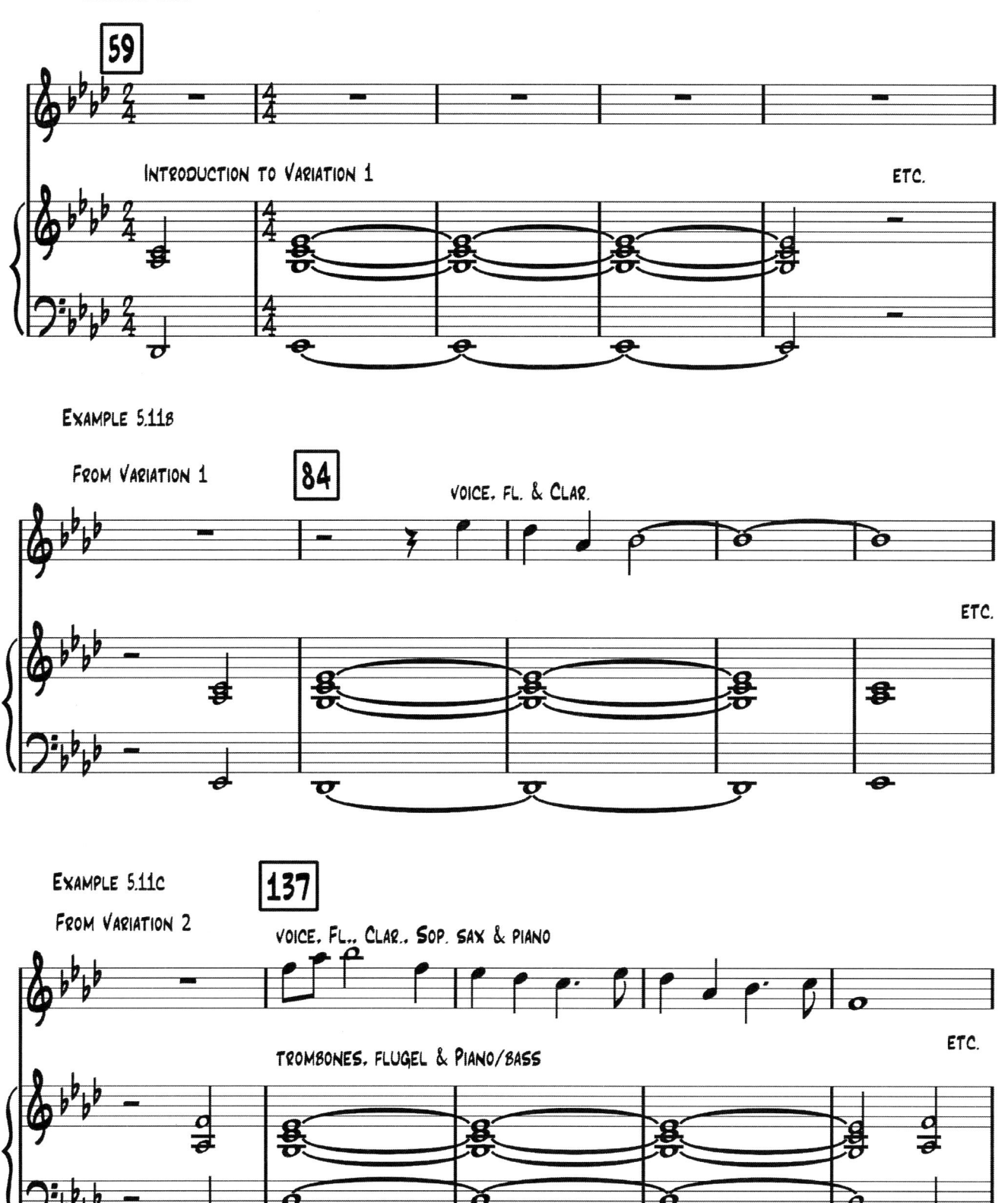

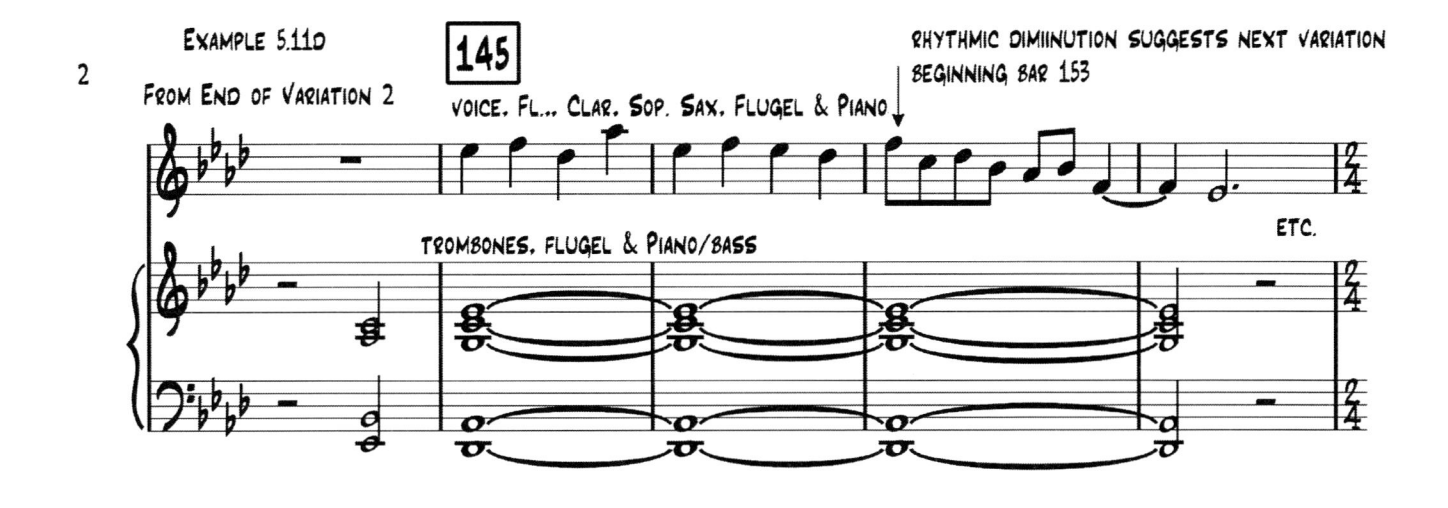

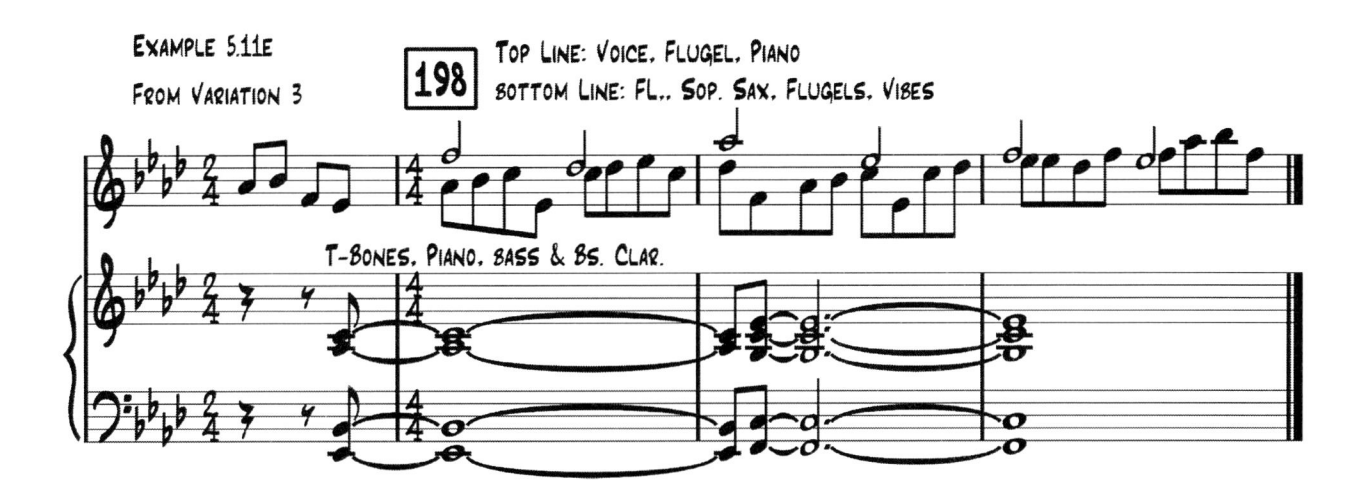

In the true Hollenbeck tradition there is no predictable harmonic design, and this keeps the listener always guessing and surprised by the unexpected.

As previously suggested, Hollenbeck provides a new tonal identity from time to time by using bass notes from another tonality, stepping away from F minor. A few examples appear as follows. Chord symbols shown are offered for analysis' sake and are not in the score. Some pitches have been enharmonically respelled to aid in clarity of analysis.

Example 5.12

It is not unusual in this score to see such out-of-key excursions move by tritone, which seems to be an important intervallic relationship throughout the piece.

The last example of bass lines that appear foreign to the home key can be seen from measures 305 to 324, where the following bass line moves in apparent random fashion toward the target goal of C–B natural. The excerpt below has been rhythmically simplified and abbreviated. The full score at this point shows no harmony through this section other than incidental harmony that is caused by the vertical collision of eighth note lines in the winds. In an interview with the composer I learned that this bass line was conceived largely as a means of moving toward the target low C and B natural in the bass because the particular bassist who premiered the piece had a bass with this extended range, and Hollenbeck wanted to take advantage of this feature.

Example 5.13

Of interest is the fact that there is no harmony or bass from m.339 until the final return of the song at measures 389–390. Only drums remain from m.339 to drive the piece to the recapitulation.

Solo Section

In an interview with the composer he divulged that this piece began as a piano piece, which explains the early interlude from measures 42 to 59, which seems less relevant to the piece and more improvisatory in nature. But in this arrangement the improvised solo section at m.214 is given to soprano saxophone. The section could be considered another variation, but an improvised one where composed thematic material takes a backseat to the soloist. Phrases based on material from the original song, however, appear in increasing frequency as the solo unfolds (measures 232, 236–237, 242–243, 248–264) but only as background material for the soloist to play off. The detail the composer provides to the soloist in this section, with specific information about background ensemble figures and when the solo is more or less important to the overall texture, is noteworthy. As with adjusting a camera lens, the depth of field constantly shifts in this section with an ever changing focal relationship of soloist to background material, or as Brookmeyer referred to them, "solo enhancements." In particular, see the score from m.232 through the end of the solo.

Example 5.14

[Musical notation: Solo Chord Progression, measures 214 onward]

The chord symbols were created only as a reference point for the soloist and not as a result of any conventional process or derived from the song. A tritone relationship between the first two chords in the reoccurring progression – D♭Ma7 and GMa7 – once again emphasizes this interval favored by the composer throughout the score.

Another interesting feature in this section is the composer's penchant for chords voiced in open 5ths and 4ths, as shown in the following example. The D♭Ma7, GMa7, and DMa7 voicings constructed of two perfect 5ths a minor second apart are exactly the same voicing Hollenbeck uses in the beginning and recapitulation of the song, where for analysis' sake they were labeled Dmi(♭6) and Fmi(♭6), respectively. This chameleon-like voicing is one of the most interesting pitch arrangements of a major 7th chord. Nearly all the voicings in this solo section are structured in open positions.

Example 5.15 – Measures 214–231

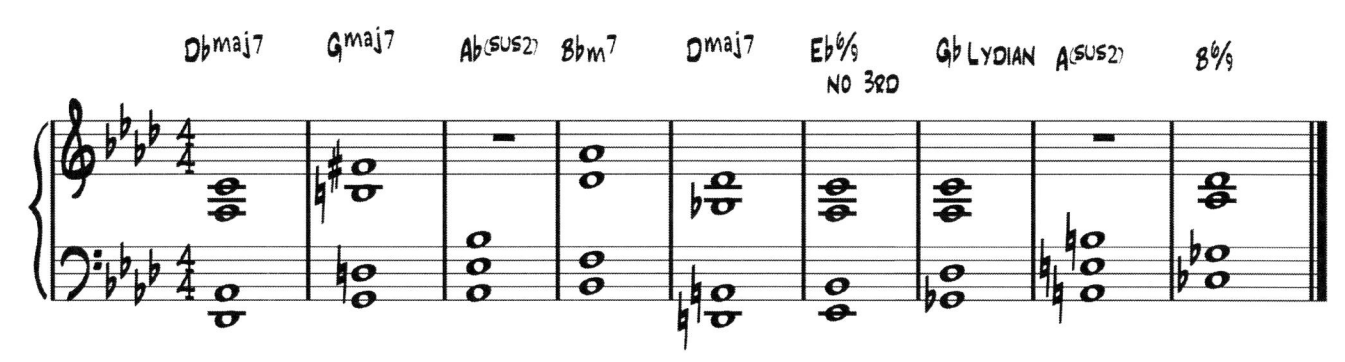

The solo section concludes much like each variation, with a four measure sustained texture that serves as an aural palate cleanser before proceeding to the next variation.

Orchestration

This score places great demands on the musicians, who likely had broad stylistic performance experiences to draw on. For example and in specific, the second and third trombonists are called upon to play very low notes as well as the challenges presented by upper register eighth note lines later in the score. Wide spacing between trombone voices is also prevalent, which presents tuning challenges. From time to time the flugelhorns are also challenged by extremely high note lines above the usual recommended top end for this instrument. Hollenbeck's approach in this regard is reminiscent of Gil Evans, who was known to orchestrate instruments in extreme, almost painful, ranges in order to achieve interesting timbres and sonic combinations that had not been heard before. It could be suggested that all four trumpet/flugelhorn players and the top three trombonists need to be principal caliber players in order to negotiate this score successfully. Passages that require long sustained brass playing, especially in the trombones, can also be very taxing.

Example 5.16

As the score becomes denser and more rhythmically active with each variation, cross section doubling of brass and woodwind melodic lines is prevalent. Harmonic pads throughout the score are largely the responsibility of the trombone and rhythm sections.

The woodwinds are employed much of the time to play melodic lines rather than voiced harmonies, with exceptions being brief interludes between variations (see m.149, for example). The saxophone section is never used in the traditional ways associated with a big band score. Instead these musicians spend most of their time playing woodwind doubles – flute, clarinet, soprano sax, and bass clarinet. The bass clarinet often reinforces double bass, left hand piano, and bass trombone notes.

The addition of pitched percussion and voice add significant color and variety. Aside from his impressive skill as a drum set player, the composer is a classically trained percussionist, so it's no surprise that mallet instruments are used throughout the score and not just as a frill.

Final Observations

Nothing about this arrangement is traditional, aside perhaps from the instrumentation, which so closely resembles a typical big band. Traditional jazz performance techniques are also absent, especially from the rhythm section. Walking bass lines, comping, swing eighth note lines, functional harmonic progressions, and so forth are all absent. Hollenbeck uses the big band more like a small wind ensemble than its historic predecessor. The score gradually moves from a sparse, mystical beginning to an ever expanding sonic landscape that culminates in a machine gun–like minimalistic texture before returning to its mystical roots. And it is difficult to imagine another drummer making this score work as well as the recording, since it requires a performer who is very sensitive to the rhythmic substructures in all parts, the complex meter changes, and the numerous subtleties throughout. Hollenbeck was meticulous in notating subtle dynamic shadings and in providing players with essential cues to indicate what is going on around them. This level of detail will be apparent in the review of the full score that follows.

Master Class Excerpt and Interview

I was fortunate to attend the first semiannual meeting of the International Society for Jazz Arrangers and Composers, held at the University of South Florida in Tampa in May 2017. John Hollenbeck was one of several outstanding guest composers in attendance, and he presented a master class and performance with his Claudia Quintet. I enjoyed the added advantage of a private interview specifically for this book. What follows is an excerpt from the master class and a transcription of my personal interview.

In response to a question from the audience during the master class, Hollenbeck spoke about his Large Ensemble and other topics:

Hollenbeck: It came down to not calling it a big band and not thinking of it as a big band. It has the same instrumentation as a big band, but it's just a large ensemble. It could be a large chamber ensemble or a wind ensemble. But thinking of it like that helped me a lot because then I didn't have to think about styles or conventions. I just think of it as a group of people, and they play these instruments, and how could [I] deal with that. So that's one thing that helped me a lot. Within that pretty traditional instrumentation that exists everywhere I just try to find a couple things that make it distinctive, that make it a little different. Having Theo Bleckmann in the band helps me stay away from what a traditional band sounds like. He can sing like an instrument, he can sing with words, and he can make sounds. Having that one musician really helped me see how to open up the music. And then having mallet percussion, nothing against guitar, got me excited about writing for the big band. It just wasn't something I'd heard that much of. I'd heard some vibes before, but this allows me to incorporate things like crotales. It also gets me closer to that wind ensemble–like vibe that I wanted. And I think I haven't even fully realized that yet. I have like ten pieces that are sort of like wind ensemble pieces.

Audience: *[Referring to "A Blessing"] Though you have trombones and all those big band sounds, you don't seem to get that traditional sound. That piece is a whole report on different things a big band can do that you don't really check out very much.*

Hollenbeck: In my band, one thing that I really think about a lot are the various groupings that exist within the whole ensemble. When you learn how to write for big bands, you first learn to treat the band sectionally. But getting back to Theo Bleckmann, when you have someone like him in your ensemble, someone who has a wide range and a great sound, you can imagine him with another person in the band, like the late Laurie Frink on trumpet, and then imagine them together. That alone could be a small group, that could be a useful sound. This approach gets you out of thinking about the trumpet section together and helps you to get to new sounds. I try to write for specific people so I actually have their sound in mind. Another aspect is that you have to let go of what you and other people have had success with. It's hard to do something new because it is possible it will be unsuccessful. So I'll say to myself, "I don't think I've ever heard anybody do this before … let me check this out." Then I'll try it and if it totally doesn't work, that's okay. I know not to do that again. Or I will break some rule that I've learned. When I was learning theory I was very frustrated because of all the rules. I understand what they're talking about now. Through trial and error, I understand that something might be an impractical idea because it is simply difficult to perform. Or it's hard to sing this particular note when someone else is singing this particular pitch. That doesn't mean you can't do it. You can still do it, but you at least know that it is difficult and you deal with the repercussions of writing something that is difficult.

Audience: *When you bring in a new piece for the large ensemble, one that you're playing on, do you hire a conductor or do you conduct from the drum set? How do you do that, because there are a lot of complexities?*

Hollenbeck: Yes. There are two real problems within that situation. One is that I can't play and conduct at the same time, and the other is that I can't be the composer and drummer at the same time. So yes, I use a conductor and that helps me a lot. I don't have to worry if someone is going to come in in the right place. I try not to worry about that at all, which helps me play better. The composer part is a little bit harder to let go, but I try to deal with that in the rehearsal situation where I can really be the composer. Then I try to let that go and just play the drums because it's pretty hard to just play the drums.

I really, really want to do something different with big band, and I'm going to try it in Montreal in July. I hope to try it, anyway. The idea would be to have a big band without a conductor where the band is not sitting and is mobile. There might be some reasons why that might be a terrible idea! But one of the things I don't like about a big band is that you have these long moments where the rhythm section and one other person is playing and the other fifteen people are just sitting there. Sometimes they can be very happy that they are sitting there. They are engaged, and as a composer I work hard at trying to engage the players, but a lot of times it looks really bizarre to me to have all those people just sitting there. I could have them playing all the time, but that has its own problems. So again, going back to the groupings, I'm thinking of when there is a grouping of, say, four trumpets, tenor sax, and trombone, that those instrumentalists could be over there [points to a place in the room] together. And the physical groupings in the space could move around according to the orchestration.

I'm going to do a new large ensemble record in June, and then after that I'm hoping to work on this new project. And I'm going to try and do it without conductor. I think what it means is that everyone has to take more responsibility. As you know, some people in some bands just don't want to count and just want to be cued.

What I found out playing with a big band is that a big band is kind of mediocre until everyone knows everyone else's part, and then it can be slammin'! I used to sub in the Village Vanguard big band and, you know, the guys that were in the band knew everyone's part, so when anyone would do something different they would stare you down! When everyone knows everyone's part you get into this special place, which is the only reason I want to have a large band because, as you probably know, running a big band just sucks! It's terrible! But when you are on stage and have that moment when everybody is in the same place and they are all playing beautifully and you can tell they are very conscious … I get chills right now just thinking about it. And that's the reason to do it, it's the only reason to do it. So not having a conductor I think will be a good thing in that it will force a lot more people to really get to know the music better and get to know each other's parts better.

Audience: *Maybe less so in your large ensemble but specifically in your Claudia Quintet music, 95 percent of jazz I've been listening to has a clear solo section and a clear beginning of that solo section and a place where it ends, and there is usually applause. We didn't get that in your Claudia Quintet music. That's a bold decision, and I want to know what led you to do that and why you like that.*

Hollenbeck: I remember there is a section in "The Blessing" where I wrote it thinking, "This will be the section that will be covered up by applause … let's see what would be appropriate for that." So I have done that before intentionally. But generally I'm not a big fan of that, though I understand for the player it might be nice. But again, what I gravitate toward naturally is not knowing … "Is that improvisation? or is that written? Or … wait, now it's definitely improv. How does that … what just happened?" For me that's what keeps me present instead of drifting away into boredom. I want to be [asking] "What's going on? … what is this? … what's happening? I really like this because I don't know what's going on!" So creating a mixture of improv and written music [is important for me]. How do you get to improv? And get out of improv? I try to meld them so you don't really know. And that gets you to the question – why is there improv? What is the formal function of an improvisation? That's why the head-solo-head form doesn't make sense to me anymore. What makes much more sense is head, solo, and then head, but the head is different now. It's in a new key, something has happened. It's evolved. It can't be the same head as you heard in the beginning because look at all that stuff that happened in between! You need something to happen in the middle, and if it does, how can you simply play the same head again? I'd much rather hear an evolution if the piece goes back to the theme.

Interview with John Hollenbeck – May 19, 2017

RL: *Who were your formal writing teachers, and what writers did you look to for inspiration? Who influenced you and your style?*

JH: My brother, Pat Hollenbeck; Bob Brookmeyer; Muhal Richard Abrams; and **Meredith Monk**.

RL: *You talked a lot earlier today about influences on your style, and I am curious if you were at all influenced by Kenny Wheeler, considering the open 5ths, modality, and the use of voice both to present a lyric and as a wordless instrument.*

JH: Yes, of course. I don't think I go there too much, and I don't feel like I have too many pieces like this ["A Blessing"]. This would be one of the few pieces that I feel like comes from two aspects of his writing – his [Kenny's] use of the voice without words as an instrument, and very simple two–three part writing where it's all trumpets in unison, trombones in unison, and saxes in unison. Obviously the whole chart isn't like that, but I did try to do that because that was a sound that I love, and I felt this tune could have that sound.

RL: *But I think you mix the orchestration within that context perhaps more than Kenny did, as much as I love his music.*

JH: Yes, yes.

RL: *In planning a piece like this, I'm curious – this is a serious sixteen minute piece, this is not a "jazz chart" – this is a pretty major work; how much organic development of music happened in the creative process, and how much of it did you have at least sketched out in your mind? You start with this basic germ that becomes the basis of the entire rest of the piece – a twenty-four bar song, which is amazing. In other words, how much material that follows the song did you have mapped out, or did you not?*

JH: I don't really remember if I had anything actually mapped out. One thing you have to deal with when you start out with a song, you know it's going to be really hard to not state the song again. But I definitely just didn't want to do the recap; what worked out is that I really based the song at the beginning and end on Theo's range. In the beginning we talked about it a lot and we found the key that he sounds very vulnerable on and not super confident – he can do it, he doesn't sound bad, but it's a vulnerable place. He has to be careful. So that was really great for the beginning. And then at the end I put him in a different key where he's much more secure, and now the band is playing this part that was just piano and vibes at the beginning, so it's much fuller. It hopefully captures the fact that something happened, has evolved. Also there is so much material in between that I think most people are like – "Oh yeah, right, that's how this piece started" [as opposed to head, solo, then head again].

RL: *That's exactly how I first heard it. I almost forgot that there was a song in the beginning.*

JH: And then after I started looking at the material, I came up with this concept where I would try to base most of the interior of the piece on the song, and at first stretch it out, and then keep compressing it. In the middle it's never actually the speed of the song. It's either much slower or much faster. It never really stays at a pace in the middle where it sounds like the original song.

I originally wrote the song on piano and performed it once with Theo, Drew Gress, and Ben Monder. Then I got this commission [IAJE Gil Evans Commission] and I wanted to showcase Theo with lyrics and also using his voice as an instrument. I wrote it for the Falconaires [Air Force Jazz Ensemble]. I checked them out and realized they had a great brass section! I also knew I needed to feature the pianist, but I didn't know him, so I chose to feature the piano but without improvisation.

I took the song apart, stretched it, fragmented it, and asked myself what else it could be. I tried to show how it evolved at the end through this process.

RL: *How do you think about when the right time for a soloist is, especially in this particular piece? There is a lot of ensemble writing in this piece, and then all of a sudden there is this great soprano sax solo emerging from the mist. And in the score you've written chord changes, which I gather you almost had to make up, which is actually the case with a number of writers I'm working with in this project. We seem to have to invent symbols because our system of symbols just doesn't work. I'm interested in your philosophy about where a solo belongs and its contribution to the piece, particularly this piece, and then how the chord changes that you did have to give him came about.*

JH: Of course Bob Brookmeyer talked about this a lot, and it was a major thing for him to instill in his students that there never had to be a solo. There doesn't have to be improvisation in a piece. After that you start thinking, if there is one it really has to have a role, it has to have a function. What do solos do? What can they do? The other thing is that he really believed that you have to force yourself to write more music than you would normally do before you come to the right moment in time for a solo. The direct opposite of a jam session, where you play a little head and then there is a huge improvisation. It's essentially the other way around. You build up this tension because usually you are a jazz band playing for a jazz audience, so they are kind of expecting something like a solo. But you keep building it up and building it up until you get ... you're looking for this place, and it's not that place where you hit a block and you can't write anymore; it's not that place, it's a place where naturally you realize that a solo would be perfect right here! Something could happen here that only a soloist could do and I can't write, and it would be really great right here. So you're always looking for that. It has a lot to do with duration and really hearing the piece in time and seeing how long this should be until it's the right moment.

As far as chord symbols, I think in this case and probably many cases, the harmony doesn't come from the tune and it's not based on functional harmony; it's a result of the development of the material. The chord symbols are just really voicings. So it's basically just showing the improviser, here are the voicings that the band is playing. Only recently have I learned that Wayne Shorter often writes voicings instead of chord symbols. There is so much start and stop in this solo and the harmony is strange enough that I expected and wanted the soloist to not just blow their brains out over it – [I wanted] more of a start and stop sort of Wayne Shorter thing. They listen to the band, then play a little and then listen – there is interaction. It's not like I made it hard but it's not so simplistic that they could just do anything over it. It's like leading them into the place where I want them to be.

RL: *One thing I noticed about the whole score is the meticulous attention to detail in the entire score. You wrote band cues in the soloist's part so that the soloist knows exactly what else is going on and where the ideal points are to emerge and make it his time. So there is this give and take, or dialogue going on. But that kind of detail exists throughout the entire score, including cues, which are so essential.*

Hollenbeck: Yes, yes!

RL: *Speaking of cues, you have the band humming in the very beginning of the piece, selecting a pitch from that open voicing [played by piano and vibes]. I didn't hear that in the recording. Is it there and I'm just not hearing it?*

JH: It might be there a little bit, but the problem is the humming is this delicate thing where if someone gets too close to the microphone it's going to be too loud. I think a couple of things happened since the time I wrote it. If we are playing in front of a "new" audience I would still play this piece, even though it is an oldie.

Now I would say I'm a little more confident in saying, "Let's go, guys, let's hear the humming." At first I realized they didn't really want to do this, and I wouldn't make them do it. And then we got into the recording studio, where it was a little bit of a problem – like how do we do this? The recording engineer always just wanted to overdub something like that and I didn't want to get into that. I think it's there a little bit on the recording, but I also think I let it go a little bit at the time. The recording is pretty old now, and it was my first session as a big band leader, so I would probably do things a little bit differently now. But it's a really nice effect live. One of the reasons that I like to do things like that is to keep the band engaged in the music. In the beginning they're picking notes from the piano, so they have to listen to the piano and try and hear those notes and hum them. And then right after that everyone is humming in unison with the bass clarinet. That one is easier and the blend of humming and bass clarinet is nice.

RL: *You have great trombone players in your band. You really challenge them. At one minute they are playing down in the basement, and in the next minute they are playing these eighth note lines that are fairly high, almost lead player lines, but written on the second or even third parts. These guys are very serious players, versatile players.*

JH: Yes, they certainly are!

RL: *Let me go in another direction. When you are writing a piece like this, or anything for that matter, do you use paper and pencil like the old days, and do you use paper without bar lines?*

JH: Yes and Yes. I think what I ended up doing in this piece was also some sort of computer Finale type manipulation that could only be done easily in Finale. I composed a lot of this on the piano. I was going between piano and paper and then putting some things in the computer, trying them out, printing them out, then going back to the piano. And I just kept moving around like that. I don't always do that and maybe I've never done that again, but it was a good process for this piece. The piece was supposed to feature this pianist who I didn't really know. The whole piece is written like a piano piece. And if you look at the piano part … [**RL:** everything is there …] Yeah. So most of the parts are just coming from the piano … a highly colorized piano sound. So because of that I wanted to write it on the piano, which I don't normally do.

RL: *The reason that I asked about that aspect of your work and the process in relation to this score is the fact that all the rhythmic hits in the bass line, which of course you reinforce on drums, in various sections throughout the piece, coupled with the changing meters, really just throws your equilibrium off, which is great. It makes it just flowing music rather than this sense of bar lines, strong beat, weak beat, and so forth; and I think when you work with paper with bar lines already there, it forces you to have to squeeze music into that space, and if you work in another way you are not bound by that visual restriction or imposition.*

JH: Yes, the downside of that, and I kind of left it this way because I'm used to it, is that I have to make a lot of bar lines and meters afterwards, and sometimes it's really hard to figure out what's better. Is it better for something to be in 4/4 and be over the bar line or if it comes on the second beat is that maybe a 5/4 bar and it's on beat one. So I made a bunch of decisions that I think were okay, but you can see how it could easily be different.

What I also wanted to say about what we were talking about before with the computer manipulation is specifically the part from after the solo to [the reappearance of] the song. That part I had some fun with in Finale, and I think it's the first time I ever did this.

I experimented with repeat signs, putting them not in the beginnings and ends of sections, but like a bar before or a bar after, just in weird places. And that created all these really interesting new phrases that came out of that. That was an exciting discovery for me.

RL: *If I'm not mistaken, that's one section where you fragment melodic material.*

JH: Yes! Just that alone sounds cool.

RL: *And you contrast the eighth note fragments with rests in between with some sustained lines, which again stem from the original tune.*

JH: Yes, yes.

RL: *What was your intent by the brief tonality/key shifts? Variety, to break away from the lengthy episodes in F minor?*

JH: Yes, to insert short breaks from the basic sound that I had been using. It is like eating some pickled ginger in between courses. Afterwards, the listener is refreshed and you can continue where you left off.

RL: *This is a bit broader topic, and you spoke a little about it in the earlier master class where you talked about the things that you do to motivate your creative process and the way you think through things where you don't even have to be at the piano. You could be sitting at Starbucks charting these ideas out. Would you attribute that process, and the different things in your life that come up, to those things that can motivate a* *piece? Would you attribute that fact, that approach, to the fact that if I hear a piece of music I may be able to safely say ... I think that's a John Hollenbeck piece, but it sure doesn't sound like anything else I've heard him do? You don't have a "thing," a sound, but you do in a way. Not like a lot of other composers where you can hear eight bars or less and draw some conclusions. Is that due to the process you apply?*

JH: Yes, at some point I started feeling strong about not repeating myself or repeating others. I felt really strongly about that and even now react very strongly when I think ... I've already heard that. This was a very natural thing. When I first started listening to the radio I couldn't really listen to anything because every piece seemed to have a backbeat on two and four. I would think, "I've already heard this piece with a backbeat on two and four. It sounds the same, or this tune sounds like this other tune." I reacted violently to it! So I realized that if I used the same process for every song there is a pretty good chance, a really good chance, that I'm going to repeat myself. And the longer that you write there's even a higher chance that you will repeat because you might not even remember what you wrote ten years ago. I've got a lot of friends who have told me – "I've written this tune and it's going real well and ... oh man, I already wrote this tune!" They totally forgot. So my theory was that by making a different process for each piece, I start differently with different material and develop it differently, I use different tools, everything is pretty different, and I'm increasing the probability that it will be its own piece. It sounds like its own thing and doesn't sound like another piece. I try to go to a place that is at least new to me and potentially new to others ... a vulnerable place, not safe. I try to write in a new way for me and stay away from others. The process is always about THIS piece, not about a style or ... I'm always looking for new things, experimental ... Every piece has its own code, process, and life.

RL: *Okay. Let me play devil's advocate just for a minute. One could say that a great painter who develops a style and is identified because of that style ... that's what made them great. They are that identifiable.*

JH: Philip Glass.

RL: *Yes, Philip is a great example. So I guess both approaches are okay by you?*

JH: Not with me. But there are a lot of composers who have developed some sort of system and they use that system maybe for the rest of their life, in the case of Stravinsky just for a period. But at some point he definitely had this feeling of needing to go somewhere else. So for me it's the same feeling, but it happens much faster. I don't like the feeling of being in the same place again and probably writing the same music again. But I do understand the non-practicality of that. So a model for me would be Ligeti, who very rarely would repeat himself and his pieces have a wide variety of styles. Every one of his piano etudes is based on some totally different thing. He would be a model, or maybe Picasso. I just really don't want to hear a piece that sounds like something I've already written.

RL: *I think you are very successful at that.*

If you were going to leave me and the readers with one suggestion about writing, what would that be? Maybe you'll have something as profound as Sammy Nestico, who replied to a similar question by saying something about the importance of learning how to use the eraser! What do you tell your students that you find yourself recycling?

JH: You have to fight to maintain openness. It's very easy to close up, which then ends up leading to repeating yourself or going to your comfort zones.

It is easy to think: "I have a deadline, so I have to use some music that I have already written." For me, I would rather miss the deadline than just write a copy of what I've done. I think you have to really fight that and also fight appropriation and derivative composing. A lot of composers are very derivative. They love this composer, so then they copy that composer. And then their pieces sound like that person's (or bad copies) and they seem to be okay with that because they love that sound. I know that most composers who hear imitations of themselves are rarely happy about it. This was a big problem for Bob Brookmeyer, since he had so many students who copied him, sometimes maybe without even knowing it!

I love the Kenny Wheeler sound, but I never wrote another piece like "A Blessing" that uses these particular orchestration ideas that I attribute to Kenny (and Bob and Bill Holman for that matter). On the new JHLE record, I include an arrangement I did of Kenny's "Heyoke." He heard it and he was very happy that I did my own thing on it! I could have easily just done his thing on his own piece and it would have been fine.

RL: *But what's the point, because he's already done that, right?*

JH: Exactly. So that's what I would say: fight to maintain openness. When you start a new piece, don't just go to your safe place but try to remain open and vulnerable, and see what possibilities come as a reward!

I know that a lot of people think in terms of style when composing. I would urge them to try to maintain a non-stylistic openness so that every piece is just about itself. Of course, I know from experience that this is very difficult!

RL: *It is, and I think it's scary.*

JH: Oh, it's super scary! It's scary for everybody. As you get older, the harder it is to maintain that openness.

RL: *Yes, the older you get, you become more and more a caricature of yourself that becomes harder and harder to avoid because you've already done all these different things.*

JH: I think one of the reasons that Philip Glass is so successful is that a lot of times when people ask him to write a piece they say, "I really love that piece that you wrote for …" With me they will say – write whatever you want, but if it were to have that thing with the trumpet and soprano sax, you know, that you did in this older piece … but write what you want! There is a lot of pressure, you know! Some composers will say, "Sure, I can do one of them again." I think Philip sees the variations in his pieces. A lot of his pieces sound very much alike to me, but I think he is okay with that, because that is his "sound."

RL: *And one final question, John. I'm curious about why you write a concert rather than transposed score, as most writers do.*

JH: I think once I saw that Ligeti writes concert scores, I thought it must be cool! It makes more sense for me that the score shows the actual pitches.

Annotated Full Score

The annotated full transposed score that follows provides additional details about "A Blessing," and includes concert pitch excerpts as reductions.

A Blessing

2001 IAJE Gil Evans Fellowship Commission

John Hollenbeck

CONCERT SCORE

9
similarity to bars 32-33
VOICE
sunshine warm u-pon your face the rains fall soft u-pon your fields May the sun shine warm u - ponyour face the rainsfall soft u-pon your fields And un-
SS/FL
CL
SS
TS/SS
BASS CL
TPT/FG 1
TPT/FG 2
FG 3
TPT/FG 4
TBN 1
TBN 2
TBN 3
BASS TBN
MALLETS
PNO
E BASS
DMS
9
10
11
12
13
14
15
16

See bars 26-27
VOICE
til we meet a - gain May God hold you in the palm of his hand of his hand
SS/FL
CL
SS
TS/SS
BASS CL
TPT/FG 1
TPT/FG 2
FG 3
TPT/FG 4
TBN 1
TBN 2
TBN 3
BASS TBN
BOWED VIBES
MALLETS
PLAY
PNO
E BASS
DMS
17
18
19
20
21
22
23
24

26
Transition & Modulation to F minor
VOICE
SS/FL
HUM with Bass Clarinet/Voice (concert pitch)
CL
PLAY (LEAD)
Transposed retrograde of bars 21/22
Transposition of bar 9
mf
SS
HUM with Bass Clarinet/Voice (concert pitch)
TS/SS
HUM with Bass Clarinet/Voice (concert pitch)
BASS CL
PLAY
mp
TPT/FG 1
HUM with Bass Clarinet/Voice (concert pitch)
TPT/FG 2
HUM with Bass Clarinet/Voice (concert pitch)
FG 3
HUM with Bass Clarinet/Voice (concert pitch)
TPT/FG 4
HUM with Bass Clarinet/Voice (concert pitch)
TBN 1
HUM with Bass Clarinet/Voice
TBN 2
HUM with Bass Clarinet/Voice
TBN 3
HUM with Bass Clarinet/Voice
BASS TBN
HUM with Bass Clarinet/Voice
MALLETS
VIBES WITH MALLETS
p
PNO
mf
E BASS
HUM with Bass Clarinet/Voice
DMS
HUM with Bass Clarinet/Voice
25
26
27
28
29
30
31
32
33
34
35
36

40
PIANO CUES
PIANO CUE NOTES IN ALL PARTS
PIANO CUE NOTES IN ALL PARTS
PIANO CUE NOTES IN ALL PARTS
PIANO CUES
solo
PIANO CUES
PIANO CUES
VOICE
SS/FL
CL
SS
TS/SS
BASS CL
TPT/FG 1
TPT/FG 2
FG 3
TPT/FG 4
TBN 1
TBN 2
TBN 3
BASS TBN
MALLETS
PNO
E BASS
DMS
37
38
39
40
41
42
43
44
45
46
47
48

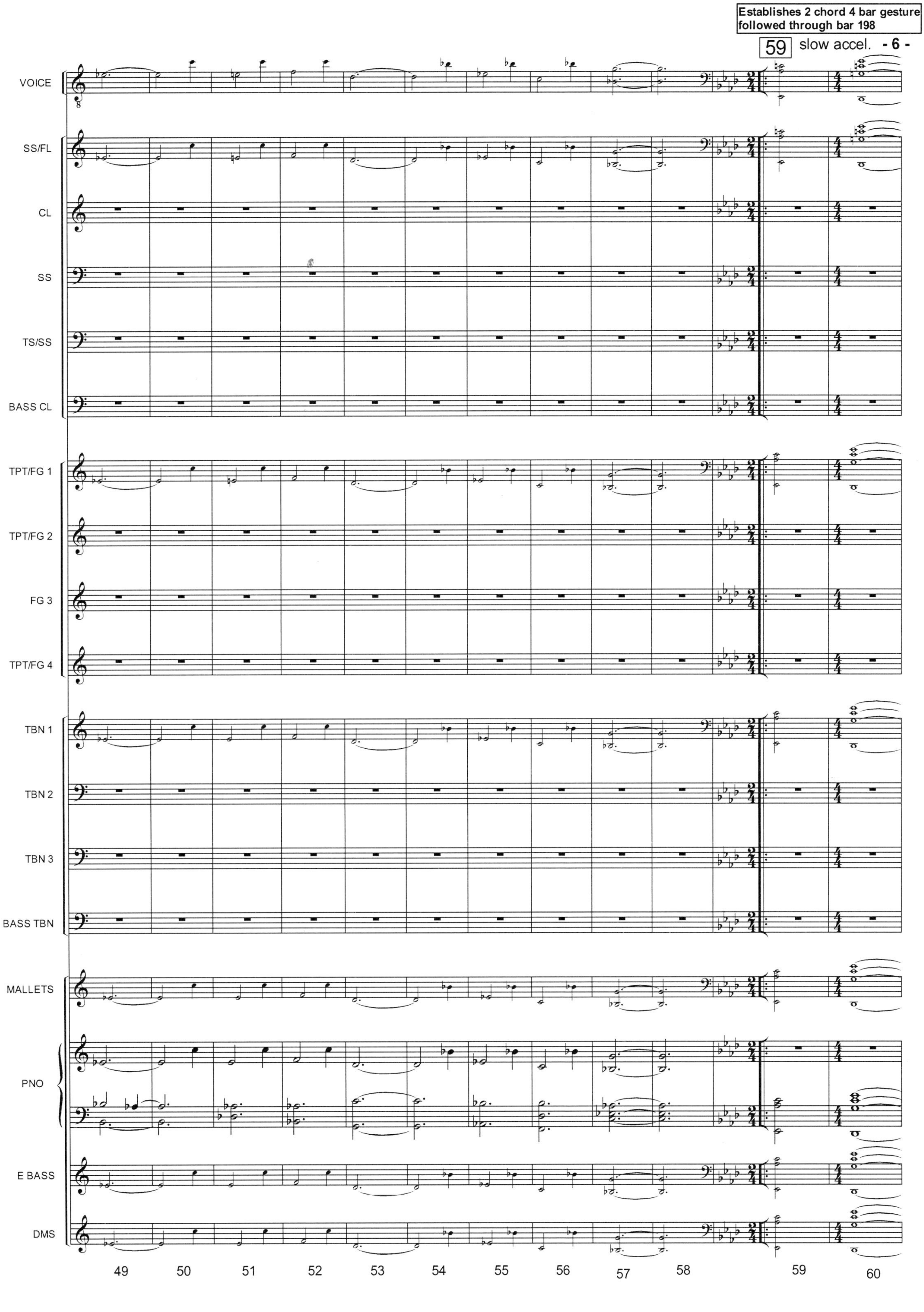
Establishes 2 chord 4 bar gesture followed through bar 198
59 slow accel. - 6 -
VOICE
SS/FL
CL
SS
TS/SS
BASS CL
TPT/FG 1
TPT/FG 2
FG 3
TPT/FG 4
TBN 1
TBN 2
TBN 3
BASS TBN
MALLETS
PNO
E BASS
DMS
49
50
51
52
53
54
55
56
57
58
59
60

Variation 1
68
Rhythmic augmentation of Song bars 4 & 5
♩= 150
STR 8TH
smooth throughout
Oh
mp
(simile)
FLUTE
mf
VOICE
SS/FL
CL
SS
TS/SS
BASS CL
TPT/FG 1
TPT/FG 2
FG 3
TPT/FG 4
TBN 1
TBN 2
TBN 3
BASS TBN
MALLETS
PNO
E BASS
DMS
PLAY
piano/bass
cymbals only
8th notes - sparse brushes or blasticks
61
62
63
64
65
66
67
68
69
70
71
72

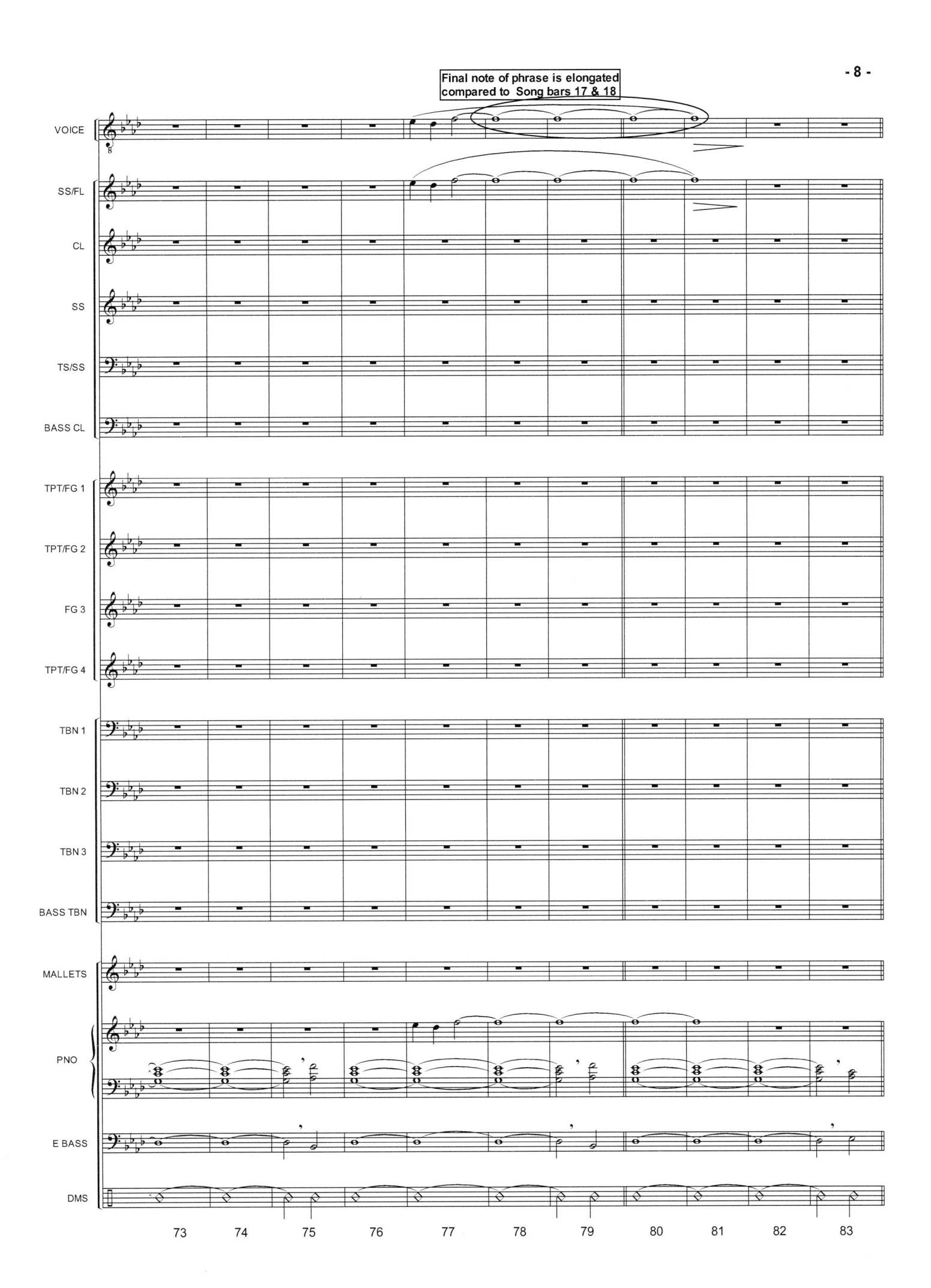

Final note of phrase is elongated compared to Song bars 17 & 18

Rhythmic variation of
Song bars 10 & 11
Rhythmic variation of
Song bars 21-23
84
VOICE
SS/FL
PLAY
CL
mp
SS
TS/SS
BASS CL
TPT/FG 1
TPT/FG 2
FG 3
TPT/FG 4
TBN 1
TBN 2
TBN 3
BASS TBN
MALLETS
PNO
E BASS
DMS
84 85 86 87 88 89 90 91 92 93 94 95 96

101
Rhythmic augmentation & diminution of Song bars 4, 7 & 8
Rhythmic augmentation of Song bars 12-14
VOICE
SS/FL
CL
SS
TS/SS
BASS CL
TPT/FG 1
TPT/FG 2
FG 3
TPT/FG 4
TBN 1
TBN 2
TBN 3
BASS TBN
MALLETS
PNO
E BASS
DMS
97
98
99
100
101
102
103
104
105
106
107
108

109
Rhythmic variation of Song bars 10 & 11
Rhythmic augmentation & retrograde inversion of Song bar 15
Rhythmic variation of Song bars 21 - 23
VOICE
SS/FL
CL
SS
TS/SS
BASS CL
TPT/FG 1
TPT/FG 2
FG 3
TPT/FG 4
TBN 1
1st chord voice enters
PLAY
mf
TBN 2
TBN 3
BASS TBN
MALLETS
PNO
E BASS
DMS
109
110
111
112
113
114
115
116
117
118
119
120

- 12 -

Variations continue based on Song with each growing longer and less space between phrases
Same melodic line as previous phrase but with different rhythms & resolves differently
137
Variation on Song; see also m105)
see m68
see m100-104
VOICE
SS/FL
CL
SS
TS/SS
BASS CL
TPT/FG 1
TPT/FG 2
FG 3
TPT/FG 4
4th & 5th accompaniment voices added
TBN 1
TBN 2
TBN 3
PLAY
BASS TBN
PLAY
mf
MALLETS
PNO
E BASS
DMS
133
134
135
136
137
138
139
140
141
142
143
144

rhythmic diminution of bars 92-95
149 Brief Transition
153 VARIATION 3
TRUMPET/SOPRANO CUES
2nd X TACET
to Soprano
TENOR
PLAY
FLUGEL
to Tpt with Cup Mute
(flugel)
Harmonic accompaniment more dense
2nd X TACET RH ONLY
add rim click sparsely
more activity
change cymbals; add SD
VOICE
SS/FL
CL
SS
TS/SS
BASS CL
TPT/FG 1
TPT/FG 2
FG 3
TPT/FG 4
TBN 1
TBN 2
TBN 3
BASS TBN
MALLETS
PNO
E BASS
DMS
145
146
147
148
149
150
151
152
153
154
155
156

Continues development & variations of previous material

- 15 -

Extreme rhythmic augmentation of thematic material in voice, tpt 4 & piano in contrast to moving wind lines
SING with Tpt 4 and Pno
VOICE
mf
SS/FL
CL
SS
TS/SS
BASS CL
TPT/FG 1
Extension & extension of bar 163
TPT/FG 2
FG 3
TPT WITH CUP MUTE
TPT/FG 4
mf
TBN 1
TBN 2
TBN 3
BASS TBN
MALLETS
PNO
E BASS
DMS
169
170
171
172
173
174
175
176
177
178
179
180

Single voice texture continues to evolve without phrase endings; line based entirely on previous material; Line is divided and passed between instruments; builds to solo section.

- 18 -

206
Brief key/tonality shift
Momentary key & tonality shift
Improvised Solo Begins
214
VOICE
1st X ONLY
SS/FL
1st X ONLY
to Flute
CL
1st X ONLY
TACET from here on 1st X
mf
D♭maj7
Gmaj7
SS
start sparse/fill-in gaps
TS/SS
f
1st X ONLY
BASS CL
TPT/FG 1
1st X ONLY
TPT/FG 2
FG 3
1st X ONLY
TPT/FG 4
1st X ONLY
MUTE OUT
TBN 1
TBN 2
1st X ONLY
TACET from here on 1st X
mf
TBN 3
1st X ONLY - - - TACET from here on 1st X
mf
BASS TBN
1st X ONLY - - - TACET from here on 1st X
mf
MALLETS
Amaj Bmaj
Cmin7sus
D♭maj Soprano Solo
PNO
(play high notes 2nd X only)
E BASS
Soprano solo/change texture/build slowly
fill in rests gently
DMS
205
206
207
208
209
210
211
212
213
214
215
216
Chords above are harmonies implied & show cadence approaching Dbmaj

VOICE
SS/FL
CL
Absus2
Bbmin7
Gbsus2
Dmaj7
Ebmaj69
Gblyd.
Asus2
Amaj7
Bmaj69
SS
TS/SS
BASS CL
TPT/FG 1
to Tpt with Cup Mute
TPT/FG 2
FG 3
TPT/FG 4
open 5th accompaniment voicings leave much to improviser & reminiscent of opening chord voicing.
TBN 1
TBN 2
TBN 3
BASS TBN
MALLETS
PNO
E BASS
DMS
217
218
219
220
221
222
223
224
225
226
227
228

232
Tpt and ww bkgrnds based on thematic material (e.g. bars 2-4, 68, 129, 153, 183, 190, 198)
VOICE
SS/FL
CL
SS
TS/SS
BASS CL
TPT/FG 1
TPT/FG 2
FG 3
TPT/FG 4
TBN 1
TBN 2
TBN 3
BASS TBN
MALLETS
PNO
E BASS
DMS
FLUTE
PLAY BOTH Xs
Cmin11
ENS.
D♭maj7
SOLO
Gmaj7
A♭sus2
ENS.
B♭min7
SOLO G♭sus2
Dmaj7
TPT WITH CUP MUTE
PLAY BOTH Xs
PLAY BOTH Xs
PLAY BOTH Xs
229 230 231 232 233 234 235 236 237 238 239 240

248
Harmonic & unison/octave linear bkgrnds thicken; more linear activity aids soloist building
- 22 -
slow moving vocal bkgrnd line accentuates harmonic color tones as indicated
7 9 7 2
VOICE
SS/FL
CL
E♭maj6 9
G♭lyd.
ENS.
Asus2
SOLO
Amaj7
Bmaj6 9
ENS.
Cmin11
D♭maj7
Gmaj7
A♭sus2
SS
TS/SS
dissonance to harmony
BASS CL
consonance w/harmony by beat 3
consonance with harmony
TPT/FG 1
TPT/FG 2
FG 3
mf
TPT/FG 4
TBN 1
TBN 2
TBN 3
BASS TBN
MALLETS
F♯ma7(#11)
A2
Ama9
PNO
E BASS
DMS
241 242 243 244 245 246 247 248 249 250 251 252

- 23 -

Bkgrnd lines continue to be derived from earlier Song material & variations

Bbmin7   SOLO Gbsus2 Dmaj7   ENS.   Ebmaj6/9   Gblyd.   Asus2   Amaj7   Bmaj6/9 Cmin11

long sustained open 5th voicing provides pause to cleanse palette before next Variation
268
Variation 4
(2+3)
Changing meters throughout variation 4 obscure bar lines and strong/weak beat emphasis
(2+2+3)
1st
2nd
VOICE
SS/FL
CL
SS
TS/SS
BASS CL
TPT/FG 1
TPT/FG 2
FG 3
TPT/FG 4
TBN 1
TBN 2
TBN 3
BASS TBN
MALLETS
PNO
E BASS
DMS
fragments of earlier material
D♭maj7 solo, fade out
PLAY 2nd X ONLY
PLAY BOTH Xs
to Bucket
BUCKET
MARIMBA
B69
(woodwinds)
almost funky-rims, etc.
bring it down
264
265
266
267
268
269
270
271
272

3 voice texture as labeled (Vx); variations based on truncated & augmented fragments of earlier material contrasted against rhythmically augmented, sustained lines.

*Drum part a melodic representation of the ensemble part

Continues 3 voice texture as labeled
Return to Fmin
(3+2)
288
(3+2)
VOICE
SS/FL
CL
SS
TS/SS
BASS CL
TPT/FG 1
TPT/FG 2
FG 3
TPT/FG 4
TBN 1
TBN 2
TBN 3
BASS TBN
MALLETS
PNO
E BASS
DMS
V1
V2
V3
to Soprano
to Soprano
Tbns. mark phrase endings with open Eb7sus chord
Fmin
play around these figures
283
284
285
286
287
288
289
290
291
292

293
4X
Maintains 3 voices but roles change as instruments added; octave dblings
300
4X
cresc. each X
cresc. each X
VOICE
SOPRANO
Play 4th X ONLY
SS/FL
Transposed momentarily for added variation
3rd/4th X 8VA
(as written)
CL
SS
SOPRANO
Play 3rd/4th Xs ONLY
TS/SS
TACET 1st X
BASS CL
TPT/FG 1
to Flugel
TPT/FG 2
Play 3rd/4th Xs ONLY
FG 3
TACET 1st X
to Fluge
FLUGEL
4th X only
TPT/FG 4
TACET 1st X
TBN 1
TBN 2
TBN 3
BASS TBN
VIBES
TACET 1st X
MALLETS
PNO
E BASS
fill around these figures (8th note grid)
bass
DMS
293
294
295
296
297
298
299
300
301
302

Return to tonality and full Ens. orchestrated cres. to final variation
Final 5th Variation
305
legato til end
Section resembles a fugue or round. Subject - mallet and piano (V1) followed by voice 2 (V2) & voice 3 (V3). A 3 part texture with independent bass line
Lines divided among instruments in constantly changing relationships and ever evolving dilogue
VOICE
SS/FL
CL
SS
TS/SS
BASS CL
TPT/FG 1
TPT/FG 2
FLUGEL
FG 3
TPT/FG 4
TBN 1
TBN 2
TBN 3
BASS TBN
MALLETS
PNO
8VB til end (bass clef only)
E BASS
DMS
V1
V2
V3
303
304
305
306
307
308
309
310
311
312

Voices shift here as labeled
VOICE
SS/FL
CL
SS
TS/SS
BASS CL
TPT/FG 1
TPT/FG 2
FG 3
TPT/FG 4
Momentary tonality shift creates dissonance
TBN 1
TBN 2
TBN 3
BASS TBN
MALLETS
PNO
Ever changing bass tones provides different modal identity to moving lines.
E BASS
DMS
V3
V2
V1
313
314
315
316
317
318
319
320
321
322

324
331
VOICE
SS/FL
CL
SS
TS/SS
BASS CL
TPT/FG 1
TPT/FG 2
FG 3
TPT/FG 4
TBN 1
TBN 2
TBN 3
BASS TBN
MALLETS
PNO
tune down 1/2 step (if needed)
tune up 1/2 step (if needed)
tune down 1/2 step (if needed)
tune up 1/2 step (if needed)
E BASS
DMS
323
324
325
326
327
328
329
330
331
332

339
Voices become more independent & doublings continually change. Greater number of different lines
VOICE
Voices begin to achieve more independence
SS/FL
CL
SS
TS/SS
BASS CL
TPT/FG 1
TPT/FG 2
FG 3
TPT/FG 4
TBN 1
TBN 2
TBN 3
BASS TBN
MALLETS
PNO
Bass drops out
E BASS
to bow/marimba OR play through *
DMS
333
334
335
336
337
338
339
340
341
342
Recording shows drums continue to play through helping to build section to climax

VOICE
SS/FL
CL
SS
TS/SS
BASS CL
TPT/FG 1
TPT/FG 2
FG 3
TPT/FG 4
TBN 1
TBN 2
TBN 3
BASS TBN
MALLETS
PNO
E BASS
DMS
343
344
345
346
347
348
349
350
351
352

- 33 -

Individual lines gradually begin to focus on more narrow intervalic motion, first in woodwinds

368
set up drones
VOICE
SS/FL
CL
SS
TS/SS
BASS CL
Rhythmic augmentation begins
TPT/FG 1
TPT/FG 2
FG 3
TPT/FG 4
single note
Tbns. reduced to single note
TBN 1
TBN 2
TBN 3
BASS TBN
MALLETS
ad. lib on this cell, add longer note values, pedal...
PNO
ad. lib on this cell, add longer note values, pedal...
E BASS
DMS
363
364
365
366
367
368
369
370
371
372

Momentum gradually slows through subtle rhythmic augmentation in all voices
379
VOICE
SS/FL
CL
SS
TS/SS
BASS CL
TPT/FG 1
TPT/FG 2
FG 3
TPT/FG 4
TBN 1
TBN 2
TBN 3
BASS TBN
MALLETS
PNO
E BASS
DMS
373
374
375
376
377
378
379
380
381
382

Settles on Fmi(b6) undulating drone that fades to end
VOICE
SS/FL
repeat this figure and grad. fade out
CL
repeat this figure and grad. fade out
SS
continue ad. lib, keep elongating note values
TS/SS
continue ad. lib, keep elongating note values
BASS CL
continue ad. lib, keep elongating note values
TPT/FG 1
repeat this figure and grad. fade out
TPT/FG 2
continue ad. lib, keep elongating note values
FG 3
continue ad. lib, keep elongating note values
TPT/FG 4
continue ad. lib, keep elongating note values
TBN 1
8VA
continue ad. lib, keep elongating note values
TBN 2
continue ad. lib, keep elongating note values
TBN 3
continue ad. lib, keep elongating note values
BASS TBN
continue ad. lib, keep elongating note values
MALLETS
bow softly - like beginning
PNO
roll softly - like beginning
E BASS
DMS
Optional bowed marimba
383
384
385
386
387
388
389

- 37 -

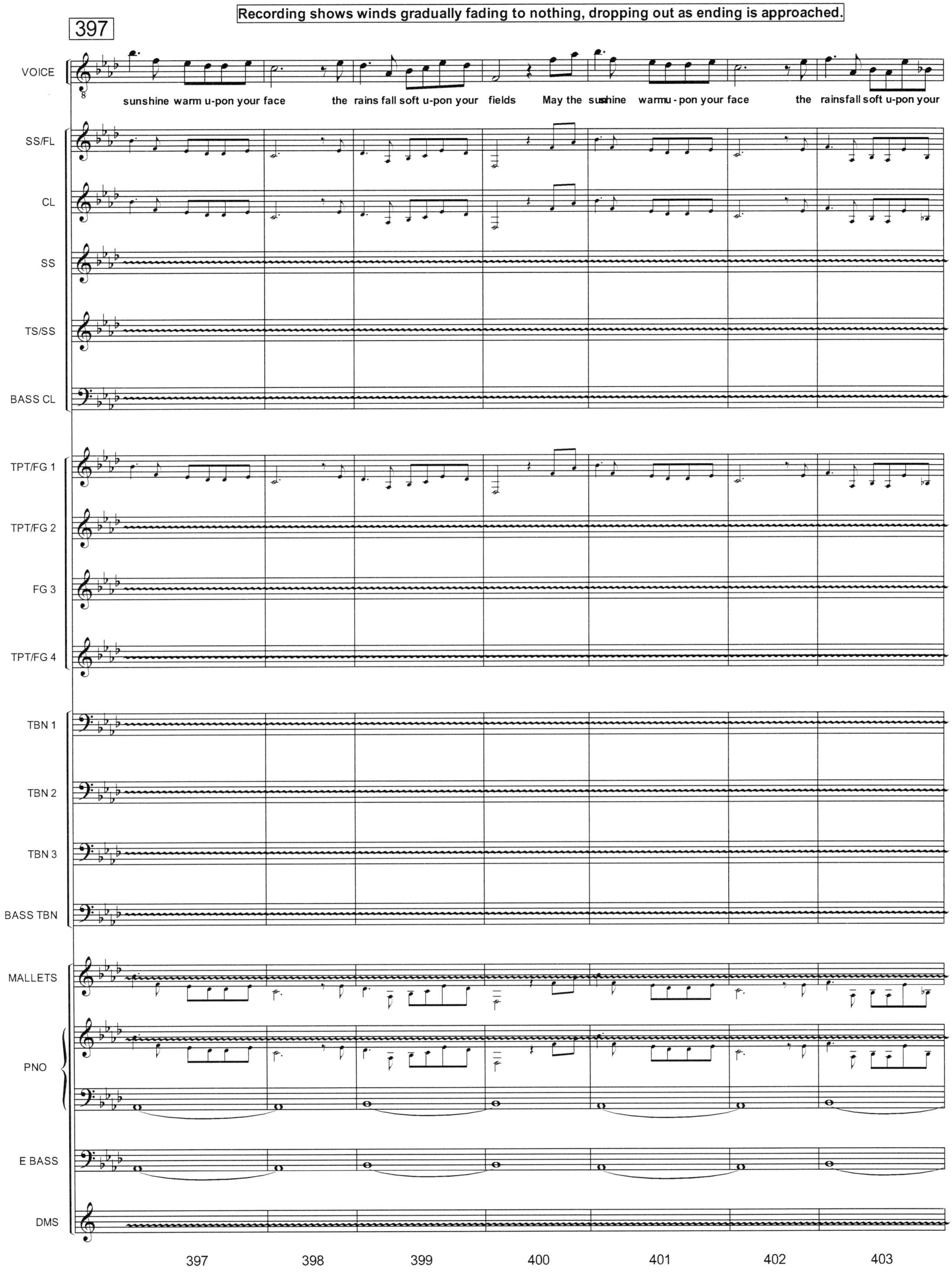

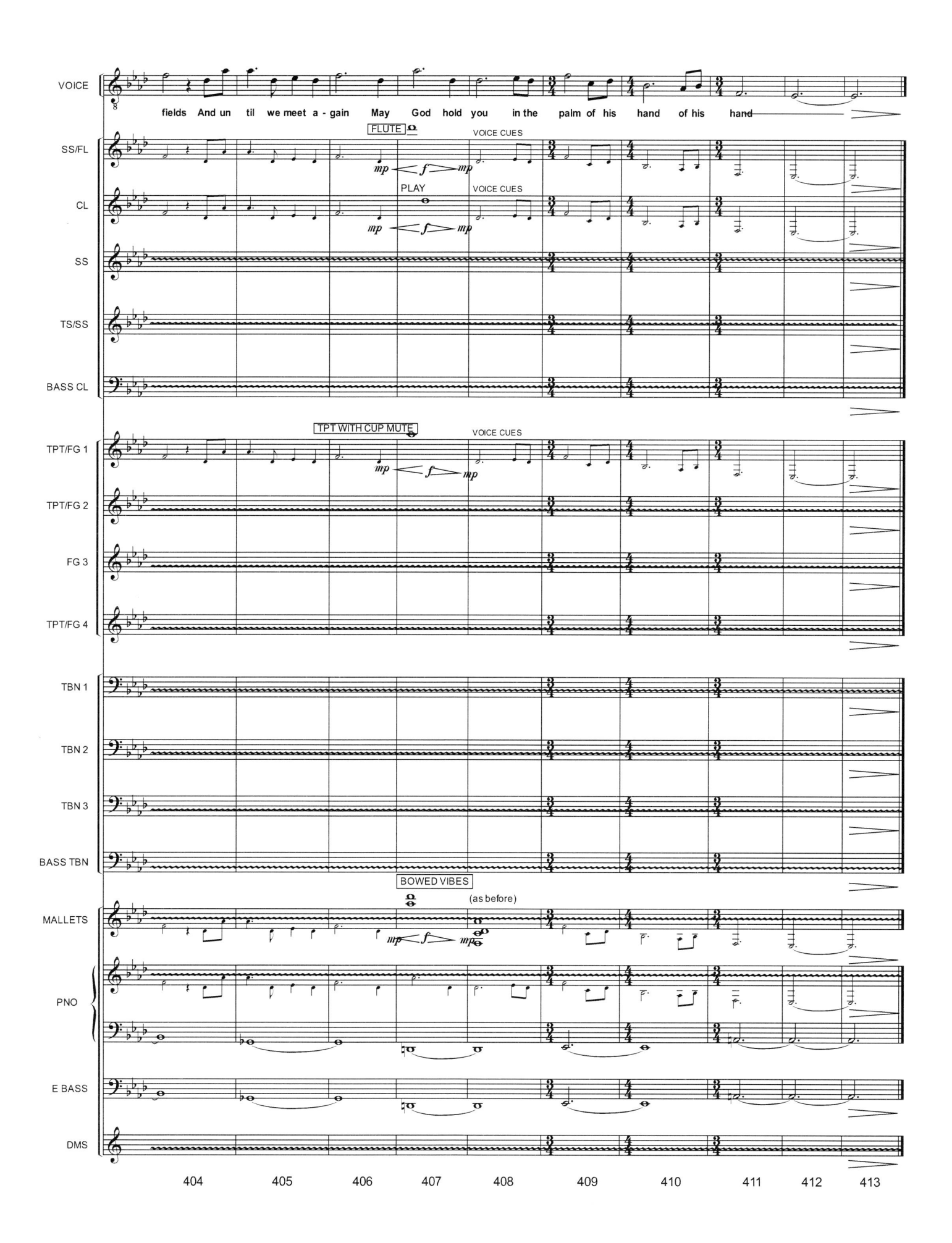

fields And un til we meet a-gain May God hold you in the palm of his hand of his hand

Photo by Lindsay Beyerstein - Composer Darcy James Argue

Chapter 6
Darcy James Argue - "Transit"

Canadian-born Darcy James Argue is one of several new generation composers who continues to prove that the big band is not a dinosaur. His compositions are "free of cliché, wary of dogma, catholic about tastes, and fastidious about details," according to journalist Larry Blumenfeld, who offered this insight in a December 2009 *Wall Street Journal* article. "His music is conceived out of the tradition but without being bound up by it; and, as relevant jazz has always been, his compositions reflect an awareness of our times without being subservient." *Newsweek* contributor Seth Colter Walls wrote that "for a wholly original take on big band's past, present and future, look to Darcy James Argue."

A native of Vancouver, Canada, Argue earned a degree at McGill University before moving to the US to study with Bob Brookmeyer at New England Conservatory. He moved to Brooklyn and studied further at the BMI Jazz Composition Workshop with Jim McNeely and Michael Abene, so it is no surprise that he has worked out a personal style that continues to evolve through his recordings — *Infernal Machines, Brooklyn Babylon* and *Real Enemies*. Each of these recordings has earned critical acclaim through consecutive Grammy and JUNO Award nominations. Argue's debut recording with Secret Society, *Infernal Machines*, brings together musical influences as far-ranging as classical, indie rock, and tango, making his music fresh, relevant, and captivating. Richard Gehr who writes for the *Village Voice* described his work as "maximalist music of impressive complexity and immense entertainment value, in your face and then in your head." "Transit," the piece chosen for this study, is included on *Infernal Machines*.

The two recordings following his inaugural release with Secret Society are based on integrated materials. The most recent release, *Real Enemies*, is self-described as a "13-chapter multimedia exploration of America's fascination with conspiracy theories and the politics of paranoia." Each chapter of *Real Enemies* is based on the composer's manipulation of 12-tone composition techniques and demonstrates a sense of musical continuity, much like *Brooklyn Babylon*, through which flows a narrative that reflects the diverse musical landscape of Brooklyn.

What separates and distinguishes artists from the crowd, regardless of their discipline, is innovation without necessarily abandoning elements of the tradition. Argue clearly falls into this category and the musicians that interpret his challenging scores help him immeasurably to achieve this distinction.

Selected Discography

Infernal Machines — New Amsterdam (2009)

Brooklyn Babylon — New Amsterdam 2013)

Real Enemies — New Amsterdam (2016)

Transit

The notes that accompany the *Infernal Machines* recording suggest a subtitle for "Transit" — "Fung Wah Rapid Transit Company." A little research revealed that this is the name of one of the first Chinatown bus services that ran from Boston to New York. The name Fung Wah came from the Cantonese pronunciation of the Chinese name 風華. Argue spent many hours on this inexpensive bus line that enabled him to commute from Boston to NYC until he moved to New York.

Argue shares a few characteristics with at least three other composers in this study — Jim McNeely, John Hollenbeck and Vince Mendoza. Since McNeely, Hollenbeck and Argue share experiences in working with Bob Brookmeyer, this is not a surprise. For example, Brookmeyer believed that improvisation should come only when nothing else would be more appropriate. In Brookmeyer's opinion, solo improvisation should never be forced and must be an integral component of the entire composition, a thread in the larger fabric — this is certainly the case in "Transit." Hollenbeck, McNeely, Mendoza and Argue all conceive of harmony as an outgrowth of linear motion and the contrapuntal interaction of voices. These four composers also employ open harmonies and incomplete harmonies where chord tones are omitted, sometimes in favor of including an extension tone instead of a key chord tone (root, 3rd or 7th). These composers also often exploit a minimum number of voices — three or four. They use large, harmonically dense voicings only sparingly, favoring open modal structures with voices doubled at the unison and octave.

Considering only the material before the improvised solo begins, "Transit" is a very long-form composition, unfolding in several contrasting sections over the course of 127 bars, or nearly three minutes — 40 percent — of the entire seven-minute piece. During this long exposition, the piece breaks from traditional structures in numerous ways.

Argue builds "Transit" by creating a series of juxtaposed dichotomies. He combines two four-measure isorhythmic ostinatos, one of which bears some similarity to the Afro-Cuban clave, providing a cohesive underpinning throughout much of the piece. The essence of the clave is that it is an unrelenting rhythm pattern, never changing, and all other aspects of the music must adhere to this rhythmic structure. This is not entirely the case in "Transit," but the ostinato isorhythms permeate much of the composition and provide rhythmic momentum.

The composer also contrasts major and minor thirds in his melodies and harmonies while maintaining a common modal D pedal point. Melodies based on the D major scale, and the D major scale with lowered 6th degree (referred to in some circles as the "harmonic major" scale) are contrasted with those based on D Dorian, D Aeolian, the D augmented scale, the 5th mode of G melodic minor. Each of these scales or modes has in common the root (D) and the 5th (A), but all other scale degrees are encountered in raised and lowered forms, including the third, which may be major, minor, or — in the case of the augmented scale — both. This approach of mixing modalities of a shared common pedal point is known as modal interchange.

The flowing rubato of the opening chorale is soon overwhelmed by the surprising uptempo A Section, and that tempo persists until the arrival of the half-time rock feel in m.220. The legato, lyrical phrases that comprise the opening chorale and the B Section (m.73) are in contrast to the more scalar and rhythmically active A Section (m.33). Each of these contrasting musical gestures, and others discussed later, create tension and resolution throughout the piece.

The following lead sheet score reduction (Example 6.1) illustrates many of these striking characteristics. (The chord symbols have been provided for analysis and are not included in the original score.

Example 6.1

TRANSIT
CHORD SYMBOLS ADDED FOR ANALYSIS PURPOSES

Darcy James Argue

© 2003 Cercopithecine Music (BMI)
All Rights Reserved

33
A Section
3-beat hemiolas
39
41
Hemiolas
Suggests D major ♭6
45
49
Hemiolas
51
57

63
69
73
B Section
Gmi
D/F#
Gmi/Bb
77
Gmi6/Bb
Gmi ma7/Bb
Bmi
81
Cma7(omit 5)
F
83
F
F+
Dmi/F
F#mi7
Gma7(#11)
Ebma7(#11)
Ebma7(#9)
C/E
90
C/E
Emi
B/D#
Bmi/D
C#ø7
96
C#ø7
Bmi9
98
D/F#
Gadd2(#11)
F#7/A#

F#7/A#
C#o7
C#o7/D
Dmi/F
D major b6
101
C Section
107
D/F#
Gmi MA7
Return to rhythmically opposing isorhythms at the octave
113
5th mode G melodic minor
Gsus2
AbMA7(#11)
D ped
120
128
Reprise of original vamp and isorhythmic ostinato prepares entrance of soloist

Lead Sheet Reduction Overview

Formal Design

"Transit" is a long-form composition that reflects traditional structures without replicating typical architecture. The opening rubato chorale is presented in two- and four-measure phrases and gives a deceptive impression of the stylistic direction the piece will take. Nonetheless, the chorale presents material that will be used and developed throughout the rest of the arrangement, albeit in a dramatically different tempo, style, and mood. A riff-like vamp following this chorale sets a bright tempo and establishes the mood for the balance of the arrangement, while introducing three distinct sections that follow — labeled A, B and C for discussion purposes. The A and B Sections are contrasting in character, which is typical even in popular songbook tunes that follow the conventional AABA song form. The concluding C Section features a synthesis of elements found in the two previous sections: scalar lines associated with the A Section along with long sustained phrases built on leaps of a major or minor third, important elements in the B Section.

Rhythmic Elements

A unifying aspect of this composition is the four-bar isorhythmic ostinato that immediately follows the opening chorale. While pitches change, and rhythms are varied based on changing harmonic and melodic context, the isorhythmic ostinato that begins in measure 16 is a constant presence throughout "Transit." The composer refers to this ostinato as the piece's clave. It also partially resembles the 2-bar son clave rhythm, as shown in Example 6.2. The character of this ostinato varies through changing orchestration and dynamics, but this rhythmic undercurrent runs for the whole of the piece. The double isorhythmic pattern that begins in measure 16 continues with some variations through the B and C Sections. The interlocking accents and syncopations between these two opposing isorhythms tend to momentarily obscure bar lines, and were it not for the fact that the two rhythms come together on the "and" of beat four at the end of each four-bar phrase, the rhythmic equilibrium would be significantly more disrupted.

Example 6.2

The re-orchestrated isorhythmic ostinato that appears in the B Section compliments the lyrical and flowing melodies, and this helps to make the B Section contrast the two surrounding sections. Note that the rhythmic activity is suspended in the fourth measure of the ostinato, in favor of sustained note values that terminate together on the "and" of beat four. The changing pitches during this section reinforce changing harmonies, which play a more important role in this contrasting section, as shown in the following example.

Example 6.3 — B Section isorhythmic accompaniment

An important third component added to the opening isorhythmic ostinato is a two-voice riff that also repeats every four measures, and emphasizes the phrase-ending "and" of beat three and "and" of beat four found in the upper voice of the ostinato. This riff, which initially suggests D major ♭6, becomes an integral aspect of the composition. The relationship of the riff to the ostinato is shown in the example that follows.

Example 6.4 — Top 2 voices along with ostinato D below suggest D major ♭6

The opening phrase of the A Section, played by the top four saxophones, has a three-beat cross-rhythm situated within the prevailing 4/4 meter, called a hemiola. It too becomes an important, reoccurring, unifying ingredient throughout the entire score.

Example 6.5

Melodic Elements

"Transit" uses melodic material from various scales and modes built on the root D. These modes might suggest either a major or minor tonality, or a combination of both. The majority of these modes begin with the tetrachord D – E – F♯ – G, or D – E – F – G. The following example illustrates these modes and scales.

Example 6.6

Melodies in the A Section are primarily constructed from eighth note lines belonging to one of these scales or modes.

The other main thematic element is a repeated two-note figure, as seen for instance in Example 6.5. This figure decorates a sustained pitch, moving away by half step, whole step, or minor third, in either direction, before returning to the original pitch.

The F♯ – A – B♭ figure that introduces the B Section echoes the opening of the chorale and foreshadows the motion by minor third in the upcoming C Section. The long, sustained melodic lines are constructed in antecedent-consequent phrases. The final four measures of this section (m.103-106) refer back to the two-note hemiola figures employed in the A Section. The rising eighth note line in m.106 (F♯ – A – B♭ – C♯

– D – E) is also derived from the opening chorale melody — with the addition of a passing C♯ — and serves to introduce the C Section.

The B Section is arranged primarily in a series of four-bar phrases, arranged into overlapping antecedent and consequent phrases. The third measure of each of these four-bar phrases contains a pick-up into the next phrase, overlapping the end of the previous phrase. The fourth phrase of the section (m.85-89) contains a one-measure phrase prolongation, making it a five-bar phrase. Beginning in measure 96, the antecedent-consequent phrases begin to overlap more closely, creating a sense of forward momentum, until they finally converge on the "and" of beat four of measure 100. Another phrase prolongation, including a measure of 6/4, creates what amounts to a five-and-a-half bar phrase (m.98-102), before reverting to a four-bar phrase to finish the B section.

An interesting feature of the melodic organization is the consistent use of a pick-up into each major section or phrase, as seen in measures 32 (pick-up to A Section), 72 (pick-up to B Section), 89 (pick-up to second half of B section) and 106 (pick-up to C section).

The melodic lines in the final C Section reflect back to both previous sections, combining active, anticipatory eighth note scalar figures with major third or minor third gestures in longer note values. The primary melody emphasizes a descending major third (F♯ – D) while the countermelody emphasizes both descending (A – F♯) and ascending (G – B♭) minor thirds. These two intervals were first introduced in the opening measure of the chorale: F♯ – A (minor third) and B♭ – D (major third). Note that this melodic motive is also a fragment of the D augmented scale.

Harmonic Elements

The harmonic analysis provided in the lead sheet reduction (Example 6.1) shows how triadic structures are fundamental to this composition. Even when extensions beyond the triad and chromatic alterations are used, they are most often expressed using three-note structures.

In the A Section, harmonic content flows from the various modes employed melodically, and their interaction with both the pedal D ostinato and the constantly varied two-note dyads used in the riff. For example, in m.49-52 (see Example 6.1), the riff pitches, in combination with the melody, suggest a chord progression of D - Emi7(♭5) – E♭MA7 - D, all over a D pedal.

The B section departs from the A Section's pedal point and begins to develop the harmonic progression first established in the chorale. For instance, take the initial harmonic progression of m.73-84 (chords in square brackets are passing chords):

Gmi – D/F♯ – Gmi/B♭ [Gmi6/B♭ – Gmi(MA7)/B♭] – Bmi – CMA7(omit3) – F [F+ - Dmi/F] – F♯mi7

Compare with the chorale progression, beginning on beat three of the first measure:

Gmi – D/F♯ – E°/B♭ [B♯+] – [C♯mi7/B] – Bmi – [Dmi/C] – Cmi – B♭/F – F♯°

While some chord qualities vary (to a lesser or greater degree) from the chorale progression, and the harmonic rhythm is considerably prolonged, the bass motion is identical. This pattern continues throughout the B Section, which is derived in its entirety from the harmonic progression used in the first eight measures of the chorale.

A slightly altered version of the isorhythmic ostinato continues to propel the B Section, but in a much more subtle way than the previous section. The pedal point is discarded for changing pitches in both parts of the clave, and these note choices interact with the melody to form changing harmonies. As a consequence of the interaction with the ostinato, most harmonic changes are either anticipated on beat four or the "and" of beat four, or delayed until the "and" of beat one.

Argue uses a highly linear, contrapuntal approach to creating shifting harmonies. Example 6.3 illustrates this with an excerpt from the abridged lead sheet.

Example 6.7 - Measures 76-81 of the abridged lead sheet. Chord symbols are added to illustrate passing harmonies created through linear motion. The Gmi6 could also be analyzed as E°/B♭, as it is in the parallel spot in the chorale.

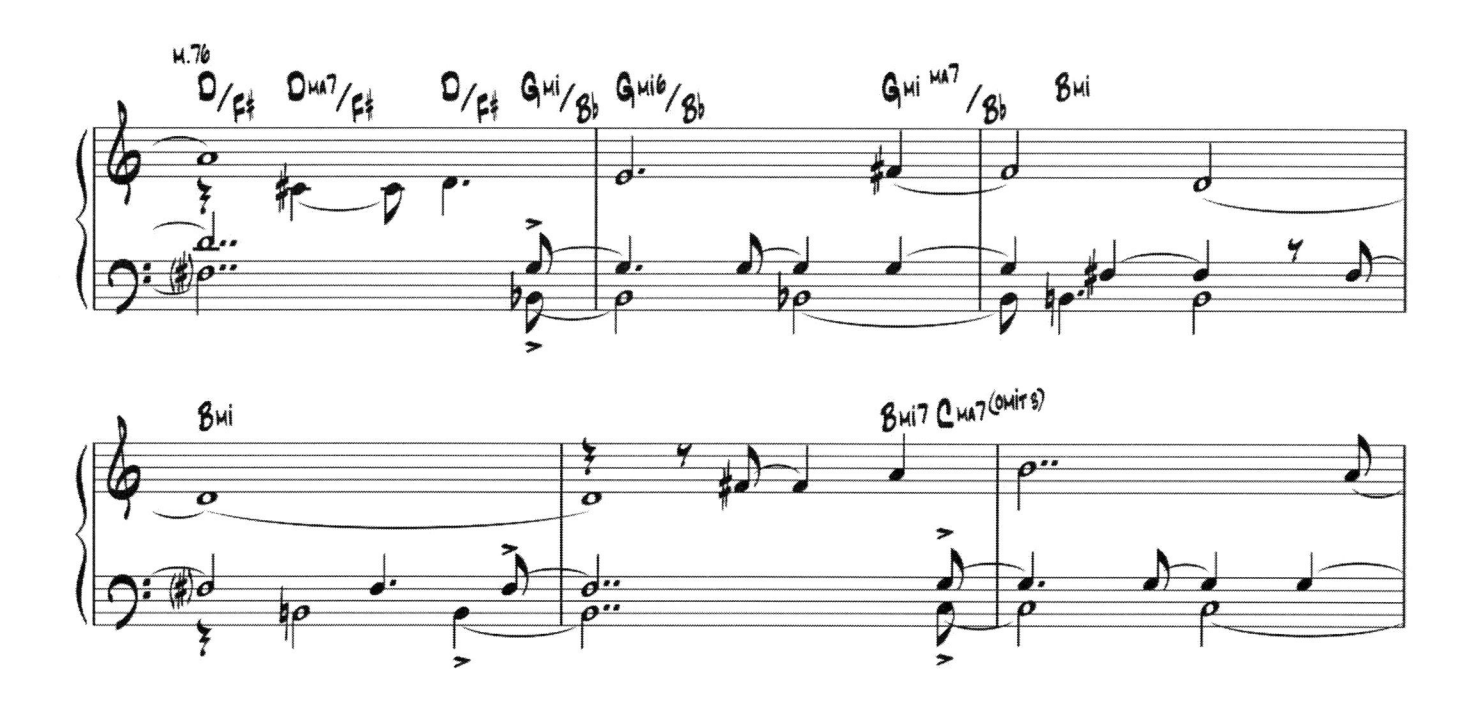

The Arrangement

The pacing of dramatic content is an important element of any arrangement. How does a composer-arranger create climactic moments, and where do they occur? How does a soloist contribute to the musical narrative? How is developmental material unfurled? These are all big picture questions. Some of these questions can be clarified by creating a timeline of musical events as they occur.

Example 6.8 — Timeline of "Transit"

The graphic analysis of "Transit" that follows provides a visual illustration of how the piece unfolds, where the high points occur, and how the composer achieves them. The climax is reached at about 80% of the way through the piece, in measures 291-304 (out of a total of 364 measures), or from 5:45 to 6:00 of the total 7-minute running time. The top row in this table shows measure numbers and timings for reference.

[1] 0:00	[16] 0:51	[33] 1:14
3-voice chorale	Introductory vamp in new tempo	A Section — Sax scalar material. Tpt responses. Tbns play ostinato isorhythmic vamp.
Three and four voices structure	Two isorhythmic ostinatos. D pedal plus 2-note reoccurring riff	Isorhythmic ostinato continues.
10 bars	*24 bars*	*39 bars*

[73] 1:54	[107] 2:28	[120] 2:41
B Section — Contrasting lyrical and harmonic content	C Section — full Ens elements using elements of A & B sections	Vamp returns.
Antecedent-consequent lines with changing rhythmic ostinato	Ostinatos return at new pitch levels	Ostinatos return to D
33 bars	*13 bars*	*8 bars*

[128] 2:48	[140] 3:12	[156] 3:28
Long Tpt solo begins on D pedal	Solo continues	Solo continues over D pedal
Ostinato continues for 16 bars	Tbn and Sax bkgrounds using vamp stretched over 16 bars	Mode changes
16 bars	*16 bars*	*16 bars*

[172] 3:44	[188] 3:59	[204] 4:13
Solo Continues over D pedal	Solo continues over D Pedal	Solo continues over D Aeolian
Bkgrnds hint at A section and build	Tonality shifts to dissonant A7/D	Ostinato moves to Gtr. Bs drops out
16 bars	*16 bars*	*16 bars*

[220] 4:30	[251] 5:02	[282] 5:33
Solo continues. Juxtaposes maj and min F/A — Fmi/A♭— E♭/G — E♭mi/G	Solo continues	Solo continues, then pauses
Drums play half-time st. 8th feel	Changing ostinato pitch. Content harmonically defines new lyrical Tbn bkgrnds	Ens builds based on C section material
31 bars	*31 bars*	*14 bars*

[296] 5:49	[304] 5:58	[328] 6:20
Solo out	Soloist re-enters, gradually winding down	Opening chorale returns
Dramatic full Ens riff	Riff continues winding down	Dual isorhythmic ostinatos accompany choral
8 bars	*24 bars*	*16 bars*

[344] 6:40
Reprise of opening vamp/riff
Settles on open 5th D harmony
21 bars

Example 6.9 — Graphic Analysis of "Transit"

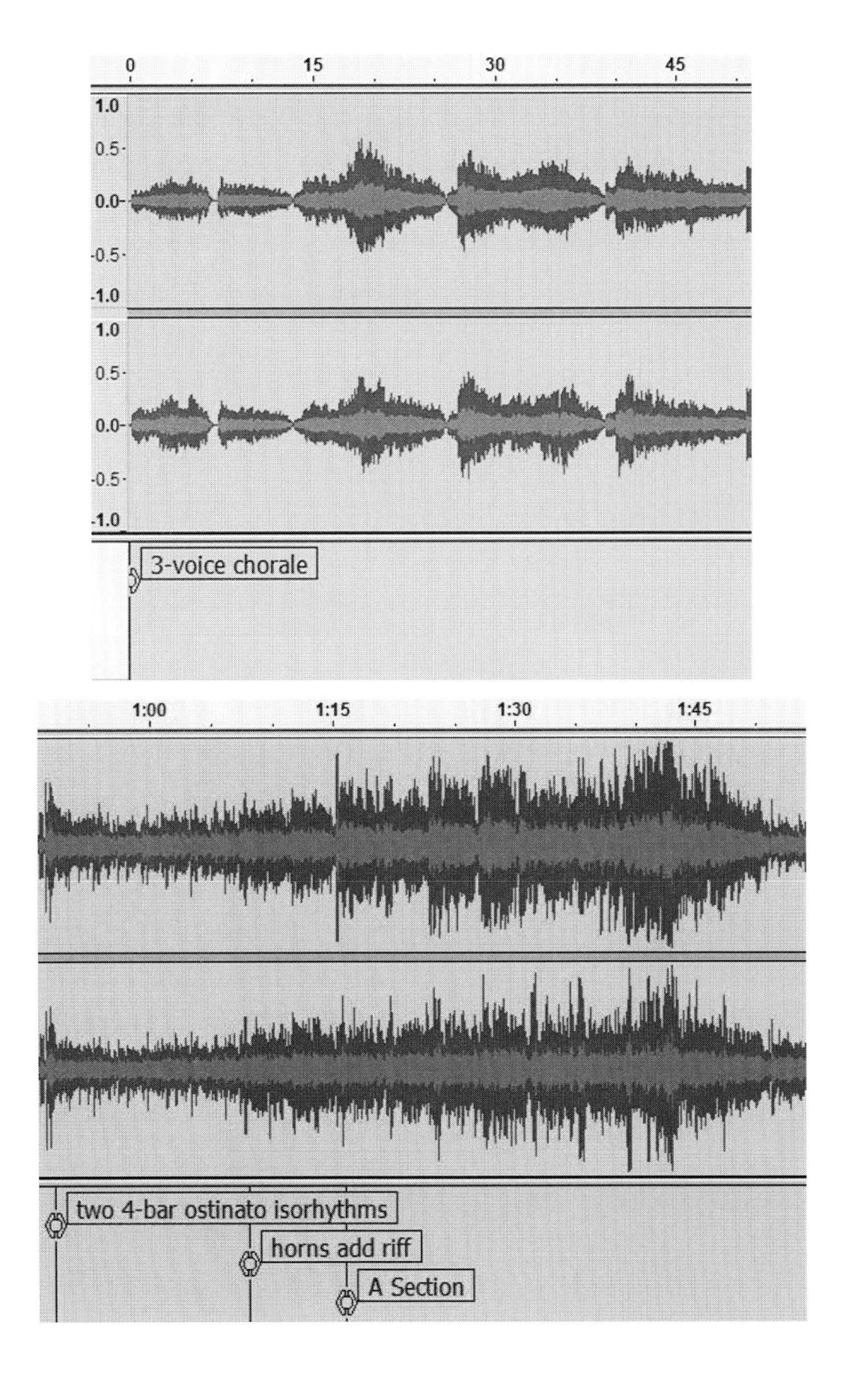

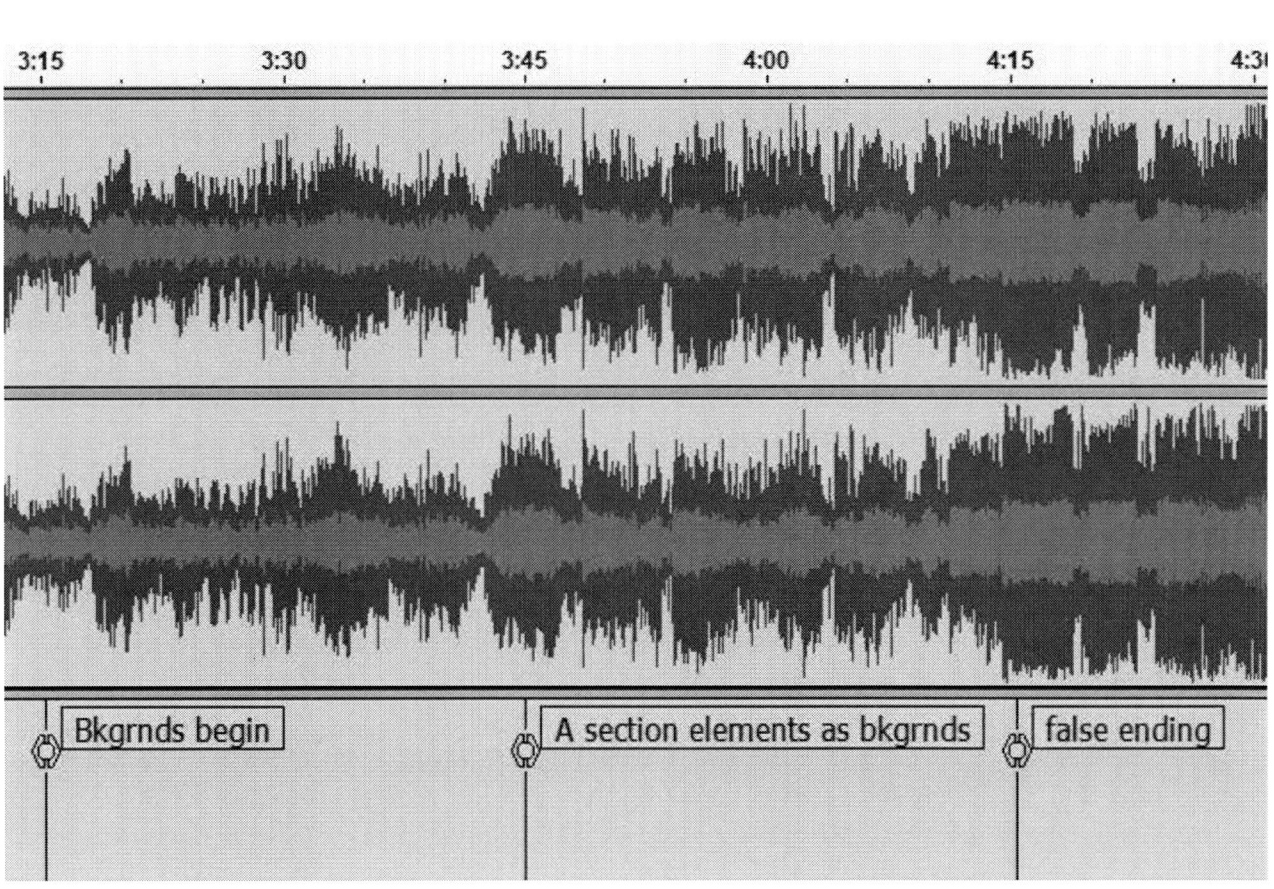

| B Section | | C Section | Riff & Isorhythms |
| | | | Tpt. solo begins |

| Bkgrnds begin | A section elements as bkgrnds | false ending |

st. 8ths section | lyrical bkgrnds

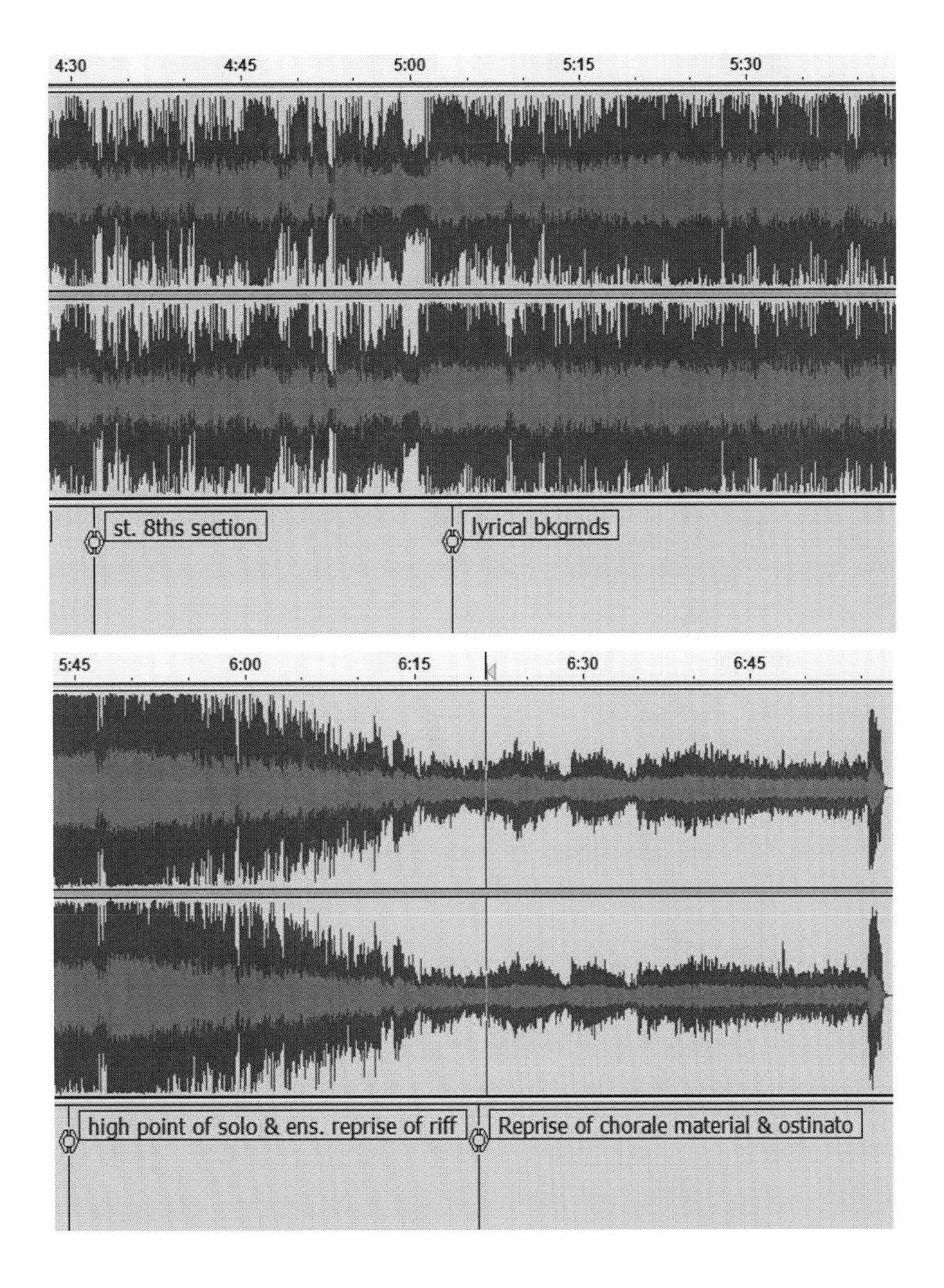

high point of solo & ens. reprise of riff | Reprise of chorale material & ostinato

General Observations

On first listening to "Transit," listeners might find themselves pondering several questions. What is the purpose of the opening chorale? Where is the typical "shout chorus," or is there such a section? What role does the very lengthy solo section play?

There is so much material between the opening chorale and the brief reprise near the end that it is easy to lose sight of this opening material. It may also not be immediately apparent how the melodic and harmonic material introduced in the chorale is used as source material throughout the entire piece. The abrupt change of tempo and style can make these connections difficult to perceive.

The extended solo section that follows the unusually long exposition seems like far more than a typical solo section, even at first hearing. The gradual introduction of ensemble background figures (or "solo enhancements," as Bob Brookmeyer referred to them) are based on prior thematic material, and the way these motives are intertwined with the soloist suggests a closer integration with the composition as a whole than is often the case.

While the composer clearly labels measure 282 as the beginning of the "ensemble shout," the soloist continues to improvise through this section, dropping out only briefly before re-emerging in the midst of the ensemble as it winds down, before the chorale is reintroduced in measure 328. Argue has effectively blurred the lines between composition and improvisation, changing the depth of field throughout the solo section.

Another distinguishing feature is the abundant use of special instrumental effects. Phrases played as fast as possible, flutter tonguing, fanning of valves, trills, false fingerings, growls, tremolos, long glissandos, and similar effects are used throughout.

It is almost impossible to neatly compartmentalize the analysis of this score by rhythm, harmony, and melody, since these components are so mutually influential. While the discussion that follows is organized according to these three elements, we will also examine related techniques, as needed.

Rhythm

The reduction provided in Example 6.1 illustrates the importance of both isorhythmic ostinatos and hemiolas to this composition. Both provide rhythmic momentum and are unifying elements throughout the score. The layered isorhythms also create subtly shifting contrapuntal harmonies through their interaction with melodic voices. This will be discussed further in the section about harmony.

The opening ostinato continues through the first 24 bars of the trumpet solo, serving as accompaniment, but from measure 132 until 203, the bass and drums are given the freedom to interact with the soloist, while guitar and piano are largely tacet. In measure 204 the guitar, now heavily distorted, unveils a new two-part ostinato, and the entire character of the piece changes, transitioning to a half-time feel with a rock backbeat in measure 220. This driving rhythmic figure is passed from guitar to the lower saxophones, trombones, and piano as the solo section develops.

The dyadic "riff" figure, imposed above the isorhythmic ostinato in measure 28, helps solidify the new tempo by emphasizing anticipations on the "and" of beat four. During the A Section, the riff pitches shift constantly, interacting with and coloring the changing melodic modes. This riff becomes a familiar ingredient. Example 6.10a shows this riff's original form, followed by one of the many permutations used throughout the piece (Example 6.10b). Note also the phrase one-measure phrase extension, transforming this "riff+ostinato" variation into a five-measure phrase.

Exampled 6.10a — "riff" appears as upper two staffs

[musical notation]

Example 6.10b

[musical notation]

The two-note hemiola figure that is so much a part of the A Section provides material used throughout the piece. This rhythmic device is influential well beyond the initial exposition, and examples of hemiola figures can be found in the following passages (among others):

        measures 172-175

        measures 180-182

        measures 188-189

        measures 196-198

One of the more interesting examples of this figure is shown as follows in Example 6.11, where the hemiolas are staggered across groups of instruments by one beat. The accents at the beginning of each 3-beat grouping make the cross-rhythms even more convincing.

Example 6.11

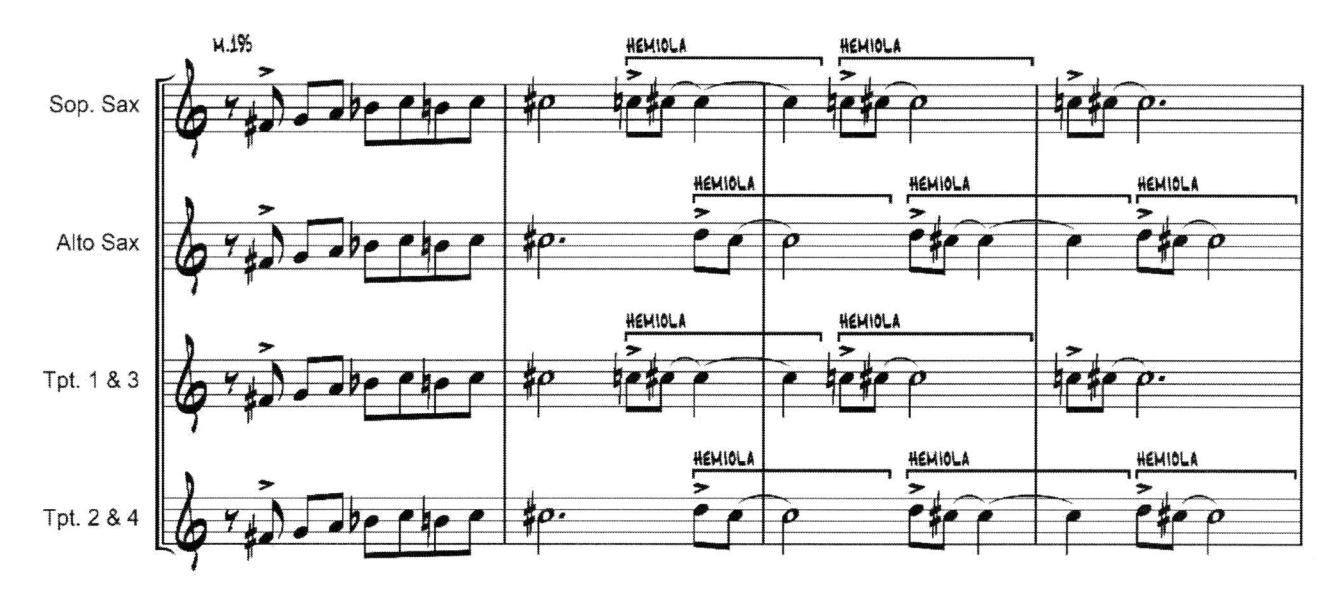

Harmony, Voicings, and Orchestration

"Transit" uses primarily spare harmonies, with frequent use of open fifths and simple triads, often in first or second inversion. This is not a harmonically dense score. Intensity and dramatic high points are achieved not through harmonic density but through orchestration and range. Harmony is frequently a result of the linear motion of voices. Chords are sometimes suggested by sparse shell voicings, where notes are omitted — including at times the third, which is traditionally expected to provide chord identity. By omitting the third, and including instead a substitute tone, such as the second, Argue obtains a very open sound that supports melodic lines that might include both major and minor thirds.

The following example illustrates the characteristic style: three-voice texture with four different rhythms, incomplete chords, and contrapuntal harmony where resolutions from one chord to another are delayed or anticipated by moving voices. It shows how harmony is created through linear motion, employing simple triadic structures (often in inversions) and incomplete chords that might lack the fifth or even the third.

In terms of orchestration, the top voice of the top staff is played by three trumpets and alto sax. The lower voice on that same staff (entering in m.76) is played by soprano sax, two trumpets, and guitar. Argue uses this "cross choir" approach to orchestration extensively, though at times groups of like instruments are also used, such as the two tenor saxophones playing the ostinato figure shown on the middle staff. The bottom staff represents trombones and bass — m.74-76 is bass alone, with Trombone 3 joining on the pickup to m.76, and Trombone 4 taking over from Trombone 3 in the pickup to m.81. Note that these pitches are the same as the lower voice of the tenor sax ostinato, but using longer note values.

Notice how harmonies change through voice leading, with some voices anticipating harmonic changes, suggesting passing harmonies, or creating suspensions before resolving to a new harmony. This technique is apparent throughout the score.

Example 6.12

The following example offers another look at Argue's ensemble voicings, where fuller chords are suggested by a small number of voices. The entire ensemble is reducible to just three voices, with the lowest doubled at the octave beginning on beat four of m.101. The very striking penultimate chord suggests a continuation of the C#°7 chord in the upper two voices, while the lowest voice has already moved on to the D minor resolution. Then, when the upper two voices resolve inward by contrary motion to A and D, the lowest voice leaps up to the minor third, F.

Example 6.13

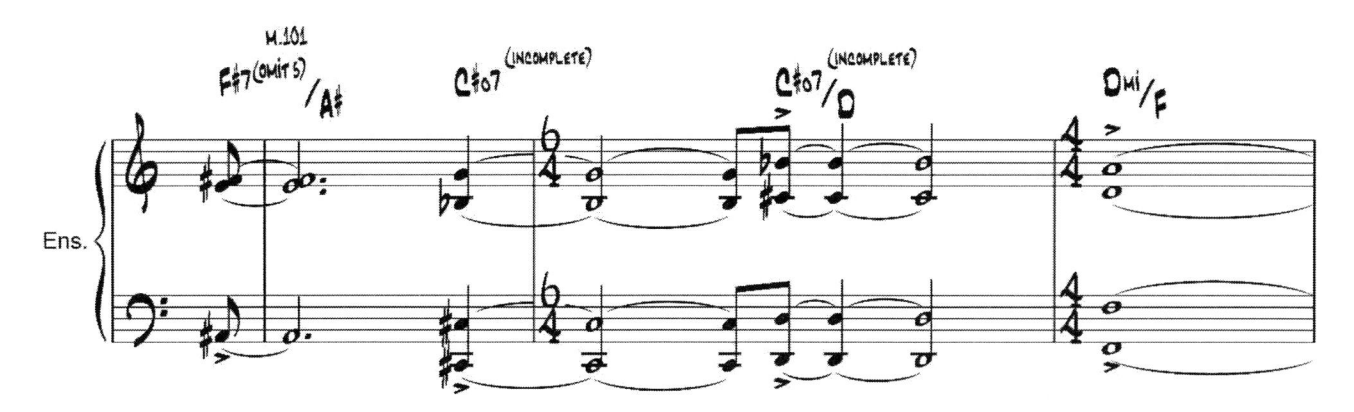

It is rare in this composition for Argue to use more than four voices. Much of the time, chords are implied without including all of the pitches. He reserves altered and extended chords for important high points, or moments that deserve to be highlighted emotionally.

The minor seventh chord with a lowered sixth first appears as a symbol for the soloist at measure 251, where the melodic material suggests the Aeolian mode. This chord, while it has become popular with contemporary jazz composers because it can be voiced in open fourths, is not voiced as a solid block in the score — it is rather suggested by the melodic lines in the accompaniment.

Example 6.14

Example 6.15 illustrates how the composer voices chords across the ensemble, frequently omitting an expected pitch and using chord inversions. Notice the use of the ongoing, relentless isorhythmic ostinato, played here by tenor sax, baritone sax, and trombone. The voicings in the trumpets and top two trombones (also doubled in the top three saxes) are made up of pure dyads, reinforced at the octave.

Example 6.15

Chords appearing at climaxes are sometimes useful substitutes for dominant seventh-type chords, such as the MA7(#11) chord, as in measures 282 and 290 in the following excerpt.

The BbMA7(#11) on the "and" of beat 4 in m.282 functions as a replacement for the substitute applied dominant chord bII7/V — Bb7 — which helps lead back into the Dmi11/A chord, which functions as a kind of cadential 6/4 chord.

The climactic chord on beat four of measure 291 has been labeled as a Bø7, though Argue suggests to the soloist that it is G7/B, which would be a IV7 chord in first inversion. This certainly makes sense, though there is no G anywhere in the voicing. It is likely that the G7 was given to the soloist in order to lead the player towards a strong, bluesy resolution to the tonic. Throughout the entire trumpet solo, the soloist is guided by the composer's solo enhancements, and suggestion of a G dominant seventh chord here is in keeping with that spirit.

Example 6.16

The movement of I to IV is heard frequently throughout this piece — the first two chords heard in the opening chorale are I (D) to iv (Gmi). This motion is also found in the pickup into the B Section, and at the beginning of the C sections. The I chord can be major, minor, or open (without a third), and the IV chord is also found in both major and minor. While the reprise of the opening chorale near the end of the piece is incomplete, and harmonized above a D pedal, it does reiterate this important I-IV motion, as illustrated in the following example.

Example 6.17 — Reprise of chorale

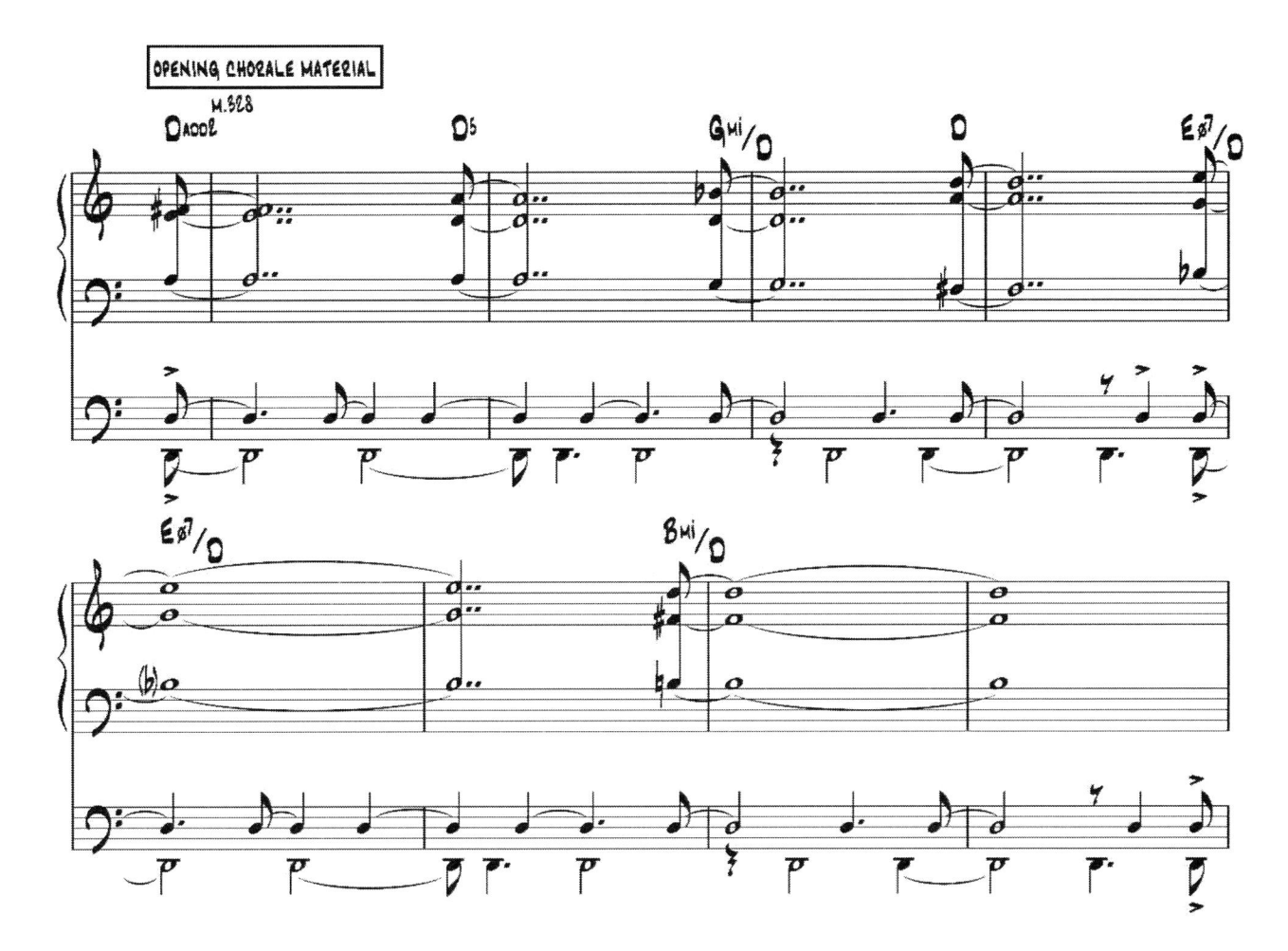

Bass Doubling

Because of the importance of pedal points and isothythmics ostinatos, it is not surprising that these bass patterns are doubled by many instruments across the ensemble. Such figures are frequently doubled by Tenor Sax 2 and Baritone Sax, Trombones 3 and 4, Guitar, Piano, and Bass, depending on the weight of the orchestration. In the more dynamically subtle B Section, the two-part isorhythm is played by the tenor saxes alone, and not doubled prior to the entrance of the baritone sax in m.90.

Solo Backgrounds and the Shout Chorus

As previously suggested, the solo section seems to evolve into something more than a typical solo section because of the high degree of ensemble activity from measure 172 on. At first it seems that background material is derived primarily from A Section material and the opening 4-measure riff, though it is manipulated to suggest other modes. The initial sax and trombone background introduced at measure 140 is a rhythmically augmented version of the riff's lower voice, as shown in the following example. The second 16 bars of this background shifts modes from D major ♭6 (or the 5th mode of G melodic minor) to D Dorian or Aeolian.

Example 6.18

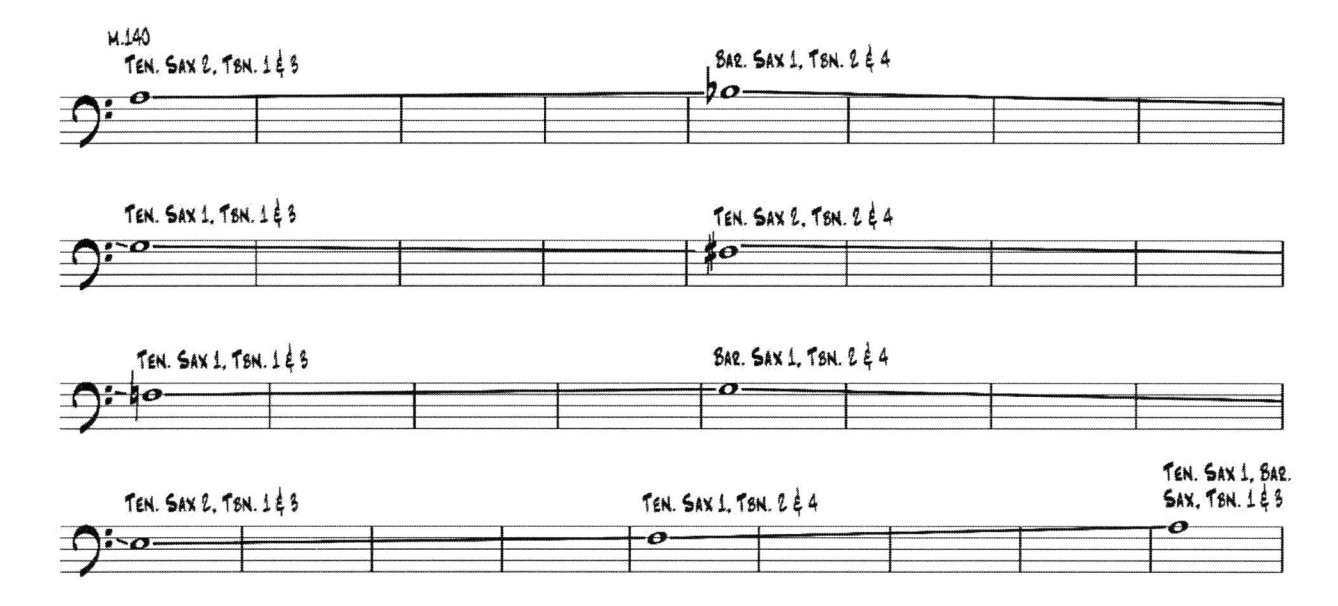

During the half-time rock section, the composer juxtaposes major and minor triads in first inversion, and introduces a new Aeolian based melodic line in trombone and saxophone parts at measure 251 (see example 6.14). It appears Argue views the entire lengthy solo section as an opportunity to reflect on all aspects of the exposition (measures 1-127). The lyrical section from 251-280 is reminiscent of the B Section without quoting it. The lyrical triplet melody is quite different from what is heard at this point in the exposition, but there is a loose similarity in the shape, the rhythmic profile (particularly the use of half-note triplets), and lyrical character. And measures 281-294 clearly recapitulates elements of the C Section before resolving to a climactic full ensemble, high-energy version of the riff. It is this section that is referred to by the composer as the "ensemble shout." The boundaries between "solo section" and "ensemble shout" are not at all clear, which makes for interesting listening.

Interview with Darcy James Argue

The composer and I met on February 13, 2018 in Princeton where he offered the following comments about "Transit," his studies with Bob Brookmeyer and thoughts on being a composer.

RL: *While I've followed your work since your first large ensemble recording, I'd like to learn more about your influences in terms of other writers and teachers. Who and perhaps what music has had an impact on you as a writer?*

DJA: Obviously the most directly impactful mentorship of my compositional career was my time spent with Bob Brookmeyer at New England Conservatory (NEC). It's extremely rare for a composer and instrumentalist of Bob's stature to also take teaching as seriously as he did. Many jazz musicians tend to do teaching as a source of income, but not something that they are going to spend an enormous amount of their limited time focusing on, at the expense of their performance career and their own compositional work. Bob was very unusual in that he thought really carefully and seriously about how to convey what was important to him. I'm sure that you've had other composers talk to you about Bob's pedagogical methods, so probably you've heard all about the white note exercise.

RL: *No I haven't heard about that. No one actually got into such specifics.*

DJA: The white note exercise is something that Bob would assign to all of his NEC students on the first day. We had to write a melody, but your melodic compass was limited from middle C to the C above, using just the white notes on the piano. It had to be in time. It had to be a certain minimum length, with a defined beginning, developmental section, and ending. It's a very challenging exercise, to have those kinds of serious constraints on you as a composer. You really have to think about what every interval means to you, and what your emotional relationship is to those intervals. Of course even with just those eight notes, you have every possible interval available to you. Sometimes only one — like, your only major seventh is C to B, but it's there. You really start to think hard about your ideas of melodic construction, unencumbered by any harmonic support, and you think about melodic continuity, and what is singable. When it came to phrasing, Bob would encourage you to get away from foursquare, antecedent-consequent "two bar phrase, then another two bar phrase" sorts of things, and focus on melodic fluidity and placement.

It's easy as a young composer to view these white note exercises very superciliously. But Bob would sit and really go over them, and at times would suggest a fermata over a particular pitch, or suggest holding something out longer, or more of this material or that. He would really try to stretch people, and get them to think about continuity, and having an emotional relationship with every interval, and with every part of the beat. Feeling an anticipation on beat four has a heaviness to it, whereas the "and" of four is lighter, and the "and" of one has sort of a stutter-step quality to it. He focused on all of those things, starting there — let's strip everything away and go back to absolute fundamentals, the diatonic C major scale and those eight pitches and let's do something with them. And then build up from there.

Bob would always encourage everyone to listen to their music "as if some other mother**** had written it." He had various expressions for that: "put your ear on the table," or "kill your babies" — meaning you can't fall in love with the first conscious melodic impulse that you have. You have to sit down and take it apart methodically, through a process of pre-compositional work. He was very insistent about composers' need to be organized and have some kind of architectural plan. He would attempt to take people who might have an interest in and a talent for writing tunes, and try to help mold them into composers by exposing them to the compositional toolkit.

I had the great opportunity while I was studying with Bob to have my music performed by the NEC Jazz Composers' Orchestra, which performed exclusively student compositions, plus Bob's music. He would sometimes bring in pieces that he hadn't yet recorded, so for instance we performed "American Tragedy" before he had recorded it with the New Art Ensemble. It was wonderful to watch him conduct, and he worked incredibly well with students, particularly drummers — he was adept at getting things out of them.

As a composer, you would bring in something to the JCO rehearsal on Tuesday and record it, something that was maybe unfinished or a work in progress. And then you'd bring it into your lesson the next day with Bob, and you would sit down and go over it for two hours and examine things from many different perspectives and vantage points and at various levels of granularity. Sometimes he would zoom right in and say "ok you put a low fifth in the chord but should it be a minor sixth, not a fifth?" or "you assigned the ninth here to the 2nd Tenor but shouldn't it be in the 1st Tenor?" and those kinds of issues. Then we'd zoom all the way back out to the drama, the narrative, when is the right time for the first solo, how do you guide the improviser through a narrative using "solo enhancements," and so on. What everyone else would call "backgrounds," he would call "solo enhancements." He was very concerned with trying to find ways to help steer the soloist in the direction that he was looking for in the piece. For Bob the worst thing was to have someone stand up and play all the shit that they had been working on in the practice room. He really wanted the improvisation to come out of the piece, and to serve that musical vision.

RL: *I've found that many of his protégés share that same philosophy. For example the way John Hollenbeck and Jim McNeely weave the improvisational moments into the larger fabric is a concept so different from the old days where there was an expected build up to a send-off for a solo and some stock backgrounds. In "Transit" that very long solo is very much an important part of the fabric of the piece rather than just a solo.*

DJA: Yes, and I think that type of holistic musical vision is certainly a thing that Bob tried to impress on me and on all of his students. He was very concerned with the necessity of patience. As a composer it is very easy to become over-familiar with your basic materials, particularly when doing the kind of pre-compositional work that Bob required all of us to do. So by the time you are actually sitting down to write the music, you've heard those themes and melodies and the developmental tangents so many times that it becomes very difficult to sit back and put yourself in the experience of listening to the music for the first time. Just on a purely practical level, when writing a piece of large ensemble music, you might take eight hours to write 10 seconds of music. So it's very easy to lose perspective in that kind of situation. One of the most important lessons that Bob had to convey was to really try to keep that kind of perspective.

There are composers who really embrace a compositional philosophy that is based on a total disregard for the experience of the listener, and it really is about "screw you I'm going to write what I'm going to write, and if you like it great, and if you don't, go f*** yourself." As embodied by that famous essay by Milton Babbitt "Who Cares if You Listen?" That's not his title, but it's a fairly accurate encapsulation of the argument that he is making: composition is a specialist activity and ought not to be apprehended by those outside the field. The only feedback that matters is that of other highly specialized composers.

Bob was not like that. It wasn't that he was incapable of writing music that did alienate the audience — he sort of wrote himself out of the Mel Lewis Orchestra in the 1980s with the kinds of experimentation that he was doing, but through all of it there was an awareness of the effect it was having on audiences, the way the art was received in the world. Even when he was deliberately setting out to be provocative in certain ways — and as a composer, as well as a commentator and a person he could be very provocative! — it was always done with an awareness of what the response was going to be, what someone's perception of the music would be. He deliberately frustrated listener expectations, but with an understanding of what those expectations *are*. As opposed to just a complete disregard for the experience of the listener, if that makes sense.

RL: *It makes complete sense.*

DJA: So my real formative experiences were with Bob, and later with Jim McNeely and Michael Abene at the BMI Jazz Composers Workshop. That was valuable not just because of the feedback I would get from Jim and Mike on my own work, but also getting outside the circle of NEC composers. It was interesting to have a peer group of composers who had not studied with Brookmeyer! After being immersed in that world for a few years at NEC, there was much more diversity in the BMI Workshop — the participating composers brought a very different perspective and a very different set of aesthetic priorities. It was great to see how Jim and Mike would try to understand what each composer was trying to do, and give them proactive and constructive advice on how they could shape things in service of that vision — which might be a vision that might be very different from their own aesthetics. I got a lot out of the feedback that Mike and Jim would give on other people's compositions, but also just hearing their compositions in the first place. Seeing how people like Joseph C. Phillips and Sherisse Rogers approached writing for large ensemble, the kinds of techniques and conceptual approaches that they brought to bear on the music, was deeply influential for me as a composer.

I also benefited from having a few lessons with Maria Schneider and those were very productive. She is also someone who is very insightful and gets right to the crux of things. I only had a handful of lessons with her over the years but they were all extremely influential and she always had useful and meaningful feedback. I remember at one point she gave what felt like, and probably was, a half-hour, blow-by-blow analysis of the beginning of *Sketches of Spain* — all the little things that Gil does in the first minute before Miles comes in, how he sets up that first entrance. That definitely stuck with me.

In terms of other composers whose work I studied, I loved Thad Jones as a teenager. The records were really difficult to get. All I could find was this one cassette, a compilation of Thad and Mel Solid State recordings, and that had to suffice for many years. I basically wore it out until the Mosaic box set came out, and that's where I heard Brookmeyer's music for the first time. Thad's music meant a tremendous amount to me as a teenager and still does today.

In terms of other influences, I include Mingus and Monk and Horace Silver and Wayne Shorter and Coltrane. Of the composers of that era, it's Mingus' music that really had an impact on me. I think I first heard Mingus when I was 13 or 14 and that had a similar impact to hearing Thad for the first time.

With Duke and Strayhorn, those came a little bit later. I had some Duke Ellington recordings as a teenager, and had one rather curious record, *First Time! The Count Meets the Duke*, with both bands together, that has a wonderful Thad Jones ballad on it, "To You." I might have heard that before I heard any other Thad Jones charts — I'm not sure that I even realized Thad had written that at first! I had it on cassette and I don't think there was much in the way of credits. But the piece definitely stuck with me.

For Ellington, it really wasn't until I got to college where we started looking at the Blanton-Webster stuff in arranging class, looking at "Ko-Ko" and "Concerto For Cootie," that the lightbulb really went off, and that was the entryway into an entire universe. Duke's stuff remains deeply mysterious. On one hand he was a populist who wrote so many hit tunes, but as a composer I think maybe it takes a certain level of maturity to really start to realize how brilliant he was — like the introduction to "Harlem Air Shaft" for instance.

RL: What do you play Darcy?

DJA: I play piano, or I should say I'm a lapsed piano player. I played trumpet in high school, primarily in the concert band. Having the experience of being a mediocre trumpet player is very helpful. [laughs] When trying to write for instruments, it can be helpful if you don't play them all that well.

RL: I'm always interested to learn about how composers work. Can you describe to us your creative process and what tools you typically use and may have used in creating "Transit? I realize that it might be difficult to answer as the process you use for one piece might vary with the next and so on.

DJA: The process is pretty similar from piece to piece. It's more about how much pre-compositional work is going to be done. If it's for a large scale work like *Brooklyn Babylon* or *Real Enemies*, well, both of those pieces required a lot of careful planning. I'm going to have to live with these musical materials for a long time, in order to generate 60 or 80 minutes' worth of music, so I have to make sure that the DNA that I'm starting with can support that kind of life-form. And then structurally, something like *Real Enemies*, the large-scale harmonic structure is a reflection of the 12-tone row that is the basis of the entire piece, so those relationships have to be worked out in advance before any writing can begin. But even for a smaller-scale piece you still have to know on a molecular level what the core of the piece is. What is the single cell organism that is going to multiply and divide and eventually evolve into a piece of music that is going to give you the length of piece you are working with?

For "Transit" there are really two things — the clave, and the chorale at the very beginning of the piece. And that chorale informs all of the harmonic choices and inflections, which are all more about subtle shadings than they are about large-scale harmonic development or making an argument through harmony. "Transit" is essentially a modal piece, so it's more about shading various scale degrees over a fixed pedal than it is about going to different harmonic places.

RL: Can I assume the chorale came first?

DJA: The clave actually came first. *[sings the rhythm of the underlying isorhythmic ostinato]* That was the initial impulse.

Beyond that, it's been so long that I don't actually recall what I did at the time! But I'll tell you what I would do with it now, if I had to start over: I might take those clave rhythms and look at the relationships between them and turn them into pitches. Can I take these durations and turn them into intervals and see what kind of intervals I get? It's possible that I did that at some point!

RL: And the chorale's final return at the end comes almost as a surprise, though it's not complete. You allude to it but not in its entirety. And much like one of the other pieces in this study, by the time you do return to the chorale, we've almost forgotten it.

DJA: Yes and that first melodic gesture in the chorale, that minor third followed by the semitone, and then major third, that gesture is part of the melodic DNA of the piece. Although the chorale isn't restated until the very end of the piece, it influences everything that comes in the middle.

RL: Yes, the ingredients are all there.

I'm always curious if composers had a plan, an outline or even a general architecture in mind before they actually begin a score. Did you have such a plan in mind when you begin scoring "Transit?" If not, at what point did you start thinking about the larger picture, or does that come more organically as part of the compositional process?

DJA: The one thing that I was always unsuccessful at was sticking to a particular fixed plan when it came to the large-scale structure of a piece. I might decide okay, it's going to go through these particular sections, and the climax is going to come in this measure, because of such-and-such a mathematical relationship. Bob would always encourage me to do all those things, and there are certain effects that you can only achieve if you get into that level of specificity in planning. And I shouldn't say I am *always* unsuccessful at sticking to the plan — I have done that on occasion. There is a piece called "Codebreaker" that I wrote for Alan Turing, that really does exploit those sorts of things in very specific ways.

But with most of the work that I do, all of the pre-compositional work leads to a sense of an array of possibilities. I have all of those possibilities in my head as I'm writing, and often the music itself pulls in a particular direction. It's really a "best-laid plans" scenario: even when I obsessively plan the architecture of a piece, I can feel myself being pulled in a different direction and the piece sort of tells me where it wants to go. So there are also times where I just skip the middle man! Once I've fully investigated all the pre-compositional material, often at that point the writing process becomes more intuitive, because I have done all of the intellectual groundwork first. Then if you get stuck you can always go back to the pre-compositional material.

RL: I remember years ago studying with Ray Wright and Manny Album and Ray in particular strongly encouraged us to do outlines, but then he was also cool if you took side trips or tangents. I think he felt that the outline, particularly for younger writers who were less experienced, gave you a safety net or something to cling to when you started what is frankly a scary process.

When you are working on a new piece and you are still in the early sketch and creative process stage, do you work with bar lines and meters? Or does it depend on the piece?

DJA: I find meter to be helpful.

RL: I do too because it involves decisions that you'd have to make later anyway.

DJA: Yes, but also because of the way I relate to music. If I'm phrasing over the bar line, I want to know where the bar line is. If something is very singing and lyrical, and nothing lands on a downbeat, for me the pulse is an important element, even if it isn't being explicitly stated. I've never felt constrained by bar lines. People talk about the tyranny of the bar line, but it's only tyrannical if you let it be!

RL: Regardless of age it seems that the computer is very much a part of our everyday lives. I'm curious how you use this tool, or don't, in your creative compositional process, or are you still, particularly in the early stages, a paper and pencil person?

DJA: I don't touch paper and pencil at all if I can help it.

RL: I guess you are of a younger generation.

DJA: Yes I've been using Finale since 1993 or '94. If I were writing a novel I would not write it by hand. I would use a word processor. It is much faster for me to sketch something out quickly in Finale and print it out and tape it next to my monitor, or on my music stand, than it is for me to write it out by hand. Occasionally I'll annotate a print-out, or I might do some of the pre-compositional sketch work by hand, but I would say 90 percent of the sketch work is done directly into the computer.

If I'm away from the computer, if I'm at the piano with a music manuscript book, then obviously I'll use paper and pencil. And occasionally when I'm working with a band in Europe and I need to sketch something out on a break at lunch or after the rehearsal, I'll jot it down that rather than break out the laptop, but at some point it all goes into the laptop anyway.

RL: Was the decision to have Ingrid Jensen, your trumpet soloist, play through the entire lengthy section one that you made at the outset, or did you arrive at that through rehearsals? Did you make any significant changes to the score after rehearsals?

DJA: No, I really didn't change it in rehearsal. The one modification that I made was to extend the solo section past the climax and to allow for a denouement before the re-entry of the chorale. Originally I left the end of the solo coincide with the climax of the piece, but that immediately proved to be unsatisfying. I realized that the band's energy has gotten to a certain point, and in order for everything to come down to a satisfying conclusion there needed to be a final gesture from the soloist that could take us from a point of maximum intensity back down to a more reflective place. That may have even been something that Ingrid decided to do on her own that I then adopted.

RL: I think it works because it's unexpected.

DJA: It's already been so long… but wait, there's more!

RL: You often seem to suggest chords without including all the expected pitches, even omitting what I would call identity tones. Can you talk a little about this particular approach to using harmony?

DJA: Harmony is a lie. It's a story we tell ourselves about how music works so we don't have to face the terrifying reality that there isn't any such thing as harmony. It's all voice leading. It's all about the horizontal relationship of one melody to another melody. We study harmony, we're taking slices, like a slice of Antarctic ice, and looking at where all these streams were going when they were frozen. This allows us to organize our thinking about voice leading in sophisticated ways. We have labels for what it sounds like when the voices arrive at this particular point, and so we're going to call that a G7(b9) chord, and when those voices resolve the way they typically want to resolve, we call that a CMA7 chord. But it's about the motion of those individual voices and their own resolution tendencies, and these labels that we put on them are labels of pure convenience.

RL: Particularly as a convenience for soloists where you have to give them some guidance.

DJA: Right. For me, particularly in the chorale, the more important way of looking at it, as opposed to chord symbols, is the motion of the three individual voices in the chorale and their own particular resolution tendencies. Yes, they suggest certain harmonies and some of those harmonies may be familiar and have a functional relationship to one another and some may not, but the shaping force in the chorale is the individuality of the three voices that make it up. They each have their own trajectory and they come together at cadences in a particular way, but I really tried to preserve the independence of their own melodic journeys. And that continues into the body of the piece, especially over pedal points — most of "Transit" is over a pedal point, giving you an enormous amount of flexibility. You can literally include any note at any given time, and all of them are supportable against that pedal point. So then it's a question of where does this voice want to go, and where does that voice want to go, do they move in contrary motion, oblique motion, similar motion? All of those things have some kind of bearing on our perception. In this piece I was not particularly thinking about functional harmony the way that I might in a different kind of piece.

RL: No that's apparent.

RL: You gave the soloist a dominant chord, a G7/B at one point, because if they think about that tonality at that point it does pull nicely back to what we will call tonic. But actually if you analyze the chord vertically it's not really a G7 in terms of what you've got sounding in what we will call backgrounds.

DJA: "Solo enhancements."[laughs]

RL: It is really like a B half-diminished, which of course is almost a G dominant. I assumed that that was a convenience for the soloist, and your effort to draw them in a way that you wanted.

DJA: You don't want to burden the soloist with too much information. That's an issue that comes up most dramatically in *Real Enemies*, where the improviser might have a 12-tone chord sounding behind them, and there is no way of describing that with a standard chord symbol. So you have to come up with some shorthand way of suggesting a relationship from the previous chord, a relationship that will take them on a trajectory into the next chord that will elicit the best possible voice leading from that soloist.

RL: That makes complete sense.

This particular composition to me appears to be based a great deal on developing different melodic relationships to D as the central pedal point. From that you superimpose material that is based on D Dorian, harmonic major and so forth.

DJA: That actually brings me to another pet peeve of mine — the so called "harmonic major" scale. There is no such thing. That scale is the Ionian mode with a ♭6th, or the major ♭6 scale. That's what I would call it. The harmonic minor scale is called that because it is the scale used to construct harmonies in a minor key. So that's why calling this altered Ionian mode "harmonic major" feels weird to me. We already have a scale used to construct harmonies in a major key: it's called "the major scale."

RL: *Going back to the compositional question, was that the idea, to juxtapose melodies that were influenced by these different scales and modes, which all have something in common, but there would be a different half-step here or whole step there?*

DJA: It's taking the idea of modal interchange to its logical conclusion. You take a piece like Billy Strayhorn's "Lush Life" and it's in D♭ major, but it is using the whole gamut of all of the pitches from the parallel minor as well. And that gives you a delicious array of notes, including the full chromatic from the fifth up to the root, as well as both the minor third and the major third. All of those borrowed pitches are used melodically and harmonically. Especially in that first melody in the refrain where Strayhorn has these very snaky chromatic melodies that outline all of the chromatic pitches between the fifth and the major seventh — they are all there.

Extending that principle, modal interchange lets you use all of the 12 tones — not just the parallel minor but all kinds of modes including the augmented scale, and symmetrical scales like the diminished scale and fragments of the whole tone scale and the augmented scale. All of those things are available.

It's sort of similar to what John Coltrane did in "Fifth House," where during his blowing, the rhythm section is just playing that C pedal, and he's playing over the descending major third Coltrane matrix progression, as applied to "What Is This Thing Called Love?" He's playing a very specific, complex harmonic progression, but the only thing underneath it is the pedal point.

So things like that were in my subconscious and a reference point for "Transit." Even if it's rarely just the pedal point! The solo begins with that, but there is usually something else going on, even if it's just trombones and saxophones smearing slowly from one one dyad to another one.

RL: *Is there anything in particular that you'd like to say about "Transit" that we haven't already covered?*

DJA: I'm using the term "clave" in a very generic sense, because it is the ground rhythm of the piece, and everything relates to it. Once the clave starts it never really goes away, although there are moments where it's cut short to a three-bar version, or it's extended for an extra bar so it becomes a five-bar version. Those are the elements that I think give it a little bit of life. Once the time comes in, there is some version of that clave happening for basically the entire piece, so I had to find ways to keep it interesting.

One of the things that helps maintain interest is that it's a two-part clave, an upper part and a lower part, and so there's always a dialogue going on. These are tricky rhythms even by themselves and it's always a challenge for bands to internalize them and to be able to really dig in. The 2nd Tenor, Bari Sax, and Trombones 3 & 4 have the clave for most of the piece. Keeping the concentration, putting it right in the pocket all the way through, is a real challenge. It requires a different type of focus and concentration than playing something more ostentatiously virtuosic — the virtuosity here is virtuosity of focus, concentration, and pocket.

That said, there are moments where the trance-like continuity of that pattern needs to be disrupted, with the odd-numbered phrase groupings I mentioned, and the 6/4 measures. Those are little strategies to keep people on their toes, so that when we return to the original form of the clave, it feels fresh.

RL: They serve as palate cleansers even for the listener.

DJA: Yes exactly.

RL: The last question I've asked all the composers that are participating in this study is more about general advice. Like all of the participants, you are also teaching some. What bit of advice, a single suggestion or two, could you leave our readers with that might help to make us all better composers and arrangers?

DJA: I think it really does come down to the ability to be able to listen to your music, as Brookmeyer said, "as if some other mother**** had written it." It's a very difficult thing to objectively assess what's in your music, what it's like to listen to it for the first time. Does the piece teach the listener how to listen to it? Are there moments where the details of your execution are letting the listener down, because *you* know what you mean but *they* don't know what you mean? Are there moments where your intent could have been clarified? Or moments where the seams show in a way that's distracting for the listener? Are there moments where the palate needs to be refreshed? Are there moments where you are overwhelming the listener too much? Is the harmony too dense, or are the lines insufficiently memorable, or the rhythmic structures too impenetrable?

As composers, we are looking to be creative, to find new things, and express ourselves in ways that are unique to us and particular to us, but in the service of that expression, you want to be sure that you are doing all that in a way that is maximally clear and maximally streamlined and focused, and that there is not extraneous stuff in your music that is distracting from your compositional goal. And that's a difficult thing to assess. We all have habits. We all have patterns that we fall into as composers. We all have assumptions about how music works based on received wisdom, or based on our experience with other pieces, but those assumptions don't always apply. Every piece is a new piece. Every piece has different parameters, different rules, and every piece makes its own demands of the listener. As a composer, you want to ask yourself what it is that I'm trying to do, and how are the gestures that I'm putting in to the music furthering that goal? And also, how are the gestures that I'm putting into the music interfering with that goal? Understanding those things is very, very challenging. There aren't easy answers, it's a life-long pursuit. You always have to keep asking yourself those questions. "I'm doing this thing that composers have done for centuries, but *why?* Is this really the right moment in this piece for this idea? Does this actually serve my goals in this piece of music, at this point in time?"

RL: Yes, I have trouble at my age sitting back and saying, "but you've done that before or almost exactly like something I'm about to write, and trying to discover new ways to do something that I may be hearing but haven't quite found, except the way I did it before and I don't want to go that way.

DJA: But that also might be the right way for the music too. There is always the desire to be personal and expressive, but that can also be at odds with what the piece wants to be, what the goal is. You want to align those two things in a way that creates an experience for the listener that is coming from a genuine place, and not coming from a place of "hey, let me show off this trick that I figured out." There is a danger with some composers, that once they got used to the idea of transformation, pre-compositional work, melodic development, and so on, their pieces just showed all of their *work.* There's no shaping. Essentially it's like a research paper where you're just showing all of your data but not drawing any conclusions. That's one pitfall that you can fall into, particularly when you are doing pre-compositional work for the first time. As a listener we want to know what *you* think is important, what conclusion *you* have drawn. We want to know that there is a reason *why* you're playing what you're playing for us.

RL: *Thank you again Darcy for sharing your thoughts with us. I'm sure our readers will gain a great deal from your words.*

Annotated Full Score

The annotated full transposed score that follows provides additional details about "Transit," and includes a three-staff concert pitch reduction.

Transposed Score

TRANSIT

Winner of the 2004 BMI Charlie Parker Composition Prize

Darcy James Argue

© 2003 Cercopithecine Music (BMI)
All Rights Reserved

TRANSIT

TRANSIT

TRANSIT

TRANSIT

TRANSIT

TRANSIT

TRANSIT

TRANSIT

TRANSIT

TRANSIT

TRANSIT

TRANSIT

TRANSIT

TRANSIT

TRANSIT

TRANSIT

TRANSIT

TRANSIT

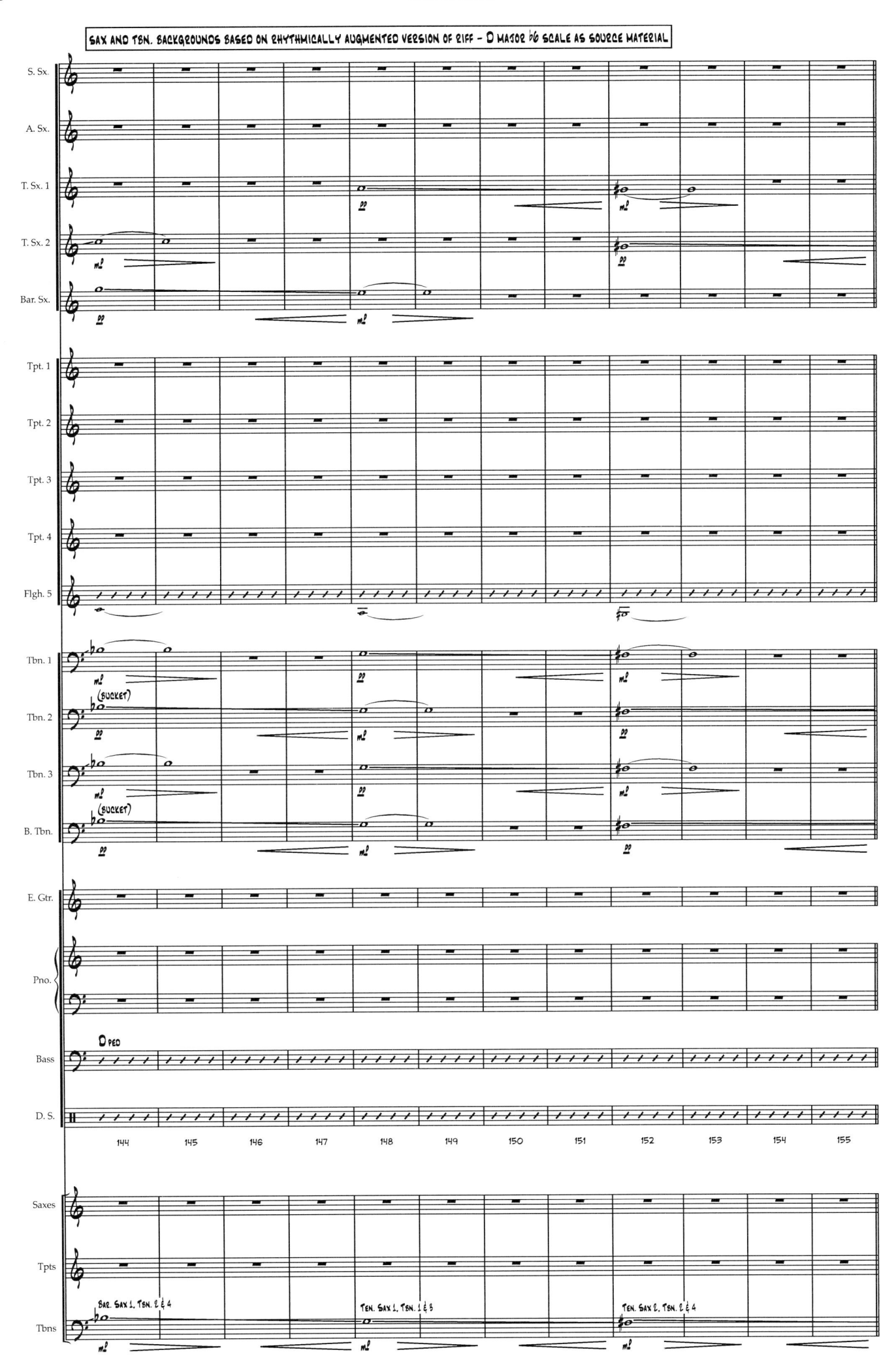

TRANSIT

TRANSIT

TRANSIT

TRANSIT

TRANSIT

TRANSIT

TRANSIT

TRANSIT

TRANSIT

TRANSIT

TRANSIT

TRANSIT

TRANSIT

TRANSIT

TRANSIT

TRANSIT

TRANSIT

TRANSIT

TRANSIT

TRANSIT

TRANSIT

TRANSIT

TRANSIT

TRANSIT

TRANSIT

TRANSIT

TRANSIT

Appendix I

Conventions, Assumptions, and Definitions

It is assumed that terms used throughout this book, such as "imitation," "sequence," "inversion," and "retrograde," and rhythmic devices such as augmentation, diminution, hemiola, and so forth, are already familiar to the reader. Brief working definitions of the following terms, however, may be useful as a quick reference for jogging memories and in clarifying concepts or analytical observations used throughout the book. Other sources should be used if these terms and their definitions that follow are not clear.

ALT – Abbreviation for altered, e.g., C7^{ALT} describes a dominant 7th chord that contains sharp and flat 5ths and 9ths. Such alterations are derived from the altered scale.

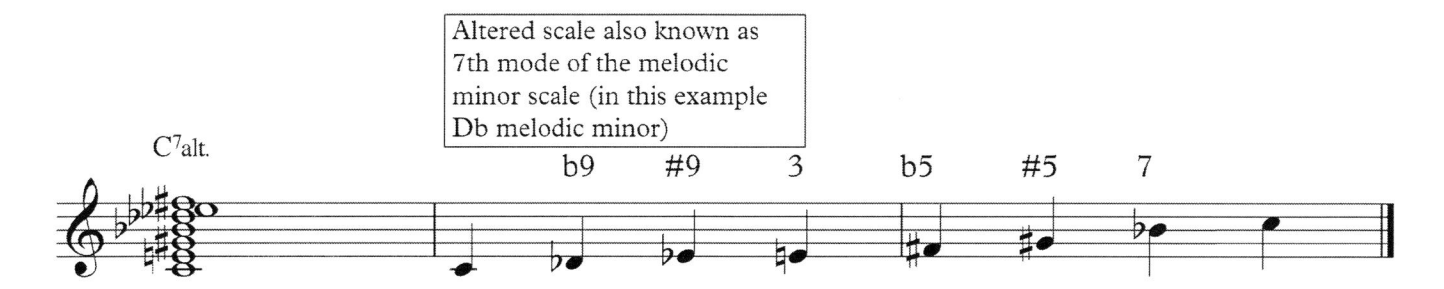

Augmentation – When longer rhythmic values are used to express a melody previously articulated over less time and with shorter rhythmic values.

Block chord – Closed position four-part harmonization of a melody.

Block voicing – Chord tones stacked from the bottom up in root position, e.g., root, 3rd, 5th, 7th.

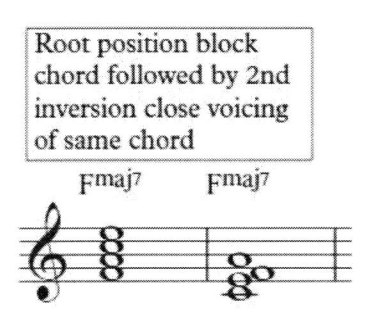

Chorale style – Open voicings where all basic defining chord tones (root, 3, 7) are included with the root as the bottommost voice followed by larger intervals by using the 3rd, 5th, or 7th of the chord.

Chorale voicing – A term used to describe a voicing that moves independently of the melodic line and usually shows larger intervals that define the chord as the bottom voices (1 and 5 or 1 and 7) with smaller intervals adding extension tones above.

Chord call – Fundamental chord of the moment.

Chord over foreign bass – Such situations typically involve a triad as the upper structure with a bass tone not considered part of the fundamental triad or its related chord scale, e.g., A♭/E bass.

Chromatic extension tones – See **Extension tones**.

Closed voicing – No more than an octave between top and bottom voices in a chord voicing. Also described as **close voicing**.

Comp – Jazz term to describe accompanying chords played by a piano or guitar in an improvised rhythmic fashion.

Concerted ensemble – A harmonized passage where all horns follow the rhythm, and usually contour, of the lead line.

Cross rhythms – See **Hemiola**.

Density – Refers to the number of different voices in a chord voicing.

Diminution – When shorter rhythmic values are used to express a melody previously articulated over greater time and with longer rhythmic values.

Ensemble or **Full ensemble** – Describes a texture or passage with all horns participating.

Extension tones – Tones that occur in the related scale above the 7th of a chord; e.g., C9 includes a D natural sounding above the B♭ and derived from the closely related C Mixolydian scale. **Chromatic extension tones** would include those occurring above the 7th, or below in the case of the 5th, and raised or lowered as compared to the most closely related chord scale. E.g., C7 $^{(\sharp 9 \flat 5)}$ includes G♯ (raised 5th and D♯ [raised 9th]).

Four part – As it suggests, refers to four chord tones in close position.

Grind – Describes a dissonance created between two voices, usually minor 2nds or minor 9ths.

Head – Primary tune or theme that serves as the basis of an arrangement.

Hemiola – The rhythmic implication of a different meter from the given, usually 3 within a context of 4, or vice versa. Such rhythmic phenomena are often referred to as cross rhythms.

Imitation – Theme, melody, or motive repeated exactly or with variation in a different voice.

Isorhythm – Usually appeared in the tenor voice in early Medieval motets and was a repeated rhythmic pattern (termed "talea") and a repeated pitch pattern, which may or may not coincide.

Lead line – Primary melody line.

Motive – A brief melodic fragment.

Open voicing – More than an octave between top and bottom voices in a chord voicing.

Ostinato – A repetitive phrase, usually relatively short, that can be a bass or upper structure pattern. The term can refer to melodic, harmonic, or rhythmic material.

Parallelism or Planing – Occurs when secondary voices move in stepwise, diatonic motion following the same direction as the lead line. Intervallic relationships do not remain exact, since movement is governed by the given scale. **Exact parallelism or planing** occurs when all intervallic motion is exactly the same as the lead line regardless of the given key or related scale.

Passing chords – Chords that fall outside the basic harmonic scheme used to harmonize a lead line. This technique is often, but not always, reserved for situations when melody notes fall outside the given basic chord of the moment.

Pedal point – A static pitch, often but not always in the bass, that functions as a constant while other harmonic structures may be changing.

Polychords – The result of superimposing one chord on another completely different chord.

Primary root movement – Strong movement created by root movement in intervals of the 4th, 5th, 2nd, and half set. All others are less strong and considered secondary movements.

Quartal voicing – Describes a collection of pitches that are spaced a 4th apart. They can be in open position or in a closed, as shown in the following example.

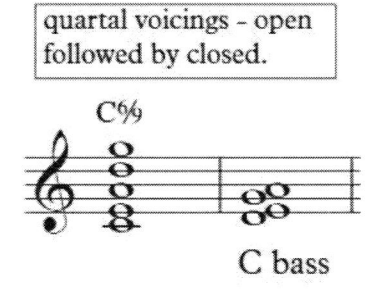

quartal voicings - open followed by closed.

C%

C bass

Reharmonization – Significant deviations from the original progression that provide a fresh, new relationship to accompanying the melody.

Repetition – Reiterating a melodic, harmonic, or rhythmic pattern.

Sequence – A melodic technique used to describe the repetition or near repetition of a motive on a different pitch level. The original motive is therefore transposed. In many instances sequences do not follow their exact model.

Shout chorus – The term commonly used to describe the jazz equivalent of a classical music score's development section. New material is presented that is typically based, sometimes loosely, on earlier thematic and harmonic material.

Span – Refers to the distance between outermost voices.

Substitute chords – Chords used in place of a chord in the original progression. Such chords may be used to replace the original chord or to delay eventual movement to the original chord.

Thickened line voicings – All voices moving in relative parallel motion to the lead, melodic line.

Tonicization – The illusion of modulation to another key that occurs when a chord momentarily serves as a new tonic when it is preceded by a secondary dominant seventh chord, or its substitute.

Weight – An approximate used to describe the number of voices (density) while also taking into account chord voice doubling in an ensemble orchestration.

In the interest of space, common abbreviations have been used in annotations in full score analysis, such as tpts (trumpets), tbn(s) (trombone[s]), bkgrnd(s) (background[s]), and so forth. These abbreviations should be obvious. The term "shout chorus" is also used to discuss that section of a score that is the equivalent of a development section consisting of new material inspired and often based on exposition material (initial presentation of the main thematic material).

For the sake of ease in interpretation, all examples included along with text are in concert pitch. The full scores are transposed; however, the specific annotated and condensed examples that appear as excerpts at the bottom of the score are in concert pitch. It is important to become conversant in transpositions, the sound of instruments in their various ranges, and the instrument's idiosyncrasies exposed by certain pitch areas. For this reason transposed full scores are included for all but the John Hollenbeck score. In the interest of being true to the composer's writing habits, this score remains as he wrote it – in concert pitch.

Appendix II
Additional Suggested Listening

The following recordings are strongly recommended as additional sources for inspiration as they feature later works by Bob Brookmeyer.

Bob Brookmeyer Composer Arranger – Mel Lewis and the Jazz Orchestra, (Gryphon, 1980)

(This recording is now available DCC Compact Classics)

Dreams – Stockholm Jazz Orchestra, (Dragon Records, 1989)

Electricity – Bob Brookmeyer and the WDR Big Band, (ACT Music, 1991)

New Works, Celebration – Bob Brookmeyer New Art Orchestra, (Challenge, 1997)

Impulsive! – Eliane Elias, Bob Brookmeyer and the Danish Jazz Orchestra, (Stunt Records, 1997)

Out of This World – Netherlands Metropole Orchestra, (Koch Records, 1998)

Waltzing With Zoe - Bob Brookmeyer New Art Orchestra, (Challenge, 2002)

Spirit Music - Bob Brookmeyer New Art Orchestra, (ArtistShare, 2006)

Clairvoyance – Ayn Inserto Jazz Orchestra featuring Bob Brookmeyer and George Garzone, (CD Baby, 2006)

Music for String Quartet and Orchestra - Bob Brookmeyer, Metropole Orchestra and Gustav Klimt Strong Quartet, (Challenge, 2009)

Get Well Soon - Bob Brookmeyer New Art Orchestra featuring Till Brönner, (Challenge, 2010)

Standards with the New Art Orchestra and Fay Claassen, (ArtistShare, 2011)

Overtime Music of Bob Brookmeyer - The Vanguard Jazz Orchestra, (Planet Arts Records, 2014)

These recordings by Kenny Wheeler are recommended. The asterisk (*) indicates that scores are available and published in a volume by Universal Edition.

Music for Large and Small Ensembles, (ECM, 1990)

Berlin Contemporary Jazz Orchestra, (ECM, 1990)

Kayak, (ECM, 1992)

The Upper Austrian Jazz Orchestra Plays Music of Kenny Wheeler, (West Wind, 1996)

Siren's Song - The Maritime Jazz Orchestra featuring Kenny Wheeler, John Taylor and Norma Winstone, (Justin Time, 1997)

A Long Time Ago, (ECM, 1999)

One More Time - UMO Jazz Orchestra with Kenny Wheeler and Norma Winstone, (A-Records, 2000)

Munich Jazz Orchestra and Kenny Wheeler – Sometime Suite, (Bassic Sound, 2001)

Now and Now Again – The Maritime Jazz Orchestra featuring Kenny Wheeler, John Taylor and Norma Winstone, (Justin Time, 2002)

Long Waiting, Kenny Wheeler Big Band, (CamJazz, 2012)

While some several of the early recordings by Maria Schneider were initially released by the ENGA label, they are now available as indicated from ArtistShare along with her more recent recordings. The asterisk indicates that scores are available and published in a volume by Universal Edition. Others may be available online for purchase from ArtistShare.

*Evanescence, (ArtistShare, 1994)

Coming About, (ArtistShare, 1996)

Allégresse, (ArtistShare, 2000)

Concert In the Garden, (ArtistShare, 2004)

Sky Blue, (ArtistShare, 2007)

Thompson Fields, (ArtistShare, 2015)

SHER MUSIC CO. - The World's Premier Jazz & Latin Music Book Publisher!

(all method books also available in digital form at www.Shermusic.com)

BEST-SELLING BOOKS BY MARK LEVINE
The Jazz Theory Book
The Jazz Piano Book
Jazz Piano Masterclass: The Drop 2 Book
How to Voice Standards at the Piano

THE WORLD'S BEST FAKE BOOKS
The New Real Book - Vol.1 - C, Bb and Eb
The New Real Book - Vol.2 - C, Bb and Eb
The New Real Book - Vol.3 - C, Bb, Eb and Bass Clef
The Real Easy Book - Vol.1 - C, Bb, Eb and Bass Clef
   (Three-Horn Edition)
The Real Easy Book - Vol.2 - C, Bb, Eb and Bass Clef
The Real Easy Book - Vol.3 - C, Bb, Eb and Bass Clef
The Latin Real Easy Book - C, Bb, Eb and Bass Clef
The Standards Real Book - C, Bb and Eb
The Latin Real Book - C, Bb and Eb
The Real Cool Book - 14 West Coast 'Cool' Jazz Octet Charts
The All-Jazz Real Book - C, Bb and Eb
The European Real Book - C, Bb and Eb
The Best of Sher Music Real Books - C, Bb and Eb
The World's Greatest Fake Book - C version only
The Yellowjackets Songbook - (all parts)
The Latin Real Book - C, Bb and Eb

DIGITAL FAKE BOOKS (at shermusic.com only)
The New Real Book - Vol.1 - C, Bb and Eb
The Digital Standards Songbook
The Digital Real Book

LATIN MUSIC BOOKS
Decoding Afro-Cuban Jazz: The Music of Chucho Valdés
   and Irakere - by Chucho Valdés and Rebeca Mauleón
The Salsa Guidebook - by Rebeca Mauleón
The Latin Real Easy Book - C, Bb, Eb and Bass Clef
The Latin Bass Book - by Oscar Stagnaro and Chuck Sher
The True Cuban Bass - by Carlos del Puerto and Silvio Vergara
The Brazilian Guitar Book - by Nelson Faria
Inside the Brazilian Rhythm Section - Nelon Faria/Cliff Korman
The Conga Drummer's Guidebook - by Michael Spiro
Language of the Masters - by Michael Spiro
Introduction to the Conga Drum DVD - by Michael Spiro
Afro-Caribbean Grooves for Drumset - by Jean-Philippe Fanfant
Afro-Peruvian Percussion Ensemble - by Hector Morales
Flamenco Improvisation, Vol. 1-3 - by Enrique Vargas
(Bilingual)
The Latin Real Book - C, Bb and Eb
101 Montunos - by Rebeca Mauleón
Muy Caliente! - Afro-Cuban Book Play-Along CD
(Libros en Español)
El Libro del Jazz Piano - by Mark Levine
Teoria del Jazz - by Mark Levine (digital only)

JAZZ METHOD BOOKS
BASS
The Improvisor's Bass Method - by Chuck Sher
Concepts for Bass Soloing - by Marc Johnson & Chuck Sher
Walking Bassics - by Ed Fuqua
Foundation Exercises for Bass - by Chuck Sher

GUITAR
Jazz Guitar Voicings: The Drop 2 Book - by Randy Vincent
Three-Note Voicings and Beyond - by Randy Vincent
Line Games - by Randy Vincent
Jazz Guitar Soloing: The Cellular Approach - by Randy Vincent
The Guitarist's Introduction to Jazz - by Randy Vincent

PIANO
Playing for Singers - by Mike Greensill
An Approach to Comping: The Essentials - by Jeb Patton
An Approach to Comping, Vol.2: Advanced - by Jeb Patton
Wisdom of the Hand - by Marius Nordal

OTHER INSTRUMENTS
Inner Drumming - by George Marsh
Method for Chromatic Harmonica - by Max de Aloe
Modern Etudes for Solo Trumpet - by Cameron Pearce
New Orleans Trumpet - by Jim Thornton

FOR ALL INSTRUMENTS
The Jazz Harmony Book - by David Berkman
The Jazz Musician's Guide to Creative Practicing -
   by David Berkman
Metaphors for the Musician - Randy Halberstadt
Forward Motion - by Hal Galper
The Serious Jazz Practice Book - by Barry Finnerty
The Serious Jazz Book II - by Barry Finnerty
Building Solo Lines From Cells - by Randy Vincent
The Real Easy Ear Training Book - by Roberta Radley
Reading, Writing and Rhythmetic - by Roberta Radley
Minor is Major - by Dan Greenblatt
Jazz Scores and Analysis - Vol.1 - by Rick Lawn
Essential Grooves - by Moretti, Nicholl and Stagnaro
The Jazz Solos of Chick Corea - transcribed by Peter Sprague

FOR STUDENT MUSICIANS
The Blues Scales - by Dan Greenblatt - C, Bb and Eb
Rhythm First! - by Tom Kamp - C, Bb, Eb and Bass Clef
The Guitarist's Introduction to Jazz - by Randy Vincent
Jazz Songs for Student Violinists - by Keefe and Mitchell

CDs
Poetry+Jazz: A Magical Marriage
The New Real Book Play-Along CDs (for Vol.1) - #1, 2 and 3
The Latin Real Book Sampler CD
The Music of Charles Stevens